AF825408

UNDERSTANDING CALIFORNIA COMMUNITY PROPERTY LAW

UNDERSTANDING CALIFORNIA COMMUNITY PROPERTY LAW

Jo Carrillo
Professor of Law
University of California, Hastings College of the Law

Carolina Academic Press
Durham, North Carolina

ISBN: 978-0-7698-5715-2
eBook ISBN: 978-1-6304-3077-1

Library of Congress Cataloging-in-Publication Data

Carrillo, Jo, 1959-
Understanding California community property law / Jo Carrillo, Professor of Law, University of California, Hastings College of the Law.
pages cm
Includes index.
ISBN 978-0-7698-5715-2 (softbound)
1. Community property--California. I. Title.
KFC125.C6C37 2015
346.79404'2--dc23 2014048414

Library of Congress Cataloging-in-Publication Data

Carrillo, Jo, 1959-
Understanding California community property law / Jo Carrillo, Professor of Law, University of California, Hastings College of the Law.
1 online resource.
Includes index.
Description based on print version record and CIP data provided by publisher; resource not viewed.
ISBN 978-1-63043-077-1 (epub) -- ISBN 978-0-7698-5715-2 (softbound) 1. Community property--California. I.
Title.
KF125.C6
346.79404'2--dc23 2014048509

This publication is designed to provide authoritative information in regard to the subject matter covered. It is sold with the understanding that the publisher is not engaged in rendering legal, accounting, or other professional services. If legal advice or other expert assistance is required, the services of a competent professional should be sought.

Copyright © 2015 Carolina Academic Press, LLC
All Rights Reserved

No copyright is claimed in the text of statutes, regulations, and excerpts from court opinions quoted within this work.

Carolina Academic Press, LLC
700 Kent Street
Durham, North Carolina 27701
Telephone (919) 489-7486
Fax (919) 493-5668
www.caplaw.com

Printed in the United States of America

2019 printing

Dedication

For my beloved parents — . . . —
in celebration of their 60th wedding anniversary
and a lifetime of being each other's true love
and son.

Acknowledgments

My thanks go out to a number of people for their assistance in producing *Understanding California Community Property Law.*

A very special thanks to Rade Vranesh, for his help with proofreading, cite checking, copyediting and nearly every other administrative task that required attention to detail. Special thanks also to: Max Carrillo-Ostrow (for acting as a student assistant and for thoughtfully reading and commenting on the manuscript), Divina Morgan (for help with all things Hastings), and Laury Ostrow (for slow food, fresh juice, and quick humor), Katherine Vranesh, Ana Beare, Amy Friedman, Angela Jamison (for a healing and intelligent perch at A2:AY), Lynne Henderson (for generously reading early drafts of Chapters 11 and 13), Robert Brownstein CPA, Chip Robertson, my family, friends, and neighbors.

My research was conducted at the Marin County Law Library, the University of California, Hastings College of the Law Library, and the University of Michigan Law Library. Thanks to Jenni Parrish, the UC Hastings Library staff, and the staff at the University of Michigan Law Library. Marin County Law Library, where I often worked, has been in existence since 1891; it is a public independent agency set up to provide free public access to legal materials. It also maintains a website, with an electronic collection. I am especially grateful to MCLL Director Jason Voelker.

Several judges, lawyers, and academics were generous with their time and perspective along the way. I wish to thank each one in private and in person, so as not to (unintentionally or inadvertently) suggest that he or she is responsible for any mistakes that I might have made. One can only hope that one's recounting is adequate, perhaps even useful. That certainly is my hope for this work.

Thanks to the UC Hastings students in my 2013 and 2014 California and comparative community property classes. They patiently allowed me to present draft chapters and examples in class. Their questions and comments, individual and collective, were exceedingly helpful. Special thanks to Sara Craig.

Finally, I am grateful for the acknowledgment and support of Dean Frank Wu, Academic Dean Elizabeth L. Hillman, Research Dean Reuel Schiller, and The Chip Robertson Faculty Development Fund. Thank you.

Preface

This *Understanding* text recounts California community property law as it now exists. The reader is asked to understand that the law is dynamic. What the Legislature and courts set down today will change by tomorrow. Change is not a flaw. It is a sign of dynamism.

This *Understanding* text can be read alone or used in conjunction with class materials. Each chapter states the law and sets out examples. The examples are a useful learning tool to help reinforce the basic concepts presented in the text. Each example presents a succinct problem and answer to help the reader gain practice in working through the issues.

Each chapter of this text corresponds to a chapter in the Carrillo community property casebook. Every chapter has a short introduction, issue by issue coverage, and a concise conclusion. Statutory language appears in bold face print, for ease of identification. Court approved formulas are fully laid out and applied. Basic property concepts are explained, where relevant.

I am pleased to report that this text extends the field in several ways. First, bank accounts are given far more extensive coverage than any other text has provided to date. Second, domestic violence and domestic violence prevention, which is fast becoming a core part of community property law practice, is explicitly covered. This text is the first of its kind to date to discuss and link domestic violence issues to the field of community property law. Third, basic topics related to elder abuse prevention and alternative dissolution processes are discussed where relevant.

I relied on traditional legal research tools to write this work. This is good news for students and bar takers who want a doctrinal recounting of California community property law. This *Understanding* text is very much for you.

At the same time, much pondering went into my effort to recount. This in turn gave me a foundation from which to rethink the field. This is good news for readers who are more interested in social and theoretical underpinnings of the law than in the doctrine itself. Community property law is (still) an under-theorized area of law. That said, it is my view — based on thousands of hours of legal and historical research — that theoretical accounts of this technically complex field fall flat if they are not based on an understanding of what the principles and rules are, and how they work in a specific case. In the field of community property law, in other words, principles, rules, facts, and theory go hand in hand.

All California statutes are available online, either through Lexis or http://legalinfo.legislature.ca.gov.

There is a 24-hour National Domestic Violence Hotline. The number is 1-800-799-SAFE (7233).

Disclaimer

I am a law professor, who is also trained as a mediator. I teach community property law, and I teach or have taught (among other topics) property law, wills and trusts, consumer lending, and mediation. My main research interest is the intersection of family law, property law, and society. To me, this intersection of property law and family law is an important subject for anyone who hopes to plan a future within the framework of an intimate partnership. As I see it, each person and each relationship is unique, which is why this material is not meant as a substitute for professional advice, legal or financial. For that reason, the information in this volume is intended for educational purposes only, and distributed on an as-is basis, without warranty. I make no legal claims, express or implied, about how the law might be applied in a particular case, by a particular judge, or in a particular judicial district. I assume no responsibility for the loss or damage caused or allegedly caused, directly or indirectly, by the use of the information contained in this book.

If you are reading this book as a student, this volume was written with your needs in mind. Even so, please understand that the law of California is exceedingly dynamic. It changes on a daily basis. This volume is up to date as of 2014, however, given the ever-changing nature of the law and the sometimes Jurassic nature of the legal educational system, please keep in mind that a judge will predictably exercise her discretion (only) on the basis of the California Family Code and the reported cases that interpret its statutes.

If you are reading this book because you are entering into or exiting from a marriage, it is my hope that you will find this volume useful. Information is a powerful tool. It can help us understand the past and present with an eye toward planning a future. It is my belief that this volume can help you ask better questions of the professionals whom you consult or hire to provide you with personalized legal advice, whether they be lawyers, mediators, therapists, clergy, or financial experts. Please understand, however, that in an actual life transition (such as, for example, a change in marital status) there is no substitute for individually delivered professional legal or financial advice.

The names in this book are street names taken from San Francisco. I intend them as an act of inclusion; it is my hope they will contribute, even if only in a small way, to repair of the world.

I look forward to hearing about the success of my readers. Please let me know how this book was helpful to you. You can reach me by sending an email to carrillo@uchastings.edu. Thank you.

Table of Contents

Table of Contents

Part I

INTRODUCTION

Chapter 1

THE CALIFORNIA COMMUNITY PROPERTY SYSTEM IN CONTEXT

This is a work of research. It makes every effort to present and explain California community property law as it exists today. This *Understanding* covers traditional topics. It also extends the field to incorporate topics relating to bank accounts, domestic violence prevention, and alternative dispute resolution.

The California community property system is a dynamic system. Today, learning about marital dissolution is a distant cry from what it used to be in the days of fault-based divorce. In the fault-based system, divorce was predicated on showing that one spouse was responsible for ending the marriage. Blaming the other spouse was the coin of the realm; and yet, at the same time, domestic violence — though so clearly present in case petitions, at least by today's California Family Code standards — was seldom acknowledged as more than one of several grounds for seeking dissolution. Today, fault is no longer a consideration in a petition for dissolution.

The California Legislature has tirelessly modified the Family Code with the intention of streamlining the dissolution and probate process. So have the courts. By the courts' own count, superior courts in the state consider well over 150,000 dissolution petitions per year, and nearly twice the number of ongoing domestic violence petitions, each of which will contain some issue of property if the parties are married, registered domestic partners [RDPs], or nonmarried cohabitants. Couples have options for how to order their intimate lives. Each one determines property rights. Each one also determines how property will get divided at the termination of the relationship.

Today the California Family Code — which is the statutory foundation of the state community property system — covers a far broader range of issues than it did in the past. In today's California family law system, knowledge of property law is a definite plus, as is sensitivity to (extended) family and social dynamics. Lawyers must familiarize themselves with basic characterization issues, fiduciary duties, disclosure laws, partnership duties, premarital and marital contracting, bank accounts, domestic violence prevention, domestic torts, elder abuse prevention, fraudulent transfers, collaborative lawyering, mediation, probate, petitions for dissolution and nullity, community reimbursements for contributions to professional education, and so forth. Accounting is central to partitioning assets. Even if parties hire forensic accounts to handle the calculation details, lawyers are called on to present and explain that information to clients and judges.

And yet, California community property law tends to get distortedly simplified by its critics. Some of whom have a personal experience with marital dissolution that has left them dissatisfied with the law, which they believe is gender-biased on its face. Some believe that judges are instructed to ignore domestic violence issues. Some assert that the court system is stacked in favor of litigation and against mediation. All of these statements are false.

The California Family Code of today is gender-neutral, and it has been for 40 years. There are formal programs to teach judges about domestic violence prevention. These programs allow judges to educate themselves about the many ways in which domestic abuse can arise, and the laws that are intended to address (if not prevent) it. In fact, California superior and criminal court judges are required to attend continuing education programs on domestic abuse. California has one of the most expansive definitions of domestic abuse, and the prevention measures apply to any number of domestic partnerships, whether the partners are married or not. Where domestic abuse is not at issue, the state expresses a strong interest in collaborative lawyering and mediation. The idea is to facilitate dissolutions in a cost effective manner, and in a way that gives parties agency in the division of their community property. A host of evidentiary and property rules are in place so as to facilitate voluntary and fair contracting over property, as well as other rights before, during and after marriage.

California community property law is enduring, but it is also responsive to changes in society: It changed in the time it took to prepare this text. This *Understanding* recounts California community property law as it exists today, knowing that by tomorrow the law will have changed yet again.

§ 1.01 WHAT IS A MARITAL PROPERTY SYSTEM?

In the state of California, as in all U.S. states, marriage and divorce are governmentally regulated activities. Marriage is a public right, not a private contractual matter. This is distinct from some religious treatments of marriage where marriage is a private, contractual or neo-contractual matter, depending on the religion.

A state marital property system regulates the property that the spouses acquire during marriage. As a matter of positive law, two marital property systems prevail in the U.S. today: the common law separate title system and the civil law community property system.

The majority of U.S. states follow the common law separate title system, which each state adopted from the English common law tradition. A minority of U.S. states follow community property law civil law tradition.

The U.S. common law separate title states follow the traditional English common law system as modified by contemporary statutes. In these jurisdictions, property acquired during marriage is individually owned by the acquiring spouse. Only a minority of common law separate title states permit spouses to opt into a unitary marital title, and then only on an asset by asset basis. At the end of marriage, property division is guided by contemporary equitable distribution statutes, in the event of divorce, or elective share statutes, in the event of death. These statutes protect the nonowning spouse from destitution or total disinheritance by replicating (to some extent) the property principles of community property law. The policy of equitable distribution and elective share statutes is to ensure a fairer division of property between the owning and nonowning spouse than would otherwise be possible without the legislation.

A minority of U.S. states follow civil law community property law. Arizona, California, Idaho, Louisiana, Nevada, New Mexico, Texas, Washington, and Wisconsin (by statute) are default community property states. Alaska and Puerto Rico allow spouses to opt into community property law with respect to a given marriage. Each of the community property states has its own community property system. Most of the states adopted their systems from the Spanish civil law tradition. Others adopted their systems as a matter of territorial extension. One — Wisconsin — adopted its system by statute.

The California system is unique among the community property systems. California's is the community property system whose precedents are most likely to be followed by other states. It is also a community property system to which significant common law modifications have been made in the interest of better operationalizing the principle that marriage is a partnership. The hybridization of California community property law with common law concepts is a matter of historical circumstance, for reasons described below.

A universal marital property system treats all property how and whenever acquired as marital property. At the end of the marriage, a hotchpot estate is formed and the marital property in that estate is divided between the parties. In the U.S., Wisconsin is perhaps the state closest to being a universal marital property system, but it too relies on community property principles.

§ 1.02 COMMUNITY PROPERTY SYSTEMS: SOME SIMILARITIES AND DIFFERENCES

There are important similarities among the community property states. The Louisiana system is closest to its traditional civil law origins. The California system is perhaps the one with the most detailed legislation and case law.

Similarities condense down to one important principle: In a community property system, property acquired during the marriage is owned by both spouses. Each spouse obtains an undivided community property interest in each asset. In California, this interest vests as it is acquired.

Another similarity is that a community property system is a default marital property system. This means that all assets, other than gifts, that are acquired during marriage are characterized as community property, regardless of whether the spouses concern themselves with the niceties of concurrent title or not. Spouses are automatically in the community property system. And they retain the contractual right to opt out of that system, either on an asset-by-asset basis or for all the property that they acquire before or during marriage.

A few major differences among the community property states are worth noting at this juncture.

One important difference concerns the default characterization of separate property rents, issues and profits. The Spanish civil law system treated all property acquired during marriage, other than gifts, as community property. By this principle the rents, issues or profits of separate property came into the marriage as community property. A minority of community property states continue to follow this rule, which is sometimes referred to as the civil law rule.

California was the first to break from this detail of the civil law tradition. In the 19th century, California adopted a common law approach to separate property rents, issues, and profits. The rule adopted was that separate property rents, issues and profits acquired during marriage are themselves separate property. Today, California still follows this so-called "American rule," as do a growing majority of community property states. Even Texas, which has historically followed the civil law rule on this issue, has vacillated back and forth on whether to — by state constitutional amendment — jump over to the American (California) rule.

Thus, a second important difference derives from how California breaks from the civil law tradition on rents, issues, and profits. Under the civil law, since separate property rents, issues and profits become community property during marriage, a strict inception of title characterization provides a useful counterbalance. Thus historically, in the civil law system, if a separate property owner permitted the community estate to assist with the purchase of a separate property asset, then that asset remained entirely separate property, but the community became entitled to a reimbursement for its contributions to purchase. The community also was given ownership of any rents, issues, or profits that the separate property earned during the marriage. California broke from this reimbursement approach in the early 20th century when the California Supreme Court decided that community property equity contributions to the purchase of a separate property asset give rise to a pro tanto equitable ownership interest in the community estate. The concurrent owners, in such an instance, are typically the separate property estate and the community property estate. Each estate owns an undivided interest in the whole. Each is entitled to possession of the whole, yet neither must pay the other for rent, absent ouster. Moreover, despite this pro-community legal development, separate property rents, issues, and profits are retained by the separate property owner.

A third important difference lies in each community property state's traditions, population, and cultures.

§ 1.03 THE CALIFORNIA COMMUNITY PROPERTY SYSTEM

[A] Three Guiding Principles

Three principles guide the California community property system.

The first is the equality principle. Spouses share an equal one-half interest in community property, no matter their actual contribution to acquisition. In a community property system, the housekeeper's contribution is conclusively presumed; it is not a question of proof. The equality principle gets carried out through the process of characterizing property as community or separate. This is the topic of Part II.

Either spouse has the right to manage and control community property, as discussed in Part IV. At marriage's end, the community estate terminates, and its holdings are distributed by right of property, not by judicial discretion. This topic is discussed in Part VI.

The second principle is the tracing principle. By this principle, property purchased or acquired during the marriage must be accounted for. Property takes on the character of its source. This means that purchases take on the character of purchase funds, and other acquisitions take on the character of their source, whether labor, investment or whatever. At the marriage's end, partition takes place, typically, by application of an array of accounting rules. The most frequently litigated of those partition rules — and the rules most often tested by bar examiners — are covered in Part III.

The third principle is the contractual modification principle. In a community property system, the legislature controls the subject of marriage. California's system is no exception. This makes marriage a public right, not a religious sacrament (which it was under the Mexican flag) or a private contractual matter (as it is under some religious legal systems). The state of California requires that valid marriages, as a matter of public right, be licensed and certified. It also "grants" dissolutions and officially returns the parties to their status as single persons, again as a matter of court action. The community property system is a default system. However, the parties, despite the fact of their marriage, retain the right — before, during, and at the end of marriage — to alter most (but not all) of the default community property rules by agreement. Contractual modification is discussed in Part V.

In California, the expectation is that all cases are to be decided in a way that is consistent with these three guiding principles. The idea is that marriage is a partnership, like any other. And yet because marriage is an intimate endeavor, marital contracting is far different from a commercial deal, where parties contract at arms' length. Therefore, as the Legislature and the state Supreme Court have consistently made clear, the state of California has a compelling interest in seeing to it that any contract that modifies the parties' default community property rights is entered into by a fair and voluntary process.

[B] Marriage as a Partnership

The definition of community property is typically linked to the spouses' efforts on behalf of the partnership. Property acquired by one or both spouses during marriage is community property. Separate property is defined by statute. Generally, separate property is property that a spouse owned prior to marriage or that one or both spouses obtained during marriage by lucrative (gratuitous or passive) means.

Community and separate property can be mixed together, or commingled. The term commingled property communicates that an asset is owned concurrently as community property and one or both spouses' separate property. With commingled property, the contributing estates (community or separate) retain their character up until the point that they can no longer be distinguished from one another. This is known as the point of confusion. At this point, the law transmutes separate property into community property by operation of law.

Despite its hybridity, the California community property system, like the systems of the other community property states, is a civil law system. This means that all cases involve the application and interpretation of statutes. California Family Code statutes cover nearly every aspect of property ownership in marriage. Cases are also important — they interpret and apply the statutes. For that reason, this *Understanding* quotes the statutory language that courts use to decide cases.

Many community property rules flow from the fact of the marriage, and most of them serve the policy of achieving equality between the spouses, as property owning partners in a confidential relationship called marriage. Key to understanding community property as a system, therefore, is that it treats marriage as a partnership, not as a guardian-ward relationship, and not as two individuals who are separately involved in the accumulation of property. Here again, critics simplify the system by complaining about the fact that the housekeeper's contribution is equal to the earning partner's contribution. The systemic response to that complaint is that a partnership is a partnership — whether partners work outside or within the home (or the firm) is not the question. Both types of labor enhance the partnership's ability to acquire assets and to satisfy liabilities.

Two philosophical — normative — starting points ground the community property system. One, the housekeeper's contribution to the marriage is a given. Unlike in a common law title system, a spouse in California who works in the home is as vested in the acquisitions of the partnership as is the spouse who works outside the home. He or she may not believe that. Neither might his or her partner. But the law treats the housekeeper's contribution to the partnership and earning spouse's contribution as one and the same. Two, unlike in a common law title system, the division of property upon dissolution or death is a matter of property right, not judicial discretion. In California, division is by halves, with half meaning an arithmetic 50-50 percent. Parties are free to agree to a different split between themselves. But if they do not, a court must step in to divide community property in 50-50 shares, on an asset-by-asset basis.

Historians attribute the community property's treatment of the housekeeper's contribution to the system's historical roots. The community property system traces from the U.S. states, back to Mexico, Spain, the Goths, and in the far distant past the Visogothic Code, where scholars note that community property rules first appeared in 693 C.E. Community property rules developed for working people, in societies where spouses labored together.

The English common law rules, by contrast, developed from the marital mergers of landed nobility. The female spouse was the ward of her husband. If and when the wife worked, whether inside or outside the home, her contributions belonged to her husband, whose own labor gave him the right to take title to the accumulations of the marriage in his name. For that reason, in the common law system, the housekeeper's contribution was disregarded, almost entirely. Today, even though U.S. common law states have modified that harsh rule by equitable distribution and elective share statutes, the housekeeper's contribution must still be alleged and established by proof. It is not a given, as it is in a community property system.

The distinction between rules that arose for working spouses as opposed to rules that arose from the merger of landed nobles who made up a minute percentage of the overall population perhaps helps understand why it is that, in a community property system, the form of record title does not determine ownership of the asset. Instead, when an asset is acquired during marriage and titled in one spouse's name only — because the housekeeper's contribution is a given — the unnamed spouse obtains an equitable ownership interest in the acquisition. Community property assets are owned by both spouses. This is true notwithstanding the form of title the spouses use.

The rationale is simple and straightforward. Marriage is a partnership. The housekeeper's contribution is a given. Partnership efforts create partnership income, acquisitions, and liabilities. And, therefore, purchases and acquisitions made with partnership income and effort belong to the partnership unless the partners have reached some other legally enforceable agreement.

[C] California's Unique History

In *Principles of Community Property,* de Funiak and Vaughn set out to show how U.S. community property systems trace back to Spain. The themes of that important volume are these: The laws and commentaries of Spain were critically important to the development of U.S. community property law. Nineteenth century judges who decided community property issues in the U.S. lacked Spanish source materials and — more importantly — the necessary civil law training and perspective to decide cases in a way that was philosophically consistent with the community property theory of marriage. And the consequence of that gap in knowledge and intention led to "frequent[ly] erroneous, indeed sometimes startling, interpretations by some of our courts."[1]

The preface to the 1850–1851 volume of California Supreme Court case reports tells the same story in a more compelling way.

Nathaniel Bennett is the court reporter.[2] He begins the first volume of the California Reports with an appeal to the reader's patience: Bennett feels the necessity of describing the conditions under which early California law was made.

According to Bennett's account the people of the newly formed state of California were "driven by extreme necessity, growing out of the political and legal chaos in which they found themselves, to the formation of a state government."[3] Bennett's point is that *in theory* California inherited its law from Spain and

---

[1] William Q. de Funiak & Michael J. Vaughn, Principles of Community Property, Preface, at xvii (2d ed. 1971).

[2] Nathaniel Bennett, California Reports, Vol. 1, 1850–1851, Preface, at v–viii. All quotations are from these pages unless noted otherwise. My account is a narrative of Bennett's account.

[3] Bennett, *supra* at v.

Mexico, but in fact the legal transitions from Spain to Mexico to the U.S. were less than orderly.

> "[M]any ordinance and decrees claim[ing] to have the force of law, had not been printed even in Mexico; and they, as well as all other books upon Spanish and Mexican laws, could be procured only with great difficulty and at great expenses, and indeed, at first, they could not be procured at all."

Before gold was discovered, California was a mission territory under Spanish rule. Then Mexico won its independence from Spain by an armed revolution. At that time, according to Bennett, California settlements were "on the out-skirts of civilization."[4] People in those settlements were governed more by custom than by "the ponderous tomes, and complicated refinements, of the civil law." Custom was determined and administered by the Alcalde system. An Alcalde being the village judge who heard oral claims within the context of summary proceedings and issued oral judgments. An alcalde's decision was generally not appealable except in grave matters. "[The alcalde system's] ready disposition of litigation," Nathaniel Bennett tells us "was strangely contrasted with 'the interminable and long drawn out proceedings of the Spanish Courts of Record."

To complicate matters, there was no mail, no dependable road system, few land surveyors (much less surveys), and few written land titles. Even if a person wanted to engage the formal legal system — for access to a judge or a written land title — he or she would have to undertake a long physical journey to a metropolitan center, over rugged country in which armed battles could erupt at any time due to the Mexican revolutionary effort.

In 1848, California became a United States territory via the Treaty of Guadalupe Hidalgo. Gold was also discovered in that same year. In 1849, the first California Constitution was formed. By 1850, over 300,000 gold seekers from every part of the world arrived in California. Among them, of course, were common law trained lawyers.

In 1850, the California Organic Act was passed. This Act protected a married woman's right to own separate property, as had been the practice under the Mexican and Spanish community property systems. Indeed, of the 66 women who were granted land — *ranchos* — during the Spanish/Mexican period of California's history, (only) 22 had their land grants confirmed and patented by the U.S.[5] Many Spanish/Mexican women lost their land holdings in the legal transitions from Spanish to Mexican to U.S. law, but of the women who managed to keep them, the California Organic Act recognized that they continued to hold their land grants in their own names, in their own right, as the heads of their own *ranchos*.

The 1850 Organic Act required that all decisions of the recently formed California Supreme Court be in writing and reported. California statutes authorized the California Supreme Court to appoint a reporter. Edward Norton, a

---

[4] *Id.*

[5] *See e.g.* California Historical Society, http://www.californiahistoricalsociety.org/ (last visited Dec. 10. 2014). Many primary sources are collected at the California Historical Society, Stanford University, and UC Berkeley.

common law trained lawyer, was named to the post. Norton reported cases from 1850 to May 1851, until — on May 4, 1851 — a fire devastated San Francisco, which was where the California Supreme Court sat. Most of Norton's court reports were destroyed or lost. Libraries "which had been collected at great cost," were destroyed. Norton resigned. Nathaniel Bennett was appointed his successor. Bennett writes from the ashes of the May 4, 1851 fire, which is why he makes a plea to his readers for their understanding: Yes, court reports are statutorily mandated. Yes, over a year of court reports are missing. But no, the loss of those records was not due to noncompliance or incompetence on either Norton's or Bennett's part. It was due to chaos, random and organized violence, and nature — fire, damp summer fog, winter rain, wind, mold, mildew, mud, and all the other elements of California's northern coastal climate that (reputedly) led Mark Twain to comment that the coldest winter he ever spent was a summer in San Francisco.

It is this history — California's history — that makes California's community property system unique among the nine community property states. The Treaty of Guadalupe Hidalgo and California law guaranteed the rights of Mexican citizens, at least on paper. And there was no dispute that the line of (European) jurisdiction — at least for property rights guaranteed under the Treaty — extended back through Mexico to Spain. But, as Bennett reports, the gold seeking population — known as the forty-niners — grew far faster than the state could establish a functioning government, and — more to the point — it grew in an area that relied on customary law and customary land titles. The forty-niners were a radically diverse population with one thing in common: they intended to extract their fortunes from the land. Before the discovery of gold, the value of land was mostly in pasturing rights. After the discovery of gold, land became valuable real estate. Perceptions about land and land title shifted, Bennett explains, thus accelerating the need to develop a stable and written property title system. One that was based on legal rules, rather than on locally administered customs.

Moreover, in this era common law trained lawyers, no matter how much they may have wanted to, could not rely on Mexican or Spanish law. It wasn't accessible or (even) available in writing. First there was the 1851 fire, which destroyed whatever library existed. Then, says Bennett, there was a notable failed attempt to gather all Mexican and Spanish law into a (single?) translated pamphlet that the courts could refer to. Obviously, this pamphlet was an incomplete, inaccurate depiction of the civil law, and as such it didn't map onto the minds of common law trained lawyers. For this reason, along with so many other others, common law rules began to insinuate themselves into the state's community property jurisprudence. Courts and lawyers, again in Bennett's words, made their decisions "generally based on Common Law grounds," which is what they were familiar with, how they had been trained, and what, in the absence of written legal authorities, seemed necessary.

Additionally, Mexican California was Catholic. The U.S. state of California was not. Once California became a state, non-Catholic residents of California, no matter their ethnicity, were required, by the 1850 Organic Act, to have their marriages certified as a matter of public civil right, not by Catholic canonical law or by Mexican

(Catholic) custom.[6] Divorce was different. Catholics could seek canonical divorces. But property division became the province of the civil state. One of the first community property cases reported is *Smith v. Smith*, which involved the division of California real estate between its community property and separate property components.[7]

This brief background helps understand why California has a civil law system in which statutes are primary and cases interpret the statutes. California did adopt the Mexican and Spanish community property system, by operation and necessity of the Treaty of Guadalupe Hidalgo. But conditions were such that when actual cases got decided, lawyers and judges *fused* the civil law with the common law. This fusion undermined the rights of wives relative to husbands, especially with respect to common law notions about gender differences.

The 1970 transition from fault based dissolution to no-fault based dissolution (irreconcilable differences) ushered in necessary and important adjustments to the community property system. So did the 1975 transition from male management to gender-neutral equal management. These two transitions alone, not to mention several others that occurred later in the 20th and early 21st century, allowed California community property law to bridge its civil law past with its present.

§ 1.04 THE CALIFORNIA FAMILY CODE

The Family Code was enacted in 1969. It took effect in 1970. Prior to that time, community property matters were governed by the general California Civil Code. Once the Family Code went into effect it became the specific law relative to which all other state codes are general law.

Stare decisis is very much alive and well in the California community property system, except that all controlling community property cases trace back to a Family Code provision, or (if before 1970) a Civil Code provision.

The Family Code has expanded since it went into effect in 1970. Today the Family Code includes the California version of model codes including the California Premarital Agreement Act [CPAA]; the Domestic Partner Rights and Responsibilities Act [DPRRA]; the Domestic Violence Prevention Act [DVPA]; (by reference) the Revised Uniform Partnership Act [RUPA]; (by implication) the Elder Abuse and Dependent Adult Civil Protection Act [EADACP]; the Uniform Parentage Act [UPA]; (by linkage to the Probate Code) the Uniform Probate Code [UPC]; and the Uniform Fraudulent Transfer Act [UFTA], to name a few.

California is a marriage equality state. Additionally, the state continues to offer Domestic Partnership as an option to those couples who qualify for RDP status. An interesting thing about California DPRRA law is that it intentionally omits a residency requirement. By this omission, DPRRA makes California community property law available to same-sex and some opposite-sex partners over a certain age, no matter their domicile. DPRRA is a robust domestic partnership law,

---

6 *Harman v. Harman*, 1 Cal. 215 (1850).

7 *Smith v. Smith*, 12 Cal. 216 (1859).

meaning that registered domestic partners are held to all the same rights (and liabilities) as spouses.

The Family Code authorizes the use of other California codes in community property cases. Two examples come to mind. Certain provisions of the Family Code synchronize with the California Multiple-Party-Accounts Law, which is part of the Probate Code. And the Family Code Domestic Violence Prevention Act synchronizes both with the Civil Code (statutory torts) and the Penal Code (criminal offenses).

§ 1.05 CALIFORNIA COURTS

Today, California has 58 superior, or trial, courts.[8] These superior courts are each located in each one of the state's 58 counties. The family court is part of the superior court system. California has six appellate districts, or intermediate courts. The California Supreme Court sits in three cities: San Francisco (its original seat), Los Angeles, and Sacramento. On select cases, the California Supreme Court sits in bank.

The six appellate districts — the map of which one can refer to online — cover a broad geographical and cultural territory.[9] Several of the districts have different divisions. The First District is the original district; it was and still is located in San Francisco, one block from where I teach. The First District serves 12 northern counties, almost all of which are on or very near the coast. The Second District serves four counties with eight divisions: Divisions 1–5, 7, and 8 are in Los Angeles; Division 6 is in Ventura. The Third District is in Sacramento; it has an official mediation program, and it serves northern rural mountainous counties. Interestingly, the 2010 Census reports that California is more than 94% rural.[10] The Fourth District has divisions in San Diego, Riverside, and Santa Ana; this district covers six counties, two which are coastal counties and four of which are inland desert counties. The Fifth District is in Fresno; it covers nine central (inland) California counties that lie at the heart of the state's agricultural industry. The Sixth District is in San Jose; established in 1984, it covers Santa Clara (Silicon Valley), Santa Cruz, Santa Benito, and Monterey counties.[11] Disagreements between the appellate courts often lead the state Supreme Court to grant review on a particular issue. For that reason, each appellate case cited has a reference to the district in which it arose.

Judicial Council data indicate that there are 200 languages spoken within the geographical boundaries of California.[12] There are over 120 languages spoken within the courts. There are 15 languages certified for court interpreters: Arabic,

---

[8] California Courts: The Judicial Branch of California, http://www.courts.ca.gov/. This discussion draws from the official California Courts website.

[9] Courts of Appeal, http://www.courts.ca.gov/courtsofappeal.htm.

[10] "I See Beauty in the Life: A Photographer Looks at 100 Years of Rural California" (information on this traveling exhibit is at http://www.californiahistoricalsociety.org/exhibitions/current_exhibitions/).

[11] California Courts: The Judicial Branch of California, www.courts.california.gov (last visited on April 10, 2014).

[12] About California Courts, http://www.courts.ca.gov/2113.htm.

Eastern Armenian, Western Armenian, Cantonese, Japanese, Khmer, Korean, Mandarin, Portuguese, Punjabi, Russian, Spanish, Tagalog, Vietnamese, and American Sign Language. Moreover, pursuant to Civil Code § 1632, there are five protected languages in the commercial sphere: Chinese (both dialects), Korean, Spanish, Tagalog, and Vietnamese.[13] Plus, within the Family Code, in some instances (premarital agreements and restraining orders), documents must be translated into the party's language of proficiency, whether or not that language is certified for court interpreters or otherwise protected by statute.

In 2011, the Judicial Council of California's Administration Office reported 160,593 family filings for dissolution, legal separation, and nullity of marriage. Child support, domestic violence, and other family filings numbered 277,207.[14] These numbers alone argue for inclusion of domestic violence into the field of community property law. In nearly every domestic violence petition, questions of property control can and do come up.

From this diversity and this volume of cases, the California Family Code is amended, applied, interpreted, amended yet again, and so forth. California community property decisional law starts at the trial court level, where judges exercise their discretion consistently with the Family Code and the community property principles and rules. When a dispute arises over the exercise of a trial court's discretion, one or both parties may appeal the decision to the intermediate court for the district. From the appeal level, a party can file a petition for state Supreme Court review. California Supreme Court decisions interpret Family Code provisions or they clarify the relationship between the Family Code and other codes. The centrality of the Family Code in California community property law means that California cases rarely cite to the cases of other jurisdictions. But the reverse is not true. The California Supreme Court writes for a vast audience of interested readers in other jurisdictions.

Some commentators assert that the courts and the Legislature are in a battle. That may have been true when the Family Law Act was adopted in the 1970s. Today, there is little extant evidence of such a battle, at least in my reading of the law. Major changes to the Family Code made from the 1970s to the 2000s caused turbulence in community law practice, which gets reflected in court opinions of that era. But even so, the courts and the Legislature have become more, rather than less, in tune with each other in this area, at least for now.

In a recent case, for example, the state Supreme Court recited the rules by which Family Code provisions are to be interpreted. By now, this recitation is an incantation found in some form or other in nearly every appellate court opinion that is about to embark on a statutory interpretation.

> "When construing a statute, our objective is to ascertain the intent of the lawmakers so as to effectuate the purpose of the statute. . . . We look first to the words of the statute, because they generally provide the most

---

[13] Jo Carrillo, *In Translation for the Latino Market Today: Acknowledging the Rights of Consumers in a Multicultural Housing Market*, 11 Harv. Lat. L. Rev. 1 (2008).

[14] Judicial Council of California, *2013 Court Statistics Report, Statewide Caseload Trends, 2002–2004 Through 2011–2012* (2013), available on the California Courts website.

> reliable indicator of legislative intent. We give the words their usual and ordinary meaning, while construing them in light of the statute as a whole and the statute's purpose. If there is no ambiguity in the language, we presume the Legislature meant what it said and the plain meaning of the statute governs. Only when the statute's language is ambiguous or susceptible of more than one reasonable interpretation may the court turn to extrinsic aids to assist in interpretation."[15]

What's more, interpretations of the Family Code are to be made in a way that is consistent with the other provisions of the Family Code.

In short, the California community property system is unique for (at least) the four reasons here identified. One, California's legal history is unique because of the state's diversity. Two, California has been diverse and abundant from its beginning, which along with the state's natural beauty, ecosystem diversity, resources, and agricultural possibility makes it one of the largest economies in the world. Three, California real estate has and continues to be valuable. That was true during the Gold Rush; it's true today. Four, California has been, and perhaps still is, the symbol of plenty, a land of imagined and real opportunity, a place of fusion and tradition, sun, sea, mountains, and deserts, a place of stability and innovation, a place that inspires literature, music, theatre, art, politics and law — all of these cultural forms inscribe California as a golden place on the cultural imagination of the country, if not the world.

What spurred California legal history forward during the Gold Rush was its cultural diversity. Customary law simply could not support the needs of the state's growing, diverse population. The same dynamic spurs the development of California community property law today, as the California Legislature and the courts to seek to develop and interpret the Family Code in a way that can be fair across cultures, languages, worldviews, lifestyles, and expectations.

I'm inspired by the idea of marriage as a partnership and by how that idea plays out in California legal history. To me, the idea of an intimate partnership as a social option that can protect the partners, as a unit, and still attend to the individuals as individuals is an enlivening idea. Additionally, I find that California history can bring up complex emotions: California history can be downright amazing, surprisingly complex, awe inspiring, sometimes, of course, exasperating, and sad. When California history is considered outside of any simplifying or cartoonizing us-them binary, it provokes thought, illuminates choices made and yet to be made, and possibly even provides guidance for our options in the future.

Community property law plays an important part in California's history. And, in turn, California's unique history is reflected in its community property law. My hope is that this *Understanding* will give readers a glimpse of how the marital property law of California seeks, within its parameters, to balance the order of law with the diversity of lived culture, as it gets played out between consenting adults who choose to make a life together.

---

[15] *Ceja v. Rudolph & Sletten, Inc.*, 56 Cal. 4th 1113, 158 Cal. Rptr. 3d 21, 302 P.3d 211 (2013).

§ 1.06 OVERVIEW OF THIS TEXT

This text was written for students of California Community Property law. It is divided into six parts. Part I is an introduction to California's unique legal history.

Part II sets out the basic characterization rules for community property (Chapter 2) and separate property (Chapter 3). In California, community property is all property acquired during marriage by effort of one or both spouses. Separate property is generally defined by statute as property that is acquired before marriage, during marriage by gift, or during marriage from the rents, issues, and profits of separate property. Some personal injury claims and recoveries, and earnings and accumulations acquired after separation can be defined as separate property, depending on the circumstances of the case.

Community property presumptions are routinely used in the California community property system. Presumptions are evidentiary leniencies, not conclusive rules. The separate property claimant has the burden to rebut any community property presumption by a preponderance of the evidence.

Part III covers approaches to apportioning commingled property. Specialized rules have developed over the years to fairly apportion property that is concurrently held between the community property estate and one or both spouses' separate property estates. These rules relate to sums on deposit in a bank account and purchases from a commingled account (Chapter 5), credit acquisitions (Chapter 6), separate property business profits (Chapter 7), life insurance proceeds (Chapter 8), and deferred work earnings (Chapter 9).

Part IV discusses management and control of community property (Chapter 10), including when domestic violence is present (Chapter 11), and debt obligations (Chapter 12).

Part V covers contractual modifications of the community property system made by prospective spouses (Chapter 13), spouses, (Chapter 14), registered domestic partners, and nonmarried partners (Chapter 15).

Part VI concludes with the disposition of property at divorce (Chapter 16) and death (Chapter 17). Federal issues are discussed throughout, where relevant.

Finally, although community property law is technical in parts, the entire push of the system is to regard marriage as a partnership, and thus to divide community property equally at marriage's end.

Each chapter includes code sections, explanatory materials, case discussions, citations, and concise examples to draw attention to the operative language in the code section at hand. All Family Code sections are indicated by section number only, as § _____. Non-Family Code sections are fully specified by Code and section number, e.g., Cal. Prob. Code § _____. Quotations are organized to facilitate reading. As always, it is important to consult the actual statute when necessary.

Part II

THE IMPORTANCE OF CHARACTERIZATION

Chapter 2

COMMUNITY PROPERTY

There are two characters of property in the California community property system: Community property and separate property.

Community property is property, wherever situated, that is acquired during the marriage by a spouse who is domiciled in California. Community property is onerously acquired through one or both spouses' work, labor, talent, industry, or other effort. Each spouse owns a vested, undivided, one-half interest in each and every community property asset as it is acquired. Either spouse acting alone can manage and control the community personal property, in all matters not testamentary. This same rule applies to community real property, except that in the interest of promoting a transparent public title record, spouses must join in signing certain transaction documents as enumerated by statute.

California has other useful designations to aid in the characterization of property at the end of a valid or void marriage. *Quasi-community property* is property that is acquired by a spouse during marriage while domiciled in another state. *Quasi-marital property* is property acquired by a putative spouse during a void marriage. A putative spouse is a person who believed in good faith in the validity of the void marriage.

A spouse's personal injury claim and recovery against a third party are generally community property during the continuance of the marriage. However, these community property recoveries are mandatorily assigned at dissolution to the injured spouse as his or her separate property. A claim that arose during the marriage but was not pursued during the marriage is also subject to the same assignment rule at dissolution. Each of these topics is discussed in more detail below.

Characterization — the act of inventorying and thus of defining the community property estate — can occur during the marriage. This happens, for example, when spouses engage in financial planning together. More typically, characterization occurs at the end of marriage when spouses (or their estate administrators) seek to partition the community property of the partnership. Disputes between the spouses may arise in the partition process.

As a general rule, the characterization of property as community or separate cannot be made solely by reference to title documents. California law relies heavily on evidentiary community property presumptions, most of which are rebuttable by tracing or by agreement. Only one presumption — the special joint form title presumption discussed below — is limited to rebuttal by agreement between the spouses that the property is not to be community property.

§ 2.01 STATUTORY DEFINITIONS OF COMMUNITY PROPERTY

The spouses, as partners, hold **"present, existing and equal interests"** in each community property asset as it is acquired.[1]

Either spouse's one-half community property interest exists in an asset notwithstanding the absence or presence of a written title. If a written title is obtained in one spouse's name only, then the unnamed spouse's community property interest exists in equitable form, notwithstanding the form of record (written) title.

Commentators sometimes make the mistake of assuming that untitled assets are items of little value. Nothing could be further from the truth. Many items of value in a marriage are untitled assets. For these assets, possession is a proxy for ownership, subject to proof of date of purchase. A piece of jewelry, furniture, a family heirloom — each of these is an example of something that would likely be untitled. A house, a car, or a boat — each of these is an example of an asset that would be titled. Indeed, title to real estate can be obtained without a written title (as in the case of adverse possession), but marketable title can only be transferred by a written deed. Community property characterization rules apply to all assets — untitled and titled.

One might visualize the community estate as a vessel that forms at the start of a marriage to hold the partnership's accumulations during the marriage. No community property exists before the marriage. It is accumulated during the marriage. If and when the marriage ends, the community estate terminates and the community property assets are accounted for and distributed. Partition is by a final dissolution order of a state superior court or by a final probate court order. In the case of dissolution, only a final judgment of dissolution terminates a marriage and returns the spouses to their status as single persons. At the end of a marriage, the Family Code and the cases that interpret it decide disputes between the spouses.

Furthermore, in a dissolution proceeding, community estate accumulations are disposed of either by agreement or as a matter of property right. Spousal support awards are by judicial discretion.

Optimally, a final judgment of dissolution is based on the spouses' enforceable private contract, which is called a *marital settlement agreement*, or MSA. An MSA divides the partnership property as the partners see fit. There is no requirement that the parties contract in furtherance of a strictly arithmetic 50-50 outcome. They are free to settle their interests in the community estate in their respective best interests, by voluntary trade and offset.

If the parties cannot reach a marital settlement agreement, a court must step in. In that case, the Family Code mandates that the court partition the community estate according to the parties' vested property interests, on an asset-by-asset basis. Every community property asset is divided in equal (50-50) arithmetic shares.[2] In dividing the property of disputing spouses, a court may, but need not,

---

[1] Cal. Fam. Code § 751.

[2] California uses an *asset-by-asset division*, which requires that each item that is or may be

take the parties' expressed considerations and preferences into account.[3] In this way, the law places an incentive on negotiating an MSA.

[A] The Basic Statute

Every characterization analysis begins with § 760 — the general Family Code definition of community property. References to community property also appear in the state civil code (§ 687) and probate code (§ 28).

Community property is defined by § 760 as **"[A]ll property, real or personal, wherever situated, acquired by a married person during the marriage while domiciled in this state. . . ."** Proof of acquisition during marriage gives rise to a general community property presumption. Rebuttal is by the separate property claimant who proves, by a preponderance of the evidence, that the property was purchased by or derived from separate property. This is the tracing principle at work. A separate property claimant can also rebut the general presumption by producing evidence of an enforceable agreement between the spouses that the disputed property was not to be community property. In such a case, the parties invoke the contractual modification principle.

The use of a community property presumption can be understood as an evidentiary leniency in favor of the community estate. Presumptions are not algorithms in the sense that they do not produce conclusive results. Rather, a community property presumption is a statement of probability that property acquired during marriage is more likely to be community property than it is to be separate property. The separate property claimant can disprove this statement of probability with actual evidence of a separate property interest.

Community property presumptions benefit the partnership in furtherance of the equality principle. Surprisingly, so too does the (low) preponderance of the evidence standard of rebuttal, a point discussed below. The use of presumptions also eases the burden on courts, lowers the cost of dissolution, and equalizes the risk of loss due to judicial error.

In any given marriage, there are three possible owning estates: the community property estate; one spouse's separate property estate; and the other spouse's separate property estate. Given these permutations, application of § 760 often requires calculating each estate's proportional ownership share in relation to the other estates. Calculating proportions can involve assessing contributions to purchase relative to purchase price, fair rates of returns relative to total growth, or other financial information. Parties often hire forensic accountants, but the lawyer is nevertheless charged with understanding, organizing, and presenting financial information.

---

community property be inventoried. Other states follow a hotchpot method, which means that parties are given a share of the community property estate, rather than an interest in each asset within the estate.

[3] Other community property states may allow a court to divide the community property on an equitable basis. *Equitable division* means that the result can be arithmetically unequal based on the needs of the respective parties. *Equal division* means that the result must be arithmetically equal.

Title documentation is important to deciding which community property presumption governs. Assets that are untitled or titled in one spouse's name only are governed by the general community property presumption. Assets that are titled in any joint title form (i.e. in both spouses' names) are governed by the special joint form title community property presumption. Sums on deposit in an account are governed by (yet) a (different) special community property presumption that applies notwithstanding the contract title to the account in which the sums are deposited. Each of these presumptions is discussed below.

Every community property presumption recognizes in each spouse a nonconclusive one-half community property interest in an asset as of the date that it is acquired. If that property interest is not recorded on a written title — as happens when title to an asset is taken in one spouse's name only — it nevertheless comes into equitable existence, thus giving its holder the right to petition for an accounting. For this reason, community property presumptions supersede the evidence code form of title presumption in a dissolution proceeding.

The general policy underlying the use of community property presumptions is to facilitate and streamline — not frustrate — private contracting or litigation between the spouses.

Example 2.1: This example illustrates the vested nature of community property. Sansome and Taylor marry. Sansome works outside of the home. Taylor is currently unemployed. Sansome's acquired earnings are community property. Each spouse obtains a vested one-half community property interest in Sansome's earnings as of the date that Sansome gets paid.

Example 2.2: This example illustrates the role of timing in defining community property. Same as Example 2.1 except that Sansome purchases a car with cash one day before Sansome and Taylor marry. Sansome's car is not community property because it was acquired before, not during, marriage.

Example 2.3: This example illustrates the role of effort in defining community property. Sansome and Taylor marry. During marriage, Taylor receives an inheritance. Taylor's inheritance is a lucrative windfall, not an onerous acquisition. As such, the inheritance is Taylor's separate property, even though it was acquired during marriage.

[B] Quasi-Community Property

Quasi-*community* property is property that is declared community property by a California court at dissolution or death.

For purposes of dissolution, quasi-community property is defined at § 125(a) as property acquired **"[b]y either spouse while domiciled elsewhere which would have been community property if the spouse who acquired the property had been domiciled in** [California] **at the time of its acquisition."** For purposes of a probate proceeding, quasi-community property is similarly defined by Probate Code § 28.

Property acquired by married persons while domiciled in another state does not automatically become quasi-community property when one or both parties move to

California. On the contrary: Any property acquired in another jurisdiction during marriage continues to be governed by the laws of that jurisdiction even after California domicile is established. What gives the state of California a substantial interest in the characterization of the petitioners' property is the voluntary act of one or both spouses filing a petition for dissolution in a California superior court.

A petition of dissolution allows a California court to declare the character of out-of-state property that the petitioners might own, even if the court has no jurisdiction over the property.[4] A court declaration appears in a dissolution judgment, which — as to quasi-community property — is interpreted as "a mere declaration of entitlement to the property which has no direct effect on the title to the property in [the other jurisdiction.]"[5]

Example 2.4: This example illustrates the concept of quasi-community property. Sansome and Taylor, a married couple, live in New York. They move to California, where they establish domicile. In California, Taylor petitions for dissolution. A few years back, while married and domiciled in New York, Sansome bought a condo on Fire Island with earnings. Taylor now seeks to have the condo characterized and declared California quasi-community property. Sansome counters that a California court has no jurisdiction over the New York property. In a dissolution dispute between Taylor and Sansome, Taylor will prevail in getting the condo declared quasi-community property. The state of California gained an interest in dissolving the marital estate, which includes the New York condo, when Taylor filed a petition for dissolution in a California rather than in New York. Had the condo been acquired while the spouses were domiciled in California, it would have been § 760 community property; thus, under California law, the condo is quasi-community property.

The same rationale holds for probate proceedings.

[C] Quasi-Marital Property

Quasi-*marital* property is property acquired during a void or voidable marriage. Quasi-marital property is defined at § 2251(a)(2) as **"property acquired during the union which would have been community property or quasi-community property if the union had not been void or voidable."** Putative spouse status and the quasi-marital property system are discussed in Chapters 15 and 16.

Example 2.5: This example illustrates the concept of quasi-marital property. Sansome and Taylor marry. Sansome works outside the home; Taylor does not. Sansome believes in good faith that the marriage is valid, as does Taylor. However, it turns out that there is an error in the licensing of the marriage: Specifically, on the date of Sansome's and Taylor's marriage, Sansome was still legally married to Laurel. Bigamy is illegal in California, which makes the second in time Sansome-Taylor marriage void as compared to the (still valid) first in time Sansome-Laurel marriage. However, if Sansome or Taylor can prove that either or both had a good faith belief in the validity of their (defective) marriage, any property that they

---

[4] *Addison v. Addison*, 62 Cal. 2d 558, 43 Cal. Rtpr. 97, 399 P.2d 897 (Cal. 1965) (in bank).

[5] *Marriage of Ben-Yehoshua*, 91 Cal. App. 3d 259, 154 Cal. Rptr. 80 (Cal. App. Ct., 5th Dist. 1979).

accumulated during that defective marriage will be deemed quasi-marital property and divided in accordance with community property law.

Quasi-community property and quasi-marital property protect the expectations of the parties. They also recognize the housekeeper's contribution as a given.

If one or both spouses from a common law separate title state — as in Example 2.4 — establish a domicile in California, any and all pre-domicile contributions to the acquisition of property during marriage will be declared quasi-community property in a California dissolution proceeding. This is the case even if those same contributions would not be recognized or accounted for under the law of the claimant's former domicile. Additionally pre-domicile housekeeping contributions will be assumed. Therefore, regardless of who acquired the pre-domicile property during marriage, each spouse's vested one-half quasi-community property interest will be recognized under California law.

Likewise, if an innocent spouse realizes that there is a defect in the certification of his or her marriage, any and all partnership contributions will be recognized as quasi-marital property in a California nullification proceeding. Housekeeping contributions will be assumed in this case as well. Regardless of who acquired the property, it will be divided equally. This is in direct contrast to nonmarried cohabitants, who must prove the existence and value of their household contributions in any contract dispute between them.

[D] Personal Injury Claims and Recoveries From a Third Party

Personal injury claims and recoveries against a third party are characterized as community property by application of § 780, a presumption that parallels the general § 760 presumption. Under § 780, property obtained from a **"cause of action for the damages** [that] **arose during the marriage"** is community property. This includes **"money and other property received or to be received by a married person in satisfaction of a judgment for damages for personal injuries, or pursuant to an agreement for the settlement or compromise of a claim for such damages."**

In the event of dissolution, a court is mandated to divide § 760 community property equally. By contrast, a court is mandated, per application of § 2603, to assign the § 780 community property to **"the party who suffered the injuries."** Damages and recoveries under § 780 include **"all money or other property received or to be received by a person in satisfaction of a judgment for damages for the person's personal injuries or pursuant to an agreement for the settlement or compromise of a claim for the damages."**[6]

A court has discretion to modify the § 2603 mandatory assignment rule in one of two situations. The first is where the personal injury recovery is **"commingled with other assets of the community estate."** No case law interprets this phrase. However, in keeping with the tracing principle, it seems most plausible that § 780

[6] Cal. Fam. Code § 2603(a); *see also Marriage of Morris*, 139 Cal. App. 3d 823, 189 Cal. Rptr. 80 (Cal. App. Ct., 4th Dist. 1983).

funds should be governed by the mandatory assignment rule so long as they remain traceable. If so, the ordinary rules of community property would come into play only if a § 780 personal injury award were to become confused with § 760 community property sums on deposit. Precedent supports this interpretation: At divorce, a traceable asset purchased with a personal injury award (§ 780 community property) is subject to the mandatory assignment rule of § 2603(b), especially if the purchase was intended to or does address the injured spouse's injury-related needs.[7]

The second instance in which a court has authority to deviate from the mandatory assignment rule is where **"the interests of justice require another disposition,"** as authorized by § 2603(b). In such a case, a court is required to take into account the **"economic condition and needs of each party, the time that has elapsed since the recovery of damages or the accrual of the cause of action, and all other facts of the case."** If a court exercises its discretion to divide the § 780 community property personal injury award between the injured spouse and the non-injured spouse, **"at least one-half of the damages shall be assigned to the party who suffered the injuries."** A personal injury recovery represents, at least in part, compensation for bodily harm to the injured spouse. For that reason, a court may be reluctant to exercise its discretion to split the recovery at dissolution between an injured spouse who is no longer fully employable and a non-injured spouse who is.[8]

Tort claims that arise during marriage but not pursued as of the time of dissolution are excluded from § 780, and instead assigned to the injured spouse as his or her separate property.[9] Also excluded from the reach of § 780 are one spouse's claims against the other spouse for domestic violence.[10] Exclusions to § 780 are discussed in Chapter 3.

Example 2.6: This example illustrates the concept of § 780 community property. While married to Sansome, a third party negligently crashes into Taylor's car. Taylor is injured and suffers damages. Taylor's personal injury claim against the third party is characterized as § 780 community property. So too are any recoveries or other property that Taylor might receive in satisfaction of that claim.

Example 2.7: This example illustrates the § 2603(b) mandatory assignment rule for § 780 community property. Same as Example 2.6 except that Sansome petitions for dissolution after Taylor is injured. At dissolution, if Taylor has not yet pursued the personal injury claim against the third party, that claim leaves the marriage as Taylor's separate property.

Example 2.8: This example illustrates the tracing principle as applied to § 780 community property. While married to Sansome, Taylor obtains a personal injury award against a third party. Taylor uses the tort recovery to purchase a wheel chair accessible residence. Title is taken in both spouses' names. Subsequently the couple

---

[7] *Marriage of Devlin*, 138 Cal. App. 3d 804, 189 Cal. Rptr. 1 (Cal. App. Ct., 3d Dist. 1982).

[8] *Id.*

[9] *Marriage of Pinto*, 28 Cal. App. 3d 86, 104 Cal. Rptr. 371 (Cal. App. Ct., 1st Dist. 1972).

[10] Cal. Fam. Code § 781

petition for dissolution. The mandatory assignment rule for community property personal injury recoveries applies both to the monetary recovery and, by application of the tracing principle, to any property that either spouse purchases with that monetary recovery. In this case, the residence was purchased with money from Taylor's tort recovery. Therefore, at dissolution, the house shall be assigned to Taylor as separate property, notwithstanding the joint form of title.

Example 2.9: This example illustrates the § 2603(b) interests of justice exception to the § 780 mandatory assignment rule. During marriage to Sansome, Taylor is injured. Sansome quits work to provide home nursing care for Taylor. Under § 2603(b) personal injury recoveries shall be assigned to the injured spouse upon dissolution unless a court finds that the interests of justice require otherwise. In this case, decisional law makes it unlikely that a court will split the personal injury award between Sansome and Taylor, notwithstanding caretaker Sansome's lost opportunity costs. Moreover, even if the court decides to split the personal injury recovery in the interests of justice, at least one-half of the § 780 property shall be assigned to the injured spouse.

[E] Exemptions

In the California community property system, a surviving *former* spouse may invoke the benefit of a community property presumption as to any of the decedent's property that was acquired during the dissolved marriage, but only if the claimant's and the decedent's marriage was dissolved less than four years before the decedent's death. If the dissolution took place more than four years before the decedent's death, a former surviving spouse may still bring a community property claim against the decedent's estate. However, in that case, § 802 shifts the burden of proof to that claimant by providing: **"The presumption that property acquired during marriage is community property does not apply . . . if the marriage during which the property was acquired was terminated by dissolution of marriage more than four years before the** [decedent's] **death."**

A second exemption, found at § 803, is known as the married woman's separate property presumption. This exemption applies only to assets that were acquired by a married woman, before January 1, 1975, by a written title in her name only. Historically, the rationale for the married woman's separate property presumption was predicated on the fact that the husband was the designated legal manager of the community property estate. If the husband transferred an asset from the community property estate to the wife in her name only, § 803 presumed that he intended to make a gift to the wife. Gifts received during marriage were and still are defined as separate property. Thus, § 803 provides that the husband's pre-1975 gift to the wife in her name only is nonconclusively presumed to be her separate property unless the husband can show that he lacked donative intent in taking title in the wife's name. The married woman's separate property presumption is a relic from a bygone male management era. Over the course of time, it decides fewer and fewer cases.

§ 2.02 THE EQUALITY PRINCIPLE

The community property system is a set of default property rules animated by principles of equality, tracing (accounting), and contract modification. *See* Chapter 1.

Within the doctrinal structure of the community property system, equality refers specifically to the spouses' property rights, not broadly to the social idea or ideal of companionate marriage. In California, marriage is a partnership. Dissolution is granted notwithstanding or regardless of personal fault. Community property is divided by agreement or, if not, on an asset-by-asset basis. And, because spousal tort immunity has been abolished, domestic abuse is actionable.

The community estate, in other words, acquires property (or not) no matter whether the partners love or respect each other in any socially unified, recognized, or acceptable way. Moreover, there is no overarching statutory requirement, at least for marriage, that the spouses conduct themselves as companionate partners, or as monogamous persons, or as persons in a committed intimate relationship. Bigamy and polygamy are illegal. And while extramarital or polyamorous affairs may be frowned upon, they do not necessarily impact community property rights in a (or the) valid marriage unless a breach of fiduciary duty has occurred. Child marriage is deemed nonconsensual as a matter of law. So too are forced marriages. In other words, the marriage partnership is voluntary and subject to the dictates of the adult spouses themselves. Parties enter into a marital partnership by a discretionary act, and they dissolve that partnership in the same way. The essential element of any partnership — commercial or intimate — must be that the partners have the right to enter and to exit the partnership, at will, with their respective contributions and obligations fully accounted for, after taking enforceable premarital and marital agreements into account.

As a general rule — with the exception of bigamy and incest — once the formal requirements for a valid marriage are met, the partners are officially married. At that point they become eligible — as spouses — to acquire community property. The spouses' sexual interaction does not generally determine their relative property rights except in the case of domestic violence, which is discussed in Chapter 11, or in the case of a voidable marriage, which is discussed in Chapter 16. In the former case, a court has discretion to assign rights of management and control to one spouse over the other so as to prevent future domestic violence. In case of voidable marriage, a court can correct the defect in the marriage certification with proof that upon learning about the defect in their marriage the parties chose to maintain an ongoing (sexual) relationship as spouses. Judgments of nullity as compared to judgments of dissolution are discussed in Chapter 16.

Otherwise, the equality principle serves to guide courts in their application of the technical rules of community property law. Implicit in the equality principle is the conclusive assumption that either spouse's housekeeping contribution adds to the community estate and thus to the partnership. Therefore, in community property jurisdictions a housekeeping contribution need not be specifically alleged or proven, as it must be in common law separate title jurisdictions. During the continuance of the marriage and at its end, each spouse enjoys a vested interest in every asset that the partnership has acquired, no matter his or her earnings or lack of earnings.[11]

Example 2.10: This example illustrates the partnership theory of marriage. Sansome and Taylor marry. Taylor works at home to care for children. Sansome's work earnings are used to purchase a house. The house belongs to both spouses, each of whom has contributed to the acquisition of the house by virtue of his or her status as a full equity partner, so to speak. Taylor's housekeeping contribution is assumed — it need not be specifically alleged or proved — and it is as valuable as Sansome's earnings contribution.

At death, a spouse retains full testamentary rights over his or her one-half community property interest, again on an asset-by-asset basis. A spouse has no legal obligation to devise his or her community property to the other spouse.

In the case of intestacy, the surviving spouse succeeds to the decedent spouse's one-half of the community property, which (added to the surviving spouse's own one-half interest) results in the surviving spouse owning 100% of the community property. By comparison, the decedent's separate property goes entirely to the surviving spouse unless the decedent is survived by issue, ancestors or collateral heirs. In the latter case the surviving spouse is statutorily required to share separate property with other intestate takers. Distribution of property at death is discussed in Chapter 17.

The general § 760 community property presumption is at once straightforward and applied against the backdrop of a thick net of regulation. Interpretation is further guided by the equality principle, the labor principle, evidentiary presumptions, the preponderance of the evidence rebuttal standard, notice requirements, and a host of other policies. Together, these considerations recognize that the state of California has a compelling interest in protecting spouses as partners during the continuance and at the end of a marriage.

Equality is achieved through tracing, or accounting. For that reason the state also an interest in articulating tracing rules, as discussed in Part III. It has an interest in preventing domestic violence, as discussed in Part IV. It has an interest in regulating the formation of contracts between intimate partners, as discussed in V. And it has an interest in dissolving the accumulations of a valid marriage, as discussed in Part VI.

Example 2.11: This example illustrates how, during marriage, the spouses obtain a present, existing, and equal ownership interest in each community property asset as it is acquired. Sansome earns $3,000 a month. Taylor works on commission. Each month, when Sansome gets paid, Sansome and Taylor each acquire a present, existing, and equal (50-50) community property interest in the $3,000. Likewise, whenever Taylor earns a commission, Sansome and Taylor each acquire a present, existing and equal community property interest in that commission.

Example 2.12: This example illustrates how the character of funds can determine the character of purchases made with those funds. During marriage, Sansome uses community property funds to buy a car. Sansome and Taylor each own a present, existing, and equal (50-50) community property interest in the funds, and

[11] Cal. Fam. Code § 751.

therefore in the car that was purchased with those funds.

Example 2.13: This example illustrates the tracing principle, this time highlighting two sources of community property: cash and creditworthiness. During marriage, Sansome buys a car with earnings and with loan proceeds. The earnings are community property, as are the loan proceeds. Sansome and Taylor each own a one-half community property interest in the car, notwithstanding the fact that only one spouse obtained the loan proceeds.

§ 2.03 COMMUNITY PROPERTY PRESUMPTIONS

In disputes between spouses, presumptions are often necessary to determine ownership of a disputed asset. California community property law recognizes one general community property presumption, two special statutory community property presumptions, and one special judicial community property presumption applicable to loan proceeds. Generally, a special presumption supersedes a general presumption.

All community property presumptions work to characterize the asset as community property. Not all of presumptions can be rebutted with the same evidence.

This Section covers the following presumptions:

- **The general community property presumption** applies to property acquired during marriage. It applies in the absence of a superseding presumption. Rebuttal is by tracing the property back to a separate property source, or by agreement. The general presumption applies in a dispute between spouses. It also applies in a dispute between a surviving spouse and a decedent spouse's estate.
- **The special § 2581 presumption for assets in joint form title** applies to property acquired during marriage in any joint form title. Rebuttal is by agreement only. This special presumption supersedes the general community property presumption. It applies only at dissolution.
- **The special California Probate Code § 5305(a) presumption for sums on deposit in an account** applies to sums on deposit in an account during marriage. Rebuttal is by tracing or by agreement. This special presumption supersedes both the general presumption and the special presumption for assets in joint form title, but only *as to sums on deposit in an account* during marriage. Cal. Prob. Code § 5305 applies at dissolution and at death.
- **The special judicially created presumption for borrowed funds** is used to assess proportional ownership shares in a secured credit acquisition. This presumption treats community property loan proceeds as a community property contribution to purchase, even if the loan has not been repaid to the lender. Rebuttal is by evidence of the lender's intent to rely solely on separate property in extending the loan. This special judicially created presumption applies at dissolution and at death.

[A] The General Presumption

The general presumption is authorized by § 760, as interpreted by decisional law. The general presumption applies to all property acquired during marriage, not covered by a superseding special presumption. Practically speaking, the general presumption applies to assets acquired during marriage that are untitled or titled in one spouse's name only. Untitled assets include cash, but not (electronic) sums on deposit in an account.

There are many reasons why spouses take title in one name only. Furthermore, it is not a breach of fiduciary duty to do so. The community interest vests upon acquisition, notwithstanding the absence of one spouse's name on a written title document.

[1] Date of Acquisition

In a dispute between spouses, the general presumption is raised by proof that the property was acquired during marriage. Date of acquisition must be established because it marks the point at which the spouses' community property ownership rights and obligations come into legal existence.

The language of § 760 expressly adopts the "acquisition-approach" to community property: A property right comes into existence when a claimant *acquires* an enforceable legal right with respect to the asset. This may or may not be the same moment when one spouse comes into possession of that asset during marriage.[12] Thus in California, for all assets except sums on deposit in an account, proof of possession during marriage is not sufficient to raise a community property presumption. Nor is possession during marriage necessarily determinative of acquisition during marriage. In the context of a long term marriage, evidence of possession may be circumstantial evidence of acquisition. But in a short term marriage, possession alone is usually not a reliable enough proxy for date of acquisition to raise the general presumption.[13]

Fidelity & Casualty Co. v. Mahoney illustrates the difference between possession and acquisition in the context of a short term marriage.[14] In that case, a spouse of two months used a small amount of out-of-pocket cash ($1) to buy a flight accident insurance policy. The insured named his son as sole beneficial designee for the policy. The plane crashed. The insured died. The insured's surviving spouse sued for a community property share of the $5,000 insurance proceeds — i.e. $2,500. The surviving spouse argued that the general presumption is raised by a showing that during marriage the decedent possessed the $1 that bought the policy. In reliance on the presumption, the surviving spouse did not introduce financial evidence as to when the cash was acquired, the nature of decedent's bank accounts, or the amount

---

[12] *Marriage of Green*, 56 Cal. 4th 1130, 1140, 158 Cal. Rptr. 3d 247, 255, 302 P.3d 562 (Cal. 2013).

[13] Texas, by comparison, has two general community property statutes: One applies to property acquired during marriage, and the other applies to property possessed during or on dissolution of the marriage. *See* V.T.C.A. § 3.002 and 3.003.

[14] *Fidelity & Casualty Co. v. Mahoney*, 71 Cal. App. 2d 65, 161 P.2d 944 (Cal. App. Ct., 2d Dist. 1945). In an accident policy, an accident is the contingency insured against; death is but one class or type of injury insured against in the event of an accident.

and frequency of the decedent's salary. The trial court declined to raise the general community property presumption: It explained that no evidence of date of acquisition had been presented. The surviving spouse appealed. The court of appeal affirmed the trial court's decision. The fact that the marriage was short (two months) required evidence, either direct (payroll records) or circumstantial (bank records), on the issue of date of acquisition for the cash ($1) that the surviving spouse alleged the decedent had used to purchase the accident insurance policy.

To sum up, in California, in a dispute between spouses as to the character of an asset, the general presumption of community ownership is raised on evidence that the disputed property was acquired during marriage. Rebuttal rests with the separate property proponent to trace the asset back to a separate property source or to produce an enforceable agreement between the parties that the property is not to be community property. Proportional ownership is permitted. The standard for rebuttal is preponderance of the evidence.

[2] Form of Title

The general presumption applies to untitled assets and to assets that are titled in one spouse's name.

It is not uncommon for community property assets to be titled, registered, or password protected in one spouse's name only. More importantly, in a dispute between spouses, the act of taking title to property in one spouse's name does not defeat the other spouse's community property ownership rights in that property. Community property vests upon acquisition. Therefore, according to general principles of property law, the unnamed spouse retains an equitable one-half interest in an asset even if it is titled in the other spouse's name only.

Sometimes trial or appellate court opinions err by applying an evidence code form of title presumption to assets titled in one spouse's name. These opinions are routinely overruled and superseded by the state Supreme Court.

[3] Rebuttal by Tracing or by Agreement

A presumption is **"an assumption of fact that the law requires to be made from another fact or group of facts found or otherwise established in the action. A presumption is not evidence."** Generally, presumptions are either conclusive or rebuttable under Cal. Evid. Code § 600; all community property presumptions are rebuttable.

In the context of § 760 the general community property presumption affects the burden of proof. Thus a spouse who claims a separate property interest in an asset must prove his or her claim. Separate property is defined by statute, as discussed in Chapter 3, but it can also be identified by tracing and by an enforceable contract.

The low preponderance of the evidence standard is the default standard used in civil actions. It is also the default rebuttal standard used by the Family Code. In disputes between spouses about the character of property, this low standard is appropriate because it allocates the risk of judicial error more or less equally between the spouses.

As the court of appeal explained in *Marriage of Ettefagh*, "since both parties have identical economic interests at risk in contesting [the method of property acquisition], it [is] appropriate to apply the preponderance standard on the issue because of its roughly equal distribution of the risk of error."[15] The *Ettefagh* view is consistent with the Legislature's rejection of fault based divorce. Moreover, it strikes a balance between protecting the community estate and protecting each spouse's right to own separate property during marriage.

Proportional rebuttal is permitted. A basic arithmetic tracing formula assists in calculating percentage shares.

The Basic Tracing Formula:

$$\frac{\text{CP contribution to purchase}}{\text{Purchase Price}} = \text{CP \% ownership}$$

$$\frac{\text{SP contribution to purchase}}{\text{Purchase Price}} = \text{SP \% ownership}$$

Example 2.14: This example illustrates the importance of timing in raising the general presumption. One day before marriage, Sansome and Taylor buy a used dining room table (an untitled asset) for their home. The purchase is made with cash earnings from Sansome's job. Five years later, Taylor petitions for dissolution. Taylor argues that the table is presumptively community property because it was purchased for the marital home. Sansome introduces evidence that the table was purchased before marriage. On these facts, the general presumption does not get raised because the table was acquired before, not during, marriage. The table is Sansome's separate property.

Example 2.15: This example involves an untitled asset acquired during marriage. One day after getting married, Sansome and Taylor buy a dining room table for their home. The general presumption is raised since the table was acquired during marriage. Rebuttal rests with the separate property claimant to show, by a preponderance of the evidence, that the table traces back to separate property.

Example 2.16: This example involves an asset acquired during marriage and titled in one spouse's name. Sansome and Taylor buy a house during marriage, taking title in Sansome's name only. Sansome contributes $25,000 of separate property as a downpayment on the $100,000 purchase price; the community contributes the remaining $75,000. At dissolution, the house is worth $200,000. In a dispute between Taylor and Sansome, the general presumption is raised because

---

[15] *Marriage of Ettefagh*, 150 Cal. App. 4th 1578, 59 Cal. Rptr. 3d 419 (Cal. App. Ct., 1st Dist. 2007), citing *Marriage of Peters*, 52 Cal. App. 4th 1487, 1491, 61 Cal. Rptr. 2d 493, 495 (Cal. App. Ct., 3d Dist. 1997).

the house was acquired during marriage. Sansome has the burden to rebut the presumption, something Sansome can do by tracing purchase funds back to a separate property source. Here, Sansome's separate property estate made a 25% contribution to the purchase of the house: This is calculated by dividing Sansome's separate property downpayment ($25,000) by the total purchase price of the house ($100,000). When the house is sold for $200,000, Sansome's separate property estate is entitled to a reimbursement for Sansome's $25,000 separate property contribution to purchase *plus* a 25% share of the market appreciation.

One final note: The house is co-owned between Sansome's separate property estate (25%) and the community estate (75%). The house may be in Sansome's name only, and the spouses may have agreed to that title designation, but the form of title — without a Family Code compliant transmutation — is not sufficient to divest the community estate of its 75% equitable ownership interest. Transmutations are discussed in Chapter 14.

Example 2.17: This example illustrates how the general community property presumption can be rebutted by an agreement between the spouses. Same as Example 2.16 except that Sansome and Taylor execute an enforceable premarital agreement that all real estate purchases titled in Sansome's name during marriage will be Sansome's separate property subject to a right of reimbursement in the community estate. Here, the house is presumed community property because it was acquired during the marriage. But Sansome successfully rebuts the general presumption entirely (100%) with the enforceable agreement, subject to the community estate's right of reimbursement for its contributions to purchase.

The main point is that in a community property system title alone does not determine ownership. Relatedly, the absence of a written title does not make an asset separate property. Nor does written title in one spouse's name only. No written title or title in a separate property contributor's name does however result in distinct benefits for the separate property contributor. One, it allows the separate property contributor to rebut the (general) community property presumption by tracing or by agreement. Two, it allows the separate property claimant to request a reimbursement for a contribution to purchase and to prove a proportional ownership claim to market appreciation. Three, it neither increases the separate property contributor's liabilities, nor diminishes the other spouse's liabilities.

[B] The Special Family Code Presumption for Assets in Joint Form Title

A special community property presumption is explained by the Legislature at § 2580 and set forth at § 2581. In a dissolution proceeding, the special § 2581 presumption applies to property that was acquired during marriage in any joint form title.

During marriage, § 750 permits spouses to hold property **"as joint tenants, or tenants in common, or as community property, or as community property with the right of survivorship."** Only tenancy by the entirety cannot be created in California. All four of these possibilities are joint form titles; but not all of these titles are community property titles. The joint title forms known as "joint tenancy" and "tenancy in common" fall outside of the community property system: for that reason they are characterized as separate property titles forms. The joint title forms "community property" and "community property with the right of survivorship" fall *within* the community property system: for that reason they are community property title forms. Joint title forms are discussed in Chapter 3.

Prior California case law on the characterization of assets in joint form title was woefully inconsistent over a long period of time.

With the enactment of § 2580 the legislature recognized that inconsistent precedent gave rise to a substantial problem: spouses could not **"have reliable expectations as to the characterization of their property held in joint form at dissolution;"** and attorneys could not give reliable advice. Plus, the conflicting precedent created an incentive for the parties in a dissolution proceeding to commit perjury. Therefore, the Legislature formally recognized — in § 2580 — that **"a compelling state interest exists to provide for uniform treatment of property"** acquired during marriage in joint form title. To further the state's interest, the Legislature adopted the special community property presumption that appears at § 2581.

Today, all U.S. community property jurisdictions except Nevada have enacted or now apply a joint form title presumption in dissolution proceedings. Arizona and New Mexico extend the presumption to estate proceedings.

[1] Joint Form Title in a Dissolution Proceeding

The special presumption in § 2581 applies in all dissolution proceedings commenced on or after January 1, 1984, as to any asset that was acquired during marriage in both spouses' names. The presumption affects the burden of proof. Rebuttal is by proof of an agreement between the parties that the asset is not to be community property.

The Legislature makes clear by the express terms of the statutory scheme that the general presumption of § 760 is superseded by the presumption of § 2581, which reads: ***"For the purpose of division of property on dissolution of marriage or legal separation of the parties,*** **property acquired by the parties during marriage in joint form, including property held in tenancy in common, joint tenancy, or tenancy by the entirety, or as community property, is presumed to be community property."** (Italics added.)

[2] Rebuttal by Agreement Only

Rebuttal of § 2581 is limited to either of the following methods:

- § 2581(a): **"A clear statement in the deed . . . that the property is separate property and not community property."**
- § 2581(b): **"Proof that the parties have made a written agreement that the property is separate property."**

The logic of the special § 2581 presumption incorporates the contractual modification principle. According to that principle, when spouses acquire property in any joint form title that act represents an initial ("first) agreement between the spouses that the titled asset will be characterized as community property in the event of dissolution. This "first" agreement is rebuttable, but only by a subsequent "second" agreement that the property is not to be community property.

The terms of § 2581(a) and (b) determine the form that a "second" rebuttal agreement must take to be enforceable. A rebuttal agreement must be in writing. That writing may either appear by express statement in the deed, or in a written document extrinsic to the deed. Proportional ownership between one or both separate property estates and the community estate is permitted, with proportions determined by the divorcing parties' rebuttal agreement (the so called "second" agreement). Tracing the divorcing parties' net character contributions to purchase (as with the general presumption) is disallowed for purposes of establishing a separate property ownership interest.

In the absence of a rebuttal agreement, the property is characterized as entirely (100%) community property. A separate property contributor is entitled to a reimbursement for any contributions to purchase of an entirely (100%) community property asset. Under § 2640, reimbursement is without interest and may not exceed the net value of the property at division. Reimbursement amounts are determined by tracing.

Example 2.18: This example illustrates the importance of timing to the special § 2581 presumption. Sansome and Taylor purchase a car before marriage. They take record title in joint tenancy. No other agreement is reached between them. In the event of divorce, the car is presumed to be concurrently owned separate property. The special § 2581 presumption applies only to property acquired *during marriage in joint form*, not to property acquired in joint form before marriage.

Example 2.19: This example applies the special § 2581 presumption. Sansome and Taylor purchase a car during marriage. They take record title in any joint title form. They reach no other agreement. In a dissolution proceeding, the car is presumed to be community property by application of § 2581.

Example 2.20: This example illustrates a § 2581 rebuttal by a clear statement in the deed. Sansome and Taylor purchase a second car during marriage. This time they take the title "*as joint tenants, as each spouse's separate property.*" In the event of divorce, the clear statement in the deed is sufficient to rebut the special § 2581 presumption. At dissolution, assuming rebuttal is successful, the car will be characterized as concurrently held separate property.

Example 2.21: This example illustrates a rebuttal by a written agreement, where there is no transmutation. Sansome and Taylor purchase a car during marriage. They take title in any joint title form. Sansome makes a separate property contribution of $2,500 to the $10,000 car purchase (25%). The community estate pays the remainder in cash. Upon taking title in both of their names, Sansome and Taylor also sign a valid written agreement that states: "*in the event of divorce, this car will be 25% separate property of the separate property contributor, Sansome, and 75% community property.*" At dissolution, the parties' agreement proportionally rebuts the special § 2581 presumption. The car is concurrently owned by Sansome's separate property estate (25%) and by the community property estate (75%). Ownership shares are determined by the rebuttal agreement itself, not by net character contributions to purchase. In this example, the rebuttal agreement happens to be identical to the character of the spouses' net contributions to purchase, which means that the second agreement need not also be analyzed for its compliance with transmutation formalities.

Example 2.22: This example illustrates a rebuttal by a written agreement, where there is a transmutation. Same purchase facts as Example 2.21 except that the spouses' agreement reads "*in the event of divorce, this car will be 10% Sansome's separate property and 90% community property.*" Here the second agreement rebuts the § 2581 presumption, just as it does in Example 2.21. However, in this example, the rebuttal agreement also purports to transmute — change the character of — Sansome's separate property into community property: Sansome made a 25% separate property contribution to purchase, but the agreement only recognizes a 10% separate property ownership share in the event of dissolution. In practical terms, this means that the rebuttal agreement will (likely) only be valid if it also meets Family Code transmutation requirements.

Example 2.23: This example illustrates the § 2640 right of reimbursement for separate property contributions to an entirely (100%) community property asset. Same purchase facts as Example 2.22 except that a court deems the second rebuttal agreement void for noncompliance with the transmutation formalities. Under these facts, the special § 2581 community property presumption stands: The car is entirely (100%) community property at dissolution. However, Sansome's separate property estate has a right to a statutory reimbursement under § 2640 for its traceable separate property contribution to the purchase of the car ($2,500). This reimbursement is without interest, and it comes out of sale proceeds, not to exceed the net value of the car. Alternatively, Sansome can elect to take an equitable lien on the car, in which case the value of the car at division (not at sale) will determine the amount of reimbursement.

Example 2.24: This example illustrates how the § 2640 reimbursement works in the case of an appreciating asset. Same facts as Example 2.23 except that the car is a classic car sought after by collectors. At dissolution the car is valued and sold for $20,000. Sansome's separate property estate contributed $2,500 to the $10,000 car purchase, which is entirely (100%) community property at dissolution by application of the § 2581 presumption. Despite the car's appreciation, under § 2640, Sansome's separate property estate is (still) only entitled to a reimbursement for its actual contribution to purchase of $2,500.

Example 2.25: This example illustrates how the § 2640 reimbursement works in the case of a depreciating asset. Same as Example 2.23 except the car is an ordinary (depreciating) car. At division the car is valued and sold for $2,000. Sansome's separate property estate contributed $2,500 of separate property to the $10,000 car purchase. Sansome's separate property estate is entitled to a no interest reimbursement under § 2640 of $2,500. Reimbursement shall be paid from the sale of the car. However, because this car has depreciated in value, Sansome's separate property reimbursement shall not exceed the net value of the property at the time of division. In this case, the reimbursement to Sansome's separate property (as determined by the sale proceeds) is limited to $2,000. Sansome loses $500 due to depreciation.

The above examples refer to a car. However, the special § 2581 presumption applies at dissolution to any asset acquired during marriage that is titled in any joint form. The § 2581 presumption does not apply to sums on deposit in an account, as discussed in Chapter 5.

[3] Retroactivity Issues

The special § 2581 community property *presumption* is retroactive: It gets raised no matter whether the property was acquired before or after the 1984 legal transition. The rationale for retroactive application is that the special presumption affects the burden of proof in a dissolution dispute between the spouses; it does not disturb vested property rights.[16]

By contrast, the statutory rebuttal requirements are not retroactive.[17] Oral rebuttal agreements made prior to January 1, 1984 to keep a separate property interest in property titled as *joint tenants* or as *tenants in common* remain enforceable notwithstanding the change in the law. Oral agreements made prior to January 1, 1987 to keep a separate property interest in property titled as *community property* also remain enforceable notwithstanding the change in the law.

The difference in treatment is due to a legislative oversight that becomes of less empirical concern to practitioners with the passage of time. That said, only rebuttal agreements that were entered into before January 1, 1984 (for assets titled as *joint tenants* or as *tenants in common*) and before January 1, 1987 (for assets titled as *community property*), are exempt from the writing requirement. All others must be in written form. The community property with the right of survivorship title form was not created until 2001; all such titles must be rebutted in writing, in accordance with § 2581.

The § 2640 right of reimbursement is not retroactive. A separate property contribution to the purchase of an entirely (100%) community property asset made before January 1, 1984 is presumed to be a gift to the community estate absent an agreement otherwise.[18] Whereas the § 2640 right of reimbursement applies to all separate property contributions to the purchase of an entirely (100%) community property asset made *on or after January 1, 1984*, absent an agreement otherwise.

[4] Different Outcome if the Marriage Terminates at Death

The special § 2581 community property presumption for joint form title applies only in a dissolution proceeding. It does not apply if the marriage terminates by the death of a spouse, which is to say it does not apply in a dispute between a surviving spouse and the decedent spouse's estate, or — at least by the terms of the statute itself — between a surviving spouse and a tax collecting agency.

---

[16] *Marriage of Buol*, 39 Cal. 3d 751, 218 Cal. Rptr. 31, 705 P.2d 354 (Cal. 1985) (in bank).

[17] *Marriage of Heikes*, 10 Cal. 4th 1211, 44 Cal. Rptr. 2d 155, 899 P.2d 1349 (Cal. 1995), distinguished by *Marriage of Koester*, 73 Cal. App. 4th 1032, 87 Cal. Rptr. 2d 76 (Cal. App. Ct., 4th Dist. 1999).

[18] *Marriage of Lucas*, 27 Cal. 3d 808, 166 Cal. Rptr. 853, 614 P.2d 285 (Cal. 1980).

When a marriage ends by the death of a spouse, joint form titles function as they are designed to with respect to the right of survivorship. Moreover, in terms of characterization, joint tenancy and tenancy in common are characterized and valued for tax purposes as concurrently owned separate property interests. Community property and community property with the right of survivorship are characterized and valued for tax purposes as community property interests. These issues are discussed in Chapter 3.

[C] A Special Probate Code Presumption for Sums on Deposit in an Account

In 1983, California adopted the California Multiple-Party Accounts Law (CAMPAL). When the probate code was repealed in 1989, CAMPAL was included in the 1990 re-adoption. CAMPAL was amended in 2012, effective January 1, 2013. The California Multiple-Party Accounts Law (CAMPAL) is discussed in detail in Chapter 5.

[1] Married Parties to an Account

CAMPAL, Cal. Prob. Code § 5305(a), states a special community property presumption. CAMPAL applies to all accounts, but the special presumption applies only to the accounts of married persons. The phrase "married persons" includes registered domestic partners.

CAMPAL § 5305(a) provides:

> **"[I]f parties to an account are married to each other, whether or not they are so described in the deposit agreement, their net contribution to the account is presumed to be and remain their community property."**

The Legislature made clear in the express terms of CAMPAL itself that the special community property presumption for sums on deposit in an account supersedes the general presumption and the special § 2581 presumption. Moreover, the Law Review Commission comments are replete with references to marriage. The policy of CAMPAL, as applied in the marriage context, is to protect the community estate's equitable ownership rights to sums on deposit from impairment due to the movement of money from account to account.

This special CAMPAL community property presumption is based on the fact of possession. It applies only to the sums on deposit in an account, not to the account itself. Possession of electronic sums on deposits is demonstrated by the presence (or absence) of the right of withdrawal to the account.

The special Cal. Prob. Code § 5305(a) presumption applies in a broad range of situations: For example, it applies regardless of whether the parties are identified on the account contract as married, It applies to all accounts, not just to accounts in both parties' names. It applies regardless of whether the account is commingled.

Some commentators suggest that Cal. Prob. Code § 5305(a) applies only at death, or only to joint accounts. The language of the CAMPAL states otherwise. To start with, the CAMPAL presumption generally applies to lifetime actions of the depositors and to methods of resolving disputes between living depositors. In addition, the Law Review Commission Comments (1990) explicitly state that Cal. Prob. Code § 5305 applies at dissolution: "The introductory clause of subdivision (b) makes clear that the [rebuttal] rule stated in subdivision (b) prevails over the rules stated in [the Family Code] with respect to the division of a joint account *upon dissolution of marriage or legal separation as well as for all other purposes.*"[19] [Italics added.] Moreover, the Preface to the Uniform MPAL suggests that CAMPAL be included in a state probate code, not because CAMPAL is limited to the estates context, but rather because CAMPAL is consistent with the Uniform Probate Code.

Therefore, at dissolution or death, the special Cal. Prob. Code § 5305(a) community property presumption applies to sums on deposit in an account. Those sums are presumed to be community property. Rebuttal rests with the separate property claimant.

[2] Rebuttal by Tracing or by Agreement

Rebuttal succeeds if either of the following is established by the separate property claimant:

- **"The sums on deposit that are claimed to be separate property can be traced from separate property unless it is proved that the married persons made a written agreement that expressed their clear intent that the sums be their community property."**
- **"The married persons made a written agreement, separate from the deposit agreement, that expressly provided that the sums on deposit, claimed not to be community property, were not to be community property."**

As the Law Review Commission Comments to Cal. Prob. Code § 5305 explain, these two rebuttal methods give spouses the flexibility to change, confirm, or trace the character of sums on deposit in an account during marriage, as well as to make written agreements about sums on deposit in a specific account. At the same time, since the special § 5305(a) presumption applies to all accounts (including business accounts, partnership accounts, and investment accounts), an additional important benefit of this special Cal. Prob. Code § 5305(a) presumption is that it protects the community estate's ownership interest in sums on deposit against loss caused by the one spouse's actions as to an account.

Thus, during marriage, if one spouse moves money from one account to another, or deposits money in one account or another, or signs or cancels a bank contract, the special presumption works to protect the community's interest in sums on deposit in the account. The community property presumption holds as to each account, and the rebuttal burden is on the separate property claimant as to each account.[20]

If the sums on deposit are withdrawn from an account and held as cash, the community is still protected, but not by Cal. Prob. Code § 5305(a), which only

[19] Cal. Prob. Code § 5305, Cal. Law Revision Comm. Report, 1990.

[20] Cal. Prob. Code § 5305, Law Review Commission Comments, 1990.

applies to sums on deposit in an account. Cash is an untitled asset governed by the general presumption; and cash purchases are presumed community property subject to rebuttal by tracing or agreement, depending on the way in which title to the purchased asset is held.

Additionally, Cal. Prob. Code § 5305(a) is consistent with prior community property law in the following ways:

- Cal. Prob. Code § 5305(a) applies to sums on deposit in an account during marriage: This leaves it to the separate property claimant to prove that certain sums on deposit were either brought to the marriage, received by gift, or else agreed not to be community property.
- Cal. Prob. Code § 5305(a), like other presumptions used in the community property system, is a presumption that affects the burden of proof in a dispute between spouses over the beneficial ownership of sums on deposit in an account. It does not transmute traceable sums on deposit.
- Cal. Prob. Code § 5305(a) can be modified by an enforceable premarital agreement or a valid transmutation agreement.
- Cal. Prob. Code § 5305(a) presumes, at death, that sums on deposit in a joint account belong to the surviving spouse, absent clear and convincing evidence of a different intent on the part of the decedent spouse.[21]

Example 2.26: This example illustrates the special presumptions for sums on deposit in an account. When Sansome and Taylor marry, Taylor has $1,000 on deposit in a bank account titled in Taylor's name only. From the date of marriage on, the sums on deposit in Taylor's account are nonconclusively presumed to be community property.

Example 2.27: This example illustrates how, upon dissolution, the special Cal. Prob. Code § 5305(a) community property presumption supersedes the special § 2581 presumption for sums on deposit in an account. When Sansome and Taylor marry, Taylor deposits sums in a joint bank account to which both Sansome and Taylor have the right of withdrawal. At dissolution, all sums on deposit are presumed to be community property by application of Cal. Prob. Code § 5305(a), not by application of § 2581 (which disallows rebuttal by tracing). The significance of this fact is that Cal. Prob. Code § 5305(a) gives the separate property claimant the full range of rebuttal methods: The claimant can either trace the disputed sums on deposit back to a separate property source, or else produce an enforceable interspousal agreement that the sums on deposit are not to be community property.

CAMPAL is discussed further in Chapter 5.

---

[21] Cal. Prob. Code § 5302(a); *Estate of Petersen*, 28 Cal. App. 4th 1742, 1750, 34 Cal. Rptr. 2d 449, 456 (Cal. App. Ct., 5th Dist. 1994).

[D] A Special Judicial Presumption for Funds Obtained on Credit

The lender's intent test is a judicially created rebuttal method that applies to situations where the lender transfers the funds borrowed by the spouses (as buyers) directly to their seller.

[1] Loan Proceeds for a Credit Acquisition

In a dispute between the spouses, the general presumption characterizes borrowed funds as community property unless the lender extended the loan *solely* on separate property information and assets.[22] Secured credit purchases are discussed in Chapter 6.

Loan proceeds transferred from the bank to a third party may not come into the possession of the spouses. So, for example, if the spouses buy a house or a car with a loan, the bank may advance the loan proceeds directly to the seller. In this case, the proceeds are presumed to be community property.

[2] Rebuttal by the Lender's Intent Test

Loan proceeds transferred from a bank to a seller on behalf of married persons remain within the possession of the lending institution. Therefore, rebuttal of the community property presumption is by the lender's intent test. The lender's intent test requires the separate property claimant to show that the lender extended the loan solely on the basis of separate property.

Once loan proceeds are distributed to one or both spouses, other presumptions apply. If the lender transfers possession of the loan proceeds to one or both spouses in the form of cash, the general presumption applies because cash is an untitled asset. If the lender deposits the loan proceeds into an account, those deposits come under the Cal. Prob. Code § 5305(a) presumption for sums on deposit in an account. Thus, where the spouses take actual possession of the loan proceeds, the lender's intent test is superseded by other rebuttal methods, depending on the facts. Still, the lender's intent test may be relevant to tracing. *See* Chapters 5 and 6.

§ 2.04 ONEROUS ACQUISITION: THE LABOR PRINCIPLE

The civil law analysis distinguished between onerous and lucrative acquisitions. An onerous acquisition was the result of labor, industry, or bargained for exchange expended during marriage. A lucrative acquisition was the result of a gratuity or a windfall received during marriage.

In disputes between spouses, California courts have long used a civil law analysis to better characterize what de Funiak and Vaughn label "equivocal assets," meaning assets that are difficult to characterize.[23] The following analysis applies to equivocal

---

[22] *Gudelj v. Gudelj*, 41 Cal. 2d 202, 259 P.2d 656 (Cal. 1953) (in bank); *Marriage of Grinius*, 166 Cal. App. 3d 1179, 212 Cal. Rptr. 803 (Cal. App. Ct., 4th Dist. 1985).

[23] de Funiak & Vaughn, *supra* Chapter 1.

assets. In terms of property theory, the onerous-lucrative distinction turns on the labor principle. It invokes a range of other property theories as well, from protecting first possession to maximizing social happiness to protecting personhood.

The onerous-lucrative distinction applies to types or categories of assets that are acquired during marriage. Work earnings and salaries, whether current or deferred, are onerously acquired, which makes them community property under § 760. Gifts received for no consideration whatsoever are lucrative acquisitions, which makes them separate property by definition of § 770.

At the end of a marriage, spouses must disclose **"all assets and liabilities in which one or both . . . may have an interest"** — (§ 2100 et seq.). An asset for these purposes **"includes, but is not limited to, any real or personal property of any nature, whether tangible or intangible, and whether currently existing or contingent."** By this standard, onerously acquired property includes but is not limited to:

- Business gifts received in lieu of work compensation;
- Business profits that result from one or both spouse's labor, managerial skill, or judgment;
- Deferred compensation;
- Adverse possession claims;
- Enforceable contract rights and proceeds;
- Contingent interests;
- Contract consideration received.

Onerous property can be vested or contingent. The fact that an interest is contingent does not necessarily make it lucrative.

Contingent property includes, for example, enforceable contract rights contingent on a future occurrence, such as contractual promises between an employer and an employee to award a bonus for reaching a productivity target.

A contingent interest is not a mere expectancy.[24] A mere expectancy might be an employer's promise of an at-will bonus; a bonus contingent solely upon continued at-will employment; or any other compensation promised by the employer on an at-will basis.[25] Employer resolutions promising to give compensation in the future (even if for past work) may be treated by the courts as mere expectancies, not as contract or contingent rights. Even so, all of these examples are onerous property once the expectancy becomes contingent.

By comparison, resolutions are not bargained for exchanges. Plus they are subject to nullification by a governing board, as with a non-profit organization. Therefore, resolutions, even once they become contingent or vest, are more lucrative than not.

---

[24] *Marriage of Brown*, 15 Cal. 3d 838, 845, 126 Cal. Rptr. 633, 544 P.2d 561 (Cal. 1976) (in bank).

[25] *Marriage of Nelson*, 177 Cal. App. 3d 150, 157–58, 222 Cal. Rptr. 790 (Cal. App. Ct., 1st Dist). 1986).

Downer v. Bramet is an example of the onerous-lucrative distinction applied.[26] In 1972, husband Keith's employer gave him an interest in an Oregon ranch; Keith did not disclose that interest in a marriage settlement agreement executed in that same year with wife, Gloria.[27] Keith had a stroke in 1976. In 1978, the ranch was sold for $1,350,000, at which time Keith's one-third of the sale proceeds was turned over to his conservator. In 1980, former wife, Gloria, learned about the sale of the ranch. She sued Keith on several grounds, one of which was to determine her community property interest in the ranch sale proceeds. Gloria argued that Keith's acquisition of the ranch was acquired during marriage in lieu of pension benefits, and therefore it fell within the definition of § 760 community property. To support her claim, Gloria introduced the following evidence: Keith and his employer did not socialize as friends; the employer offered no pension benefits to its employees; and the employer made similar gifts to similarly situated employees. Keith, through his conservator, moved to dismiss Gloria's claims on the theory that a gift received during marriage, by definition, is separate property. The trial court granted Keith's motion. Gloria appealed. The court of appeal reversed and remanded, holding that the trial court erred in dismissing Gloria's characterization claim. According to the court of appeal "although the conveyance of the ranch interest to former husband was in the form of a gift, the evidence would support, indeed strongly suggests (sic), that it was in whole or part a remunerative gift in recognition of the former husband's loyal and skillful efforts and services to his employer."[28]

The case was remanded so that the trial court could determine whether the ranch was onerously acquired by Keith during the marriage. If it was, then the general presumption would be raised in Gloria's favor as to the proceeds obtained from the sale of Keith's interest in the ranch.

Furthermore, the court held that Keith had a duty to disclose the existence of the ranch at the time of the 1972 marriage settlement agreement: The community property *might* have had an interest in it. Without disclosure, however, that interest would or could not be identifiable.

§ 2.05 PROPERTY INVENTORIES

California, Idaho, Nevada and Texas permit a married person to delineate separate property by use of an inventory, or list of assets.

If the inventory is compiled before marriage, most of the assets on the inventory will remain separate property during the marriage, *unless they have been commingled.* Inventories can be updated during marriage as assets are acquired.

The benefit of a separate property inventory is that it can identify property by date of acquisition, by type of property, by net contribution to purchase, and so forth. These factors, along with the existence of the inventory itself, can aid a court in characterizing property in the event of a dispute between the spouses.

---

[26] *Downer v. Bramet*, 152 Cal. App. 3d 837, 199 Cal. Rptr. 830 (Cal. App. Ct., 4th Dist. 1984).

[27] Cal. Fam. Code § 770.

[28] *Downer, supra* at 841.

Furthermore, an inventory puts each spouse on notice of the other spouse's expectations as to the character of listed and omitted assets. An inventory can also serve as notice to third parties. An inventory is not a premarital or marital agreement, although it can be incorporated into one. For that reason an inventory, standing alone, does not trump the rules of the Family Code, but it can be useful for establishing expectations and for identifying contributions to purchase.

§ 2.06 SUMMARY

"Community property" is property, wherever situated, that is acquired during marriage by the onerous activity of a spouse, while domiciled in California. California has two additional categories of community property: "quasi-community property" and "quasi-marital property." Quasi-community property is property acquired by a spouse while domiciled elsewhere that would have been community property had it been acquired while domiciled in California. Quasi-marital property is property acquired during a putative marriage.

A personal injury claim that arose during marriage against a third party results in a special category of community property that is subject to a mandatory assignment rule at dissolution. Special community property shall be assigned to the injured spouse as separate property unless it has been commingled to the point of confusion with ordinary community property, or where the interests of justice demand otherwise.

The basic statute that defines community property gives rise to a general presumption, not a rule. The general presumption applies in the absence of a special presumption. The general community property presumption is raised by proof of acquisition during marriage. Rebuttal requires the separate property proponent to trace the property back to a separate property source. An agreement may also rebut the general presumption.

Property acquired during marriage in both spouses' names is presumed to be community property for purposes of a dissolution proceeding only. Rebuttal is by agreement only. A spouse who seeks to rebut this special joint form title presumption must point to a clear statement in the deed or to a written interspousal agreement — separate from the deed itself — that confirms the separate property character of the jointly titled asset. Tracing cannot be used to rebut this special joint form title presumption. This special presumption applies only in a dissolution proceeding to disputes between spouses. Disputes between a spouse and a third party do not fall under the ambit of the special presumption.

Sums on deposit in an account during marriage are presumed to be community property. This is so no matter whether one or both spouses are named on the bank account contract, and no matter when and how the sums on deposit were acquired. Rebuttal rests with the separate property proponent to either trace the sums on deposit back to a separate property source, or to produce a written interspousal agreement that confirms the separate property character of disputed sums on deposit. The interspousal agreement must be extrinsic to the deposit agreement between the account owner and the financial institution.

The civil law system provides an additional aid for characterizing assets. This analytic is the onerous-lucrative distinction. An asset is community property if it is acquired by one or both spouses during the marriage with labor, industry, judgment, talent, consideration, managerial skill, or effort. By contrast, an asset is separate property if it is acquired by one or both spouses during marriage by gift or windfall.

Chapter 3

SEPARATE PROPERTY

Separate property is protected by the California Constitution.

The Family Code defines separate property in a number of provisions. The general definition of separate property is property acquired before marriage or during marriage by gift, bequest, devise or descent. In California, rents, issues and profits of separate property are also characterized as separate property. Personal injury claims (and recoveries) that arose before marriage and after separation are separate property of the injured spouse. Interspousal domestic violence monetary awards and personal injury claims (and recoveries) are separate property of the injured spouse.

The policy supporting the protection of separate property rests with recognition of individual property rights, as well as personhood, as in the case of personal injury awards. The separate property claimant generally has the burden to rebut any applicable community property presumption. He or she does that by proving that the disputed property falls within or has its source in a statutory definition of separate property. In some cases, rebuttal can also be made by an enforceable agreement that the property is not to be community property, or by a valid transmutation.

§ 3.01 STATE CONSTITUTIONAL PROTECTION

Article XI, Section14 of the California Constitution of 1849, protected the separate property of a married woman. The Organic Act of 1850 recognized the community property system and the separate property rights of the wife, but then gave the husband the legal right to manage and control the wife's separate property during the continuance of the marriage. The wife's interest in the community property was not calculable unless and until a dissolution or the husband's death. The California Constitution of 1879, Article XX, Section 8 continued to recognize the community property system by broadening its definition and its guarantee of separate property rights from the wife to both spouses, but the wife remained restricted in her rights of management and control. Until 1975, the husband was the legal manager of the community property estate.

The 1979 California Constitution continues to define and guarantee the separate property rights of both spouses to separate property. Article 1, Section 21 reads: **"Property owned before marriage or acquired during marriage by gift, will or inheritance is separate property."**

Additionally, the Family Code protects a married person's right to separate property, a married person's right to community property, and a married person's right to be free from bodily harm. Management and control is gender neutral: Either spouse has the right to manage and control community property, as discussed in Chapter 10.

The basic separate property definition appears at § 770. Personal injury claims and awards are specifically defined as either community property (§ 780) or as separate property (§ 781), depending on when the claim arose and whom the claim can be brought against (a third party or the other spouse).

A spouse has exclusive rights to manage and control his or her separate property. Additionally, § 770(b) provides: **"[a] married person may, without the consent of the person's spouse, convey the person's separate property."**

However, once separate property is commingled with community property, Family Code rules of management and control apply to the commingled property. This protects against the impairment of the community property interest.

§ 3.02 THE BASIC STATUTE

Time and manner of acquisition are relevant to the characterization of property.

[A] Time and Manner of Acquisition

The general rule is that property acquired before marriage or during marriage by lucrative acquisition is the separate property of the acquiring spouse.

[1] Before Marriage

Before the date of marriage, all accumulations are owned as individual property. Unmarried persons are not within the community property system.

When property acquired before marriage is brought to a marriage, § 770(a)(1) defines it as separate property: **"Separate property of a married person includes . . . all property owned by the person before marriage."** This is the case no matter whether the property was acquired onerously or lucratively.

Example 3.1: This example illustrates that property brought to the marriage is characterized as separate property. Larkin and Mason plan to marry. Prior to marriage, Larkin owns a parcel of real estate. Mason owns a car. These assets are the individual property of their respective owners. When Larkin and Mason marry, the real estate is characterized as Larkin's separate property. The car is characterized as Mason's separate property.

Example 3.2: This example illustrates the California separate property rents, issues and profits rule. Larkin owns an unencumbered rental before marriage. That rental is individual property. On the date of Larkin's marriage to Mason, the rental is characterized as Larkin's separate property, as are rents, issues and profits derived from the rental during marriage.

Commingled property retains its character. If separate property rents — as in Example 3.2 — are deposited into an account with community property sums on deposit, all of the sums on deposit are presumed community property. The separate property owner of the rent producing asset then bears the burden of rebutting that presumption as to the deposited rents. Rebuttal can be by tracing or by an agreement between the spouses that the rents, notwithstanding their deposit into a specific account during marriage, are not to be community property.

[2] By Gift

Under § 770(a)(2), **"[A]ll property acquired by the person after marriage by gift, bequest, devise, or descent"** is separate property.

[a] Gifts from Third Parties

Any gift received during marriage is the donee spouse's separate property. This is so whether the gift is received by inter vivos transfer, by testamentary transfer, or by intestate succession.

A brief review of the common law of gifts is perhaps useful at this point. This law interacts with community property law.

An inter vivos gift is valid if it meets three elements. The donor intends to divest him or herself of the property — typically this element requires proof of a present donative intent. The donor delivers the property to the donee in such a way as to part with dominion and control of it. And the donee accepts the property. When all three elements are met, title to the property transfers from the donor to the donee.

Generally, a valid inter vivos gift, once made, is irrevocable. However, the law of gifts allows a donor to make a gift revocable. A donor exercises this option by expressly conditioning the gift on the occurrence or nonoccurrence of a future event, thus demonstrating the donor's conditional donative intent. A conditional gift is one in which the donor retains a reversionary interest. If the contingency named is satisfied, title to the gift passes to the donee. But if the contingency does not come to pass, then the donor retains title to the property, notwithstanding proof of delivery or acceptance. Without donative intent, there can be no gift. The policy underlying the donative intent requirement protects the donor from fraud. The same is true of the delivery requirement.

Delivery can be manual, constructive, or symbolic. The donee has the burden of proving delivery. Therefore, it is generally agreed that the clearest delivery method is the one that best suits the character of the property. Courts typically require manual delivery. But manual delivery is not always practicable. When it isn't, constructive or symbolic delivery can be made. Constructive delivery allows the donor to make a gift by delivering an object that provides the donee with access to the item: For example, a key can be constructive delivery of a car. Symbolic delivery allows the donor to make a gift by delivering to the donee an object that symbolizes the gift: For example, a title document (pink slip) can be symbolic delivery of a car.

Acceptance by the donee is presumed if the gift is valuable.

In the community property system, property acquired by a spouse from a decedent's estate is considered a lucrative acquisition. A testamentary gift is made by valid will to a decedent's beneficiaries. In the case of intestate succession, the state distributes the decedent's property to his or her heirs or next of kin. Gifts in trust are non-testamentary transfers made to the settlor's trust beneficiaries. All of these transfers, if received during the marriage, are characterized as the recipient spouse's separate property under § 770(a)(2).

Gifts of cash are untitled property, governed by the general presumption. Once cash is deposited into an account, it is presumptively community property under the special Cal. Prob. Code § 5305(a) presumption. If a recipient spouse is concerned with his or her ability to trace a monetary gift back to a separate property source, he or she can rebut the community property presumption for sums on deposit either by tracing or by agreement. A rebuttal agreement for this purpose must be specific to a particular account, as well as to the particular sums on deposit in that account. Either rebuttal approach for Cal. Prob. Code § 5305(a) — by tracing or by agreement regarding sums on deposit in an account — likely requires the recipient spouse to produce proof of the original gift. Accounts are discussed in Chapters 2 and 5.

[b] Wedding Gifts

The Family Code is silent on how to characterize wedding gifts. Nonetheless, § 770(a)(1) and (2) make clear that all property acquired by the person before marriage and after marriage by gift, bequest, devise, or descent is the person's separate property. By this language a gift made before or (even) during marriage falls within the statutory definition of separate property.

Before marriage, an engagement or a wedding gift is received by the prospective spouses as individuals, not as spouses.

Generally, an engagement gift made by a third party is irrevocable. The donor can change this outcome by expressly making the gift conditional upon the occurrence of the marriage. Such a condition must be established by direct proof; it will not be implied merely from the fact that the recipients of the gift were intending to marry.

The controlling case is *Simonian v. Donoian*.[1] In that case, a prospective mother-in-law delivered a diamond set wristwatch to her son's fiancée at an engagement announcement party. The prospective mother-in-law delivered her gift to the donee with these words: "This is from dad and I." A short time later, the prospective husband canceled the wedding. He sued his former fiancée for return of the diamond set wristwatch. The court held that the defendant-donee had the superior right to the property. Title passed from the donor to the donee upon delivery, notwithstanding the cancellation of the marriage. The donor expressed unconditional donative intent along with her delivery of the property.

Under the common law of gifts, a donor has the right to expressly condition a wedding gift on the occurrence of the marriage. If so, the donor retains a reversionary interest in the gift, which is conditional on the marriage ensuing. If the wedding is called off, the donor is entitled to return of the gift, or its value. But

---

1 *Simonian v. Donoian*, 96 Cal. App. 2d 259, 262, 215 P.2d 119, 121 (Cal. App. Ct., 2d Dist. 1950).

if the wedding takes place, then the gift is received by the spouses as concurrently held separate property.

Two theories support these outcomes. The first covers engagement gifts to the couple. A contingent engagement gift creates an enforceable property right prior to marriage; therefore under § 770(a)(1) the gift — despite its contingent nature — is defined as property acquired before marriage. The alternative theory applies to a wedding gift received during marriage. A wedding gift acquired by each spouse during marriage, is a lucrative acquisition, which means that it is defined as separate property under § 770(a)(2).

A conditional gift cannot be made by an expression of future donative intent ("I *will* give you a car when you get married.") If oral, such an attempt would be void; and if made by writing, such an attempt would be an invalid testamentary transfer. A conditional gift, such as one made contingent on the occurrence of the parties' marriage, must be made by an expression of *present* donative intent, and it must be accompanied by an express condition. ("I give you this gift conditional on the occurrence of your upcoming marriage.") In practical terms, this means that for a conditional gift to be valid, a donor must intend to give the prospective spouses an enforceable right as of the date of delivery, even if the condition that triggers vesting (the occurrence of the marriage) will not occur until a future date.

Sometimes donors attempt to get around this problem by expressing the present intent to make a gift, but then withholding possession of the gift until after the prospective spouses are married. Here, proof of donative intent is present, but proof of delivery is not. A donor can get around this delivery problem by explicitly expressing the condition upon which the gift is made, and only then relinquishing possession. Or a donor can deliver title to the gift by symbolic means (a writing), but then retain the right of possession until a later date.[2] Or a donor can deliver the gift of personal property to a proxy-donee with the intention of retaining a reversionary interest in the gift until the occurrence of the wedding.[3]

Some commentators suggest that a donor can deliver a gift with the manifest intention that it be accepted by the donee-spouses as community property. While this may be the case in other community property systems, no California case has so held. In light of the state constitutional protections for and the statutory definitions of separate property, the more likely legal outcome is that wedding gifts, because they are lucratively acquired, are defined as separate property, whether acquired before or during the marriage. If a donor wishes to affect the characterization of a gift, he or she can perhaps reliably do so by delivering the gift to the spouses during the marriage in joint title form; or by exchanging the gift for some (nominal) consideration from the parties after they have married. An alternative approach is that the parties can agree by premarital contract or by valid transmutation to change the character of the wedding gifts from separate property to community property upon the occurrence of the marriage.

---

[2] *See, e.g.*, *Gruen v. Gruen*, 68 N.Y.2d 48, 496 N.E.2d 869 (N.Y. 1986).

[3] *See, e.g.*, Restatement (Second) of Property: Donative Transfers § 31.2 (1992) (Gift of Personal Property in Which Donor Retains Reversionary Interest applies to gifts that are made without transfer documents).

Received during marriage, a gift titled in one spouse's name raises the general presumption. Rebuttal is by tracing. If rebuttal is successful, the spouse whose name is not on title retains an equitable interest in the wedding gift as concurrently owned separate property under § 770(a)(2).

A wedding gift received by the spouses during marriage in any joint form title is governed by the special § 2581 community property presumption in a dissolution proceeding. This special presumption is rebuttable only by a subsequent agreement between the spouses that the asset is not to be community property in the event of dissolution. At the death of a spouse, the special § 2581 presumption does not apply; instead, the character of a jointly titled asset will depend upon its joint title form. A gift titled in the tenancy in common or in joint tenancy is concurrently held separate property. A gift titled in community property or community property with the right of survivorship is community property. Characterization is relevant for succession and tax valuation, as discussed in Example 3.29 and Example 3.30 below.

Wedding gifts of cash are characterized differently than is other personal property. Cash is an untitled asset. As such, cash is subject to the general community property presumption unless and until it gets deposited into a bank account. But once deposited, the gift of cash is governed by the special Cal. Prob. Code § 5305(a) presumption for sums on deposit in an account. This is so regardless of whether the cash gift was received before or during marriage.

The Restatement Second of Property, Donative Transfers, § 31.2 protects the donor's reversionary interest in a conditional gift of personal property even if the gift is oral, which is to say made without a document of transfer, or even if the condition is not expressly stated. The rationale is that a donor may intend to make a gift of personal property conditional on the occurrence of nonoccurrence of a wedding — our topic here — but then not take the extra step of expressing that intention in writing. The outcome in *Simonian* might have been different had the court applied this Restatement approach.

In light of the social sensitivity of the wedding context, the Restatement specifically protects the reversionary rights of a donor in a number of wedding gift related transfers. It protects the donor's reversionary rights in making a gift of personal property explicitly conditional upon the occurrence of the donee's or donees' contemplated marriage. It protects the reversionary rights of the donor when he or she makes a gift of personal property to a proxy-donee with the manifest intention that the proxy-donee return that property to the donor at a certain time: A paradigmatic example of this occurs when the donor is a prospective spouse who gives the wedding ring to a person in the wedding party with the intention that it be returned to the donor during the wedding ceremony. Cases involving personal property gifts made by one prospective spouse to the other prospective spouse are covered by Restatement § 31.2.

The tracing principle assures that property received in exchange for separate property is itself separate property. By this principle, rents, issues and profits of separate property gifts are themselves characterized as separate property under § 770(a)(3).

Example 3.3: This example illustrates how inter vivos gifts acquired during marriage by one spouse meet the § 770(a)(2) definition of separate property. Larkin and Mason are married. During marriage Larkin receives a collectible guitar from a parent. This guitar is Larkin's separate property.

Example 3.4: This example illustrates how testamentary bequests received during marriage meet the § 770(a)(2) definition of separate property. During marriage to Larkin, Mason's grandparent leaves him registered securities. On the grandparent's death, the securities are Mason's separate property.

Example 3.5: This example illustrates how testamentary devises received during marriage by one spouse meet the § 770(a)(2) definition of separate property. Larkin's mother dies. She leaves the family ranch to Larkin in her will. This devise is Larkin's separate property.

Example 3.6: This example illustrates how gifts in trust received during marriage are the separate property of the beneficiary-spouse. Mason is an income beneficiary for a trust settled by Mason's grandparent. During marriage to Larkin, Mason's interest in the trust property is Mason's separate property under § 770(a)(2). If Mason deposits trust income into an account, those sums become governable by the special Cal. Prob. Code § 5305(a) presumption. Mason can (easily) rebut by tracing the sums on deposit back to the trust, or by producing an agreement between the spouses that Mason's trust fund distributions are not to be community property.

[c] Gifts Made by a Party to a Contemplated Marriage

The validity of title to property that is exchanged by gratuitous transfer is governed by the common law of gifts. A gift made by a third party to a person in contemplation of the donee's marriage is an engagement gift as discussed in the text above at § 3.02[2][a]. A gift made by a third party to a couple on the occasion of their marriage is a wedding gift, as discussed in § 3.02[2][b]. For the purposes of consistency of coverage, gifts exchanged between persons who are contemplating marriage to each other are discussed herein at § 3.02[2][c].

Between parties to a contemplated marriage, gifts made during the engagement period (i.e., before marriage) are the donee's individual property. Upon marriage, these gifts gets redefined within the community property system as the donee's § 770(a)(1) separate property.

If the upcoming marriage is canceled during the engagement period, however, the California Cal. Civ. Code § 1590 modifies the common law of gifts by making the transfer potentially revocable by the donor.

Early unmarried cohabitant cases raised the issue of whether Cal. Civ. Code § 43.5 — California's anti-heart balm statute — barred the enforcement of a pooling contract between nonmarried cohabitants. In 1976, the California Supreme Court case of *Marvin v. Marvin* put an end to that line of inquiry when it held that nonmarried cohabitants have the right to enter into enforceable pooling contracts as a general civil matter.[4] The rights of unmarried cohabitants are discussed in Chapter 15.

Today, disputes over gifts made in contemplation of marriage can occur in the context of a nullified marriage for which the parties are not permitted to use the quasi-marital property system. They can also occur in the context of engaged cohabitants who break-up before they can marry.

The anti-heart balm statute prevents various lawsuits arising from a break-up. Cal. Civ. Code § 43.5, was added to the civil code in 1939, it provides:

No cause of action arises for:

(a) Alienation of affection.

(b) Criminal conversion.[5]

(c) Seduction of a person over the age of legal consent.

(d) Breach of promise of marriage.

Cal. Civ. Code § 1590 takes a slightly different tack. It recognizes two empirical facts about gifts that are exchanged between parties to a contemplated marriage. One: Such gifts are often made conditional on the occurrence of the marriage. Two: The donor often neglects to express that condition clearly enough to retain a reversionary right under the common law of gifts. Thus, Cal. Civ. Code § 1590 makes a gift exchanged by a party in contemplation of his or her marriage to the donee conditional by operation of law. And it applies whether the parties are living together or not.

Cal. Civ. Code § 1590 provides:

> **Where either party to a contemplated marriage . . . makes a gift of money or property to the other on the basis or assumption that the marriage will take place, in the event that the donee refuses to enter into the marriage as contemplated or that it is given up by mutual consent, the donor may recover such gift or such part of its value as may, under all of the circumstances of the case, be found by a court or jury to be just.**

The gender-neutral code section has both a fault and a no-fault mechanism. The fault mechanism applies when the donee breaks the engagement. The no-fault mechanism applies when both parties mutually decide to break the engagement.

Cal. Civ. Code § 1590 contains no explicit time limits. This implies that, depending on the nature of the gift, the donor's claim is subject to the general

---

[4] *Marvin v. Marvin*, 18 Cal. 3d 660, 134 Cal. Rptr. 815, 557 P.2d 106 (Cal. 1976) (in bank).

[5] Black's Law Dictionary 430 (9th ed. 2009) (acknowledges that criminal conversion is archaic, and defines it as "a tort action for adultery, brought on by a husband against a third party who engaged in sexual intercourse with his wife."). Criminal conversion has been abolished in most jurisdictions. Historically, the action was distinct from that of enticement, and it "was no doubt a necessity when dissolution" was fault based.

statute of limitations.[6] Moreover, failure to return property after a demand can be alleged as a claim for recovery under Cal. Civ. Code § 1590 *and* as a common law conversion claim. To date, only a few cases have been brought under Cal. Civ. Code § 1590, most of them over a half century ago. Recently, a complaint was filed on Cal. Civ. Code § 1590 grounds after one party obtained a judgment of nullity.

Simonian controls on the issue of gifts between parties who are contemplating marriage.[7] In *Simonian* the prospective groom "put the ring on the respondent's finger" at an engagement party. The prospective groom did not condition his delivery of the ring on the occurrence of the wedding. As discussed above, the prospective mother-in-law also made a gift at that engagement party. When the prospective groom canceled the engagement, he sued his former fiancée for return of the engagement ring and for return of the diamond set wristwatch that his mother had given her at their engagement party. The trial court decided that Cal. Civ. Code § 1590 did not apply to the donor's gift since the donor was not a party to the contemplated marriage. (Nor was she the donor's agent for delivery.) However, it held, that Cal. Civ. Code § 1590 did apply to the engagement ring since it was given by a donor who was contemplating marriage to the donee. By operation of Cal. Civ. Code § 1590, the donor was held to have delivered the ring conditional on the occurrence of the marriage, notwithstanding the fact that he did not express his conditional donative intent, as would be otherwise required by the common law of gifts. The donee appealed the holding that the prospective groom's gift was conditional by operation of law.

The trial court next took up the issue of whether the donor was entitled to revoke the engagement ring gift. The court found that the donor was responsible for the nonoccurrence of the marriage, while the donee remained willing to marry the donor. This established the donee's superior right to the engagement ring (or its value) as against the donor. The donee's vested property right to the ring came into existence on the date that the wedding would have occurred had it not been canceled by the donor. The donor appealed the holding that his cancellation of the wedding voided his reversionary interest in the engagement ring.

Both results were affirmed on appeal in a decision that interpreted Cal. Civ. Code § 1590 to mean a gift exchanged in contemplation of marriage is contingent by operation of law: Hence, "the donee of an engagement ring is entitled to retain possession thereof when the marriage contract is breached by the donor without any fault on the donee's part." Additionally, the court of appeal made clear that proof of refusal to go through with the marriage can be shown "by any words or conduct although there is neither verbal nor written refusal to marry."[8]

In *Stienback v. Halsey* a donor sued a donee for replevin of various items of personal property, as well as for reconveyance of a parcel of real property jointly titled in the donor's and donee's names.[9] The donor alleged he had given the property to the donee in reliance and in contemplation of marriage to her, thus

---

[6] *Shaw v. Shaw*, 227 Cal. App. 2d 159, 38 Cal. Rptr. 520 (Cal. App. Ct., 2d Dist. 1964).

[7] *Simonian, supra*, at 262.

[8] *Simonian, supra*, at 261.

[9] *Stienback v. Halsey*, 115 Cal. App. 2d 213, 251 P.2d 1008 (Cal. App. Ct., 4th Dist. 1953).

making each gift conditional by operation of Cal. Civ. Code § 1590. He also alleged that the marriage did not take place; and therefore that he was entitled to return of the property from the donee. The trial court ordered the donee to return and reconvey all of the property (or its value) that the donor had transferred in contemplation of his marriage to the donee. This included an engagement ring, a car, silverware, a vacuum cleaner, a sewing machine, and various cash advances. The donee was permitted to retain a few tangible items of a personal nature such as monogrammed luggage, perfume, clothing, and petty cash. The court's rationale was that the latter items were irrevocable inter vivos gifts not made in contemplation of marriage, and thus not made conditional by operation of Cal. Civ. Code § 1590. The court of appeal affirmed.

Gifts between spouses are treated differently because of the transmutation possibility. Gifts between spouses are covered in Chapter 14.

To sum up, after the cancellation of an engagement, the parties cannot sue for lost affection (i.e. a claim against a third party for interfering with the romantic relationship), criminal conversion, seduction of an adult, or breach of a promise to marry. Either party can sue the other, however, to recover any property or gifts that were conditionally transferred in contemplation of their upcoming marriage. If the engagement was canceled by mutual consent, either party has a right to recover gifts or property that he or she transferred to the other party. But if the engagement was canceled by the donor, then the donor relinquishes his or her reversionary interest to any property that was transferred to the donee in contemplation of the marriage. Additionally, if the parties lived together without marriage, either can sue the other to enforce an oral or implied pooling contract. These permitted actions are filed in civil court, not in family court.

Example 3.7: This example illustrates how Cal. Civ. Code § 1590 implies a condition of marriage to a gift made by a party contemplating marriage. According to that condition, if legal title is transferred to the donee, the transfer date is the date that the canceled wedding was to have taken place. Assume that Larkin owns IT Corp., a closely held corporation. In November, Larkin makes an engagement gift to Mason of 100 shares of IT Corp. stock. The market value of the stock is $5,000 per share. The wedding is set for June. Larkin subsequently cancels the wedding in April. Mason is still willing to go through with the marriage. In June, the market value of the IT Corp. stock soars to $50,000 per share. If Larkin, the donor, sues Mason, the donee, for return of the stock under Cal. Civ. Code § 1590, Mason will prevail. The rationale is that the donor is at fault for canceling the engagement, not the donee; thus it is the donor's voluntary act that nullifies the donor's reversionary right in the gift. Donee-Mason has a vested right to the 100 shares of stock (or their value) as of June, the date that the planned wedding was to have occurred.

Example 3.8: This example illustrates how an implied condition of marriage does not attach by operation of Cal. Civ. Code § 1590 to an engagement gift made by a third party. Larkin's parents give Mason a piano as an engagement gift with these words: "Mason, we want to give you this piano." Larkin and Mason cancel the wedding. Larkin's parents sue Mason for return of the piano. The donors are not parties to the contemplated marriage, nor did the donors expressly condition the gift on the occurrence of the wedding. Therefore, under the law of gifts, title to the piano passed to Mason upon delivery.

Example 3.9: This example illustrates the ambiguity surrounding engagement gifts. At the couple's engagement party, Larkin's mother explains to Larkin that she wants to give Mason a brooch that has been in Larkin's family for generations. Larkin assents to the gift. While delivering the brooch, Larkin's mother says: "Mason, you're a part of our family now, so I want you to have this." If Larkin and Mason marry, Mason can argue that the brooch is Mason's separate property under § 770(a)(1). If Larkin and Mason break up before they marry, Mason can argue that Larkin's mother made an irrevocable gift of the brooch. To this argument, Larkin's mother will counter that the words "Mason, you're part of our family now, so I want you to have this" were an expression of her conditional donative intent. If Mason is responsible for the break-up, Larkin can allege that the gift was made by Larkin, through his mother as agent, thus invoking Cal. Civ. Code § 1590.

The fact that the brooch is (or is not) a family heirloom is not relevant to the gift analysis. What is relevant is the donor's intent.

A third party donor must express conditional intent upon delivery. In Example 3.9, did Larkin's mother intend to condition her gift on the occurrence or non-occurrence of Larkin's marriage to Mason (*you're part of our family now, so I give you this brooch on condition that Larkin decides to go through with the marriage to you*)? Or, did Larkin's mother intend to condition the gift on Mason's marriage to Larkin (*you're part of our family now, so I give you this brooch on condition that you decide to go through with the marriage to Larkin*)?

Whereas for a donor who is a party contemplating marriage, the law assumes that he or she transfer's title on condition that the upcoming marriage occurs. The donor can cancel the wedding, of course, but doing so indicates a waiver of the reversionary right that Cal. Civ. Code § 1590 creates.

Example 3.10: Same as Example 3.9, except that while delivering the brooch Larkin's mother says: "Mason, you're a part of our family now, so I want you to have this brooch. But if you ever break up with Larkin, I want this brooch back." Larkin and Mason marry. Several years later they separate. In a dispute between Larkin's mother and Mason, superior title to the brooch (or its value) belongs to Larkin's mother as of the date that the gift was made. Larkin's claims, if any, under Cal. Civ. Code § 1590 expired once the (valid) marriage did, in fact, take place.

Example 3.11: Same as Example 3.10, except that Larkin's mother delivers the brooch to Mason during the marriage, saying "Mason, you're a part of our family now, so I want you to have this. But if you ever get divorced, I want this brooch back." Now, as between Larkin and Mason, the brooch is Mason's separate property under § 770(a)(2) because it was lucratively acquired by Mason during marriage. However, given the express condition that Larkin's mother placed on the gift to Mason, if Larkin and Mason dissolve the marriage, as between Larkin's mother and Mason, Larkin's mother is entitled to return of the brooch (or its value), as of the date that the gift was made. Larkin has no Cal. Civ. Code § 1590 claim since the brooch was delivered to Mason after the (valid) marriage occurred.

Value to an item of personal property is determined by what a willing buyer will pay for the item on the used personal property market. In Example 3.11, the brooch's value as a family heirloom likely far exceeds its fair market value on the used personal property market (e.g. Craig's list, garage sale, e-bay).

[3] During Marriage: Separate Property Rents, Issues, and Profits

Among community property jurisdictions, there is a doctrinal split as to whether separate property rents, issues, and profits obtained *during* marriage are separate or community property. The majority of community property states characterize separate property rents, issues, and profits obtained during marriage as separate property. Arizona, California, Nevada, New Mexico and Washington follow this approach. A minority of community property states characterize the same as community property, in line with the traditional civil law approach. Idaho, Louisiana, Texas, and Wisconsin follow this approach.

In California, the **"rents, issues and profits"** of separate property are themselves separate property under § 770(a)(3). [10]

Example 3.12: This example illustrates the difference between the California rule and the civil law rule. Prior to marriage, Larkin owns a cow that weighs 800 pounds. During marriage, Larkin's cow gains 1,000 pounds and gives birth to a calf. Under § 770(a)(3), all 1,800 pounds of the cow is Larkin's separate property, as is the calf: the extra 1000 pounds on the cow is a natural increase (appreciation) while the calf is the cow's offspring (issue). By contrast, under the civil law rule followed by some other U.S. community property states, the extra 1,000 pounds on the cow (appreciation or natural increase) remains separate property, but the calf (issue) is community property. This rule applies to other appreciating and income producing property as well.

Example 3.13: This example illustrates the basic rule that the rents of separate property are also defined as separate property. Larkin owns unencumbered real estate prior to marriage. The real estate is rented out. The real estate and its pre-marital rents are Larkin's separate property under § 770(a)(1). During Larkin's marriage to Mason, any rents from the real estate are also Larkin's separate property under § 770(a)(3). But these rents may be subject to adjustment for community property labor that goes into managing the property. Adjustments are discussed in Chapter 7. Additionally, if the rents are deposited into an account during marriage, Larkin — the separate property claimant — has the burden to prove their separate property origin.

Example 3.14: This example illustrates the basic rule that separate property income is also characterized as separate property. Larkin obtains a personal injury award one day prior to marriage. The award is settled in a trust and invested in securities. The award is Larkin's separate property by definition of § 770(a)(1). During marriage, any income (in the form of issues and profits) derived from Larkin's invested trust funds are also Larkin's separate property under § 770(a)(3). These funds may be subject to adjustment for community property labor that goes

---

[10] *George v. Ransom*, 15 Cal. 322 (Cal. 1860).

into their management. *See* Chapter 7. Larkin can deposit these funds into an account subject to an agreement that they are not to be community property. *See* Chapter 5.

Example 3.15: This example illustrates the basic rule that the profits of separate property are also defined as separate property under § 770(a)(3). Larkin owns a business prior to marriage. The business and its profits come to the marriage as separate property under § 770(a)(1). During marriage, business profits traceable to the underlying capital are separate property under § 770(a)(3). By contrast, business profits that are traceable to community property labor belong to the community property. *See* Chapter 7.

[4] From Separation to Divorce

"[T]he earnings and accumulations of a spouse . . . while living separate and apart from the other spouse, are the separate property of the spouse" per § 771. By application of § 772, so too are earnings or accumulations **"[a]fter entry of a judgment of legal separation of the parties."**

For purposes of § 771 and § 772, the word **"earnings"** means more than mere wages or salary. In *Marriage of Imperato* and *American Olean Tile Co.*, for example, **"earnings"** was held to encompass income from a sole proprietorship.[11]

The definition of **"accumulations"** is similarly broad. For example, land acquired by adverse possession during a period of separation would be an **"accumulation"** under § 771 and § 772.

[a] Living Separate and Apart

The phrase living separate and apart is defined by case law, and judicial definitions have changed over time. The most reliable line of precedent holds that for purposes of characterizing earnings and accumulations during a disputed period, the date of separation is determined by a subjective test.[12] The subjective test is referred to here as the *Hardin-Manfer* test: the reason being that *Marriage of Hardin* states the test, and *Marriage of Manfer* clarifies and applies it.[13]

In *Marriage of Manfer*, husband Samuel moved out of the marital home in 2004, after 31 years of marriage. At that time, wife Maureen made up her mind that the marriage was over. For the sake of their children the parties mutually agreed to keep their separation a secret until after the holidays. During the disputed period, the parties did not engage in sexual relations, commingle property, or support each other. In 2005, Samuel filed a dissolution petition. Citing *Marriage of Baragry*, he alleged that 2005 was the date of separation because it was when third parties learned about the break up.[14] The trial court made an inconsistent ruling. It found

---

[11] *Marriage of Imperato*, 45 Cal. App. 3d 432, 119 Cal. Rptr. 590 (Cal. App. Ct., 2d Dist. 1975); *American Olean Tile Co. v. Schultze*, 169 Cal. App. 3d 359, 215 Cal. Rptr. 184 (Cal. App. Ct., 1st Dist. 1985).

[12] *Marriage of Manfer*, 144 Cal. App. 4th 925, 50 Cal. Rptr. 3d 785 (Cal. App. Ct., 4th Dist. 2006).

[13] Cf. *Marriage of Norviel*, 102 Cal. App. 4th 1152, 126 Cal. Rptr. 2d 148 (Cal. App. Ct., 6th Dist. 2002).

[14] *Marriage of Baragry*, 73 Cal. App. 3d 444, 140 Cal. Rptr. 779 (Cal. App. Ct., 2d Dist. 1977).

by a preponderance of the evidence that the Manfers' marriage ended in 2004, but that the date of separation was 2005 for purposes of § 771. Maureen appealed. The court of appeal reversed and remanded on the ground that the trial court had reached its decision "by expressly utilizing an 'objective test' standard, i.e. '[W]ould society at large consider the couple separated?' "[15] The court of appeal explained that there is no objective test for determining when a spouse begins to live separate and apart from the other spouse for purposes of § 771. It then cited *Marriage of Hardin* as "most helpful" in understanding why this is so.[16]

According to *Manfer* if a spouse, during the disputed time, perceives that the rift in the marriage is final, forms the intention not to resume the marriage and then acts on that intention, any evidence reflecting that party's words and actions is "to be objectively considered by the court."[17] This test is often discussed as having only two elements, but actually it more accurately breaks down into three elements. Together these (three) elements establish the date after which the separating spouse's earnings and accumulations become his or her separate property under § 771.

Thus, under the *Hardin-Manfer* test, a spouse begins to live separate and apart from the other spouse when the following elements are simultaneously present:[18]

> (1) *The Spouse Perceives a Break in the Marriage:* One or both spouses perceive that the marriage has broken down due to problems which "there is no reasonable possibility of eliminating, correcting, or resolving." This prong may seem like a so-called objective element that calls for evidence of third party perception, but it isn't. Rather, this prong confirms, at the very least, that the spouse who seeks to rely on § 771 perceived, as of a certain date, that there was a break in the marriage from which he or she could infer that the marriage was over.[19]
>
> *(2) Intent:* The spouse "does not intend to resume the marriage." This element requires a showing that the spouse has formed the intention not to resume or repair the marriage.
>
> (3) *Conduct:* The spouse acts to further his or her intention not to resume the marriage.[20] Any evidence of conduct is relevant.

During marriage the acquisition and characterization of property concerns the community estate, its accumulations, and (perhaps) its dissolution, not the broader public. For that reason, living separate and apart under § 771 requires a court to consider the claimants' perceptions, intentions, and conduct, not societal (third party) perceptions.

---

[15] *Manfer, supra*, at 928, citing *Hardin*, 38 Cal. App. 4th 448, 451, 45 Cal. Rptr. 2d 308 (Cal. App. Ct., 4th Dist. 1995).

[16] *Manfer supra*, at 930, discussing *Hardin, supra*, at 451.

[17] *Hardin, supra*, at 452.

[18] *Id.*

[19] *Id.*

[20] *Manfer, supra*, at 930, 933, citing *Hardin, supra. But see Marriage of von der Nuell*, 23 Cal. App. 4th 730, 28 Cal. Rptr. 2d 447 (2d Dist. 1994).

Under the *Hardin-Manfer* test, evidence of one or both spouse's perception can come in any form. "No particular facts are per se determinative,"[21] but any evidence that is admitted "is to be objectively considered by the court."[22] Hence a trial court can and must consider evidence of "'all factors bearing on either party's intentions to return or not to return'" to the marriage.[23] In practical terms, as between the spouses, this means that the pivotal *perception* is that the marital relationship was irreparably broken, and the pivotal *intention* is that one or both spouses did not want to resume the marital relationship. There is no one pivotal form of conduct: To the contrary, any conduct that takes place contemporaneously with the claimant's intention not to resume the marriage is relevant. *Manfer* recognized that physical separation can be dispositive of a party's intention to end a marriage, but — at least until the California Supreme Court decides otherwise — physical separation is only one factor among many from which a judge can draw a reasonable inference that the claimant was living separate and apart from the other party for purposes of § 771.

The strength of the *Hardin-Manfer* test is that it leaves it to one or both spouses to decide when the marriage has come to an end, not to third parties. The clear drawback of the test is that it can work against an indecisive party who later decides to claim a separate property interest in the accumulations of a disputed period. Additionally, there is a line of cases that raises the issue of whether a spouse who continues to reside as a housemate with the other spouse can be living separate and apart for purposes of § 771. This line of cases ends most recently with *Marriage of Davis*.[24]

In *Marriage of Davis*, the parties, Xavier and Sheryl, were married in 1993. In 1999, after their second child was conceived, the parties stopped having sex together. Sheryl testified that she perceived the marriage to be over in 2000. There was an altercation in 2005. In 2006, Sheryl announced to Xavier that the marriage was over. At that time, she presented Xavier with a detailed ledger, the purpose of which was to transform the parties' finances from the shared obligations of a married couple to the segregated, individual obligations of housemates who were also co-parents. Sheryl offered the ledger as evidence that she was living separate and apart from Xavier. From that point forward, the parties had separate responsibilities as to the family finances. In addition, Sheryl removed Xavier's name from her credit card accounts, and no longer made charges on his credit card accounts. She also moved into a room of her own in the family residence. In 2008, Sheryl petitioned for dissolution. In 2011 she moved out.

Sheryl alleged 2006 as the date of separation for purposes of § 771. She testified that she "continued to live in the home after 2006 because it was her home just as much as Xavier's, but she made an effort to keep their interactions to a minimum." From Xavier's point of view, Sheryl's segregation of the parties' finances was merely

[21] *Manfer supra*, at 930.

[22] *Manfer*, *supra*, at 930, citing *Hardin*, *supra*, at 451–53.

[23] *Manfer*, *supra*, at 930.

[24] *Marriage of Davis*, 220 Cal. App. 4th 1109, 163 Cal. Rptr. 3d 695 (Cal. App. Ct., 1st Dist. 2013).

a symptom of a dysfunctional relationship that had not yet ended when Sheryl presented the expense ledger to Xavier.

Xavier challenged Sheryl's 2006 date of separation claim on the ground that the parties' were still living together as spouses until either 2009 (the year that Sheryl filed for dissolution) or 2011 (the year that Sheryl left the family home). The trial court accepted Sheryl's 2006 date of separation. Xavier appealed. He argued for the application of *Marriage of Norviel,* a case in which the husband announced to the wife that he wanted to dissolve the marriage, but then took several months to untangle and segregate the parties' finances. Under the *Norviel* standard, Xavier argued, Sheryl's expense ledger was not evidence of a substantial change in the marriage and, therefore, it was not evidence from which the trial court could draw an inference of separation.

Sheryl successfully relied on the *Hardin-Manfer* test according to which a party begins to live separate and apart from the other party when he or she perceives that the marriage is over, intends not to resume the marriage, and takes action to further that intention. Sheryl argued that after she perceived that there was a break in the marriage, she formed the intention not to resume the marriage, and she manifested her intention to live separate and apart from Xavier in ways that included presenting him with the expense ledger in 2006. The expense ledger, in other words, was a form of conduct sufficient from which a court could draw an inference that Sheryl was living separate and apart from Xavier for purposes of § 771.

The court of appeal opinion in *Marriage of Davis* agreed with *Marriage of Manfer* that the trial court has discretion to determine the date of separation, and that the standard of review on appeal is the substantial evidence standard, not the de novo standard used when there is an error of law. *Manfer* cites *Hardin* for the proposition that date of separation is based on three *subjective* factors (perception, intention, and conduct). *Manfer* subsequently explains that evidence of all three factors is to be broadly admitted and *objectively* considered by a court. *Davis,* by contrast, "disagree[s] with the bright -line rule drawn by the majority in *Norviel*" in dicta, according to which living apart physically becomes an "indispensable threshold requirement to separation." However, *Davis* goes on to cite *Norviel* for the proposition that when parties are living together as housemates "the evidence would need to demonstrate unambiguous objectively ascertainable conduct amounting to a physical separation under the same roof."[25] The *Davis*'s court's reliance on the phrase "unambiguous objectively ascertainable conduct" suggests that in the absence of physical separation, a party who makes a § 771 claim, while living in the same residence with the other spouse, must produce evidence of conduct from which a third party could draw the inference that a separation has occurred. If so, such a suggestion contradicts the *Hardin-Manfer* rule, which directs the court to focus on the claimant's subjective intention not to resume the marriage.

Davis affirmed the trial court judgment, citing *Manfer.* The California Supreme Court has granted review limited to this question: "for the purpose of establishing the date of separation under Family Code section 771, may a couple be 'living

[25] *Norviel, supra,* at 1164.

separate and apart' when they reside in the same residence?"[26]

In any event, it appears that *Hardin-Manfer* states a general test, while *Noviel-Davis* attempts a specific test that applies where the party who claims separation has not physically left the family residence. Until the state Supreme Court clarifies the issue, for both lines of cases, the question of how a separating party goes about proving his or her intention not to resume the marriage is a question of fact that can be established by any relevant evidence. To date, living separate and apart for purposes of § 771 has been found upon proof of: physical separation; living as housemates and maintaining separate financial lives; the filing of legal documents; and a judgment of legal separation. Claims of living separate and apart have been denied where: parties maintain joint accounts; keep joint credit cards; jointly contribute to family expenses; live in the same house while trying to repair the marriage; live in different countries while trying to repair the marriage; reside in different places for economic or social reasons, such as with a commuter marriage; acquire real property together during the disputed period; take joint vacations during the disputed period; and otherwise conduct themselves as if there were possibility of reconciliation.[27]

Sometimes spouses have multiple periods of separation during marriage. In *Marsden*, the court of appeal held that the parties were not living separate and apart where there had not been a complete break in the marriage. Periods of conflict, without more, are not sufficient evidence of living separate and apart purposes of characterizing property.[28]

[b] After Entry of a Judgment of Legal Separation

The entry of a judgment of legal separation occurs on a date certain. After that date, according to § 772, **"the earnings or accumulations of each party are the separate property of the party acquiring the earnings of accumulations."**

After dissolution, property acquired by the now former spouses is no longer within the community property system. Rather, it is the individual property of the acquiring person. The analog for individual property in any community property system is separate property.

In *Estate of McDaniel*, one spouse died after the petition for dissolution was filed but before the final judgment of dissolution was issued. The other spouse petitioned for surviving spouse status under the Probate Code; that petition was denied.[29] A spouse who is living separate and apart from the other may not be

---

[26] *Marriage of Davis*, 167 Cal. Rptr. 3d 656, 317 P.3d 1183 (Cal. Feb. 11, 2014).

[27] *See, e.g.*, *Makeig v. United Security Bk.& T. Co.*, 112 Cal. App. 138, 143, 296 P. 673 (Cal. App. Ct., 1st Dist. 1931) (no separation where spouses "are residing temporarily in different places due to economic or social reasons"); *Baragry*, *supra* (no separation where one spouse is living with sexual partner while maintaining non-sexual marital-type relationship with spouse); *Marriage of Marsden*, 130 Cal. App. 3d 426, 435, 181 Cal. Rptr. 910, 914 (Cal. App. Ct., 1st Dist. 1982) (no separation where spouses attempt to reconcile while living in different countries); *Norviel*, *supra* (no separation where parties purchase real estate together and take joint title as spouses).

[28] *Marsden*, *supra*, at 435.

[29] *Estate of McDaniel*, 161 Cal. App. 4th 458, 73 Cal. Rptr. 3d 907 (Cal. App. Ct., 3d Dist. 2008).

eligible for surviving spouse status under the Probate Code.

The tracing principle ensures that property received in exchange for separate property is itself characterized as separate property.

Example 3.16: This example illustrates the effect of the spouses' physical separation on their earnings and accumulations. Larkin and Mason are married, but Mason perceives that the marriage has broken down. During this period, Mason decides to not repair the marriage. Mason moves out of the marital home. Under § 771, Mason's earnings and accumulations become Mason's separate property as of the date that Mason leaves the marital home.

Example 3.17: Same as Example 3.16 except that Mason does not move out of the marital home. Instead, in 2005, Mason tells Larkin that the marriage is over. In that same time period, Mason moves into a separate bedroom in the family home, segregates the couples' finances, cancels all joint credit cards, and comes up with a ledger that clarifies each party's individual obligation to the running of the household. The parties live as housemates until 2010. Under the *Hardin-Manfer* test, Mason plausibly begins to live separate and apart from Larkin in 2005, the year that Mason perceives a break in the marriage, intends not to resume the marriage, and takes action to further that intention. Until the California Supreme Court decides otherwise, leaving the marital home is relevant but not necessary for purposes of establishing the date on which one spouse begins to live separate and apart from the other spouse for purposes of § 771.

Example 3.18: This example illustrates the importance of perception and intent in the *Hardin-Manfer* test. Larkin and Mason are married. Larkin takes a job in another state. Mason remains in California. Mason is unhappy about this decision and contemplates ending the marriage, but decides to continue on with the marriage instead. To that end, Mason comes up with a detailed budget for how the parties can contribute to their California home while Larkin lives out of state. In this case, there is no break in the marriage, Mason intends to continue with the marriage (as does Larkin), and thus the compilation of Mason's budget does not support an inference that Mason is living separate and apart from Larkin for purposes of § 771. The parties earnings and accumulations continue to be community property under § 760.

Example 3.19: This example illustrates the effect of the spouses' legal (formal) separation on the characterization of earnings and accumulations. Same as Example 3.16 except that Mason obtains a judgment of legal separation just before leaving the marital home. Under § 772, the entry of the judgment of legal separation marks the formal separation period after which Mason's earnings and accumulations become Mason's separate property. By that same provision, Larkin's earnings and accumulations become Larkin's separate property on the date that the judgment of legal separation is obtained.

Property acquired while living separate and apart or after a judgment of legal separation is defined as separate property. The phrase "living separate and apart from the other spouse" is not merely a colloquialism. Rather, it appears in § 771 as the mechanism by which a separate property proponent can establish the date on which his or her earnings and accumulations become separate property. After the entry of a judgment of legal separation (§ 772) all earnings and accumulations become the separate property of the accumulating spouse.

Generally, separate property is defined by statute. All property owned before marriage is separate property. All property obtained during marriage by gift is separate property. In California, the rents, issues, and profits of separate property are separate property. However, as with community property, there are some assets that are difficult to characterize. For these assets, the onerous-lucrative test may be used.

[B] By Lucrative Acquisition

The Spanish *ganancial* system concerned itself with how property was acquired rather than with when it was acquired. As discussed in Chapter 2, onerously acquired property was community property, whereas lucratively acquired property was the separate property of the acquiring spouse. Today that same logic holds. A lucrative acquisition is one obtained with no effort. A true gift is acquired for no consideration whatsoever.

During marriage, a true gift from a third party is distinguishable from a so-called business gift made in lieu of compensation. Federal income tax cases lend some insight into the issue of when and how a business gift is considered a taxable event. Tips and gratuities, exchanges for services, and other bargained for exchanges are onerous. Additionally, third party transfers made in lieu of retirement compensation are deferred compensation, which makes them onerously acquired.

[C] Separate Property Inventories

An inventory or an asset-specific declaration allows one or both spouses to proactively designate and identify separate property relative to community property as of a certain date, such as for example the date of the marriage. A separate property inventory is not a premarital contract. However, an existing separate property inventory can be incorporated by reference into an otherwise enforceable premarital or marital contract.

At the start of the marriage, an inventory can identify property that was brought to the marriage as separate property. It can also identify rents, issues and profits of separate property, or establish asset values for purposes of proportional allocation in the event of dissolution.

During a marriage, a separate property inventory can identify property received by gift or otherwise identify property that is traceable to separate property.

California, Idaho, Nevada and Texas permit a married person to delineate separate property by use of an inventory, as discussed in Chapter 2. Nevada has the most extensive legislation for creating, maintaining and establishing the authenticity of a separate property inventory. Louisiana allows spouses to make a declaration of a separate property interest on an asset-by-asset basis. Thus, in Louisiana, when a spouse acquires an asset during marriage, he or she can declare in writing that the acquisition was made with separate funds.

§ 3.03 PERSONAL INJURY CLAIMS AGAINST A THIRD PARTY THAT AROSE AFTER SEPARATION

Personal injury claims that arise after the injured party separates from the other spouse are the injured spouse's separate property. So too is money or property received in satisfaction of such a claim.

The character of a personal injury claim depends on party and timing. Section § 781(a) specifically defines personal injury *claims* as separate property if the claim arose in one of two instances: **"After the entry of a judgment of dissolution of a marriage or legal separation of the parties"** or **"[W]hile either spouse, if he or she is the injured person, is living separate from the other spouse."** These distinctions apply as well to **"money or other property received or to be received by a married person"** in satisfaction of a judgment for damages, a settlement agreement, or a compromise of the claim. Thus, personal injury *damages* that are received from a **"cause of action that arises after the entry of judgment or dissolution . . . or legal separation . . .** [or] **while either spouse . . . is living separate from the other spouse"** are separate property under § 781(a).

A personal injury recovery is made up of five elements:

- Compensation for future earnings;
- Reimbursement for past medical expenses;
- Compensation for pain, suffering and disfigurement;
- Payments for loss of body parts; and
- Disability payments.

As discussed in Chapter 2, during the marriage, personal injury damages from a third party are characterized as § 780 community property. At dissolution, all § 780 community property is mandatorily assigned to the injured spouse as separate property. The mandatory assignment rule is in recognition of the fact that damages are intended to compensate the injured spouse for bodily harm, loss of future earnings, and loss of future employability.

A personal injury cause of action that arose during the marriage, but was not pursued or settled by the end of the marriage is the separate property of the injured spouse.[30]

The community is entitled to reimbursement for expenses that it paid from the § 760 community property to the injured spouse's creditors. Reimbursement is authorized by § 781(b) and (c), which apply notwithstanding the fact that the cause of action arose after the judgment of dissolution or legal separation of the parties, or during a period in which the injured person was living separate and apart from the other spouse.

Example 3.20: This example reviews the mandatory § 2603 assignment rule for § 780 community property discussed in Examples 2.6 through 2.9. Assume Larkin is injured by a negligent driver during marriage to Mason. Larkin pursues the tort claim and obtains damages in the amount of $100,000. Soon thereafter, Larkin and

---

[30] *Pinto, supra.*

Mason dissolve the marriage. During marriage, the $100,000 is § 780 community property, but at dissolution that award is mandatorily assigned to Larkin as separate property by application of § 2603, the underlying policy of which recognizes that personal injury awards are for injuries to Larkin's person. If the community property or Mason's separate property covered any of Larkin's injury related expenses, a statutory right of reimbursement arises.

Example 3.21: This example reviews the commingling exception to the § 2603 assignment rule. Same as Example 3.20, but the damage award was received quite a long time ago. Larkin and Mason have been living off of the personal injury award to such an extent that the § 780 sums on deposit have been confused with § 760 sums on deposit. Assume that no records exist to trace the § 780 sums on deposit, and no extrinsic agreements have been reached by the spouses that the § 780 sums on deposit are not to be treated as ordinary § 760 community property. Upon dissolution, § 2603 mandates that Larkin be assigned the § 780 damages as separate property unless the § 780 sums on deposit were commingled with § 760 sums on deposit. Here, § 780 and § 760 sums on deposit were commingled to the point of confusion. At dissolution, there is no personal injury award left to assign to Larkin as separate property.

Example 3.22: For a review the equitable exception to the § 2603 assignment rule, see Example 2.9.

Example 3.23: This example reviews the reimbursement provision related to the § 2603 assignment rule. Same as Example 3.20 except that Mason pays for Larkin's past medical expenses with separate property and with § 760 community property. The personal injury damages — as § 780 community property — are assignable to Larkin at dissolution. However, Mason's separate property estate is entitled to a reimbursement for the injury related expenses that it paid to third party creditors on Larkin's behalf. Likewise, the community is entitled to a reimbursement for any injury related expenses that it paid on Larkin's behalf; community property reimbursements are divided equally between the spouses at dissolution.

Example 3.24: This example illustrates that any cause of action for damages that arose but was not pursued during the marriage belongs to the injured spouse at dissolution. Larkin is injured by a negligent driver during marriage, but does not pursue the claim for damages until after the parties are living separate and apart. At dissolution, the personal injury claim is Larkin's separate property, notwithstanding the fact that it arose during marriage to Mason. Had Larkin pursued the claim during marriage, the award would have been § 780 community property subject to the separate property assignment rule (as in Example 2.6).

§ 3.04 PERSONAL INJURY CLAIMS AGAINST A SPOUSE

A personal injury claim that arose during marriage against a spouse **"is the separate property of the injured spouse"** by definition of § 781(c). This is so even if the claim arose during marriage. So too is money and other property received or to be received by the injured spouse from the other spouse in satisfaction of a judgment for damages, a settlement agreement, or a compromise of the claim. The existence of § 781(c) separate property depends upon party, not timing.

A majority of states have abolished the doctrine of interspousal tort immunity. California adopted the spousal tort immunity doctrine in 1909; but subsequently abolished that doctrine as applied to intentional torts in *Self v. Self*, and negligent torts in *Klein v. Klein*.[31] Thus, a spouse can sue the other spouse for intentional and negligent torts during marriage, during periods of separation, and after dissolution. Historically, immunities did not apply in domestic violence cases; plus, immunities increasingly became inapplicable in actions by one spouse against the other spouse for property, economic, and financial harms. These issues are discussed further in Chapter 11.

One important function of the rules on separate property is to protect a spouse from injuries that are caused by the other spouse during marriage. To this end, § 781(c) characterizes any money received or to be received by one spouse from the other spouse for a civil claim that arose during marriage *as the injured spouse's separate property*.

This rule is subject to an important caveat. If a § 781 monetary award is deposited into a bank account during marriage, the sums on deposit become governable by the special Cal. Prob. Code § 5305(a) presumption. Rebuttal would require the separate property claimant (the injured spouse) to trace the funds back to the monetary award, or else to produce a written agreement that the award sums on deposit are not to be community property. This issue is a function of the interaction between the separate property definition rules and the special presumption that applies to sums on deposit in an account. *See* Chapters 2 and 5.

Nonmarried cohabitants are outside of the community property system. Monetary awards and tort damages obtained by one cohabitant against the other cohabitant are individually owned.

§ 3.05 BY CONTRACT

A valid agreement between the spouses that certain property will not be community property trumps the general rules of the Family Code. For assets in any joint form title, ownership is determined by the agreement, not by tracing. For sums on deposit, a rebuttal agreement must declare that certain sums on deposit are not to be community property. *See* Chapter 5.

[A] By Premarital Agreement

An enforceable premarital agreement trumps the Family Code. *See* Chapter 13.

Prospective spouses and spouses may execute premarital and marital agreements that include separate property clauses. A separate property clause can provide, for example, that specifically identified assets or streams of assets are or become the separate property of the acquiring spouse upon acquisition during marriage. Or, it can incorporate by reference a separate property inventory into

[31] *Peters v. Peters*, 156 Cal. 32, 103 P. 219 (Cal. 1909), overruled by *Self v. Self*, 58 Cal. 2d 683, 26 Cal. Rptr. 97, 376 P.2d 65 (Cal. 1962) (in bank); *Klein v. Klein*, 58 Cal. 2d 692, 26 Cal. Rptr. 102, 376 P.2d 70 (Cal. 1962) (in bank).

the contract. Or, it can provide that a certain asset be characterized as separate property upon dissolution or the death of a spouse.

A private contract clause that (re)defines property onerously acquired during marriage as separate property is no small matter. Importantly, any assets that are defined in a premarital contract as separate property come under the exclusive management and control of the owning spouse, unless those assets have been commingled with community property.

[B] By Marital Agreement

A valid transmutation trumps the Family Code.

During marriage the spouses are in a confidential relationship to each other as a matter of law. Thus each spouse must meet his or her general fiduciary duties under § 721(b) in any transaction between the spouses. Keeping that in mind, property can be transmuted from community property to separate property during marriage.

A valid transmutation is one that complies with § 852(a) (written express declaration formalities) as well as the standards of § 721(b) (fiduciary duties in transactions between spouses). Other more specific fiduciary formalities or duties may apply when a spouse interacts with a third party using community property. These issues are discussed in Chapters 10 and 14.

§ 3.06 BY COMMON LAW JOINT TITLE FORMS AT THE DEATH OF A SPOUSE

Common law title forms are not part of any community property system. Even so, § 750 provides that **"A husband and wife may hold property as joint tenants or tenants in common, or as community property, or as community property with a right of survivorship."**

Historically, the *tenancy in common* title form and the *joint tenancy with the right of survivorship* title form were characterized as separate property. Today, this is still the case, but only when the marriage ends by the death of a spouse.

[A] Types of Joint Form Titles

A joint title represents an agreement between the spouses to hold the property concurrently. Any additional terms of that initial agreement depend on the type of joint title used. The title document itself is evidence of the spouses' agreement as to the titled asset.

Four joint title forms are commonly used in California. (Tenancy by the entirety cannot be created in the jurisdiction.) All are presumptively community property at dissolution. At death, however, each title form functions in accordance with how it is traditionally characterized.

At death, tenancy in common and joint tenancy titles are characterized as separate property interests.

Community property and community property with the right of survivorship are characterized as community property interests.

[B] Common Law Joint Title Forms

This section distinguishes the common law title forms from community property title forms.

[1] Tenancy in Common

The *tenancy in common* is a common law title form. The tenancy in common is the default common law concurrent title form for assets, but not for sums on deposit in an account.[32]

The specific agreement of the tenancy in common title form is that the parties own the property by their net contributions to purchase, and they retain all rights of devise and descent in relation to each other. For an asset titled as tenancy in common, at the death of the first spouse, his or her share passes by devise or descent.

In the context of the termination of a marriage by death, an asset titled as tenants in common will be characterized as concurrently held separate property. Each spouses' interest is characterized as separate property for any necessary tax purposes. *See* Example 3.29.

Example 3.25: This example provides a model for how tenancy in common works upon the death of a spouse. Record title to Blackacre reads "*Larkin and Mason as tenants in common.*" Larkin leaves a valid will devising Blackacre to Truett. In a contest between Truett and Mason, Larkin's interest in Blackacre passes to Truett by devise. Additionally, Blackacre is characterized as separate property for purposes of calculating Mason's income tax basis in the year of Larkin's death.

[2] Joint Tenancy with the Right of Survivorship

The *joint tenancy with the right of survivorship* — joint tenancy for short — is a common law concurrent title form that the tenants must opt in to.

For an asset titled as joint tenancy, the spouses agree to waive rights of devise and descent for the titled asset, as to each other, by right of survivorship. At the death of the first spouse, the surviving spouse is guaranteed to succeed to the decedent's one-half share of the asset as against the decedent's estate. The decedent spouse's interest in the asset vanishes; the surviving spouse takes full ownership of the title asset by right of survivorship. Joint tenancy is popular among married persons and registered domestic partners as a probate avoidance title form.

When spouses are joint tenants, they own the property in equal interests, notwithstanding actual contributions to purchase.

A joint tenancy must be created by the requirements of Cal. Civ. Code § 683. A joint tenancy can be created by a single will or transfer that expressly declares the

---

[32] Cal. Multiple-Party Accounts Law, Cal. Prob. Code §§ 5301–5307.

joint tenancy. It can be created by a transfer from a third party to the joint tenants. It can be created unilaterally by an owner who conveys to herself and another as joint tenants. It can be created by a transfer from a spouse or spouses holding community property to themselves as joint tenants. Likewise, a joint tenancy title can be unilaterally severed as when O, who owns Blackacre as a joint tenant with A, conveys O's interest "to O".

Real and personal property can be owned in joint tenancy. Joint tenancy in real property is and must be reflected in the record title. Joint tenancy in personal property is and must be created by a written transfer, instrument, or agreement between the joint tenants.

At the death of a joint tenant, the surviving tenant automatically becomes the owner to the titled asset by right of survivorship. The property is characterized as concurrently owned separate property. *See* Example 3.29.

Example 3.26: This example provides a model for how joint tenancy works upon the death of a spouse. Larkin and Mason are married to each other. Record title to Blackacre reads "*Larkin and Mason as joint tenants with the right of survivorship.*" Larkin leaves a valid will devising Blackacre to Truett. At Larkin's death, Mason takes Blackacre by right of survivorship as against Larkin's estate. Additionally, Blackacre is characterized as separate property for any necessary tax purposes.

[C] Community Property Title Forms

California spouses have the option to use two community property title forms. Community property is the default community property title form. Community property with the right of survivorship is an optional title form.

[1] Community Property

When an asset is titled as *community property*, the spouses own that asset in equal one-half shares. Each spouse retains full testamentary rights to his or her one-half of a community property titled asset: A spouse can freely devise his or her one-half of an asset titled in community property. Or, a spouse can forego a will with the knowledge that the deceased spouse's one-half community property share shall descend to the surviving spouse by intestate succession.

For purposes of recording title, only married couples and registered domestic partners are permitted to use the community property title form.

At the death of a spouse, an asset titled as community property is characterized as community property for necessary tax purposes.

Example 3.27: This example provides a model for how community property works upon the death of a spouse. Larkin and Mason are married. They take record title to Blackacre as "*Larkin and Mason as community property.*" Larkin devises Blackacre to Truett. At Larkin's death, Truett succeeds to the ownership of Larkin's *one-half interest* in Blackacre. Mason retains a one-half share. Title to Blackacre, between Mason and Truett who are not spouses or registered domestic partners, defaults to the tenancy in common form. For purposes of calculating Mason's income tax basis in the year of Larkin's death, Blackacre is characterized as community property (as in Example 3.30).

[2] Community Property with the Right of Survivorship

The *community property with the right of survivorship* title form is authorized by Cal. Civ. Code § 682.1, effective July 1, 2001.[33]

Such an interest "[S]**hall, upon the death of one of the spouses, pass to the survivor, without administration, pursuant to the terms of the instrument, subject to the same procedures, as property held in joint tenancy. Prior to the death of either spouse, the right of survivorship may be terminated pursuant to the same procedures by which a joint tenancy may be severed. . . .**"

Community property with the right of survivorship attempts to replicate the function of the common law joint tenancy from within the community property system. The community property with the right of survivorship title form is available only to married couples and registered domestic partners.

The right of survivorship indicates that each spouse agrees to waive testamentary rights to the titled asset in exchange for a guarantee that the surviving spouse will succeed to the decedent spouse's one-half interest in the titled asset, as against the decedent's estate, and without the need for probate. At death, each spouse's interest in the titled asset is characterized as community property for purpose of calculating the survivor's income tax basis (as in 3.30).

Example 3.28: This example provides a model for how community property with the right of survivorship works upon the death of a spouse. Larkin and Mason are married. They take record title to Blackacre as "*Larkin and Mason as community property with the right of survivorship.*" Larkin devises Blackacre to Truett. At Larkin's death, Mason succeeds to sole ownership of Blackacre, as against Larkin's estate: Title passes automatically and immediately to Mason, thus avoiding the need for including Blackacre in Larkin's probate estate. In a contest between Mason and Truett, Mason prevails. Furthermore, Blackacre is characterized as community property for purposes of calculating Mason's income tax basis in the year of Larkin's death.

Examples 3.25 through 3.28 walk through the technical outcomes of the different joint title forms when a marriage ends by the death of a spouse. For assets titled as joint tenancy with the right of survivorship and as community property with the right of survivorship, the surviving spouse takes *the titled asset* by non-probate transfer, as against the decedent's estate. For assets titled as tenants in common and as community property, the decedent's share of the asset is included in the decedent spouse's probate estate.

In accordance with the Internal Revenue Code, a surviving spouse may find it necessary to establish that an asset in joint form title is community property in the year that the marriage ends by the death of the other spouse. This is because the decedent's and the surviving spouse's one-half interest in community property

---

[33] Cal. Prob. Code §§ 5100 and 5301 through 5307 were passed before Cal. Civ. Code § 682.1.

receive a new basis if at least one-half of the community property was includible in the decedent spouse's gross estate for federal estate tax purposes.[34] Only community property qualifies for this double basis step up for both spouses' one-half of the property. Other forms of joint ownership do not.

The Tax Court has correctly held that California law treats joint tenancy and community property as mutually exclusive interests at the death of the first spouse.[35] Furthermore, pursuant to I.R.C. § 1014(a) and § 1014(b)(6), the basis of property in the hands of the surviving spouse is generally the value of the property upon the decedent's death.[36] Therefore, when a marriage ends by the death of a spouse, the surviving spouse's separate property interest does not qualify for a stepped up basis; whereas the surviving spouse's community property interest does. Calculations are made in the year of death, but realized gains occur when the surviving spouse sells the property. The survivor's taxable capital gain is calculated by subtracting the original basis from the selling price. A higher basis is generally advantageous to the surviving spouse because it results in a lower taxable capital gain for that (surviving) spouse's income tax in the year the asset is sold.

Example 3.29 and Example 3.30 illustrate the tax differences between common law concurrent titles and community property titles.

Example 3.29: Larkin and Mason buy a condo in San Francisco for $500,000 in 2005. They take title as joint tenants, a title form by which they hold equal concurrent interests. Mason dies in 2014. At Mason's death, Larkin is able to sell the condo for $1,000,000. The property is titled in joint tenancy (a separate property title form). The original fair market value for decedent Masons' interest in this property was $250,000 (or one-half of the 2005 purchase price of $500,000). At Mason's death, Mason's new (stepped-up) basis is $500,000 (one-half the 2014 sale price of $1,000,000). Since the property is separate property, only the decedent's one-half of the condo qualifies for a stepped-up basis at termination of the marriage by death in 2014, not the survivor's. Thus when surviving spouse Larkin sells the condo at a profit, Larkin's adjusted basis for income tax purposes is $750,000: ($250,000 for Larkin's original basis plus $500,000 for Mason's stepped-up basis). In the year that the condo is sold, Larkin realizes taxable income of $250,000:

2014 sale price – (Larkin's 2005 SP basis + Mason's 2014 SP basis) =
Larkin's capital gain of $250,000

$1,000,000 - $750,000 = $250,000

Example 3.30: Same facts as in Example 3.29 except that Larkin and Mason hold title to the condo as community property at Mason's death. Now, both spouses' one-half interest in the property qualifies for a step up in basis to fair market value at the termination of the marriage by death. Decedent Mason's step up in basis is $500,000. Surviving spouse Larkin's step up in basis is $500,000. In other words, the entire community receives a stepped-up basis for the date-of-death value of

---

[34] I.R.C. § 1014

[35] *Young Est. v. Comr.*, 110 T.C. 297, 300-01 (1998).

[36] *See also* Treas. Reg. § 1.1014-2(a)(5); Rev. Rul. 68–80, 1968-1 C.B. 348.

$1,000,000. In 2014, when Larkin sells the condo for § 1,000,000, Larkin realizes taxable income of $0.

2014 sale price – (2014 CP basis for entire property) = Larkin's capital gain

$1,000,000 – $1,000,000 = $0

§ 3.07 SUMMARY

Separate property is protected by the California Constitution and defined by a general statute and several specific statutes. The general statute defines separate property as anything owned by the person before marriage, or acquired by the person during marriage by gift, bequest, devise, or descent. Rents, issues, and profits of separate property received during marriage are characterized as separate property. Personal injury recoveries may or may not be separate property, depending on when the underlying claim arose; however, at dissolution, all personal injury recoveries obtained by an injured spouse from a third party are assigned to the injured spouse as separate property, with few exceptions. Domestic violence awards and personal injury claims and recoveries obtained by an injured spouse against the other spouse are the injured spouse's separate property.

By the tracing principle, any property acquired with separate property during marriage is separate property.

The earnings and accumulations of a spouse become that spouse's separate property on the date that he or she begins to live separate and apart from the other spouse. Often both spouses live separate and apart from one another at the same time. Occasionally one spouse begins to live separate and apart from the other, while the other spouse continues in the marriage. When that happens, the earnings and accumulations of the spouse who is living separate and apart are characterized as that party's separate property.

The earnings and accumulations of either spouse are also — perhaps even more clearly — characterized as that spouse's separate property after judgment of legal separation, an enforceable marital settlement agreement, or a final judgment of dissolution. The community property analog for individually owned property is separate property. Once a marriage terminates, the parties acquire property outside of the community property system, in their respective status as single individuals.

Parties can agree to characterize certain acquisitions as separate property. An enforceable agreement trumps the community property laws that it modifies. A valid transmutation can change the character of property from community to separate.

When a marriage ends by the death of a spouse, jointly titled assets are characterized by their joint title forms. An asset titled as tenants in common or as joint tenancy is characterized as separate property. An asset titled as community property or community property with the right of survivorship is characterized as community property.

From start to end of marriage, for any property obtained during marriage, the burden of proof is on the spouse who claims a separate property interest.

Part III

COMMINGLED PROPERTY

Chapter 4

AN OVERVIEW OF TERMS, PRINCIPLES, AND ISSUES

Commingling means the admixture of community property and separate property. Commingled property retains its character, notwithstanding the admixture. Special rules apply for apportioning or otherwise identifying the community property component of an asset from the separate property component.

§ 4.01 COMMINGLING

Commingling occurs when property of one character is mixed with property of a different character. Commingling can involve the admixture of separate property with community property, the admixture of the separate property of one spouse with the separate property of the other spouse, or the admixture of § 760 community property with § 780 community property.

Commingled property does not lose its character by the mere fact of being mixed with property of another character. But when it becomes impossible or impractical to identify the respective characters of the commingled asset, § 852(d) transmutes the confused property entirely into community property by operation of law. The doctrine of confusion is codified in § 852(d), and discussed further in Chapter 14.

§ 4.02 THE TRACING PRINCIPLE

The tracing principle is a core principle of community property law. The tracing principle holds that the source of the property determines its character. Community property traces back to community property. Separate property traces back to separate property.

Property acquired during the marriage is presumptively community property. As discussed in Chapter 2, there are different community property presumptions that may apply. The general community property presumption applies to property that is acquired during marriage and either untitled or titled in one spouse's name only. The special § 2581 presumption applies for purposes of dissolution only to property that is acquired during marriage and titled in both spouses' names. The special Cal. Prob. Code § 5305(a) presumption applies to sums on deposit in an account during marriage. Of these presumptions, the general presumption and presumption for sums on deposit in an account are rebuttable by tracing or by agreement. The basic tracing formula covers many assets (*supra* § 2.03[A][3]); plus, the California courts have also developed specialized tracing formulas as discussed in Part III. Financial records are always helpful, if not required, to conduct a successful rebuttal by tracing.

§ 4.03 INCEPTION OF TITLE

Generally, property is characterized as of the inception of title. For titled assets, the date of inception is the date that title was acquired. For untitled assets, the date of acquisition ordinarily correlates with the date of purchase or first possession.

When an asset is purchased with a secured loan, the date of acquisition is the inception of title. This is so even though the record title is encumbered by a lien, a mortgage, or a deed of trust. For a secured transaction, all community property jurisdictions recognize that the date of acquisition determines the asset's initial character. Community property jurisdictions differ, however, on how to treat such an asset. Some jurisdictions reimburse the community for any contribution it makes to the purchase of a separate property asset. California gives the community estate a pro tanto share of the asset.

When a community property loan is repaid with community property earnings, all community property states recognize that no commingling has occurred. The asset is entirely community property.

When a separate property loan is repaid with community property earnings, there is a split in authority among community property jurisdictions. Arizona, Idaho, Louisiana, Texas and Washington follow the classic civil law approach sometimes called the "inception of title rule." By that rule, property purchased with a separate property loan is characterized as separate property as of the inception of *record* title, and community property contributions to the repayment of the loan principal are reimbursed.

The California approach — sometimes referred to (by courts in other jurisdictions but not by California courts) as the "buy in" approach — is different. In California, property purchased with a separate property loan is characterized as separate property as of the inception of title. But any community contributions to the purchase of the asset give rise to an equitable ownership interest in the community. This ownership share is proportional to the community's contributions to the purchase of the asset.

Two rationales support the California approach.

The first is the implied agreement theory. This rationale presumes the existence of an implied agreement between the separate property owner and the community (i.e., the spouses). The terms of that agreement are that the separate property owner promises to transfer equitable title to the community estate in exchange for its contributions to purchase. Ordinarily, contributions to purchase come in the form of loan principle payments, but they can come in other forms as well.[1]

The second rationale is the inchoate title theory. This rationale recognizes that record title to an asset securing a loan is not perfected until the loan is repaid and the lender's lien is canceled. By repaying the loan principal, the community estate helps the separate property owner perfect title to the property. Therefore, when a separate property loan principal is repaid by the community, equity demands that

---

[1] *See, e.g., Marriage of Marsden*, 130 Cal. App. 3d 426, 435, 181 Cal. Rptr. 910, 914 (Cal. App. Ct., 1st Dist. 1982) (discussed in Chapter 6); Cal. Fam. Code § 2640.

the community be recognized as a co-owner of the asset. Again, the community's interest is proportional to its contribution to purchase.

§ 4.04 APPORTIONMENT

Apportionment refers to the process of determining the percentage character ownership of the asset. When commingling occurs, the law requires that the proportional ownership shares be identified and separated out. Apportionment methodologies can differ by asset and by context. In all cases, however, the law attempts to balance Family Code protections for community ownership with constitutional protections for separate property ownership. Proportionally owned assets are concurrently owned by one or both separate property estates and the community estate.

§ 4.05 ACQUISITIONS VERSUS FAMILY EXPENSES

Community property law distinguishes between acquisitions and expenses. An acquisition is a gain, investment, purchase, or accession. Houses, cars, shares of stock, time shares, securities, interest and dividends from sums on deposit, businesses, retirement benefits, life insurance policies, life insurance proceeds, jewelry, furniture and so forth are examples of acquisitions rather than expenses.

An expense is a cost of living. Typically an expense covers consumable goods. Medical bills, food, utilities, transportation costs, interest payments, taxes, insurance, clothing, medical expenses, vacation expenses, and so forth are examples of family expenses.

Rent is an expense; a new couch is an acquisition. Cable access accounts are an expense; a cell phone (as an object) is an acquisition. Mortgage payments are made up of principal and interest components: mortgage principal payments are a contribution to purchase (and thus an acquisition); mortgage interest payments are a family expense, as are real estate taxes and property insurance. Therefore, the payment of mortgage principal payments can give rise to an ownership share, while the payment of ordinary maintenance expenses related to real estate ownership shall not factor into the determination of proportional ownership. Community funded capital appreciation improvements will also give rise to an equitable ownership interest in the community estate.

When a separate property contributor declines or fails to rebut a community property presumption, the asset is characterized as entirely (100%) community property and the separate property estate is entitled to a reimbursement for any contributions to the purchase. By contrast, a separate property estate's contribution to family expenses may not give rise to a right of reimbursement absent a contrary agreement between the spouses.

Chapter 5

ACCOUNTS AND PURCHASES MADE FROM A COMMINGLED ACCOUNT

The California Multiple-Party Accounts Law, or CAMPAL, covers the ownership of accounts, sums on deposits in accounts, protections for financial institutions, and creditors' rights.

CAMPAL is synchronized with the community property system in that it includes a rebuttable community property presumption that applies not to accounts, but to sums on deposit in an account.[1] The policy underlying the CAMPAL community property presumption is to protect against the impairment of community property by the movement of money. Moving money from account to account during marriage can affect a spouse's right of withdrawal, or even a spouse's succession rights. But, thanks to CAMPAL, it cannot defeat the community estate's ownership of sums on deposit in an account.

Today, CAMPAL is consistent with case law rules for characterizing purchases from commingled accounts. Sums on deposit are presumed community property subject to rebuttal. Only if rebuttal is successful as to specific sums on deposit can the separate property claimant succeed in rebutting the general presumption as to a purchase from that commingled account. In term of recovery, the main difference between CAMPAL and *See v. See* and its progeny is that CAMPAL allows a separate property claimant to recapture excess withdrawals (i.e., the CAMPAL remedy is *monetary*) whereas the *See* line of cases allows a separate property claimant to recapture an *asset* that was purchased from a commingled account with separate property sums on deposit (i.e., the *See* remedy is in rem). This distinction is discussed below.

CAMPAL applies to all multiple-party accounts, whether the parties are married or not. Only Cal. Prob. Code § 5305(a) applies to the accounts of married persons. For convenience, the word "spouse" is used, but the special CAMPAL community property presumption applies to the accounts of registered domestic partners as well.

§ 5.01 THE CALIFORNIA MULTIPLE-PARTY ACCOUNTS LAW (CAMPAL)

An account is made up of two components: The account itself and the sums on deposit in the account.

---

[1] Cal. Prob. Code § 5305(a)

[A] Type of Account: The Issue of Access

A contract of deposit is an agreement between the depositor and the financial institution. The depositor gives the financial institution the use of money (in the form of deposits). In exchange the financial institution — as a debtor of the depositor — promises to repay those sums upon demand. A depositor calls on the debt by exercising his or her right to withdraw deposits from the account.

In the marriage context, a deposit contract determines which of the spouses has the right to withdraw the sums on deposit from the account during his or her lifetime. A spouse has the right of access to an account if he or she is named on the contract of deposit as an account owner. Access means that the spouse can withdraw funds from the account and obtain information about the account. The financial institution is liable for the misdelivery of funds. Therefore, a financial institution will not deliver funds to someone who is not named on the account absent special authorization.

In order to determine whether a spouse has the right to access an account it is necessary to label the account in question.

CAMPAL defines an **"account"** as **"[a] contract of deposit of funds between a depositor and a financial institution. . . ."**[2] By this definition, an account can include a checking, account, savings account, certificate of deposit, share account, or **"[o]ther like arrangement."** Sums on deposit are owned by the depositor or depositors to the account. The right of withdrawal as to an account is determined by the contract of deposit.

A sole account is one in which only one spouse's name is on the bank account contract. With a sole account, the financial institution is authorized to deliver funds (including interest and dividends) to the named depositor during life. At the death of the depositor, the sums on deposit pass by beneficial designation or through the decedent's estate. If the sums on deposit are community property in character, they remain subject to the beneficial ownership of both spouses even if only one spouse has access to the account.

Example 5.1: This example illustrates the difference between access and ownership of a sole account. Before marriage, Baker has a sole bank account. During marriage to Clay, Baker makes deposits into the account. Baker has the contractual right to withdraw sums on deposit from the account. However, because the sums are presumptively community property, Clay has a one-half equitable ownership interest in all sums on deposit in the account.

A **"joint account"** is defined in Cal. Prob. Code § 5130 as **"[a]n account payable on the request of one or more of two or more parties whether or not mention is made of right of survivorship."** In the marriage context, a joint account is an account payable on the request of one or both spouses, meaning that both spouses have access to the account during their respective lifetimes. The spouse may or may not have the right to name a beneficial designee upon death, depending on whether the account is by right of survivorship or not.

---

[2] Cal. Prob. Code § 5122.

A joint account **"embraces all of the following"**:

- **"Joint accounts with right of survivorship."** This is the default account under CAMPAL.[3] The right of survivorship indicates that the depositors have agreed that at the death of one depositor, the surviving spouse is to succeed to all deposits.
- **"Joint account without right of survivorship."** Also known as a tenancy in common account, this account requires clear and convincing evidence of the depositors' intent not to have survivorship.[4] The absence of the right of survivorship indicates that at the death of a depositor, that decedent's net contributions pass by beneficial designation in the deposit contract or through the decedent's estate.
- **"Joint account held by** [spouses] **with right of survivorship that cannot be changed by will."** This is a contractually designated "community property with the right of survivorship account." Spouses must opt into this account by agreeing to the right of survivorship.[5] The right of survivorship indicates that the depositors have agreed that, while the account is a community property account, at the death of a depositor, the surviving spouse is to succeed to all deposits.
- **"Joint account held by** [spouses] **that is specifically designated as a 'community property' account."** This is the default community property account under CAMPAL.[6] This account is a contractually designated "community property account." It does not include the right of survivorship. The absence of the right of survivorship indicates that the decedent's net community property contributions and all (100%) provable net separate property contributions pass by beneficial designation in the deposit contract or through the decedent's estate. With a community property account, either spouse retains full rights of management and control over all sums on deposit during life, and full testamentary rights over his or her one-half (50%) interest in the net community property deposits on the date of death.

The phrase **"multiple party account"** is defined by Cal. Prob. Code § 5132 to include a **"joint account, a P.O.D. account, or a Totten trust account."**

As discussed above, a joint account is payable on request of any of the depositors named on the contract agreement.

"A P.O.D. account" means an account payable to a beneficial designee — or P.O.D. — upon the death of the depositor.[7] A P.O.D. designee is generally named on the contract of deposit. A P.O.D. beneficiary has no access to or beneficial ownership of the sums on deposit during the lifetime of the depositor. (Although, depending on the contract, the depositor may authorize an at-will debit card for

---

[3] Cal. Prob. Code § 5301(a)(1) and § 5302(a).

[4] Cal. Prob. Code § 5203(a)(6) and § 5306.

[5] Cal. Prob. Code § 5203(a)(4).

[6] Cal. Prob. Code § 5203(a)(5) and § 5307.

[7] Cal. Prob. Code § 5140.

use by the P.O.D. designee.) Upon the death of a depositor, the financial institution delivers the sums on deposit to the P.O.D. designee absent clear and convincing evidence of a different intent on the part of the depositor.

A **"Totten trust account"** functions like a simple revocable trust where the depositor is the trustee for a beneficiary or beneficiaries.[8] The "trust" relationship is established by the form of the account, not by a trust document; and there is no trust property other than the sums on deposit. Upon the death of the depositor, the sums on deposit are payable to the beneficial designee on the account contract absent clear and convincing evidence of a different intent on the part of the depositor.

Example 5.2: This example illustrates the difference between access and ownership of a joint account. During marriage to Clay, Baker opens a "joint account." The joint account contract gives either Baker or Clay access to the account. Additionally, by operation of the CAMPAL, beneficial ownership of the sums on deposit are presumptively community property. Assume that Baker moves money from the joint account to a sole bank account. Clay no longer has the right to access the sums on deposit in Baker's sole account, nor does Clay have a right of survivorship to those sums that Baker moved from the joint account to Baker's sole account. Nevertheless, Clay continues to own a one-half community property interest in the deposits whether they are in the joint account or in the sole account. Now assume that Baker withdraws money from the sole account and deposits it into the joint account. Baker's act of moving money reinstates Clay's access to the deposits — as those sums are now in a joint account — and Clay's rights of survivorship as to those sums. The mere act of moving money, however, does not affect either spouse's community property rights to the sums on deposit. Clay continues to have a one-half interest in the sums on deposit in both accounts, as does Baker.

Once a deposit account is opened, a financial institution is authorized to deliver sums on deposit, together with interest and dividends, to all named depositors during their joint lives. For a sole account, only one depositor is named. For a joint account, two (or more) depositors are named.

Access to an account includes the right to name a beneficial designee who will take upon the death of the depositor. The contract of deposit authorizes the financial institution to deliver sums on deposit to the depositor's survivor(s) or beneficial designee, depending on the type of account. For a sole account, the named depositor has the right to name a beneficial designee, but only as to his or her one-half of the community property deposits. For a joint account, the depositors can either elect to take by right of survivorship, or else each can name a beneficial designee for his or her net contributions to the account. A deceased depositor's net contributions include his or her one-half (50%) of net community property deposits and all (100%) of his or her provable net separate property deposits.

Joint depositors — including spouses — may enter into an enforceable written agreement as to how each may exercise his or her right of withdrawal; however, the

[8] Cal. Prob. Code § 80.

financial institution is not a party to such an agreement. CAMPAL protects financial institutions from misdelivery claims in disputes between joint account owners.[9] Overdrafts are the joint debt of the depositors.

[B] Deposits: The Issue of Beneficial Ownership

The general rule appears at Cal. Prob. Code § 5301. Sums on deposit are proportionately owned as measured by the parties' net contributions to the account. This rule applies during the lifetime of the parties, whether they are married or not.

Example 5.3: This example illustrates the general rule as applied to friends. Clay and Baker are roommates during law school. They open a joint bank account for household business. Clay deposits $75 into the account, Baker deposits $25. Both Clay and Baker have access to all sums on deposit in the account — either or both can withdraw $100 from the account. However, Clay has beneficial ownership of $25 (Clay's net contribution to the account) and Baker has beneficial ownership of $75 (Baker's net contribution to the account).

Cal. Prob. Code § 5305(a) extends the Cal. Prob. Code § 5301 proportionate ownership rule to married depositors: As between spouses, sums on deposit in an account are presumptively community property. A spouse can rebut the Cal. Prob. Code § 5305(a) community property presumption in one of two ways, no matter whether the account is a sole account or a joint account. The first way is to trace sums on deposit back to a separate property source. The second way is to produce an enforceable interspousal agreement that the sums on deposit are not to be community property. Rebuttal is by the preponderance of the evidence standard.

Example 5.4: This example illustrates the general rule as applied to spouses who open a joint account. Clay and Baker are married. They open a joint bank account for household business. Clay deposits $75 into the account, Baker deposits $25. Both Clay and Baker have access to all sums on deposit in the account — either or both can withdraw $100 from the account. However, Clay has beneficial ownership of one-half of the community property deposits ($50) and Baker has beneficial ownership of the other one-half ($50).

As between the spouses, it is of little consequence how an account is titled. All sums on deposit in an account during marriage — sole or joint — are presumed to be community property.

Example 5.5: This example illustrates the general rule as applied to spouses who move money from account to account. Clay and Baker are married. They open a joint bank account for household business. Clay deposits $75 into the account, Baker deposits $25. Both Clay and Baker have access to all sums on deposit in the account — either or both can withdraw $100 from the account — and each owns a one-half community property interest in net deposits. If Baker withdraws $100 from the joint account and deposits it into Baker's sole account, that act does not impair Clay's community property ownership of the $100. By operation of the CAMPAL community property presumption, all sums on deposit continue to be

[9] Chapter 4, Cal. Prob. Code §§ 5401–5407.

presumptive community property, on an account-by-account basis.

Beneficial ownership remains constant. Access rights, survivorship rights, and other testamentary matters may change depending on the type of account.

CAMPAL recognizes the joint tenancy account as the default account. Adding a spouse's name as a P.O.D. does not necessarily create a joint tenancy account. Nevertheless, the joint account is the default account because it gives joint depositors access to all sums on deposit during their lifetimes, and it gives surviving depositors access to all sums on deposit at the death of a joint depositor.

Depositors can limit access and testamentary access right by using a tenancy in common account. Married depositors can do the same by using a community property account. Both types indicate the parties' agreement to open an account without survivorship. Both limit the surviving depositor's access to his or her net contributions at the death of the other depositor; the depositor's net contributions either pass by beneficial designation in the deposit contract or by probate.

To create a community property account, spouses must use the term "community property" in the deposit contract. The mere use of the word "or" on a financial institution signature card does not necessarily create a community property account. It certainly doesn't create a community property with the right of survivorship account. To create a tenancy in common account, spouses must indicate on the deposit contract that the joint account is "without survivorship." To create a community property with the right of survivorship account, depositors must indicate on the deposit contract itself that the account is community property and that the parties have expressly opted into the right of survivorship.

Once an account is opened, the spouses may terminate or recreate the right of survivorship in several ways, including:

- By closing a joint account and reopening it under terms that make clear that the account is without survivorship;
- By modifying the bank contract, in compliance with the agreement contract terms, so that survivorship rights are eliminated (or recreated). Modifications must be in writing and signed by all parties with rights of withdrawal to the modified account.
- By withdrawing deposits from a joint account and moving them to a sole account. In the marriage context, this is typically an act undertaken by one spouse. As discussed in Examples 5.4 and 5.5, this act defeats the other spouse's access rights to sums on deposit. It may also defeat the other spouse's survivorship rights to the withdrawn sums. But it does not enhance or defeat either spouse's one-half community property ownership interest in those sums, despite the fact that they were moved from one account to another.

At the death of a spouse, the existence or absence of the right of survivorship has important consequences for the disposition of the remaining sums on deposit. The right of survivorship indicates that the sums on deposit in the joint account belong entirely (100%) to the surviving spouse as against the deceased spouse's estate. Rebuttal is permitted by clear and convincing evidence of a different intent on the decedent spouse's part.[10]

CAMPAL has a special rule for community property accounts. As indicated above, the default community property account is one without survivorship.[11] A **"[c]ommunity property account"** is one that is described in a contract agreement as payable on the request of either or both spouses. Under Cal. Prob. Code § 5307, if an account **"[i]s expressly described in the account agreement as a 'community property' account, the ownership of the account during lifetime and after death of the spouse is governed by the law governing community property generally."**

This is yet another way that CAMPAL is synchronized with the California community property system. When a contract of deposit designates a "community property" account, the spouses retain all testamentary rights to the sums on deposit — as they did pre-CAMPAL — unless one of the following occurs: The bank agreement expressly provides otherwise; or the spouses expressly describe the account — in the agreement contract itself — as "community property with the right of survivorship."

Consistent with the Uniform Probate Code, a judgment of dissolution or nullity terminates the former spouse's right of survivorship upon the first spouse's death. Living separate and apart may not.[12]

[C] Net Character Contributions

The net deposit concept of Cal. Prob. Code § 5301 is modified by the community property presumption of Cal. Prob. Code § 5305(a), which states a rule about net *character* deposits. In the marriage context, the phrase net contributions — which applies generally — is modified to mean net *character* contributions.

"Net contribution" is defined at Cal. Prob. Code § 5134 as:

- Deposits less withdrawals.
- A pro rata share of interest or dividends earned, **"[w]hether or not included in the current balance."**
- **"Any proceeds of deposit life insurance added to an account by reason of the death of the party whose net contribution is in question."**

The net contribution concept resolves ownership controversies between the parties, their creditors, and their successors. Otherwise it has "no bearing on the power of withdrawal of these persons as determined by the terms of the account contract."[13]

---

[10] Cal. Prob. Code § 5302(a).

[11] Cal. Prob. Code § 5307.

[12] The Cal. Prob. Code § 5302 survivorship rule is expressly made subject to Cal. Prob. Code § 5600 (failure of nonprobate transfer to former spouse).

[13] *See Stevens v. Tri Counties Bank*, 177 Cal. App. 4th 236, 99 Cal. Rptr. 3d 188 (Cal. App. Ct., 3d Dist. 2009).

A joint account gives either spouse power of withdrawal to the sums on deposit in the account, while a sole account gives only one spouse power of withdrawal to the sums on deposit in the account. Regardless of which spouse has access to an account, CAMPAL makes the following steps operative:

- All sums on deposit are presumed to be net community property contributions.
- Once proved, net separate property character contributions are owned as net separate property deposits.
- A commingled account is made up of net contributions of different characters, as demonstrated by the existence of commingled net character deposits. Net character deposits retain their character despite being commingled. They are owned proportionally in relation to total deposits on a given date. Net *separate property* deposits are owned by the separate property claimant. Net *community property* deposits are owned by the spouses by halves. Proportional shares may change on a daily basis depending on deposits and withdrawals made to the account and net character deposits may dissipate by paying family expenses.
- The family expense presumption holds that family expenses are paid for first from net community property deposits. Separate property deposits become liable once community property deposits are exhausted.
- Purchases are presumed to be made from available net community property deposits. Only if net community property deposits are exhausted on the date that one or both spouses purchase a disputed asset, is the inference that the purchase was made from net separate property deposits upheld. Records must be kept contemporaneously with net character deposits and withdrawals; they are inadmissible if prepared in anticipation of dissolution.
- If on the date of a disputed purchase from a commingled account, both net contributing estates had sufficient sums on deposit to make the purchase, then the purchase is presumed to be community property. A separate property claimant can rebut this presumption by declaring an intention to purchase the asset with separate property sums on deposit. A declaration of intent must be extrinsic to the account records, and it must have been made on or near the purchase date. Additionally, the account records must reflect the declaration of intent by subtracting the purchase from net separate property deposits rather than from the net community property deposits. Records must be kept contemporaneously with net character deposits and withdrawals; they are inadmissible if prepared in anticipation of dissolution. Disclosure may also be necessary to avoid a breach of fiduciary duty.

Example 5.6: This example illustrates how the net deposit concept of Cal. Prob. Code § 5301 is modified by the community property presumption of Cal. Prob. Code § 5305(a), which states the rule about *net character deposits*. Clay and Baker are married. They open a joint bank account. Clay deposits $7,500 of an inheritance into the account; Baker deposits $2,500 of work earnings. Both Clay and Baker have the right of withdrawal to all sums on deposit in the joint account. On the date of Clay's deposit, all sums on deposit in the account (including Clay's $7,500) are presumed to be community property, unless Clay rebuts the presumption by tracing or by an agreement between the spouses that the certain deposits are not to be community property. Assume Clay can rebut the community property presumption by $7,500 on a date when sums on deposit in the account equal $10,000. On that date, the sums on deposit in the account are owned in proportion to the net character deposits. Clay owns 75% of the sums on deposit as separate property ($7,500 net separate property deposits divided by total deposits of $10,000); and the community estate owns 25% of the sums on deposit ($2,500 net community property deposits divided by total deposits of $10,000).

[D] Net Character Deposits: Deposits Less Withdrawals Plus Interest

The phrase **"sums on deposit"** is defined at Cal. Prob. Code § 5150 as:

> **(a) The balance payable on an account, including interest and dividends earned, whether or not included in the current balance.**
>
> **(b) Any life insurance proceeds added to the account by reason of death to a party.**

The phrase **"whether or not included in the current balance"** was added by a 2012 amendment to cover the situation where interest or dividends have been earned but not yet credited to the account.

"Withdrawal" means the right to take out cash, as well as the right to make a payment to a third person through a check or other directive as provided Cal. Prob. Code § 5152.

Generally, only the party or parties who have a present right of withdrawal to an account **"[s]hall be considered as having a net contribution."**[14] However, Cal. Prob. Code § 5305(a) carves out an exception to that rule for spouses by treating the community estate as having a net contribution to any account on which one or both spouses is named on the contract of deposit.

As discussed in Chapter 2, Cal. Prob. Code § 5305(a) provides: **"[i]f parties to an account are married to each other, whether or not they are so described in the deposit agreement, their net contribution to the account is presumed to be and remain their community property."**

This presumption may be rebutted **"notwithstanding Sections 2581 and 2640 of the Family Code . . . by proof of either of the following . . .":**

- **(1) The sums on deposit that are claimed to be separate property can be traced from separate property unless it is proved that the married persons made a written agreement that expressed their clear intent that the sums be their community property.**
- **(2) The married persons made a written agreement, separate from the deposit agreement, that expressly provided that the sums on deposit,**

[14] Cal. Prob. Code § 5134.

> **claimed not to be community property, were not to be community property.**

Additionally, Cal. Prob. Code § 5301 provides that a multiple-party account belongs, **"[d]uring the lifetime of the parties, to the parties in proportion to the net contributions of each, unless there is clear and convincing evidence of a different intent."** This provision anticipates the possibility of a commingled account, thereby confirming that Cal. Prob. Code § 5305(a) is not a transmutation rule.

Even when the spouses commingle sums on deposit in an account, the entirety (100%) of the sums on deposit in that account are presumed community property. However, because commingled property retains its character, separate property sums on deposit remain separate so long as they are traceable or identifiable by a written agreement between the spouses. CAMPAL requires, at the very least, that a rebuttal agreement be extrinsic to the deposit agreement.

Cal. Prob. Code § 5305(a) make one simple point: Sums on deposits are owned by the spouses absent evidence otherwise. If this presumption is rebutted, then net *character* contributions determine the spouses' beneficial ownership rights. Net community property sums on deposit, including interest and dividends paid and yet to be paid, are owned by the community, with each spouse having a, present, existing, and equal undivided interest in the those sums. Net separate property sums on deposit, including interest and dividends paid and yet to be paid, are owned entirely by the separate property claimant.

To facilitate multiple-party banking, CAMPAL protects financial institution in two ways. First, the net character contribution concept determines ownership rights in dissolution proceedings between the spouses, or in probate proceedings between a surviving spouse and a decedent spouse's estate. Second, the duty to keep records rests with the parties. Legally speaking, in the marriage context, the separate property claimant — not the financial institution — has the duty to keep net character contribution records. CAMPAL specifically relieves a financial institution from any such a duty.

Cal. Prob. Code § 5401 provides:

> **(c) A financial institution is not required to do any of the following . . . :**
>
> **(1) Inquire as to the source of funds received for deposit . . . or inquire as to the proposed application of any sum withdrawn from an account, for purposes of establishing net contributions.**
>
> **(2) Determine any party's net contribution.**
>
> **(3) Limit withdrawals or any other use of an account based on the net contribution of any party, whether or not the financial institution has actual knowledge of each party's contribution.**
>
> **(d) All funds in an account, unless otherwise agreed in writing by the financial institution and the parties to the account, remain subject to liens, security interests, rights of setoff, and charges, notwithstand-**

ing the determination or allocation of net contributions with respect to the parties.

This Cal. Prob. Code § 5401 provision is consistent with *See v. See*: Sums on deposit in an account are presumptively community property unless a separate property claimant produces contemporaneous character specific records that can establish otherwise.[15] It is also consistent with liability rules insofar as it makes clear that all sums on deposit in an account are subject to encumbrances created by one spouse acting alone and equitable liens such as those that might arise in a dissolution proceeding.

[E] Right of Reimbursement for Excess Withdrawals

CAMPAL was amended in 2012, effective January 1, 2013. The most recent amendment better defines the general reimbursement remedy made operative by Cal. Prob. Code § 5301(b). This reimbursement remedy comes into play when a party makes **"[a]n excess withdrawal from an account, . . . unless there is clear and convincing evidence of a contrary agreement between the parties."**

An **"excess withdrawal"** is defined as **"the amount of a party's withdrawal that exceeds that party's net contribution on deposit in the account immediately preceding the withdrawal."**[16]

In the case of an excess withdrawal by one party, the other party or parties **"[s]hall have an ownership interest in the excess withdrawal in proportion to the net contributions of each to the amount on deposit in the account immediately following the excess withdrawal, unless there is clear and convincing evidence of a contrary agreement between the parties."**[17]

During the marriage, CAMPAL is superseded by the Family Code when the parties have mutual obligations of support. However, at the termination of a marriage by the death of a spouse, CAMPAL's remedy of reimbursement likely supersedes Family Code remedies.

The following examples illustrate CAMPAL basics. Assume that all examples take place in the context of a marriage between Clay and Baker. For ease of illustration, Baker is the separate property owner in all examples.

Example 5.7: This problem illustrates how sums on deposit retain their character even when commingled. During marriage, Clay deposits $10,000 of earnings into a bank account — no matter how titled. That same bank account also holds $5,000 of Baker's separate property. Once deposited during the marriage, the Cal. Prob. Code § 5305(a) presumption is raised as to the sums on deposit in the account, which has $10,000 of community property commingled with (assuming Baker's records are clear) $5,000 of Baker's separate property. Consistent with the idea that Baker's $5,000 retains its separate property character relative to the $10,000, CAMPAL permits Baker to rebut the community property presumption as

---

[15] *See v. See*, 64 Cal. 2d 778, 51 Cal. Rptr. 888, 415 P.2d 776 (Cal. 1966) (in bank).

[16] Amended Stats. 2012 ch. 235 § 1 (AB 1624), effective January 1, 2013; Cal. Prob. Code § 5301(f).

[17] Cal. Prob. Code § 5301(b).

to sums on deposit in the account either by tracing or by an interspousal agreement. Assuming adequate tracing records or an enforceable agreement, Cal. Prob. Code § 5134 requires that the community estate **"[s]hall be considered as having a net contribution"** of $10,000, and Baker's separate property estate **"shall be considered as having a net contribution"** of $5,000.

Example 5.8: This problem illustrates how transmutation by operation of law can occur in a commingled account under the doctrine of confusion, codified in § 852(d). Assume that during marriage Clay deposits $1,000 of earnings each month into a joint bank account. That same bank account also holds an unknown sum of Baker's separate property deposits. Neither spouse keeps financial records. Baker's separate property sums on deposit can no longer be traced relative to the community property sums on deposit. All of Baker's separate property sums on deposit, no matter how or when obtained, are transmuted into community property. The rationale is gift-based: the law presumes that Baker intends to make a gift of Baker's separate property sums on deposit to the community on the date that Baker allows those deposits to get confused relative to the community property deposits.

Example 5.9: This problem illustrates how the beneficial ownership theory works in the context of marriage. Assume that during marriage Clay deposits $200 of earnings into a bank account titled in both Clay's and Baker's names. That same bank account holds $400 of Baker's provable separate property deposits. Once deposited, the account becomes commingled. On that date, Baker's net separate property deposits are two-thirds of the total deposits:

$$\$400 \text{ net separate property deposits} \div \$600 \text{ total deposits} = 2/3$$

On that same date, the net community property deposits are one-third of total deposits:

$$\$200 \text{ net community property deposits} \div \$600 \text{ total deposits} = 1/3$$

Example 5.10: This problem illustrates a CAMPAL right to reimbursement. Assume the same as in Example 5.9 except that the day after making the community property deposit of $200, Clay withdraws $300 from the account. Clay has access to the account, because the contract of deposit is in both spouses' names; and, on the date in question, two-thirds of the sums on deposit are net separate deposits. Baker's records show that Clay's $300 withdrawal exceeded the net community property deposits in the amount of $100. Under CAMPAL, Baker's separate property estate has a right of reimbursement from the community property. The reimbursement due is in proportion to the net separate property deposits that were available **"immediately after"** Clay's excess withdrawal was made.

Example 5.11: This example extends the explanation of Example 5.10. Under CAMPAL, the account had $600 "immediately preceding" Clay's withdrawal of $300, but only $300 "immediately after" Clay's withdrawal. On the date of Clay's withdrawal, Clay had the right to exhaust the $200 of net community property deposits. Clay exercised that right. Clay also had the right — since this is a joint account — to withdraw Baker's net separate property deposits. Clay exercised that right. But Clay did not have beneficial ownership to Baker's separate property deposits. Therefore, by withdrawing more than Clay owned, Clay made an excess withdrawal — i.e., Clay wrongfully withdrew $100 of Baker's net separate property deposits from the account.[18] Assume that Clay used the money for non-family related expenses — say gambling.

Under the CAMPAL excess withdrawal rule, Baker's is entitled to 100% of the excess withdrawal ($100), as determined by Baker's separate property proportionate ownership of the account immediately after Clay's excess withdrawal was made. In this case, Baker had $400 of separate property funds out of $600 total deposits. Clay withdrew $300 from the $600 total deposits, leaving $300 of deposits remaining. That $300 was entirely (100%) Baker's net separate property contribution to the account. Baker's reimbursement is calculated by the percentage of net deposits that were owned by Baker's separate property estate *immediately after* Clay's excess withdrawal — in this case that percentage equals 100%. Therefore, of the $100 excess withdrawal, Baker is entitled to a reimbursement for all $100.

Example 5.12: This example illustrates a possible inconsistency between the CAMPAL reimbursement remedy and application of the family expense presumption of community property law. Same as Example 5.10 except that it becomes known that Clay made the excess withdrawal to pay for a legitimate family expense. Cal. Prob. Code § 5301 (b), CAMPAL appears to give Baker's separate property estate a right of reimbursement *regardless* of why Clay made the excess withdrawal. However, under community property law, whether Clay's withdrawal is deemed excess (or not) would depend on why the withdrawal was made. On these facts, Clay's withdrawal was made to pay for a family expense, and it was made after community property sums on deposit were exhausted. Therefore, under community property law, Baker has a spousal duty to apply available separate property sums on deposit to the payment of family expenses when community property sums on deposit fall short. Additionally, Baker's separate property estate is not entitled to a reimbursement absent an agreement otherwise.

Whether the CAMPAL excess withdrawal provisions could be interpreted in line with community property law depends upon the interpretation of **"net contribution . . . ."** Cal. Prob. Code § 5134(a)(1) defines net contributions to mean **"all deposits thereto made by or for the party, less all withdrawals made by *or for the party* that have not been paid to or applied to the use of any other party."** (Italics added.) Arguably, a separate property withdrawal, to pay family expenses, even if made by the non-owning spouse, benefits the separate property proponent. Indeed, it is the obligation of the separate property owner to ratify this withdrawal if community property sums on deposit were exhausted on other purchases and expenses on the date in question. If so, under Cal. Prob. Code § 5134(a)(1), such a withdrawal is **"for the party"** — meaning the separate property owning spouse — even though the withdrawal was made by the other spouse. This interpretation would make the CAMPAL right of reimbursement

---

[18] In this case, the excess withdrawal was $100: $400 SP Baker – ($200 CP + $100 SP Baker) = $100 excess withdrawal of Baker's separate property sums on deposit.

consistent with community property law as defined by § 720 and the family expense presumption articulated in *See v. See*.[19] As of yet, no case so holds, but interpreting Cal. Prob. Code § 5134(a)(1) in this way would bring CAMPAL in line with community property law in the sense that Clay's withdrawal of Baker's separate property to pay for family expenses would not be deemed excessive if the withdrawn separate property funds were used *for Clay's and Baker's benefit as a family* or *for Baker's benefit* (as a member of the family).

From these examples, one can better understand why and how it is that a commingled account is a presumptively disputed account. Under community property law, a general principle is that the sums on deposit in a commingled account become disputed when funds of a different character (or the net contributions of a different character in CAMPAL terms) are commingled. By the same principle, any asset that gets purchased with sums on deposit in a commingled account is also a disputed asset.

§ 5.02 PURCHASES MADE FROM A COMMINGLED ACCOUNT

The Restatement (First) of Restitution (1937) and the Restatement (Third) of Restitution and Unjust Enrichment (2011) speak to the equitable claims that arise when the money of one person is wrongfully mingled by another person, and subsequently used to purchase property. The Restatement recognizes that the injured party has a claim against the purchased property, either in the form of an equitable lien or a constructive trust. Additionally, the injured party may be entitled to an equitable lien against remaining sums on deposit in the commingled bank account. Liability for conversion arises at the point of commingling. The rationale is that regardless of innocence or blame, the commingling converter obtains advantages from the act of commingling. Those advantages come from sidestepping disclosure, negotiation, contracting, and accounting. Advantages may also come from securing purchase opportunities at the expense of the other beneficial owner.

In the context of marriage, § 721(b) addresses these issues by providing that the spouses are in a confidential relationship as to each other, in transactions between themselves. Additionally, § 1100(e) incorporates § 721(b) into all provisions regarding the spouses' management rights and responsibilities of community personal property. Disclosure duties exist until the end of the marriage.

The Restatement view is evident against this background: A commingled or undisclosed account is by definition a disputed account.[20] A commingling spouse gains a benefit in relation to the other spouse. That benefit, to reiterate, derives from sidestepping disclosure, negotiation, contracting, accounting, and mutual decision making about sums on deposit, purchases, and the order in which expenses are (or should be) paid. Without disclosure, the non-benefitted spouse cannot meaningfully consent to or ratify the benefit that the commingling spouse obtains for him or herself from the act of commingling.

---

[19] *See, supra*, at 785.

[20] *See, supra*.

For the above reasons, when it comes to a commingled account or to making purchases from a commingled account, disclosure requires financial records. Those records must identify net community property deposits, relative to provable net separate property deposits on a specific date in question. The Restatement is consistent with CAMPAL's definition of an excess withdrawal as determined by the net contributions on deposit in the account *immediately preceding* the withdrawal. Both are consistent with the holding in *See v. See*, which applies the general community property presumption to purchases made from a commingled account absent evidence that community funds were exhausted on the date of the purchase.[21]

[A] The Requirement of Specialized Rebuttal Records

See v. See held that property purchased during marriage from a commingled account is presumed to be community property unless the separate property claimant can establish otherwise, as of the date of the purchase. To successfully carry that burden as to purchases governed by the general presumption, the separate property claimant must show that, on the date of purchase, the community property sums on deposit in the account were exhausted. Rebuttal by the exhaustion method goes forward on an asset-by-asset basis. Rebuttal requires specialized records for the account in question. Records must have been kept contemporaneously with deposits and withdrawals, and they must be character specific. *See* disallows total recap accounting; *Mix* and *Marsden* disallow records prepared in anticipation of a dissolution proceeding.[22]

For a disputed purchase made from a commingled account, *See* makes clear that the ordinary tracing rules are too general to determine whether an asset was purchased by community or separate property sums on deposit. Instead, contemporaneously kept specialized records are required. Characterization occurs at the inception of title. Therefore, the aim of character specific account records is to identify net character deposits on the date immediately preceding and immediately following the date of the disputed purchase.

To quote from the opinion in *See*, records are sufficient to rebut the general presumption if they "establish the balance of community income and expenditures at the time an asset is acquired with commingled property."[23] Practically speaking, this means that *See*-compliant rebuttal records are sufficient when they:

(1) Keep track of the character of deposits, as they are made.

(2) Keep track of the character of withdrawals, as they are made.

(3) Keep a running balance of net character deposits, which is to say separate property and community property sums on deposit after application of the family expense presumption.

---

[21] *See, supra*, at 784.

[22] *Marriage of Mix*, 14 Cal. 3d 604, 122 Cal. Rptr. 79, 536 P.2d 479 (Cal. 1975) (in bank); *Marsden, supra*, at 441.

[23] *See, supra*, at 784.

When an asset is purchased from a commingled account — and the remedy sought by the separate property claimant is ownership of the asset itself — the first step is to determine whether the asset is subject to the general presumption (i.e., it is an untitled asset or an asset titled in one name only) or to the special community property presumption for an asset in any joint form title. The general presumption can be rebutted by tracing. Rebuttal of the special joint form presumption is by agreement only, and then only in a dissolution proceeding. For a 100% community property asset, tracing can be used to establish a reimbursement under § 2640, for contributions to purchase, without interest, and subject to a value limitation.

Under the rule in *See*, the first spouse who commingled funds in an account has a legal duty to create and maintain specialized account records. By dicta in *See*, the duty to keep records likewise falls on the spouse who fails to disclose the existence of an account.

Rebuttal rests with the separate property proponent to show that the community funds were exhausted on the date of the purchase. And, rebuttal is *for the disputed item* only. Records are adequate for purposes of rebuttal when they support the inference that separate property funds were used to make the purchase because community property funds were insufficient to do so on the date of purchase.

One rationale for requiring contemporaneous records rests with the inception of title doctrine. Community property acquired during marriage vests upon the date of acquisition. Therefore, under *See*, a purchase from a commingled account presumptively belongs to — that is, vests in — the community estate, unless the separate property proponent can prove otherwise.

A second rationale for requiring contemporaneous records has to do with the fiduciary nature of the spousal relationship. Even if spouses informally sidestep disclosure on a day-to-day basis for financial activities large and small, under *See*, the legal outcome of doing so is that purchases from a commingled account are presumptively community property. A spouse who seeks to establish any greater percentage of ownership in a disputed asset can do so, but only by showing that he or she kept contemporaneous records that allow a court to determine that the net community property deposits were exhausted on the date of the disputed purchase. The inference here is that there was no breach of duty on the purchasing spouse's part because that spouse did not obtain a benefit relative to the community property estate on the date of purchase.

The relationship between the general presumption and a *See* rebuttal for an asset purchased from a commingled account is this: If the community owned sufficient net deposits in the account on the date of purchase, then purchase would have (*automatically*) been made by and benefitted the community estate. Due to insufficient funds, however, the community was not able to make the purchase. In such a case, it is fair — under § 721(b) — to allow the separate property estate of a record-keeping commingling spouse to reap any opportunities that might come from such a purchase relative to the community property estate.

Above and beyond CAMPAL and the Restatement, the California Family Code provides spouses with statutory remedies for any breach of fiduciary duty that results in the impairment of property in which the claimant spouse has or may have a community property interest. This cause of action appears in § 1101(a): **"A spouse has a claim against the other spouse for any breach of the fiduciary duty that results in impairment to the claimant spouse's present undivided one-half interest in the community estate . . . ."** Available § 1101 remedies for impairment include, but are not limited to, a formal accounting, a court order to add a spouse's name to record title, damages, attorney's fees and court costs.

In addition to personal injury and property damage, domestic violence can and often does result in financial harm to the community estate. The California Domestic Violence Prevention Act (DVPA) provides a remedy for community property impairment claims, but only if the remedy is deemed to be proximately caused by the (tortious) act of abuse upon which the DVPA claim is based. And yet, a multitude of more general financial and economic harms can result from living in an abusive relationship. Thus lawyers are well advised to consider general Family Code impairment claims in domestic violence cases. Impairment claims are discussed in Chapter 10. The DVPA is discussed in Chapter 11.

[B] The Family Expense Presumption

During marriage, the spouses have a duty to support each other. Family support presumptively is paid for by the community property. If there are insufficient funds to pay for family expenses, the separate property of either spouse becomes liable.

In sorting through bank records, the family expense presumption is an evidentiary rule that deducts family expenses from available community property sums on deposit in an account. Separate property sums on deposit pay for family expenses only if and when community property sums on deposit are exhausted. The separate property owner is not ordinarily entitled to a reimbursement for paying family expenses, absent an agreement otherwise.

Statutory authority for the family expense presumption comes from basic principles of support and liability.

On the support side, § 720 obligates the spouses to duties of **"[m]utual respect, fidelity, and support."**

On the liability side, § 914 provides that **"[a] married person is personally liable for . . . a debt incurred for necessaries of life of the person's spouse while the spouses are living together . . .** [and for] **common necessaries of life of the person's spouse while the spouses are living separately."**

These same statutes, along with either spouse's rights to manage and control community property, authorize either spouse to use separate property funds to pay for family expenses when community property funds are insufficient or exhausted.

[C] Rebuttal Methods

The following methods rebut the general presumption for a purchase from a commingled account. These methods can be used when a marriage ends by dissolution or by the death of one spouse.

[1] *See v. See* Exhaustion

See v. See allows rebuttal by the exhaustion method of accounting.[24] Under *See*, if on the date of a disputed purchase, the separate property proponent can show that community property sums on deposit in the disputed account were exhausted (i.e., insufficient to make the purchase), then the rebuttal is successful. A successful rebuttal supports an inference that, at purchase, title to the asset vested in the separate property estate. *See* § 5.02, *infra*.

Proportional rebuttal is permitted.

[2] *Hicks-Mix* Direct Tracing

Hicks-Mix allows rebuttal by a direct tracing method coupled with a declaration of intent.[25] By this method, a successful rebuttal is made when the separate property proponent can show all the following:

(1) On the date of the disputed purchase, both community property sums on deposit and separate property sums on deposit were sufficient to make the disputed purchase.

(2) On or near the date of the disputed purchase, the separate property proponent declared an intention, in a writing separate from the account records, to make the purchase with separate property sums on deposit; and

(3) Immediately after the purchase, the amount of that purchase was withdrawn from the separate property sums on deposit.

Proportional rebuttal is permitted. Disclosure is also necessary, as discussed in Chapter 10.

After *Mix*, the use of records prepared in anticipation of litigation is disallowed.

The separate property proponent tested the direct tracing method in *Marriage of Marsden* by arguing that — even after the decision in *Mix* — a trial court has discretion to approve the use of records prepared in anticipation of a dissolution proceeding. The California Supreme Court disagreed. In so doing it took the opportunity to clarify the policy underlying the *Hicks-Mix* rebuttal method:

> Husband's arguments along this line would be persuasive if the Court were satisfied as to the truth of husband's contention, but it is not. The Court cannot find that husband has carried his burden of proof in establishing what stocks were purchased from funds in the Great Western

---

[24] *See, supra; see also Estate of Murphy*, 15 Cal. 3d 907, 918, 126 Cal. Rptr. 820, 544 P.2d 956 (Cal. 1976) (in bank) (permitting rebuttal by exhaustion method when a marriage ends by the death of a spouse).

[25] *Hicks v. Hicks*, 211 Cal. App. 2d 144, 27 Cal. Rptr. 307 (Cal. App. Ct., 4th Dist. 1962); *Mix, supra*.

> account. Husband could have avoided this difficulty by some rudimentary record keeping, but he kept virtually no records in this respect and it is far too late to reconstruct them with any degree of persuasive proof.[26]

Hick-Mix direct tracing is consistent with CAMPAL Cal. Prob. Code § 5301(b) in three key ways. First, a declaration to purchase an asset with separate property sums on deposit requires knowledge of the net character contributions on deposit in the account immediately preceding the withdrawal: Both *Mix* and CAMPAL require that the separate property proponent know, on the date of the purchase, that there are sufficient separate property *and* community property sums on deposit to make the purchase. Second, a declaration of intent (not necessarily an agreement) must be made, on or near the date of purchase, by a writing that is separate from the specialized account records. Third, the separate property claimant's specialized account records must confirm that the sums on deposit that were used to make the purchase were in fact deducted from the separate property sums on deposit immediately after the purchase was made.

Example 5.13: This problem illustrates how presumptions can simplify the characterization of a purchase made with sums from a commingled account. Clay and Baker purchase a car during marriage with cash from a commingled bank account. Title to the car is taken in joint tenancy. Clay and Baker now seek a dissolution. In this example, the car is community property under the special § 2581community property presumption. The § 2581 presumption is rebutted only if the separate property proponent can produce a written agreement to keep a separate property interest in the car. Neither the *See* exhaustion method nor the *Hicks-Mix* direct tracing method can be used to rebut the special § 2581 presumption. Therefore, as to this car, a net character deposit analysis is not relevant.

Example 5.14: Same as Example 5.13, except that the car is titled as tenants in common. At dissolution, the car is community property for the same reason stated in Example 5.13.

Example 5.15: This problem analyzes an untitled purchase from a commingled account when no (or inadequate) financial records are kept. During marriage, Clay purchases a $2,000 untitled stereo system during marriage with cash from a commingled account. Assume that no financial records are available to identify net community property deposits relative to net separate property deposits. On these facts, the stereo system is community property by application of the general community property presumption. Additionally, the funds that were used to buy the stereo are presumed community property under CAMPAL, and thus the stereo purchase also traces back to community property purchase funds.

Example 5.16: This problem characterizes an untitled purchase from a commingled account when adequate exhaustion method records are kept. Same as Example 5.15 except Baker is the first to commingle the bank account. Baker keeps specialized rebuttal records, as required by *See v. See*. Assume a dispute arises over ownership of the stereo system. The analysis starts by applying the general presumption to the stereo system. If Baker's records show that community funds were exhausted on the date that the stereo system was purchased, then the general

---

[26] *Marsden, supra*, at 441; *Mix, supra*, at 611.

presumption is rebutted as to the stereo. In such a case, the stereo system is entirely Baker's separate property because it traces back to a separate property source of purchase funds, as of the date of its purchase. Baker's records will be sufficient to rebut the community property presumption applicable to the stereo *only* if they are also sufficient to rebut the CAMPAL community property presumption as to sums on deposit in the account.

Example 5.17: This problem illustrates proportional rebuttal using *See v. See* records. Same as Example 5.16 except that Baker's rebuttal shows that on the date that Clay purchased the $2,000 stereo system, the community property sums on deposit in the commingled account were sufficient to pay for only one-third of the purchase. Based on Baker's rebuttal, the stereo system is two-thirds Baker's separate property and one-third community property. Again, Baker's rebuttal of the general presumption as to the stereo depends upon a successful rebuttal as to the sums on deposit in the account.

Example 5.18: This example illustrates the application of the family expense presumption in an exhaustion method accounting problem. On January 1, immediately preceding the purchase of a $2,000 stereo system with sums on deposit in a commingled account, Baker's records show that the community sums on deposit totaled $2,000 and the separate property sums on deposit totaled $2,000. Rent came due in the amount of $2,000 on the first day of the month, immediately preceding the purchase of the stereo system. Applying the family expense presumption, the $2,000 rent payment must be deducted from the available community property sums on deposit. Immediately after paying the rent, the community had $0 on deposit, which means that on the date that the stereo system was purchased, the community property estate had insufficient funds to make that purchase. The separate property sums on deposit, on the other hand, were sufficient to make the purchase because Baker's separate property estate had $2,000 on deposit on the date that the stereo system was purchased. Assuming Baker's records are deemed to be *See* compliant, Baker successfully rebuts the community property presumption as to the stereo system by 100%.

Example 5.19: This example illustrates a *Hicks-Mix* direct tracing method rebuttal. Same as Example 5.18 except that Baker's records also show that immediately after the rent was paid by community property sums on deposit, an automatic deposit of $5,000 was made by Clay's employer and an automatic deposit of $5,000 was made by Baker's employer. Now, on the date that the $2,000 stereo system was purchased, and even after the rent was paid, the community property sums on deposit totaled $10,000: specifically, the community had $2,000 on deposit on Jan 1, it withdrew $2,000 to pay the rent, leaving it with $0; but it then received salary deposits totaling $10,000. Baker also had $2,000 of separate property sums on deposit on the date of the stereo system purchase. Therefore, on that date, both community and separate property sums on deposit were sufficient to make the purchase. The stereo system goes to the community property estate unless Baker can also show that on the date of the purchase Baker declared an intention — in a writing extrinsic from the specialized account records — to make the purchase from Baker's separate property sums on deposit.

The *Hicks Mix* analysis starts with the general presumption: The stereo system is presumed to be community property because, on the date of the purchase, the community estate had sufficient funds to make the purchase. But on the date of the purchase, Baker could elect to make the purchase with separate property funds. To do this, Baker had to: (1) show from *See*-compliant specialized records that immediately before the purchase, both the community property and Baker's separate property funds were sufficient to make the purchase; (2) declare an intention, in a writing, extrinsic from the account records, to use separate property sums on deposit to buy the stereo system; and (3) show that immediately after the purchase, the amount of the stereo system purchase ($2,000) was withdrawn from Baker's separate property sums on deposit.

Example 5.20: This example illustrates that *See*-compliant records must be kept contemporaneously with deposits and withdrawals. Same as Example 5.18 except that Baker does not declare an intention to claim the stereo system until a year after the purchase is made, a time during which the parties are going through a dissolution. Looking back, Baker realizes that the purchase of the stereo system could have been with separate property. In anticipation of trial, Baker, who was the first party to commingle the sums on deposit, retroactively declares an intention to purchase the stereo system with separate property sums on deposit. With the help of an accountant Baker then retrospectively adjusts the account balances to show sufficient separate property sums on deposit immediately before the stereo system was purchased. In this case, Baker's financial records do not meet the *See* standard: Specifically, Baker's records are not contemporaneous with deposits and withdrawals. Nor do Baker's records meet the *Hicks-Mix* standard: Specifically, Baker's declaration to purchase the stereo was made well after the purchase, at a time when the parties were disputing the ownership of the stereo system. Baker's records are additionally disallowed because they were prepared in anticipation of dissolution. As such they heighten the risk of perjury. Additionally, to paraphrase the *Marsden* court, the separate property proponent (Baker) "could have avoided this difficulty by some rudimentary record keeping, but kept virtually no records in this respect and it is far too late to reconstruct them with any degree of persuasive proof."[27] Under *See*, *Hicks*, *Mix*, and *Marsden*, Baker's attempt to rebut the community property presumption must fail. The stereo system is entirely (100%) community property.

Example 5.21: This example illustrates why *See*-compliant records identify the character of the sums on deposit in the account in question. Same as Example 5.20 except that five years after the purchase, at dissolution, Baker can (only) produce standard-form bank statements. The bank statements show deposits and withdrawals, but they do not identify the net character deposits, on any particular date. Without more, standard bank statements are insufficient to rebut the general community property presumption as to any disputed purchase from the commingled account. Both *See* and CAMPAL make clear that the burden for keeping adequate records rests with the parties, not with the financial institution; and specifically with the first party to commingle the sums on deposit in the account. The purpose of specialized records is to disprove a community property presump-

---

[27] *Marsden*, *supra*, at 441.

tion. Standard bank records simply do not contain the necessary information to serve that purpose.

§ 5.03 JOINT SAFE-DEPOSIT BOXES

Safe deposit boxes are rented pursuant to a form agreement provided by the bank to the box lessee. Some bank form agreements may provide that, where two people contract for the safe-deposit box, the box contents are held in joint tenancy by the co-tenants of the box.

In California the rule is otherwise.

Cal. Civ. Code § 683.1 provides: **"No contract . . . between any person, firm, or corporation engaged in the business of renting safe-deposit boxes and the renter or renters of a safe-deposit box, shall create a joint tenancy in or otherwise establish ownership in any of the contents of such safe deposit box."** Any contract that attempts to do so is void by application of Cal. Civ. Code § 683.1. In other words, a bank contract for the rental of a safe-deposit box cannot decide the ownership of the contents of that box.

§ 5.04 SUMMARY

Bank accounts and sums on deposit are separate assets, each necessitating their own analysis.

Ownership of a bank account is designated by a contract between the financial institution and the depositor or depositors. A deposit contract determines who has the right to access the account.

Ownership of the sums on deposit in an account is determined by each party's net contributions to the account. In the community property context, sums on deposit are presumed to be community absent proof otherwise. With proof, sums on deposit are owned as net character contributions. Any sums on deposit obtained during marriage from work, talent, industry, the sale of a community property asset, or any other community property source, are characterized as community property deposits. Any sums on deposit obtained from a separate property source or from the sale of separate property are characterized as separate property deposits.

Net character contributions allow for the application of the *See* family expense presumption, which recognizes that community property is liable for support obligations of the current marriage. In terms of accounting methods, the family expense presumption requires that family expenses be deducted from available community property funds *before* they are deducted from available separate property funds. The separate property is entitled to a reimbursement for family expenses; but only if, on the date the disputed payment was made, community property funds were available but not used. The separate property is not entitled to a reimbursement if those funds are used to pay for family expenses on a date when the community property sums were insufficient to cover the expenses, absent a contrary agreement.

Commingled sums on deposit in an account retain their character so long as they can be identified relative to each other. The mere act of commingling will not transmute the sums on deposit. But once it is no longer possible to (re)trace sums on deposit to their separate property source, the doctrine of confusion applies, as codified in § 852(d): In that instance, all of the sums on deposit are transmuted into community property by operation of law.

A commingled bank account is by definition a disputed account. Disputes might arise over the ownership of the sums on deposit; over the ownership of assets that were purchased with the commingled sums on deposits; or over whether the sums on deposit are liable for family expenses, and if so whether a reimbursement is due. Bank generated records allow parties to keep track of their account balances, but those records do not identify community property sums on deposit relative to separate property sums on deposit. Therefore, standard bank account records are not legally adequate for purposes of rebutting the CAMPAL community property presumption or the general presumption as applied to an eligible purchase made from a commingled account.

Upon acquisition, purchases from a commingled account are characterized as community property. Statutory and case law obligates the first spouse who commingles to keep specialized records of net character deposits. Specialized records are: (1) a contemporaneously maintained records; (2) of net character contributions in the account; (3) on the date of the disputed purchase.

The legal duty to keep such records falls on the first spouse who commingles funds in the account. However, the financial risk of not keeping adequate records falls squarely on the separate property depositor. Often these are one and same person; but sometimes they are not. The general principle here is that the community property edifice favors the family. Thus when commingling occurs, absent specialized contemporaneously kept records, the following rules serve to protect the community estate, both in its ownership of sums on deposit and in its ownership of assets purchased from commingled accounts:

- The act of commingling is a breach of fiduciary duty that creates a disputed account. If that breach of fiduciary duty impairs the other spouse's community property interest, a claim arises in favor of the impaired spouse. Remedies include a formal accounting; amended account title records; ownership of purchases made from the account; or damages. In the event that damages are awarded, the claimant spouse can also claim attorney's fees and court costs. Any recoveries are defined as the claimant spouse's separate property.
- An asset purchased from a commingled account is presumptively community property. Which presumption applies depends how title to the purchased asset is held.
- *See* allows for rebuttal of the general community property presumption by the exhaustion method accounting. By this method, a separate property depositor must introduce *See*-compliant records to show that, on the date of purchase, the community property sums on deposit were exhausted. This allows a court to support the inference that the disputed purchase was made with available separate property funds.

- *Hicks-Mix* allows for rebuttal of the general community property presumption by the direct-tracing method. By this method, a separate property depositor must introduce *See*-compliant records along with a written declaration of intent made on or near the date of the purchase to buy the asset with separate property funds. The *See*-compliant records prove that, on the date of purchase both community and separate property sums on deposit were sufficient to make the purchase, and that the purchase was nevertheless made with separate property funds. The date-specific written declaration of intent reduces the risk of perjury during a legal separation or dissolution proceeding. Disclosure may (and probably is) also required.

Chapter 6

CREDIT ACQUISITIONS

Secured credit purchases are an important part of modern life.[1] In the context of marriage, credit acquisitions are often commingled. This happens, for example, when loan proceeds of one character are repaid with payments of another character. What gets commingled in such a case is the asset's appreciation.

This chapter discusses the case law on credit acquisitions. The decisional framework has taken nearly a century to develop. It starts with *Vieux v. Vieux* in 1926 and extends through today. *Vieux* stands for the principle that the community obtains an equitable ownership interest for its equity (or capital) contribution to the purchase of a separate property asset. This interest is often referred to as the community's pro tanto interest. A pro tanto interest gives each concurrent owning estate an undivided right to the whole.

The policy behind recognizing the community's interest lies in contract, in equity, and in community property law, as discussed in detail below.

§ 6.01 A SECURED CREDIT PURCHASE MADE DURING MARRIAGE

When a purchase is made during marriage, the asset purchased is presumptively community property. The separate property claimant can establish proportional ownership by rebuttal. Rebuttal can proceed in one of two ways. The separate property claimant can show that inception of title was in the claimant's separate property estate, leaving it to the community to establish its equity contribution. Alternatively, assuming inception of title was in the community property estate, the separate property claimant can rebut with proof that it made an equity contribution to the community property purchase.

Sometimes a separate property claimant's proof is insufficient to establish an equity position in the asset. When this happens, traceable separate property contributions to the purchase of an entirely (100%) community property asset are reimbursed as a matter of right under § 2640. Reimbursements are made for **"[d]ownpayments, payments for improvements, and payments that reduce the principal of a loan used to finance the purchase or improvement of the property . . . ."**

[1] For information on lending and types of loans, see the U.S. Housing and Urban Development website, www.hud.gov.

Vieux and its progeny apply to separate property acquisitions to which the community estate makes an equity contribution to purchase.[2] For application of these cases, contributions to purchase are not defined by reference to § 2640. Rather they are defined by reference to case law. *Moore* defines the phrase contribution to purchase as a payment that was applied to loan principal reduction; not as a payment applied to interest, taxes, or insurance. This is the P of PITI formula. *Marsden* adds to that definition: A contribution to purchase includes payments that "may be relevant in determining [the asset's] market value from which in turn the owners' equity is derived by subtracting the outstanding obligation."[3]

[A] The Basic Tracing Formula

The basic tracing formula is an arithmetic expression of the tracing principle. The tracing principle is one of three animating principles of the California community property system. Thus the basic tracing formula determines proportional ownership shares between a separate property estate (or sometimes both separate property estates) and the community property estate.

The basic tracing formula is used when an asset is purchased, with cash, by the community estate and by one or both separate property estates.

When the community estate purchases (acquires) an asset during the marriage, characterization is governable by a general or a specific presumption. Rebuttal of the special joint form title presumption is by agreement only. Rebuttal of the general community property presumption is by tracing purchase funds back to a separate property source.[4] Once rebuttal proof is made, proportional shares are calculated by dividing each estate's contribution to purchase by the historic purchase price.

---

[2] *Vieux v. Vieux*, 80 Cal. App. 222, 251 P. 640 (Cal. App. Ct., 2d Dist. 1926), *Marriage of Aufmuth*, 89 Cal. App. 3d 446, 152 Cal. Rptr. 668 (Cal. App. Ct., 1st Dist. 1979), *Marriage of Moore*, 28 Cal. 3d 366, 168 Cal. Rptr. 662, 655, 618 P.2d 208, 211 (Cal. 1980) (in bank), *Marriage of Marsden*, 130 Cal. App. 3d 426, 435, 181 Cal. Rptr. 910, 914 (Cal. App. Ct., 1st Dist. 1982); *Bono v. Clark*, 103 Cal. App. 4th 1409, 1428, 128 Cal. Rptr. 2d 31, 45 (Cal. App. Ct., 6th Dist. 2002).

Marriage of Geraci, 144 Cal. App. 4th 1278, 51 Cal. Rptr. 3d 234 (Cal. App. Ct., 2d Dist. 2006).

[3] *Marsden*, *supra*, at 438, citing *Moore*, *supra*, at 372.

[4] The special Cal. Fam. Code § 2581 presumption cannot be rebutted by tracing.

The Basic Tracing Formula:

$$\frac{\text{CP contributions to purchase}}{\text{Purchase Price}} = \text{CP\%}$$

$$\frac{\text{SP contributions to purchase}}{\text{Purchase Price}} = \text{SP\%}$$

[B] The *Aufmuth* Formula for Credit Acquisitions

Marriage of Aufmuth adjusts the basic tracing formula to credit acquisitions.[5] *Aufmuth* was decided in 1979, when joint titles could be rebutted by tracing; the case was decided by application of *See v. See*, which allowed the separate property claimant to trace the purchase of a house to the use of separate property funds. Today, by operation of § 2581, joint title forms at dissolution are presumed community property, with rebuttal by agreement only. Marcia and Lawrence Aufmuth did not have an agreement that their house would be community property upon dissolution. Therefore, today — by application of § 2581 — the house would be deemed entirely (100%) community property, subject to a non-interest reimbursement to Marcia for her separate property contribution to purchase in the form of a downpayment.

Notwithstanding the above changes in the law, the *Aufmuth* adjustment to the basic formula, discussed below, is still good law.

In *Aufmuth*, wife Marcia used separate property during marriage to make a downpayment on a house. The remainder of the purchase price came from a community property loan executed by both Marcia and husband Lawrence. At dissolution, Marcia contended that the house was entirely her separate property, subject to a reimbursement for the community. Lawrence argued for apportioning the house between the community property and Marcia's separate property estate; Lawrence also argued that all community contributions — loan proceeds, taxes, maintenance, and related expenses — should factor into determining the community property's percentage ownership share.

The trial court exercised its discretion to apportion the house. It determined ownership shares by identifying each estate's equity contribution to purchase; and then dividing that equity contribution to purchase by the original purchase price of the house. Marcia's equity contribution to purchase was her separate property downpayment. The community property's equity contribution to purchase was in the form of loan proceeds that the spouses — as a community — had their lender advance to their seller. Next, the trial court took the respective estate's percentage ownership share and multiplied each by the house's appreciation. Finally, the trial

[5] *Aufmuth, supra*, at 457 (affirming the trial court's recognition of the loan proceeds as an equity contribution to purchase).

court reimbursed the respective estates for their equity contribution to purchase; the trial court also gave each its percentage ownership of the commingled appreciation. Marcia appealed. Lawrence responded with a cross-appeal.

The court of appeal upheld the trial court's formula; by so doing the court of appeal affirmed the trial court's treatment of credit (i.e., loan proceeds) as an equity contribution to purchase. (This was despite the fact that the loan had not yet been repaid.) The result was the *Aufmuth* formula: The basic tracing formula as applied to a secured credit purchase. Under the *Aufmuth* formula, equity contributions are indentified, used to calculate percentage ownership shares, and then reimbursed. Percentage ownership shares are then used to apportion commingled appreciation.

Appreciation for purposes of the basic tracing formula means that the underlying capital has increased in value over time. Depreciation means that the underlying capital has decreased in value over time.

The* Aufmuth *Tracing Formula:

$$\frac{\text{CP loan proceeds*}}{\text{Purchase Price}} = \text{CP\%}$$

$$\frac{\text{SP contributions to purchase}}{\text{Purchase Price}} = \text{SP\%}$$

* The *Aufmuth* formula allows loan proceeds to be factored in as an equity contribution to purchase.[6]

The following examples all involve an asset that was purchased during marriage with a separate property contribution.

In these examples, the analysis starts with the general community property presumption. Rebuttal is by proof of a traceable separate property contribution to purchase. Both the basic tracing formula and the *Aufmuth* formula allow parties to determine their proportional ownership shares by dividing the original purchase price by their respective contributions to purchase. The *Aufmuth* formula allows loan proceeds to be factored in as an equity contribution to purchase; but it disallows the use of insurance, taxes, maintenance and other non-equity expenditures. The resulting percentages are used to apportion commingled appreciation.

Example 6.1: This example involves a cash purchase. It illustrates rebuttal of the general presumption with the basic tracing formula. Cesar buys a car during marriage for $12,000. The car is titled in Cesar's name only. Cesar uses $10,000 from earnings and $2,000 of traceable separate property cash. Cesar is permitted to use the basic tracing formula to rebut the general community property

[6] *Aufmuth, supra*, at 457.

presumption. A successful rebuttal establishes Cesar's separate property ownership share in the car.

> ***Example 6.1: Cesar's Tracing Rebuttal: Basic Formula:***
>
> $\frac{\$10{,}000 \text{ CP cash contributions to purchase}}{\$12{,}000} = 83\% \text{ CP}$
>
> $\frac{\$2{,}000 \text{ SP contributions to purchase}}{\$12{,}000} = 17\% \text{ SP}$

Example 6.2: This example involves a secured credit acquisition; it illustrates rebuttal of the general presumption with the basic tracing formula, as approved by *Aufmuth*. During marriage, Cesar borrows $10,000 to buy the $12,000 car. Cesar takes title in his name only. The lender advances the loan proceeds directly to the car dealership. In addition, Cesar contributes $2,000 of traceable separate property cash. Over time, the fully amortizing loan is repaid with community property funds.

> ***Example 6.2: Cesar's Tracing Rebuttal: Basic* Aufmuth *Formula:***
>
> $\frac{\$10{,}000 \text{ CP loan proceeds*}}{\$12{,}000} = 83\% \text{ CP}$
>
> $\frac{\$2{,}000 \text{ SP contributions to purchase}}{\$12{,}000} = 17\% \text{ SP}$
>
> * Under *Aufmuth* the community property gets credit for its ability to obtain $10,000 in loan proceeds from the lender. The *Aufmuth* formula allows the community property to define loan proceeds as an equity contribution to purchase for purposes of determining its percentage ownership share of the asset.

In Examples 6.1 and 6.2, the separate property's percentage share is calculated from its cash contribution to purchase, which in this case is a downpayment. The community's contribution, on the other hand, is calculated in Example 6.1 from its cash contributions and in Example 6.2 from its credit contribution. Cash contributions implicate the basic tracing formula. Credit contributions in the form of loan proceeds implicate the *Aufmuth* tracing formula.

In Examples 6.2 and 6.3, the *Aufmuth* tracing formula is used because the asset was acquired during the marriage with a community property loan. An asset acquired during marriage is presumptively community property. Tracing is only permitted if title is in one spouse's name.

Example 6.3: This example highlights the meaning of equity contribution to purchase in the context of a secured credit acquisition. Cesar borrows $10,000 to buy a $12,000 car. Cesar takes title in his name only. Cesar contributes $2,000 of separate property cash as a downpayment. Because Cesar is expecting a large bonus, he decides to use *an interest-only loan.* The interest component of the loan is repaid each month with community property funds. As in the Example 6.2, the car is presumed community property because it was acquired during marriage; rebuttal is permitted. This leaves it to Cesar to offer evidence of a separate property contribution of $2,000. In this case, however, *notwithstanding the fact that the loan is interest-only (i.e., it does not amortize over time), Aufmuth* permits the community estate to count as its contribution to purchase borrowed funds in the amount of $10,000.

Example 6.3: Cesar's Tracing Rebuttal: Basic* Aufmuth *Formula:

$$\frac{\$10{,}000 \text{ CP contributions to purchase*}}{\$12{,}000} = 83\% \text{ CP}$$

$$\frac{\$2{,}000 \text{ SP contributions to purchase}}{\$12{,}000} = 17\% \text{ SP}$$

* Example 6.2 is different from 6.3 only in the type of loan Cesar used. In Example 6.2, Cesar used a fully amortizing loan. In Example 6.3, Cesar used an interest-only loan. Nevertheless, in both Example 6.2 and 6.3, the *Aufmuth* formula gives the community a $10,000 credit for its contribution to purchase. The take-away being, that the community's ability to obtain loan proceeds is its contribution to purchase.

Example 6.4: This example uses the *Aufmuth* tracing formula to apportion ownership interests in a mixed character (commingled) real estate. During marriage, Cesar and Dolores buy a house for $100,000. They use Cesar's $25,000 inheritance as a downpayment, and a $75,000 loan for which the lender takes a deed of trust on the house. Title is in Cesar's name only. The general presumption starts the analysis: At inception of title, the house, which was acquired during marriage, is presumed to be community property. Cesar rebuts the general presumption by tracing the downpayment back to a separate property source (Cesar's $25,000 inheritance). The community's contribution to purchase is a credit contribution equal to the loan proceeds advanced by Cesar's and Dolores's lender to the seller ($75,000). Applying the *Aufmuth* formula, the house is owned 25% by Cesar's separate property estate, and 75% by the community estate.

Example 6.4: Cesar's Tracing Rebuttal: Basic* Aufmuth *Formula:

$$\frac{\text{\$75,000 CP contribution*}}{\text{purchase price}} = 75\% = \text{CP \% ownership}$$

$$\frac{\text{\$25,000 SP contribution}}{\text{purchase price}} = 25\% = \text{SP \% ownership}$$

* The *Aufmuth* formula gives the community estate credit for the community property loan proceeds that were advanced to the seller.

Example 6.5: This example extends the rationale of Example 6.4 by illustrating how the percentage ownership interest is used to apportion the commingled real estate appreciation. Same as Example 6.4 except that during the marriage the house appreciates (increases in value) by $100,000. By application of the *Aufmuth* formula, this house is 25% Cesar's separate property and 75% community property (as illustrated in Example 6.4). These percentages can now be used to apportion the $100,000 of real estate appreciation.

Here is the *Aufmuth* tracing formula applied:

Step #1: Apply the *Aufmuth* Tracing Formula:

$$\frac{\text{\$75,000 CP loan proceeds}}{\text{\$100,000}} = 75\%\ \text{CP}\ \%$$

$$\frac{\text{\$25,000 Cesar's SP contribution}}{\text{\$100,000}} = 25\%\ \text{SP}\ \%$$

Step #2: Apportion the Commingled Appreciation:

At the time of trial, the fair market value of the house is $100,000 greater than the original purchase price. This commingled appreciation is a divisible asset, and it is owned proportionally 75% by the CP and 25% by Cesar's SP.

75% x $100,000 appreciation = $75,000 of appr. owned by the CP

25% x $100,000 appreciation = $25,000 of appr. is owned by SP

Reverse Calculation: Working backwards, after the house is sold for $200,000, once all of the proceeds are accounted for, $0 dollars should remain.

$200,000 sale proceeds - $75,000 reimbursement to CP for loan proceeds* = $125,000 funds remaining

$125,000 funds remaining - $25,000 reimbursement to Cesar's SP for downpayment = $100,000 funds remaining

$100,000 funds remaining - $75,000 CP share of appreciation = $25,000 funds remaining

$25,000 funds remaining - $25,000 Cesar's SP share of appreciation = $0 funds remaining

* The CP has the obligation to repay the mortgage loan in full.

§ 6.02 A SECURED CREDIT PURCHASE MADE BEFORE MARRIAGE

When a separate property estate purchases an asset, the inception of title rule characterizes the asset — in the first instance — as separate property. Under the traditional civil law approach, characterization occurs at inception of title. Therefore, any subsequent community property contributions to purchase (can only) give rise to a reimbursement, not to an ownership interest. California does not follow the civil law approach, for reasons discussed below.

[A] A Premarital Purchase

Assume a disputed asset that was purchased *prior* to marriage with borrowed funds. The general community property presumption cannot be raised because the asset was not acquired during marriage. Instead, the asset comes to the marriage as separate property. But what if, during marriage, the community contributes to the purchase of that separate property asset? Is the community contribution treated as the basis for an ownership claim? Or is the community reimbursed, without interest?

The traditional civil law approach would reimburse the community for its contribution to the purchase of the otherwise entirely separate property asset.

California veered off the civil law path on this issue with *Vieux* (1926), where a court of appeal held that community property contributions to the purchase of an otherwise separate property asset give rise to an equitable title in the community estate.[7] This is sometimes called the "buy-in approach" by the courts of other states — although "buy-in" is not a term typically used by California courts.

In *Marriage of Moore*, the California Supreme Court brought *Vieux* into the jet age in a case involving a separate property loan whose principal was repaid with community property contributions. *Moore* gave the separate property estate credit for (1) its downpayment, and (2) its separate property loan minus any community property loan principal payments that reduced the separate property estate's indebtedness on that loan. The total of (1) and (2) became the separate property's

[7] *Vieux, supra.*

equity contribution to purchase. That contribution was then divided by the purchase price to identify the separate property's proportional ownership share of the asset. On the other side of the partition table, the community's ownership share of the asset was its equity contribution to purchase in the form of the loan principal payments it made to reduce the indebtedness on the separate property loan. This contribution to purchase was then divided by the purchase price of the asset.

Marriage of Marsden extends the *Moore* formula. Upon proof of premarital appreciation, a hybridized *Moore/Marsden* formula can be used to distinguish marital appreciation from *pre*marital appreciation. Marital appreciation is subsequently apportioned. Premarital equity and appreciation are reimbursed to the separate property owner.

[1] The Community Estate's Equitable Ownership Interest: *Vieux*

A few conceptual baselines are helpful:

An entirely (100%) separate property asset is not a commingled asset. So, for example, when a separate property asset is purchased prior to marriage with a loan that is repaid during marriage with separate property, that asset remains entirely separate property. Authority for this outcome is found at § 770(a)(1) and § 770(a)(3).

Example 6.6: This example illustrates the outcome when a separate property loan is repaid with separate property during the marriage. Cesar acquires a house before marriage with a loan that Cesar obtains before marriage. Record title is in Cesar's name only. During marriage, Cesar repays the loan with a separate property inheritance. The house and its appreciation, respectively, belong entirely (100%) to Cesar's separate property estate.

Apportionment formulas set forth below are law, not math. Each formula applies straightforwardly in a paradigmatic case. But where facts get complicated, keep in mind that each formula aims to accomplish two things. The first is to require proof of traceable contributions to purchase. The second is to calculate percentage ownership shares that can be used to partition commingled appreciation.

Vieux states the apportionment rule. *Vieux* was decided in 1926, long before the widespread use of residential mortgages. Yet, even today, *Vieux* remains important both for its holding and its rationale.

Vieux involved a premarital purchase involving prospective spouses who "shortly prior to marriage . . . discussed and considered the purchase of [real estate], and together viewed said property, and it was agreed between them that said property would be desirable to purchase."[8] Martin purchased the real estate on credit prior to the marriage, expending in terms of "outlay" from his separate property about "somewhat less than one-tenth of the purchase price."[9] During the marriage, Martin and Coralyn used community funds to repay Martin's premarital purchase obligation, which was secured by the real estate; the community "expended . . .

---

[8] *Vieux, supra*, at 224.

[9] *Id.*

approximately one-fifth of the purchase price."[10] When Martin and Coralyn divorced, Martin contended that the real estate was his separate property, that the property had not been transmuted, and that the property, at most, was subject to a reimbursement in the community in accordance with the traditional civil law approach. Coralyn argued that the community was entitled to an equitable ownership interest for its equity contribution to purchase. Coralyn based her argument on the fact that the parties had agreed to buy the property together before their marriage, that they reduced Martin's (pre-marital) indebtedness on the property with community property funds, and hence that the community had a reasonable expectation of an equitable ownership interest in the property, notwithstanding the inception of title rule.

The trial court deemed the property Martin's separate property. Coralyn appealed. The court of appeal reversed and remanded the case to determine proportional ownership shares between Martin's separate property estate and the community estate. The *Vieux* court of appeal held that the community established an equitable ownership right in the property by its contributions to purchase, notwithstanding the inception of title doctrine. The *Vieux* rationale was multi-pronged.

First, the court recognized the fact that Coralyn and Martin went shopping for the property before marriage — together. When they found the property, they entered into an implied agreement to own the property together as a married community, in partnership with Martin's separate property estate. The purpose of the partnership was to perfect inchoate (i.e., encumbered) title by using community property funds to reduce Martin's separate property note, which was secured by the property. Quoting from *Vieux*:

> In the circumstances here present, it requires no wild stretch of the imagination to perceive a 'meeting of the minds' without the form of express words, either spoken or written, to the effect that the property in question was not considered by the parties as exclusively in the husband, with the wife having absolutely no material right, title, or interest therein; but, to the contrary that the property was 'theirs,' each of the parties enjoying equal rights and privileges, at least as far as the community funds contributed to the payment of the purchase price thereof. *In effect it was somewhat in the nature of a partnership relationship that existed between the parties — the husband on the one side, and the community consisting of the husband and wife, on the other side.*[11] (Italics added.)

Second, the court was persuaded by the reasonableness of the community's expectancy interest. The community (i.e., married partnership) — as articulated by Coralyn — expected that its contributions to the purchase of that property would give it an equitable property right in the property, not just a no-interest reimbursement. The court explained that when the community helps purchase a separate property asset during marriage, equity demands apportionment, not merely interest-free reimbursement. This equitable rationale builds on the implied part-

---

[10] *Vieux, supra*, at 225.

[11] *Vieux, supra*, at 227.

nership rationale. To cite again from *Vieux*: "justice demands that the rights of the parties should be measured by the direct contributions made by the respective parties to the purchase price of the property."[12]

Third, the court explained that the California Civil Code defines property in this way: "the ownership of a thing is the right of one or more persons to possess and use it to the exclusion of others."[13] This provision applies generally, but it must be interpreted differently in relation to spouses. In other words, the provision applicable to spouses supersedes the general provision.

Then, with a single passage, *Vieux* rejected the traditional civil law inception of title doctrine as applied to secured credit acquisitions. The following paragraph is one of the more important passages of California community property law because it steered California community property law at once away from its civil law origins and toward a partnership theory of marriage.

The idea was that the California Legislature would not define separate property in a way that might lead to a "disastrous and unjust" outcome for the community property estate. Inception of title was important since it set the original character of the asset. But the spouses — as partners — could choose to modify the inception of title rule through the voluntary act of allowing the community to contribute to the purchase of the separate property asset. If the spouses made such an agreement — as demonstrated by the use of community property funds to make an equity contribution to purchase — then fairness demanded that a court enforce that agreement, notwithstanding the statutory definition of separate property as that which is acquired by a spouse before marriage.

Here is the passage:

> The confidential relationship existing between [spouses] . . . forbids such strict construction to be placed upon the statute as will destroy the probable intent of [the spouses] with reference to the manner in which the ownership of property is to be enjoyed. Any other construction in these days of liberal terms with reference to installment purchase price contracts for the sale of real property, including the possible provision of "a dollar down and a dollar per week," would permit a [spouse] or a prospective [spouse] to buy or to agree to buy any reasonable quantity of lots or lands on the payment by him from his separate funds of a comparatively insignificant sum and thereafter to pay practically the entire purchase price from community funds, and yet successfully maintain that because in its inception the naked right to purchase, carrying with it the right of use and possession, was his separate property, it so remained. It would seem improbable that through general definition of terms, the intention of the lawmakers was to bring about a result which, in many if not a majority of instances, would be of so disastrous and unjust a consequence. Rather should it be assumed that when the legislature undertook to define separate property as that owned by the [spouse] before marriage, even though in

---

[12] *Vieux, supra*, at 229.

[13] Cal. Civ. Code § 654.

> other statutes the right of exclusive possession and use was specified as the indicia of "ownership," the "ownership" in [one spouse] through and by virtue of which the [other spouse's] interest would be entirely excluded, would necessarily be an absolute ownership, as distinguished from a limited ownership, and that, *so far as community funds might participate in the acquisition or protection of vested rights, to that extent proportionally should the property be considered "community."*[14] (Italics in the original.)

The practical effect of the rule in *Vieux* is that if and when the community estate contributes to the acquisition of separate property, the community obtains an equitable ownership interest in that property as measured by its equity contributions to purchase.

Example 6.7: This example illustrates how the community's right to apportionment is established. Cesar buys a house on Packard Street before marriage. He makes the purchase with a downpayment and mortgage. Shortly thereafter, Cesar marries Dolores. During marriage, Dolores uses her earnings to help pay off Cesar's loan. The spouses' use of community property funds to pay off Cesar's separate property mortgage principal gives the community estate an equitable ownership interest in the Packard Street house.

Example 6.8: This example illustrates a case where the community does not establish an ownership position in the underlying real estate. Cesar buys a house before marriage on Olivia Street. He uses a downpayment and trust fund income. During marriage to Dolores, the couple use earnings to pay for real estate taxes on the Olivia Street property. In this case, the community property does not establish an equitable ownership interest in the house on Olivia Street. Real taxes are an expense, not an acquisition to purchase.

Example 6.9: This example illustrates another case where the community does not establish an ownership position in the underlying real estate. Before marriage, Cesar buys a house on Prospect Street with the use of an interest-only mortgage loan. During marriage to Dolores, the couple use earnings to pay the (interest-only) mortgage payments. In this case, the community property does not establish an equitable ownership interest in Cesar's house on Prospect Street. This is because mortgage interest is an expense, not an acquisition to purchase. Only equity contributions to purchase give rise to an equitable ownership interest in the community.

[2] Commingled Appreciation: The *Moore* Formula

Vieux left unanswered how to apportion ownership interests between a separate property estate and the community estate. A half-century later, *Marriage of Moore* reaffirmed the *Aufmuth* formula as well as the rationale of *Vieux*.[15] Together, these cases establish that each contributing estate's proportional ownership share is measured by its equity contribution to purchase.

---

[14] *Vieux, supra*, at 227–28.

[15] *Moore, supra.*

In a paradigmatic *Moore* case, the separate property contribution to purchase is in the form of a downpayment and a separate property loan, the property is purchased close to marriage, and the community property equity contribution to purchase is in the form of principal payments on the separate property loan. As with the *Aufmuth* tracing formula, contributions to purchase are defined as downpayments, credit contributions (loan proceeds advanced from a lender to a seller), mortgage loan principal payments, and any other payments that "may be relevant in determining [the asset's] market value from which in turn the owners' equity is derived by subtracting the outstanding obligation."[16]

Taxes, maintenance, insurance, or any other variety of expenses that may be incurred in maintaining real property are not contributions to purchase, they are family expenses under § 720.[17] Maintenance costs are not relevant in the *Aufmuth/ Moore* formula. Nor are they relevant in the *Moore/Marsden* formula.

To return to the holding in *Moore*: The *Moore* formula requires proof of reimbursable equity contributions to purchase. From this proof, pro tanto ownership percentages can then be calculated. The resulting percentage shares are subsequently used to partition the commingled appreciation or depreciation. Percentages are calculated by identifying each estate's contribution to purchase (the reimbursable numerator) and dividing it by the historic purchase price (the denominator).

The California Supreme Court articulated its holding *Moore* as follows. This is yet another important paragraph of California community property law.

> The separate property percentage interest is determined by crediting the separate property with the down payment and the full amount of the loan less the amount by which the community property payments reduced the principal balance of the loan. . . . The separate property interest would be . . . the amount of capital appreciation attributable to the separate funds added to the amount of equity paid by separate funds . . . This sum is divided by the purchase price . . . The community property percentage interest is found by dividing the amount by which community property payments reduced the principal by the purchase price. The community property share would be . . . the amount of capital appreciation attributable to community funds added to the amount of equity paid by community funds.[18]

Here is the *Moore* holding expressed as a formula:

---

[16] *Moore, supra*, at 372.

[17] *Aufmuth, supra*, at 457, *Moore, supra*, at 372.

[18] *Moore, supra*, at 373, 374.

The* Moore *Formula:

Step #1: Determine ownership interests by reference to reimbursable equity contributions to purchase:

$$\frac{\text{SP downpayment} + (\text{SP loan} - \text{CP contributions to purchase})}{\text{Historic Purchase Price}^{19}} = \text{SP \%}$$

$$\frac{\text{CP contributions to purchase}}{\text{Historic Purchase Price}} = \text{CP \%}$$

Step #2: Apportion appreciation (or depreciation):

Appr. = (FMV @ divorce - Historic Purchase Price)

SP % × appr. = SP ownership share of commingled appr.

CP % × appr. = CP ownership share of commingled appr.

Step #3: Partition:

Reimbursements for equity:

- The SP estate is reimbursed for its original equity contribution to purchase in the form of a downpayment and the loan proceeds.
- The CP estate is reimbursed for its original equity contribution to purchase in the form of its principal repayments to the separate property loan.

Commingled appreciation is apportioned depending on each estate's percentage ownership share:

- SP% × appr. = SP% of the commingled appr.
- CP% × appr. = CP% of the commingled appr.

FMV = Fair Market Value, which is defined as what a willing buyer would pay for the property after full disclosure.

Example 6.10: This example illustrates an application of the *Moore* apportionment formula in a paradigmatic case. It is a useful model for understanding the *Moore* formula, which identifies original contributions to purchase and then uses them to calculate ownership percentages. Those percentages are used to apportion any appreciation (or depreciation).

---

[19] The use of the word "historic" comes from this passage in *Marsden, supra*, at 438: "It is clear that part of our confusion results from the use of the word 'equity.' The fair market value at or near the time of purchase is usually equivalent to the purchase price. In short, the appraised value equals the cost value. Such was the case in *Moore*, where the respondent wife had purchase the property eight months before the marriage, and thus no question of the fair market value of the home at the time of marriage was posed. (*Id.* 28 Cal. 3d at p. 370)." (Citation in the original.)

Example 6.10: Cesar's Tracing Rebuttal:* Moore *Formula:

Cesar buys a house *immediately* before marriage to Dolores. The contract price of the house is $100,000. Cesar puts $20,000 down and assumes a fully amortizing mortgage of $80,000. During the marriage, community property repays $10,000 of the separate property loan principal. At dissolution, Cesar and Dolores sell the house for $200,000.

Step #1: Calculate ownership interests based on contributions to purchase:

$$\frac{\$20{,}000 \text{ SP dpmt} + (\$80{,}000 \text{ SP loan} - \$10{,}000 \text{ CP contribution})}{\$100{,}000 \text{ HPP}} = 90\% \text{ SP}$$

$$\frac{\$10{,}000 \text{ cp contribution}}{\$100{,}000 \text{ HPP}} = 10\% \text{ CP}$$

Step #2: Apportion the commingled appreciation:

Appr. = $200,000 FMV @ trial - $100,000 HPP = $100,000 appr.

SP% of appr. = 90% x $100,000 = $90,000

CP% of appr. = 10% x $10,000 = $10,000

Step #3: The Partition Outcome:

- Cesar's SP estate is *reimbursed* for its downpayment ($20,000), and for the loan it obtained minus the community property contributions to the repayment of that loan ($70,000); a total of $90,000. *In addition*, Cesar's SP *ownership share* of the asset's appreciation is $90,000 (per Step #2). Thus, Cesar's SP estate is entitled to $180,000 of the $200,000 sale proceeds.
- The CP estate is *reimbursed* for its contribution to the repayment of Cesar's SP loan principal ($10,000). *In addition*, the community's *ownership share* of asset appreciation is $10,000 (per Step #2). The community is entitled to $20,000 of the $200,000 sale proceeds. This amount is divisible by half at dissolution.

Reverse Calculations: Working backwards from the sale:

When the house is sold for $200,000, Cesar must first pay the creditor the $70,000 loan balance:

$200,000 sale proceeds - $70,000 repay loan balance = $130,000 remaining funds

From the remaining funds, Cesar's separate property estate is entitled to an equity reimbursement of $20,000 for its SP downpayment:

$130,000 - $20,000 Cesar's SP equity
reimbursement = $110,000 remaining funds

From the remaining funds, the community is entitled to an equity reimbursement of $10,000 for its contributions to the repayment of the SP loan principal:

$110,000 - $10,000 CP equity
reimbursement = $100,000 remaining fund

From the remaining funds, Cesar's separate property estate is entitled to $90,000 of appreciation for increased market value of the property as measured from the time of purchase to the time of divorce:

$100,000 - $90,000 Cesar's SP ownership share
of appr. = $10,000 remaining funds

From the remaining funds, the community is entitled to $10,000 of appreciation for the increased market value of the property as measured from the time of purchase to the time of divorce:

$10,000 - $10,000 CP share of appr. = $0

Transaction costs are the sellers' proportionally shared responsibility. The separate property estate repays the lender.

Both Cesar and Dolores must sign the transfer deed, so as to release all separate and community interests in the property.

Marsden does not apply in this example because there was no measurable appreciation from the time of purchase to the time of marriage, as the house was purchased immediately before marriage.

[3] Premarital Appreciation: The *Moore/Marsden* Formula

In *Marriage of Marsden*, husband, Sullivan, the separate property proponent, lived in the disputed house nine years prior to marriage.[20] Upon dissolution, the trial court erred in the formula it used to calculate the community's interest in the property. On appeal Sullivan advanced two arguments to establish the correct apportionment formula. Sullivan's first argument was that he was entitled to a reimbursement for premarital equity and for premarital appreciation; his second argument was that, to reflect premarital equity and premarital appreciation, the denominator in the *Moore* formula should be changed from the (historic) purchase price ($38,300) to the fair market value of the house on the date of marriage ($65,000). Sullivan's adjusted formula would have given his separate property estate a larger percentage of marital appreciation (85.85%) than the percentage (75.98%) that was ultimately approved by the court of appeal.[21] In apportioning the house, the *Marsden* court of appeal agreed that Sullivan was entitled to a reimbursement for premarital equity and premarital appreciation. But it rejected, as non-compliant with the holding in *Moore*, Sullivan's second argument to change the denominator

[20] *Marsden, supra.*

[21] *Marsden, supra,* at 437, 439.

in the *Moore* formula from the historic purchase price to the fair market value of the house at marriage.[22]

The court of appeal explained: "[Sullivan] contends and we agree that he should have the benefit of approximately nine years of appreciation in the value of the property before the marriage in 1971."[23] The more precise question for the *Marsden* court, however, was how to account for that pre-marital benefit given that "[t]he *Moore/Lucas/Aufmuth* formula makes no provision for prenuptial appreciation on property and therefore offers no guidance."[24] Thus *Marsden*, "bound by the *Moore/Lucas/Aufmuth* formula," set out to offer an "adjustment" that would "fit within that formula."[25] Ultimately, the *Marsden* court held that *Moore* requires the use of the historic purchase price as a denominator to calculate ownership percentages. *Marsden* identified this historic price as "the fair market value at or near the time of purchase [which] is usually equivalent to the purchase price. In short the appraised value equals the cost value."[26]

To account for premarital appreciation, *Marsden* split total appreciation of the house (i.e., the appreciation of the house from purchase to divorce) into two temporal periods: Appreciation before marriage and appreciation during marriage. This split hybridized the original *Moore* formula, resulting in a formula now commonly referred to as the *Moore/Marsden* formula.

To take a step back, in a *Moore* accounting, the separate property proponent's original equity contribution is accounted for in the form of its downpayment and the loan proceeds that it obtained to purchase the property. The crux of the paradigmatic *Moore* problem, then, is that the separate property proponent makes no claim for premarital appreciation (i.e., increase in market value before marriage). For that reason, the *Moore* formula accounts only for the reimbursement of marital equity and marital appreciation.

In a paradigmatic *Moore/Marsden* problem, by comparison, the separate property proponent is able to prove the existence of both premarital equity and *premarital appreciation*. Proof of premarital equity takes the form of information about the separate property proponent's downpayment and the separate property loan proceeds — just as in *Moore*. Plus there may be evidence of (separate property) repayments of loan principal that were made before marriage. Whereas proof of premarital appreciation, must take the form of an appraisal report dated on or near the date of marriage (best evidence) or expert testimony reconstructing past housing markets (found not persuasive in *Marsden*). Assuming persuasive proof, premarital appreciation is subsequently calculated by subtracting the original contract price (i.e., the historic purchase price) from the fair market value of the asset at the time of marriage. Marital appreciation is calculated by

---

[22] *But see Patrick v. Alacer Corp.*, 201 Cal. App. 4th 1326, 136 Cal. Rptr. 3d 669 (Cal. App. Ct., 4th Dist. 2011) (holding that the trial court did not err when it declined to extend *Marsden* to a separate property business characterization dispute).

[23] *Marsden, supra*, at 437.

[24] *Marsden, supra*, at 437.

[25] *Marsden, supra*, at 438.

[26] *Marsden, supra*, at 438.

subtracting the fair market value of the asset at the time of marriage from the fair market value at the time of trial.

Taking a Family Code centric view of *Moore/Marsden*: premarital equity and premarital appreciation are properly defined as separate property under § 770. Marital appreciation is properly characterized as commingled § 760/§ 770 property. The *Moore* part of *Moore/Marsden* apportions commingled marital appreciation; this first step of the *Moore/Marsden* formula divides contributions to purchase (equity) by the historic purchase price. (*Marsden* held that the asset's original (historic) purchase price is the legally correct denominator even if the asset was purchased long before the marriage, as it was in the *Marsden* case.) The *Marsden* step of the *Moore/Marsden* formula identifies premarital equity and premarital appreciation, and labels as premarital appreciation any asset appreciation that occurred between the time of purchase and the date of marriage. Both are properly characterized as separate property under the definition in § 770.

Here is *Moore/Marsden* expressed as a formula:

The* Moore/Marsden *Formula:

Step #1: Start with *Moore*:

$$\frac{\text{SP downpayment} + (\text{SP loan} - \text{CP contribution})}{\text{HPP}} = \text{SP \%}$$

$$\frac{\text{CP contribution}}{\text{HPP}} = \text{CP \%}$$

Step #2: Apportion Marital Appreciation:

Marital appr. = FMV@ time of trial – FMV @ time of marriage

SP % × Marital appr. = SP % of commingled marital appr.

CP % × Marital appr. = CP % of commingled marital appr.

Step #3: Account for Premarital Equity and for Premarital Appreciation:

Premarital *equity* (i.e., contributions to purchase) is reimbursed to the SP under § 770(a)(1).

Premarital *appreciation* (i.e., the increase in value from the time of purchase to the date of marriage) is reimbursed to the SP under § 770(a)(1).

Premarital appr. = FMV* @ date of marriage - HPP

The total SP premarital reimbursement is represented by this formula:

SP reimbursement =
FMV @ time of trial - (premarital equity + premarital appr.)

- Note: FMV = Fair Market Value, meaning what a willing buyer would pay for the property after full disclosure.

- Note: only appreciation *during* marriage is subject to apportionment, since only marital appreciation can become commingled.

Example 6.11: This example illustrates application of the *Moore/Marsden* formula. Cesar buys a house before marriage for $38,300. Cesar purchases the house with an $8,300 downpayment and a $30,000 loan. During the 9 years that Cesar lived in the house prior to marriage, Cesar pays $7,655 of loan principal. On the date of marriage, Cesar obtains an appraisal of the house. The house appraises at $65,000. During marriage, Cesar repays $9,200 of loan principal with work earnings. Eventually, Cesar and Dolores decide to dissolve their marriage, at which time the appraised value of the house is $182,500. The house is sold. How should the sale proceeds be divided?

Example 6.11: Cesar's Tracing Rebuttal:* Moore/Marsden *Formula:[27]

Step #1: Start with *Moore*:

$8,300 SP dpmt +
<u>($30,000 SP loan - $9,200 CP contr.)</u> = 75.98% = SP % of marital appr.
$38,300 HPP

<u>$9,200 CP contr.</u> = 24.02% = CP% of marital appr.
$38,300 HPP

Step #2: Apportion the Commingled Marital Appreciation:

Marital appr. = $182,500 FMV @ trial –
($38,300 HPP + $26,700 premarital appr.) = $117,500

75.98% SP × $117,500 = $89,276.50

24.02% CP × $117,500 = $28,223.50

Step #3: Account for Premarital Appreciation:

Premarital appr. = $65,000 FMV @ marriage -
$38,300 HPP = $26,700 premarital appr.

Balance remaining on the loan at time of trial = $13,145

Working backwards from the sale:

When the house is sold for $182,500, Cesar must first repay the lender:

$182,500 sale proceeds - $13,145 SP loan balance =
$169,355 remaining funds

From the remaining funds, Cesar is entitled to a (premarital) equity reimbursement of $15,955. This figure *includes* Cesar's $8,300 downpayment plus $7,655 of premarital loan repayments. For purposes of Step #1

[27] *Marsden, supra,* at 439.

of the formula, Cesar's $7,655 of premarital loan repayments is included in the $30,000 of loan proceeds credit that he got for obtaining the loan.

$169,355 - $15,955 premarital equity reimbursement =
$153,400 remaining funds

From the remaining funds, Cesar is entitled to the premarital appreciation.

$153,400 - $26,700 SP premarital appr. = $126,700 remaining funds

From the remaining funds, Cesar is entitled to SP marital appreciation.

$126,700 - $89,276.50 = $37,424.50 remaining funds

From the remaining funds, the community is entitled to a $9,200 reimbursement for its contribution to purchase.

$37,424.50 - $9,200 CP contribution = $28,224.50 remaining funds

From the remaining funds, the community is entitled to its share of marital appreciation

$28,224.50 remaining funds - $28,223.50 = $0

Transaction costs are the sellers' responsibility. The SP repays the remaining loan principal.

Both Cesar and Dolores must sign the transfer deed, so as to release all separate and community interests in the property.

Moore/Marsden is used here because the SP proponent established the fair market value of the house at marriage and thus proved the existence of premarital appreciation.

Use of the *Moore/Marsden* formula requires proof of the fair market value of the asset at marriage so that premarital appreciation can be established. If the trial court decides not to allow the use of *Moore/Marsden*, it can still allow the use of *Moore*. If the trial court declines to allow *Moore*, the asset is deemed entirely community property; in this case, the separate property contributor is entitled to a § 2640 no-interest reimbursement.

Additionally, where the financing record has become so confused that neither *Moore* nor *Moore/Marsden* can practicably apply, a court can exercise its discretion to characterize the house as entirely (100%) community property. The rationale for this outcome is threefold. One, the doctrine of confusion holds that at the point that a commingled asset can no longer be apportioned, it is transmuted into community property by operation of law. Two, § 852(d) codifies the doctrine of confusion. Three, *Marriage of Geraci* places the burden of clarifying the financing record on the separate property claimant; where the record is unclear, the trial court has discretion to deem the property entirely community property by application of the doctrine of confusion as codified in 852(d).[28]

If an asset is deemed to be entirely community property, the separate property proponent is entitled to a statutory reimbursement under § 2640 for traceable

28 *Geraci, supra.*

contributions to purchase.

[B] Transmutation

Moore is deemed the correct approach in a case where the separate property acquisition occurs before marriage. However, *Aufmuth/Moore* can apply also to acquisitions made during marriage, by transmutation. Any community property purchase contributions from the date of acquisition forward go toward establishing the community's equitable ownership share under the *Moore* formula. Depending on the evidence, the separate property proponent can make a claim for pre-acquisition contributions to purchase and appreciation using the *Moore/Marsden* formula.

In *Broderick*, the *Aufmuth/ Moore/Marsden* line of cases was approved for use in a valid transmutation.[29] In *Broderick*, wife transmuted her community property interest in the family home to the husband by quitclaim deed. In exchange, the husband gave the wife $4,000. The court of appeal upheld the use of *Moore* and, if necessary, *Moore/Marsden*. But it remanded the case to the trial court to determine the correct community property ownership share. The separate property acquisition date was the date of the transmutation; the rationale being that a valid transmutation divests the adversely affected spouse of the entirety of the transmuted property. In *Broderick* that transmutation included possession of the house, its market appreciation, and the wife's share of the community's pre-transmutation contributions to purchase. Yet, as the appellate judge made clear: ". . . I continue to have serious doubt that this transaction is legally conscionable: a quick three (or four) thousand dollars in exchange for an equity interest having at least triple that value." That said, assuming the transmutation was deemed valid, use of *Moore* and *Moore/Marsden* were permitted.

[C] An Improvement Made with Community Funds

Generally, when the non-owning spouse consents to the use of community property to improve the other spouse's separate property, no gift is intended.[30] It is unclear, however, whether the community is entitled to a proportional ownership interest for its contributions to improvements.[31]

[1] Capital Improvements: The *Bono* Formula

The threshold issue in deciding whether to apportion or to reimburse turns on whether there is in fact a *capital* improvement. A capital improvement is one that increases the separate property's fair market value. If there is, *Bono* holds that the community estate is entitled to an equitable ownership interest in the property, as measured by its contributions to the total investment.[32] To quote the court of appeal in *Bono*: "The principal effect of our holding is to put capital improvements on the

---

29 *Marriage of Broderick*, 209 Cal. App. 3d 489, 257 Cal. Rptr. 397 (Cal. App. Ct., 1st Dist. 1989).

30 *Marriage of Allen*, 96 Cal. App. 4th 497, 116 Cal. Rptr. 2d 887 (Cal. App. Ct., 2d Dist. 2002).

31 *Marriage of Wolfe*, 91 Cal. App. 4th 962, 110 Cal. Rptr. 2d 921 (Cal. App. Ct., 3d Dist. 2001).

32 *Bono, supra*, at 1428.

same footing as expenditures for property acquisition or for mortgage reduction."

Here is the *Bono* approach expressed as a formula:

Step #1: Find the total investment in the property:

Total investment = HPP + premarital (or preimprovement) appr. + community improvements

Step #2: Find the Ratio of Ownership Interests:

$$\frac{\text{Purchase price + Premarital (or preimprovement) appr.}}{\text{Total Investment}} = \text{SP \% ownership}$$

$$\frac{\text{Community Improvements}}{\text{Total Investment}} = \text{CP \%}$$

Step #3: Apportion Marital Appreciation:

Equity is fair market value less encumbrances.

Marital Appr. =
Equity at date of separation - Equity at date of improvements

[2] Maintenance and Non-capital Improvements

Maintenance falls under the category of family expenses.

Improvements must be classified as capital improvement or non-capital improvements. A non-capital improvement is one that does not enhance the property's fair market value. A tennis court without drainage that cracks and sink over time; a pool built without a permit atop of a hill; an addition that disrupts the flow of the home; an addition made with faulty construction; and so on. These represent material changes to the real estate, but they do no enhance real estate's fair market value over time. As the court in *Reed v. King* held, fair market value assumes a willing buyer with knowledge of all the issues and purposes to which the realty is adopted.[33] Therefore, as non-capital improvements must be disclosed to a prospective buyer, it is as likely as not that they will diminish (rather than enhance) the fair market value of the property.

The community is entitled to a reimbursement for its contributions to construction for non-capital improvements.

[33] *Reed v. King*, 145 Cal. App. 3d 261, 193 Cal. Rptr. 130 (Cal. App. Ct., 3d Dist. 1983).

§ 6.03 SEPARATE PROPERTY CONTRIBUTIONS TO AN ENTIRELY COMMUNITY PROPERTY ASSET

Cal. Fam. Code § 2640 creates a right of statutory reimbursement that applies **"In the division of the community estate . . . unless a party has made a written waiver of the right of reimbursement or has signed a writing that has the effect of a waiver."** Absent such a waiver, **"[t]he** [separate property contributor] **shall be reimbursed for the party's contributions to the acquisition of** [entirely community] **property. . . ."**

Tracing determines the amount of the reimbursement, which, also under § 2640(b), **"[s]hall be without interest or adjustment for change in monetary values and may not exceed the net value of the property at the time of the division."** If the property has appreciated in value, the community gets the appreciation; the separate property contributor gets a reimbursement. According to the Law Review Commission Revised Comment, "If the property has depreciated in value, reimbursement may not exceed the value of the property; if both parties are entitled to reimbursement and the property has insufficient value to permit full reimbursement of both, reimbursement should be on a proportionate basis."

Prior to January 1, 1984, when former Civil Code § 4800.2 went into effect to reverse the gift presumption in *Marriage of Lucas*, the separate property contributor was presumed to make a gift absent an agreement otherwise.[34] From January 1, 1984-on, the separate property became statutorily entitled to a no-interest reimbursement for any contribution to the purchase of an entirely community property asset. In 1992, § 2640 was enacted in the Family Code and amended effective 1993. Retroactive application of former Civil Code § 4800.2 (current Family Code § 2640) was held to be unconstitutional in *Marriage of Heikes*, 10 Cal. 4th 1211, 44 Cal. Rptr. 2d 155, 899 P.2d 1349 (1995).[35] Retroactive application means application to cases arising before January 1, 1984.

Marriage of Walrath held that the § 2640 right to reimbursement carries over in the event that the original property is refinanced and the (refinanced) loan proceeds are used to a secure a community asset.[36]

Consistent with the case law understanding of contributions to purchase as principal payments to a loan § 2640 defines **"Contributions to the acquisition of property"** as including **"[d]ownpayments, payments for improvements, and payments that reduce the principal of a loan used to finance the purchase or improvement of the property"** By the same statute, contributions to purchase **"[d]o not include payments of interest on the loan or payments made for maintenance, insurance, or taxation of the property."**

In *Marriage of Geraci*, the separate property proponent's *Moore/Marsden* attempt failed.[37] Consequently, the separate property proponent, John, sought a

---

[34] *Lucas, supra.*

[35] *Heikes, supra.*

[36] *Marriage of Walrath*, 17 Cal. 4th 907, 72 Cal. Rptr. 2d 856, 952 P.2d 1124 (Cal. 1998).

[37] *Geraci, supra.*

reimbursement for premarital equity under § 2640. The trial court disallowed the reimbursement on the ground that John failed to establish the fair market value of the property on the date of marriage. The record showed that John owned a property that he acquired (in a former dissolution) in 1973 for $43,000. In 1980, John razed the original house and built an entirely new 3,100 square-foot replacement house. Evidently John did not re-appraise the replacement house at the time of his marriage to Jane in 1983. Seventeen years and many mortgage refinances and home equity lines of credit later, Jane and John dissolved their marriage. To that end, they sold the house for $974,000. After all costs and loans were paid, the house netted sale proceeds of $354,000. Of this, John claimed the entire amount as a reimbursement for his premarital equity for the years 1973–1983.

John presented expert testimony of the house's probable market value in 1983. He also presented and testified as to his own calculations about the house's probable fair market value in 1983. He did not, however, clarify the financing history for the trial court. After several days of trial, the court held that John failed to carry his burden of adequately tracing his separate property contribution to purchase. The court exercised its discretion to enforce the parties' own pretrial settlement agreement, which gave John $194,000 — approximately $35,000 more than Jane received — in recognition of his prior ownership of the house. John appealed. The court of appeal affirmed. It held that what John failed to establish was "any evidence of how the rebuilding project in 1980 was financed and any evidence of John's *equity* in the property at the time of marriage." (Italics in the original.)[38]

The above cases seem complicated. Keep in mind, however, that if the financial picture is not adequately explained, the court can exercise its discretion in favor of finding that the purchase is community property. It is the duty of the separate property claimant (1) to establish the fair market value of the property on the date of marriage; and (2) to make the financing history of the property clear for the court. If the record is confused, § 852(d) allows a court to rule that the asset has been transmuted into community property by operation of law. If reimbursement is permitted, it is without interest and subject to value limitations in the case of depreciation.

In this case, the separate property proponent is entitled to a § 2640 reimbursement for traceable contributions to purchase. Otherwise, *Moore* calculates proportional shares of commingled appreciation. *Moore/Marsden* calculates proportional shares of commingled marital appreciation, while also reimbursing the separate property proponent for *pre*marital equity and premarital appreciation. *Geraci* establishes that, in order to obtain a *Moore/Marsden* reimbursement, the separate property claimant must prove that there was premarital appreciation.

Bono applies *Moore* to capital improvements made to separate property with community property funds.

Example 6.12: This example illustrates the separate property claimant's burden of proof. Cesar buys a house before marriage for $38,300. Cesar keeps no records. Cesar lives in the house for 9 years prior to marriage, but does not appraise the house on the date of marriage. Prior to and after marriage various refinance and

---

[38] *Id.*

home equity loans are obtained, all secured by the property. During marriage, Cesar repays the most recent mortgage with work earnings. Eventually, Cesar and Dolores decide to dissolve their marriage, at which time the appraised value of the house is $182,500. Cesar, not the community, has the burden to prove Cesar's premarital equity and premarital appreciation amounts. On these facts, such proof appears to be confused at best and absent at worst. Consequently, a court has the discretion to disallow a *Moore/Marsden* formula and apply the *Moore* formula; or, alternatively, to characterize the house as entirely (100%) community property, subject to the separate property claimant's traceable § 2640 no-interest reimbursement, if any.

Example 6.13: This example illustrates the § 2640 reimbursement when an asset appreciates in value. Assume that Cesar and Dolores buy a house during marriage for $100,000. Cesar uses $20,000 of separate property to make the downpayment. The spouses obtain a mortgage for $80,000. Record title to the house reads: *"Cesar and Dolores as a married couple."* At divorce, the house sells for $200,000. The loan principal is $79,000. Application of § 2581 characterizes the house as entirely (100%) community property. Application of the § 2640 right of reimbursement gives Cesar's separate property estate a reimbursement of $20,000, without interest or adjustment for change in monetary values, for its downpayment.

From the $200,000 sale proceeds, the mortgage creditor is paid first. This releases the deed of trust:

$200,000 sale proceeds - $79,000 SP loan repayment =
$119,000 remaining funds

From the $119,000 remaining, Cesar is entitled to a no-interest reimbursement of $20,000 for the separate property downpayment:

$119,000 - $20,000 SP reimbursement = $99,000 remaining funds

The remaining $99,000 is community property, to which each spouse is entitled to a one-half community property share.

Example 6.14: This example illustrates the § 2640 reimbursement where the asset depreciates in value. Same as Example 6.13 except that now the house must be sold for at a loss for $79,000. The house is community property per § 2581, just as in Example 6.13. But since the $79,000 sale proceeds barely cover the mortgage obligation, Cesar's § 2640 reimbursement cannot be made due to insufficient funds.

§ 6.04 THE LENDER'S INTENT TEST

For purposes of liability, a contract obligation is characterized temporally, according to when the obligation was incurred.

Prior to marriage, by this temporal analysis, a loan is a separate obligation; as such it results in entirely (100%) separate property loan proceeds (cash in the form of the borrowed funds).

During marriage, a loan is a community property contract obligation. A community property loan produces entirely (100%) community property loan proceeds. Cash obtained from a community property loan is credited to the community property.

In a secured transaction, where the lender pays the seller directly, the community property presumption as to borrowed funds may only be rebutted by the lender's intent test. According to the lender's intent test, if "the lender intended to rely *solely* on a spouse's separate property [in extending the loan] and in fact did so," then the loan is properly characterized as a separate property loan.[39] (Italics added.)

As a factual matter, the lender's intent test is difficult to meet for a loan obtained during marriage. This is because creditworthiness during marriage is a community asset. If a lender runs a spouse's credit history, that credit report will contain information that was accumulated on a chronological basis. Information generated during marriage, at least under the lender's intent test, is a community property asset. Similarly, if the lender extends credit based on a spouse's current earnings, or current employment, then the lender is relying on community property income and projections of income in making the loan. And even if the lender relies on a separate property business (like a taxable investment account), that loan will more likely than not be characterized as a community property loan, especially given that separate property businesses are easily commingled with community labor.

Example 6.15: This example illustrates application of the presumption that loan proceeds obtained during marriage are community property unless the lender relied solely on separate property in extending the loan. At the start of their marriage, Cesar and Dolores obtain a mortgage loan to buy a house. The lender originates the loan based on both spouses' earnings, credit histories, and credit scores. The proceeds obtained from this loan are community property funds.

Example 6.16: This example illustrates application of the lender's intent rebuttal. Cesar and Dolores want to buy a house. The lender originates the loan based solely on income from Trust 111, a trust to which Dolores is a beneficiary. Trust 111 makes the downpayment on the property from Trust 111 property. Each month, Trust 111 pays the mortgage principal with trust property that is transferred directly to the lender: The trustee takes this precaution to ensure that no commingling can occur by the act of depositing trust funds into the account of either or both spouses. Here, the analysis starts with the presumption that the loan proceeds are community property. Dolores rebuts this presumption by showing that the lender intended to rely solely on Trust 111 in making the loan. The loan proceeds are separate property.

To reiterate, the estate that obtains the borrowed funds gets full credit for those funds. Practically speaking, this means that when the sale proceeds are being distributed, the contractually bound estate's proportional share, which is based on loan proceeds, is sufficient to repay the loan. The prior statement assumes that the indebtedness on the property does not exceed its fair market value.

---

[39] *Gudelj v. Gudelj*, 41 Cal. 2d 202, 259 P.2d 656 (Cal. 1953) (in bank); *Marriage of Grinius*, 166 Cal. App. 3d 1179, 212 Cal. Rptr. 803 (Cal. App. Ct., 4th Dist. 1985).

In distributing sale proceeds, the mortgage lender (or servicing company) is paid first. This releases the lender's deed of trust on the property. Next, other outstanding obligations, including transaction costs, are paid so as to release any other liens on title. And then, only if there are sale proceeds remaining, do separate property and community property shares (finally) get distributed. In the event of default, a lender can demand repayment from the community property as well as from a co-signing spouse's separate property estate. Liabilities are discussed in Chapter 13.

§ 6.05 SUMMARY

Obviously valuation questions can be complicated, especially given real estate market twists and turns.

Therefore, the take-aways — plural — from this chapter are the principles of how best to apportion commingled credit acquisitions. The basic principles are more critical to one's understanding than are the arithmetic details. Also key is the relationship between accounting and full disclosure, as discussed in Parts IV and V. In a complicated case, parties will dispute over appraisal value, and over other financial details; they will also hire forensic experts.

Notwithstanding the use of experts, lawyers shape their client's case and introduce the evidence related to purchase details. For that reason, lawyers are called on to understand basic principles. Therefore, here is where the burdens currently lie:

- **The basic tracing formula:** The property is presumed community property. Thus, the burden is on the separate property claimant to establish a proportional ownership share. The separate property proponent does this by tracing all or some of the purchase back to separate property funds. Percentage ownership shares are used to apportion commingled appreciation. The basic tracing formula is in § 6.01[A].
- **The *Aufmuth* formula:** *Aufmuth* permits credit contributions (loan proceeds) to be counted as equity contributions for purposes of apportioning ownership. The *Aufmuth* formula is like the basic tracing formula except that the community estate's equity contribution to purchase is in the amount of the loan proceeds that were advanced by the lender to the seller. The *Aufmuth* formula is in § 6.01[B].
- **The *Moore* formula:** The property is brought to the marriage as separate property. Building on *Aufmuth*, Moore allows credit contributions (loan proceeds) to be counted as equity contributions to purchase. The separate property estate's percentage share is based on its downpayment, plus its total loan proceeds minus any community property principal repayments, divided by the historic purchase price. The community estate's equity contribution to purchase is the amount by which it reduced the principal portion of the separate property loan divided by the historic purchase price. This calculation results in proportional ownership shares for the respective estates. Equity

contributions to purchase are reimbursed. Percentage ownership shares are used to apportion commingled appreciation (or depreciation). The *Moore* formula is in § 6.02[A][2].

- **The *Moore/Marsden* formula:** Just as with *Moore*, the property is brought to the marriage as separate property. Assuming loan payments are made from earnings during marriage, the community property proponent has the burden to produce mortgage or loan payment records. From these records, the community contribution to purchase can be calculated. Each estate's contribution to purchase is divided by the historic purchase price. This calculation results in proportional ownership shares of *marital* equity. Premarital appreciation is defined as the fair market value of the asset on the date of marriage minus the fair market value of the asset on the date of purchase. Premarital equity (i.e., provable contributions to purchase) and premarital appreciation — once proved — are reimbursed to the separate property claimant. The community is likewise reimbursed for its contributions to purchase in the form of loan principal payments. Percentage ownership shares are used to apportion commingled marital appreciation.

In addition to the burdens discussed above, the burden is on the separate property proponent to establish: (1) financing history for the property and (2) for purposes of *Moore/Marsden*, the fair market value of the property on the date of marriage. However, if a record becomes so confused such that the separate property's interest cannot be distinguished from the community property's interest, or if the separate property cannot credibly establish fair market value on the date of marriage, then a trial court has discretion to deem that the asset is entirely community property, subject to a reimbursement, without interest, for the separate property contributor as authorized by § 2640. The *Moore/Marsden* formula is in § 6.02[A][3].

Chapter 7

SEPARATE PROPERTY BUSINESS GROWTH

A business characterization dispute can arise when a spouse comes to the marriage with separate property business and subsequently devotes community property labor to the business during marriage. At dissolution, the question becomes how to account for the business growth.

California law provides two alternatives. The community estate is either entitled to its share of the excess profits of the business (by apportionment) or, alternatively, it is entitled to a reimbursement for its labor contribution, minus family expenses. This is so regardless of which spouse's activities made the business enterprise profitable during marriage, since labor belongs to the community estate. Thus, either spouse can add community property labor to a separate property business.[1]

Which of the approaches is used is left to the discretion of the trial court.

The basic concept of community property is that marriage is a partnership. Thus any community property labor that goes toward improving the financial lives of the partners must be accounted for at the termination of the marriage. The trial court has discretion to decide, at the end of the marriage, how best to account for a separate property business that one or both spouses worked in. It does so by deciding which approach furthers substantial justice between the parties.

§ 7.01 CONCEPTUAL ELEMENTS

Four conceptual elements are useful in understanding California's approach to separate property business apportionment.

- Labor is community property.
- The underlying business capital is separate property.
- Commingling occurs when the community labor investment increases the fair market value of the business during marriage.
- Commingled assets retain their character notwithstanding the admixture.

Generally, a commingled business is apportioned between the separate property owner and the community estate when to do so would achieve substantial justice between the parties. Apportionment is commonly by the *Pereira* approach. Otherwise, the community can be reimbursed by application of the *Van Camp* approach.

---

[1] *Marriage of Dekker*, 17 Cal. App. 4th 842, 851, 21 Cal. Rptr. 2d 642, 647 (Cal. App. Ct., 4th Dist. 1993).

§ 7.02 THE UNDERLYING BUSINESS

The separate property claimant has the burden of proving that the business is in fact a separate property business. A separate property business is defined as one that either came to the marriage or that was started during the marriage with separate property funds. Once a separate property business is established, the burden shifts to the community to show that community labor contributed to the growth of the business during the marriage.

For example, in *Austin v. Austin*, defendant, Jerome claimed that he was the sole owner of a welding business that he started during marriage. In support of his claim, Jerome sought to account for the business under the *Van Camp* rule.[2] To that end, Jerome testified that he used about $1,800 of separate property funds to buy an interest in a welding business during marriage. Otherwise Jerome produced no financial records. The trial court found that Jerome did not establish a separate property business. The court of appeal upheld the trial court. In doing so, it distinguished Jerome's welding business from the businesses covered by *Pereira* or *Van Camp*.

In *Pereira*, the husband owned a profitable saloon business before marriage; the business became even more profitable during marriage.[3] In *Van Camp*, Frank Van Camp moved his extensive meat packing business from Indianapolis to California. Subsequently, Frank married and divorced. At dissolution, Frank proved that he owned $150,000 of the $200,000 total capital that was used to start Van Camp Sea Food Company before his marriage. Van Camp Sea Food Company "employed" Frank, thus paying him a salary for his (nonessential) services to the corporation. Frank's salary was modest in comparison to his vast wealth and to his stock, which paid handsome dividends before and during his marriage.[4]

In *Austin*, by contrast, Jerome could not prove that his welding business was separate property at inception. But even if he could have established that fact, Jerome failed to convince the trial court that what he had was a "business" subject to *Pereira* or *Van Camp* apportionment. What the court found instead is that Jerome had a community property income stream that was based on his personal services, and welding tools that were community personal property subject to division at dissolution. The trial court's decision states the distinction well:

> In the present case, the welding business had no operating capital whatever except through earnings. In the beginning the business was only bringing in $7 or $8 a day, and it had no value whatever except in the equipment of a welding shop. That was all defendant purchased. . . . Defendant worked long hours, from 7 a.m. until late in the evening, estimating for prospective jobs and managing and supervising the work. All the earnings of the business were due to his labor, skill, and management. There was no one else to take his place. It is true that he was on salary of $1,000 per month, and that in recent years he had withdrawn from the

---

[2] *Austin v. Austin*, 190 Cal. App. 2d 45, 11 Cal. Rptr. 593 (Cal. App. Ct., 2d Dist. 1961).

[3] *Pereira v. Pereira*, 156 Cal. 1, 156 Cal. App. 11, 103 P. 488 (Cal. 1909).

[4] *Van Camp v. Van Camp*, 53 Cal. App. 17, 199 P. 885 (Cal. App. Ct., 2d Dist. 1921).

> business about $27,000 per year, but it would be unrealistic to say that this was the full measure of the value of his services, and that the increase in value, or any part of it, was due to capital supplied by the defendant and used in the business. . . . If the value of his entire services were withdrawn from the value of the business there would be nothing left as separate property attributable to the use of capital as a contribution to the earnings and the value of the business. The situation was much the same as that of a professional man who invests in equipment in an office and library, or of an artisan who acquires the tools of his trade. As the business is developed the value it takes on is not due to the equipment itself aside from the labor, judgment and skill with which it is used. It must be presumed that the trial court concluded that the value which it placed upon the business of $100,000 was due to the personal services of the defendant, and to nothing else. It is a conclusion with which we agree, and it supports the further conclusion that the stock representing defendant's interest in the business was community property.[5]

The value of a separate property business on the date of the marriage or inception (if during marriage) represents the underlying § 770 separate property capital investment. Subject to the general rule, a separate property business retains its character during marriage, absent a premarital contract or a valid transmutation.

The fact of marriage does not automatically transmute a profit making enterprise from a separate property business into a community property one; nor does the fact that community property labor was added to the business transmute it.[6] Added labor, without more, does not necessarily signal commingling.

In a separate property business, the underlying capital is § 770 separate property, as is the intrinsic business appreciation that traces back to that original capital. Rents, issues, and profits that trace back to the underlying § 770(a)(1) or (2) capital are also separate property under § 770(a)(3). But where the community has contributed a certain amount of labor to the growth of the business, then at the end of the marriage, the community estate may be entitled to an equitable accounting.

The community estate's right to apportionment or, alternatively, to reimbursement is not dependent upon the form or the nature of the underlying business. A bricks and mortar business that one spouse brings to the marriage is clearly a separate property business eligible for equitable accounting at the termination of marriage.[7] So too are: a business started during marriage with separate property funds;[8] a taxable security investment account;[9] a "labyrinth of interlocking and interrelated corporate entities, family trusts, and closely owned holding compa-

---

[5] *Austin, supra*, at 51.

[6] *Patrick, supra*, at 1343–44.

[7] *Pereira, supra* (saloon business); *Van Camp, supra* (publicly traded seafood packing enterprise); *Tassi v. Tassi*, 160 Cal. App. 2d 680, 325 P.2d 872 (Cal. App. Ct., 1st Dist. 1958) (meat business during wartime).

[8] *Dekker, supra* (closely held corporation, originally funded with $1,000 of wife's separate property, valued at dissolution at $927,000, and having only two stockholders, the spouses).

nies;"[10] an agricultural enterprise;[11] shares held in a private investment group;[12] a fractional royalty producing interest in an oil drilling partnership;[13] and so forth.

What connects these examples is that each was a bona fide separate property profit making enterprise with a capital base that grew during the marriage. Once a court is satisfied that a separate property business is involved, the question becomes which method should apply.

§ 7.03 THE COMMUNITY PROPERTY LABOR CONTRIBUTION TO BUSINESS GROWTH

The California rule is that if the one or both spouses devote "more than minimal effort" to a separate property business, the community estate is entitled to excess profits from that business.[14] Other community property jurisdictions set the bar at substantial effort. The line between minimal and more than minimal (i.e., "minimum-plus") can result in conflicting case law.[15] Hence, the cornerstone issue for deciding whether to apply the *Pereira* apportionment formula versus the *Van Camp* reimbursement formula is not one of abstract line drawing, but rather one of achieving substantial justice between the parties.[16] Practically speaking, the minimum-plus labor contribution standard together with the substantial justice standard requires a judge to exercise discretion in favor of the approach that produces the better result for the party who prevails on the issue of what contributed — community labor or market forces — to the business's growth.

To isolate the issue of labor contribution, a conceptual baseline is helpful.

On the side of finding no labor contribution is *Estate of Ney*, a case in which a trial court held that the deceased husband Ira's efforts had not contributed to the growth of his separate property stock portfolio, even though Ira made his living from the portfolio income.[17] At Ira's death, the record showed that Ira had made approximately 150 stock transactions in a 10-year period. No special stock trading ability was established on Ira's part, but the record showed that Ira visited his

---

[9] *Beam v. Bank of America*, 6 Cal. 3d 12, 98 Cal. Rptr. 137, 490 P.2d 257 (Cal. 1971) (in bank) (taxable investment portfolio).

[10] *Marriage of Zaentz*, 218 Cal. App. 3d 154, 160, 267 Cal. Rptr. 31, 34 (Cal. App. Ct., 1st Dist. 1990) (movie production enterprise).

[11] *In re Pepper's Estate*, 158 Cal. 619, 112 P. 62 (1910) (plant nursery enterprise), overruled in part by *Estate of Nielson*, 57 Cal. 2d 733, 22 Cal. Rptr. 1, 371 P.2d 745 (Cal. 1962) (in bank) (farm enterprise).

[12] *Weinberg v. Weinberg*, 67 Cal. 2d 557, 63 Cal. Rptr. 13, 432 P.2d 709 (Cal. 1967) (in bank) (stock investments in five related corporations that were held by a private investment group in which the separate property owner, a partner in the investment group, was deemed minimally involved).

[13] *Kenney v. Kenney*, 128 Cal. App. 2d 128, 274 P.2d 951 (Cal. App. Ct., 2d Dist. 1954) (a one-eighth royalty producing interest in an oil drilling partnership).

[14] *Beam*, *supra*, at 17.

[15] *See, e.g.*, *Tassi*, *supra*; *Marriage of Shelton*, 118 Cal. App. 3d 811, 815, 173 Cal. Rptr. 629, 631 (Cal. App. Ct., 3d Dist. 1981) (court held that the community's profits or increased value after separation is community property if the increase is not due to any significant efforts on the part of either spouse).

[16] *Beam*, *supra*, at 17; *Dekker*, *supra*, at 851; *Patrick*, *supra*, at 1340–41.

[17] *Estate of Ney*, 212 Cal. App. 2d 891, 28 Cal. Rptr. 442 (Cal. App. Ct., 1st Dist. 1963).

broker on the average of once a week, sold stock on the average of once a month, and read the Wall Street Journal at home on a daily basis. In 14 years, the decedent's estate grew from $39,000 to $73,000 (not quite double growth); during that same period, the Dow Jones industrial average increased from 207.60 to 582.69 (almost triple growth). Ira's surviving spouse, Loretta, claimed a community property interest in the excess profits of Ira's separate property stock portfolio. The trial court ruled that the increase in Ira's portfolio was not the result of community labor during marriage. Loretta appealed. The court of appeal affirmed on the rationale that Loretta could have countered with how the labor that was identified in the trial record in fact contributed to the growth of Ira's investment portfolio, but she choose not to.

Contrasted to *Ney* is the case of *Beam*, where the separate property business owner conceded in the dissolution proceeding that he spent nearly all of his time managing his taxable investment portfolio.[18] Also contrasted to *Ney* is the case of *Patrick*, where the trial court decided for use of *Pereira* accounting on a general finding that the husband was involved in "virtually every aspect of the company."[19]

The point is that the burden lies with the separate property claimant to prove that the business is in fact a separate property business. Once that element of proof has been made, the burden shifts to the community to show that community labor contributed to the growth of the business during the marriage.

§ 7.04 SEPARATE PROPERTY BUSINESS APPRECIATION, RENTS, ISSUES, AND PROFITS

Once a separate property business is established, two questions arise. Did a minimum-plus amount of community labor go into enhancing the value of the business? And, as between *Pereira* and *Van Camp*, which method best effects "substantial justice" between the parties in light of which party prevailed on the issue of contribution to growth?[20] If the growth of the separate property business is attributable to community property labor, then the *Pereira* formula is the preferred formula. If separate property business is not attributable to community efforts, then the *Van Camp* formula provides a formula by which to reimburse the community for its labor, minus family expenses.

The *Pereira* apportionment method allocates a fair return to the separate property capital investment; the balance of the increased value of the business is allocated to community property. The *Van Camp* approach determines the reasonable value of the community's labor contribution (minus family expenses) and allocates that amount to the community; the balance of the growth is allocated to the separate property.

---

[18] *Beam, supra*, at 16.

[19] *Patrick, supra*, at 1340.

[20] *Beam, supra*, at 18.

There is no legal requirement that the separate property business transfer the community's equitable share of business profits in the form of shares of stock.[21] Neither *Pereira* nor *Van Camp* is a transmutation rule. Therefore, business stock remains separate property, leaving it up to the business entity to decide how best to satisfy the community's claim to excess profits.[22]

[A] The *Pereira* Apportionment Formula

Pereira v. Pereira is the case that articulates the formula for separate property business apportionment.[23] The formula is a total recapitulation accounting method: It takes account of the fair market value of the business at the start of marriage relative to the value of the business at the end of marriage. The value of the business at the start of marriage represents the business owner's § 770(a) separate property capital. The fair rate of return [FRR] on that separate property capital represents the business owner's hypothetical § 770(a)(3) separate property rents, issues, and profits calculated using a simple interest formula (P × r × t). Any business profits in excess of the § 770(a) and § 770(a)(3) components are characterized as community property on the rationale that those excess profits trace back to a § 760 labor contribution.

Pereira recognizes that appreciation, rents, issues, and profits are what get commingled in a separate property business. As a result, the *Pereira* formula attempts to draw a line between appreciation and profits that trace back to the original separate property capital investment, and those that trace back to community property labor. Separate property appreciation and profits are determined by reference to a hypothetical fair rate of return calculation. By that calculation, the fair rate of return is defined as what the separate property capital contribution to the business would have earned had it been invested during the marriage in securities of reasonable safety.[24] Securities of reasonable safety are defined as conservative (low risk) investments.

The fair rate of return on the separate property's original investment ("FMV @ start of marriage" in the formula below) is calculated at simple interest, so as to account for family expenses.[25] The legal interest rate is used in the absence of evidence as to an actual interest rate.

Typically, *Pereira* calculations are offered through expert testimony.

---

21 *Patrick, supra*, at 1340, citing *Dekker, supra*, at 852–53.

22 *Patrick, supra*, at 1343–44.

23 *Pereira, supra*.

24 *Id.*

25 *Marriage of Frick*, 181 Cal. App. 3d 997, 1018–1019, 226 Cal. Rptr. 766, 778 (Cal. App. Ct., 2d Dist. 1986).

Here is the* Pereira *holding expressed as a formula:

FMV @ dissolution – (FMV @ marriage + FRR)* = CP excess profits

*Fair rate of return (FRR) on the original investment (FMV @ marriage) is calculated at simple interest:

FRR = Principal × interest
FRR = P × r × t, where r is rate of interest

Here is* Pereira *expressed in terms of Family Code sections:

(§ 770/ § 760) – (§ 770(a)(1)* + § 770(a)(3)) = § 760

* Assumes a business brought to the marriage.

Example 7.1: This example applies the *Pereira* formula. Pierce owns a widget business before marriage. The value of the business at marriage is $100,000. During a 10 year marriage Franklin manages the business. The business increases in value to $1,000,000. Pierce and Franklin decide to dissolve their marriage. Assume an interest rate of 4%.

$1,000,000 – ($100,000 × .04 × 10) = excess profits

$1,000,000 FMV @ dissolution - ($100,000 FMV @ marriage + $40,000 SP FRR) = $860,000 CP

Here, Pierce gets a reimbursement for her original capital investment ($100,000), plus a fair rate of return on that original investment, calculated at 4% simple interest for the 10 year marriage ($40,000). The fair rate of return represents what Pierce would have made had her $100,000 been invested in reasonably safe securities over her 10 year marriage. Under *Pereira,* the separate property investment that Pierce brought to the marriage as § 770(a)(1) ($100,000), plus a fair rate of return on that investment during the course of the 10 year marriage ($40,000) entitles Pierce to a total of $140,000 of a separate property allocation from the $1,000,000 business. This leaves excess profits of $860,000 for allocation to the community. Excess profits are characterized as community property in which each spouse has a one half interest ($430,000 per spouse).

[B] The *Van Camp* Reimbursement Formula

The alternative method is a reimbursement based on the classic case of *Van Camp v. Van Camp.*[26] *Van Camp* formula recognizes that separate property business growth can be due to forces other than community labor.

For example, when a business grows primarily because of inflation or other market forces, that business growth is due not to community labor, but rather to the ownership of the underlying capital.[27] Likewise, when a separate property business owner hires an outside manager, community property labor is not necessarily responsible for business growth.[28] In *Van Camp*, defendant Frank was a founding shareholder in Van Camp Sea Food Company, a successful corporate entity. Frank earned a small salary from his business, but most of his wealth came from stock ownership. The growth of the business, which led Frank's stock to appreciate, was not due to a community property labor contribution; it was due to other market conditions. Thus, the court in *Van Camp* declined to apply *Pereira*, and it decided instead to credit the community for the value of Frank's services to the corporation, minus family expenses.

As to family expenses, the court said: "In the absence of any evidence showing a different practice, and there is none, the rule is that the community earnings of husband and wife are chargeable with the family support."

Here is the* Van Camp *holding expressed as a formula:

FMV @ divorce - (CP labor - family expenses)* = SP

* Labor contribution = annual benchmark salary × number of years
Family expenses = annual expense × number of years

Here is the* Van Camp *formula expressed in terms of Family Code sections:

§ 770 – (§ 760 – § 720 family expenses) = § 770

Example 7.2: This example applies the *Van Camp* formula. Pierce owns a widget business before marriage. The value of the business at marriage is $100,000. During marriage, the business increases in value to $1,000,000. Pierce and Franklin are married for 10 years. During that ten year period, Pierce minimally manages the business. Family expenses are paid from the business at an estimated

[26] *Van Camp, supra.*

[27] *Tassi, supra.*

[28] *Weinberg, supra.*

amount of $10,000 per year. Assume that a benchmark salary for the work that Pierce did would be $35,000 per year.

$1,000,000 - [($35,000 × 10) - ($10,000 × 10)] = $750,000 Pierce's SP

The community gets a reimbursement of $250,000.

Here, the business is entirely separate property. But it must reimburse the Pierce-Franklin community estate $250,000 for the use of community labor during the marriage ($35,000 × 10 years of marriage = $350,000). Family expenses are subtracted from the community labor component ($10,000 × 10 years of marriage = $100,000). Each spouse has a one-half interest in the $250,000 community reimbursement at dissolution.

[C] *Pereira* or *Van Camp*?: The Substantial Justice Standard

Generally speaking, a separate property business is one that is brought to the marriage or else started during the marriage with separate property capital. The fact of marriage does not automatically transmute a profit making enterprise from separate property to community property. Nor does it necessarily signal commingling. Nor does the fact that the separate property business owner added labor to the business transmute a separate property business into community property one: "California law does not require apportionment of community efforts devoted to separate property on an ongoing basis, upon pain of transmuting the separate property into community property. Courts account for community efforts toward separate property through equitable apportionment after the marriage, not transmutation during the marriage."[29]

A separate property business retains its character during marriage, absent a community labor investment, a premarital contract, or a valid transmutation.

At the end of the marriage, whether by dissolution or death, the community estate is entitled to an equitable accounting. That accounting determines what, if any, proportion of the increase in the value of the business is due to community efforts, and what is due to market or inflationary growth.

A judge has discretion to decide whether to apportion or reimburse the community depending on which approach achieves substantial justice between the parties.[30] Practically speaking this would require the judge to exercise discretion in favor of the approach that produces the better result for the party who prevails on the issue of what contributed — community labor or market forces — to the business's growth.

In the following examples, a single item — a horse — is analyzed as the business.

Keep in mind that labor is § 760 community property; and appreciation, rents, issues, and profits that trace back to labor are also community property.

---

[29] *Patrick, supra*, at 1343–44, citing *Dekker, supra*, at 852–53.

[30] *Beam, supra*, at 17.

The underlying capital, by contrast, is defined as § 770(a)(1) or (2) property; appreciation, rents, issues and profits that trace back to separate property are also, by definition of § 770(a)(3), separate property.

Example 7.3: This example illustrates the basic idea of how appreciation traces back to the underlying asset. The concepts apply to businesses, of course. But for simplicity's sake, the illustration uses one appreciable, issue producing asset — a young horse. Pierce owned a young horse before marriage. That horse weighed 800 pounds on the date of marriage, and it was valued at $1,000. Pierce pastured the horse. At dissolution, five years later, the horse weighs 1,800 pounds; and the horse has a market value of $1,500. Pierce's horse is the same horse at the start as at the end of marriage, even if it has gained 1000 pounds and appreciated $500 in market value. In a dispute between the spouses, the horse is entirely Pierce's separate property.

Example 7.4: This example illustrates the basic concept of how rents, issues, and profits are separate property if they trace back to separate property. Same as Example 7.3, except during Pierce's marriage to Franklin, Pierce's horse gives birth to a foal. In California, Pierce's horse is separate property, as in Example 7.3. So too is the foal. The foal is an issue that traces back to Pierce's separate property horse. These concepts apply to any business, no matter the form. Ordinarily, as in Example 7.3 and 7.4, natural appreciation is an inseparable part of the original asset (although it can be hypothecated). The (now more valuable) horse is (still) Pierce's separate property under § 770(a)(1) whether it weighs 800 pounds or 1,800 pounds. The foal, however, is distinct from the original separate property horse. Nevertheless, in California, the foal is also defined as separate property within the rents, issues, and profits phrase of § 770(a)(3).

Example 7.5: This example illustrates the *Pereira* elements, with a focus on what gets commingled. Same as Example 7.3, except that instead of pasturing the horse, Pierce trains the horse to be a champion show horse. Training occurs during Pierce's marriage to Franklin. During marriage, the horse earns $100,000 per year; moreover, it has a fair market value of $1,000,000 at dissolution. Each year, Pierce and Franklin apply the income from the trained horse ($100,000 per year) to family expenses. When dissolution occurs five years after marriage, the horse is still Pierce's separate property, as in Example 7.3. However, the horse's market value has significantly appreciated thanks to Pierce's training efforts (labor). The horse's fair market value at the start of the marriage was $1,000. By the added value of community property labor — namely Pierce's training efforts — the horse appreciated in value to $1,000,000; it also produced income during the marriage. Thus, in California, Pierce's horse can be analyzed as a profit making enterprise (a business). At dissolution, the horse has a fair market value of $1,000,000. Pierce's separate property is the original investment ($1,000) plus a fair rate of return on that investment over five years at simple interest (FRR = $1,000 × r × 5). The fair rate of return on Pierce's original investment (FRR) will depends on the rate of interest applied. The total is subtracted from the fair market value of the horse at dissolution. The remainder equals the excess, which belongs to the community estate.

> FMV of horse at dissolution – (FMV of horse at marriage + FRR* over 5 years) = CP excess
>
> * Where FRR = $1,000 × r × 5.

In a dispute between the spouses, the *Pereira* formula identifies each estate's apportioned share of the business. Pierce's original investment plus a fair rate of return on that investment get returned; simple interest is used so as to account for family expenses, with the rate of interest also left to the court's discretion. Excess profits are award to the community estate, with each spouse taking a one-half share.

Example 7.6: This example illustrates a *Van Camp* outcome, with a focus on how the horse's appreciation remains entirely separate property during marriage. Same as Example 7.5, except that Pierce contracts the training of the horse out to a famous horse trainer. Training occurs during Pierce's marriage to Franklin, but the horse trainer is paid with Pierce's separate property funds. During marriage, the horse earns $100,000 per year, and has a fair market value of $1,000,000 at the end of marriage. In this case, the horse is still Pierce's separate property, and the horse's market value has significantly appreciated thanks to the famous trainer's efforts. However, those training efforts were not supplied or paid for by the community estate. In a dispute between the spouses, the horse's appreciated value as well as its earnings are entirely Pierce's separate property under § 770. The community is entitled to a reimbursement for any provable labor that Pierce or Franklin may have devoted to the horse's training during the marriage minus family expenses that income from the horse may have paid over the course of the marriage.

California does not follow the traditional civil law rule that characterizes rents, issues and profits — no matter the source — as community property. Therefore, the keynote here is that a separate property business becomes commingled when the accumulations (appreciation, rents, issues, and profits) of separate property capital are partially due to a contribution of community property labor.

[D] Salary

Whether the community's interest in the separate property business is apportioned or reimbursed does not depend upon the actual compensation that one or both spouses received from the business. In *Patrick v*, the court of appeal held that a trial court need not limit the community's interest in a business to salary actually received: This is the case even if the separate property business generously compensated the community for its labor contribution.[31]

---

[31] *Patrick, supra.*

The *Patrick* rationale was that the *Pereira* apportionment formula does not reduce the community property's interest to a salary component. Indeed to do so would be reversible error because it would not address the fact that what has been commingled, in a contested business, is business *appreciation and profits*. As a conceptual matter, appreciation is merged with the business, while profits are independent from the element of salary (fair market compensation for labor). Therefore, whether the community property was undercompensated or overcompensated for the value of its labor during marriage is separate from the issue of whether the business appreciated in value over the course of the marriage.

Additionally, keep in mind that the *Pereira* formula and *Van Camp* formula are legal holdings, not mathematical exercises. Thus in *Zaentz*, the trial court's exercise of discretion in favor of the *Pereira* formula was upheld in a case where the trial record established that the business came to the marriage as separate property, but otherwise that the facts were too complicated and uncertain to plug any numbers into a formula.[32]

Marriage of Imperato allows for reverse-*Pereira* apportionment. In such a case, accretion to a community property business allegedly comes from an infusion of labor during a period when the spouses are living separate and apart. For purposes of § 771, post-separation labor is characterized as the laboring spouse's separate property.[33]

§ 7.05 SUMMARY

In California, two competing accounting methods are recognized by the courts to compensate the community for its labor investment to a separate property business. These methods are closely followed in other community property jurisdictions that that treat separate property rents, issues, and profits as separate property.

To recap, in California:

- The separate property proponent has the burden to show that the business was started with separate property capital. If this burden is met, the business is initially characterized as separate property.
- The labor of a spouse — no matter the form it takes and no matter which spouse expends the labor — is community property under § 760.
- The appreciation of the underlying separate property business is ordinarily itself separate property. However, when community labor is responsible for any part of the increase in the business's market value at dissolution, then the business becomes commingled.
- Appreciation, rents, issues, and profits that trace back to separate property are characterized as separate property under § 770. Appreciation, rents, issues and profits that trace back to the community's equitable share of a business are characterized as community property.
- If and when business rents, issues and profits are used to pay family

[32] *Zaentz, supra.*

[33] *Imperato, supra.*

expenses, they are either community property earnings applied to spousal support obligations, or they are separate property contributions for which the separate property estate is generally not entitled to a reimbursement absent an agreement otherwise. The *Pereira* approach addresses the family expense presumption by using simple interest to calculate the separate property's fair rate of return on the initial investment over the disputed period (typically that period is the length of the marriage). The *Van Camp* approach subtracts family expenses from the community's labor reimbursement.

- A court has the discretion to choose either *Pereira* or *Van Camp* depending on what will achieve substantial justice between the parties.

Chapter 8

LIFE INSURANCE

This chapter covers term life insurance and whole life insurance.

Term life insurance is a contract liability that expires at the end of the specified contract term. Whole life insurance is also a contractual liability with an added savings component. A life insurance contract names a beneficial designee or designees. Upon the death of the insured, the policy premiums are paid to the beneficial designee subject to any equitable claimant.

§ 8.01 BASIC TERMS

A *policy owner* or *policy holder* is the person or business that owns the policy.

A married person has an *insurable interest* in all community property, including that which is commingled with separate property. Every person has an insurable interest in his or her own life and in the life of his or her spouse. A person does not have an insurable interest in the life of the former spouse unless certain elements of proof are met. Under the law of California, an insurance company may not issue a policy to a person unless he or she has an insurable interest in the property insured, or an insurable interest in life of the person insured.

The *insured* is the person whose life is insured by the life insurance. Often the insured and the policy owner are one and same person. Sometimes they are not.

The *beneficial designee* is the person whom the policy owner designates to receive the insurance proceeds upon the occurrence of the peril insured against. In the case of property insurance, the peril insured against is the loss of the property. In the case of life insurance, the peril insured against is the insured's death.

The *face amount* or stated value of the life insurance policy refers to the amount of insurance coverage that the policy provides. A term life insurance policy in the amount of $75,000, for example, will pay out $75,000 of proceeds if the insured dies during the policy term. A whole life policy in the amount of $10,000 with a saving component of $2,000 will pay out a total of $12,000 on the death of the insured; the policyholder might be permitted to borrow against the policy in the amount of $2,000 during his or her life. Policies are defined by the terms of the contract, hence there are many possible permutations of this basic structure.

A *premium* is a contract debt that the policy owner owes the insurance company to keep the policy in force. Premium amounts are determined by actuarial tables, meaning professionally prepared statistics tables that determine the probability of death based on the insured's characteristics. During a policy term, a person can become uninsurable due to illness or age. When this happens the person cannot (easily) obtain a new life insurance, but he or she may continue to maintain (pay the premiums) on any existing life insurance policy.

Policy *proceeds* are paid to the named beneficial designee once the peril insured against comes to pass. Contract beneficiaries take subject to equitable interests. For married persons, the character of policy premiums determines the character of the life insurance, which in turn determines the character of any proceeds that might pay out. Depending on the life insurance contract, policy proceeds may be paid out in a lump sum or in an annuity (monthly payments).

In the California community property system, term life insurance proceeds are characterized by *the last premium rule*. The last premium rule holds that the character of the last premium payment determines the character of any insurance proceeds that pay out during that term. When community property funds pay the last premium, the proceeds are community property. If separate property pays the last premium, the proceeds are separate property. Proportional ownership is permitted as measured by contributions to the last premium payment.

§ 8.02 INSURABLE INTEREST

For property insurance, an insurable interest is defined as an interest in property. An insurable interest extends to any relation that the policy owner has with the property, or any liability that he or she has with respect to the property.

Under the California Insurance Code, the property interest must be of a nature that it might be diminished by a **"contemplated peril that might directly damnify the insured."**[1]

An insurable interest may exist in:

- property that the policyholder owns;
- property that the policyholder will own once certain contingencies are met; or
- an expectancy interest in the policyholder that is coupled with an existing property interest.[2]

Each spouse has an insurable interest in the entirety of the community property. Under Cal. Ins. Code § 286, an insurable interest in property **"must exist when the insurance takes effect, and when the loss occurs, but need not exist in the meantime . . . ."**[3]

For life insurance, an insurable interest is defined under Cal. Ins. Code § 10110:

Every person has an insurable interest in the life and health of:

(a) Himself [or herself].

---

1 Cal. Ins. Code § 281.

2 Cal. Ins. Code § 282.

3 Cal. Ins. Code § 286.

(b) Any person on whom he depends wholly or in part for education or support.

(c) Any person under a legal obligation to him for the payment of money or respecting property or services, of which death or illness might delay or prevent the performance.[4]

(d) Any person upon whose life any estate or interest vested in him depends.

Cal. Ins. Code § 286 provides: "**. . . an interest in the life . . . of a person insured must exist when the insurance takes effect, but need not exist thereafter or when the loss occurs.**" Absent an insurable interest, a life insurance policy is considered a wager on the life of the person insured: Wagers on the life of another are void as against public policy.[5]

The issue of insurable interest is raised by the insurer. During the lifetimes of the spouses, a life insurance company will typically confirm the existence of the prospective policyholder's insurable interest in the life of the insured. Confirmation is required because, even though a spouse has an insurable interest in the life of the other spouse, under California law an insurance company may not issue an individual life insurance policy to an applicant on the applicant's spouse "**unless the applicant's spouse has signed the policy application or has otherwise been notified in advance of the issuance of the policy.**"[6] After the insured's death, the insurer can elect to waive the issue of insurable interest and pay out the proceeds to the named beneficiary, or not.

Example 8.1: This example illustrates the relationship between insurable interest and beneficial designee status. Langston and Natoma are dating. As a general matter, each has an insurable interest in his or her own life, but neither has an insurable interest in the other's life absent proof to the contrary. Natoma owns an insurance policy on her own life. She names Langston as her beneficial designee. Upon the occurrence of the peril insured against — Natoma's death — Langston will be entitled to the insurance proceeds even though he does not have an insurable interest in Natoma's life. The policyholder must have an insurable interest in the life of the insured; the beneficial designee need not.

Example 8.2: This example illustrates that each spouse has an insurable interest in him or herself and in the other spouse. Langston and Natoma are married. Each has an insurable interest in his or her own life and in the other's life. Natoma can purchase life insurance on Langston's life. Langston can purchase life insurance on Natoma's life.

---

[4] *Jimenez v. Protective Life Insurance Co.*, 8 Cal. App. 4th 528, 10 Cal. Rptr. 2d 326 (Cal. App. Ct., 4th Dist. 1992), interpreting Cal. Ins. Code § 10110(c) to be based on a bright line rule measured by the amount of the debt, plus the refund on the initial premium, plus interest on these two amounts.

[5] *Warnock v. Davis*, 104 U.S. 775 (1881), followed by *Jimenez, supra*, at 536, citing Cal. Ins. Code §§ 252, 280, and 10110.

[6] Cal. Ins. Code § 10110.3 (applies to policies with face amounts exceeding $50,000 issued on or after July 1, 2004).

Example 8.3: This example illustrates that each spouse loses his or her insurable interest in the other spouse upon dissolution, absent evidence otherwise. Langston and Natoma seek dissolution. After dissolution, neither has an insurable interest in the other, which means that neither can purchase a new life insurance policy on the life of the other.

§ 8.03 TERM LIFE INSURANCE

Term life insurance is sometimes referred to as pure life insurance. The insured pays a premium amount that is priced using actuarial data. There is no savings component to term life insurance.

Actuarial data determines the probability that the insured will die during the policy term. Many factors can be used to assess probability of death. Common risk factors include age, health, occupation, tobacco use, excessive risk taking, and so forth. A Formula 1 race car driver, for example, will pay more for a life insurance policy than will a literature professor of the same age who engages in no risky endeavors. It's not that Formula 1 racing is more exciting than professing literature; it's just that Formula 1 racing is more likely to result in a fatal accident.

After assessing the prospective insured's actuarial data, the life insurance company makes a decision to issue a term life policy. The premium amount is due **"as soon as the subject matter insured is exposed to the peril insured against."**[7] If a policy is issued, it comes into existence when the first premium payment is made. Based on this rule, the continued timely payment of insurance premiums is a material condition of an insurance contract; and the payment of premiums to maintain a term life insurance policy is often (properly) the subject of agreements between spouses.

A married person has the right to name a nonspousal beneficial designee on his or her life insurance policy. Designations are ambulatory, which is to say revocable. The policy owner has the right to name a beneficial designee up until his or her death so long as the change is made in accordance with the terms of the insurance contract. Once named, the beneficial designee acquires an expectancy interest in the policy proceeds. The expectancy vests at the death of the insured, at which point the beneficiary is contractually entitled to the life insurance proceeds.

Term life insurance is typically renewable during the life of the insured. This means that as a person ages the policy ordinarily renews, notwithstanding the increased likelihood of death due to illness or age. Premium payments reflect the increased probability of death. Sometimes, often due to the passage of time or the presence of disease, a life insurer decides not to renew a policy. When this happens, the insured may no longer be considered insurable.

Depending on the contract terms, a life insurance policy can include a savings element. A policy that has a savings component along with a life insurance component is called a whole life insurance policy. Whole life insurance policies are discussed below.

---

[7] Cal. Ins. Code § 480.

Before the death of the insured, the policy premium is a contract debt of the policyholder.[8] Upon the death of the insured, the insurance company becomes the debtor to the beneficial designee and any equitable takers. At that time, the insurance company is obligated to deliver the policy proceeds to the beneficiary, minus unpaid premiums.

Under § 1100(a), a married policyholder can use community property funds to pay for a life insurance premium **"with like absolute power of disposition, other than testamentary, as the spouse has of the separate estate of the spouse."** This provision allows for the use of community property funds to pay for life insurance premiums even if the policyholder names a nonspousal beneficiary. Naming a beneficiary is testamentary matter, and spouses have full testamentary rights — including the right to use nonprobate transfers — notwithstanding the fact of marriage. Therefore, a married policyholder is free to name a beneficial designee for his or her one-half of the community property proceeds only. The other one-half of the proceeds belong to the other spouse. The named policy owner does not have the authority to create an obligation as to the other spouse's one-half of the proceeds. Nor does the policy owner have the right to limit how the other spouse decides to receive proceeds (lump sum or annuity).[9]

Likewise, if a policy owner names a nonspousal beneficiary, then, by contractual right, that third party (only) obtains the decedent's one-half interest in the community property proceeds. The surviving spouse retains an equitable right to any proceeds that trace back to community property premiums, notwithstanding that his or her name does not appear by beneficial designation on the policy.

As a general matter, dissolution divests a person of an insurable interest in his or her former spouse. An exception arises when a former spouse retains a pecuniary interest in the other former spouse, as defined by Cal. Ins. Code § 10110 reproduced above. A former spouse retains an insurable interest in the other spouse when, for example, a former spouse is ordered to pay spousal or child support to the other former spouse: The person receiving support has a pecuniary interest in the former spouse's life that lasts as long as the support obligation lasts. Additionally, a court can formalize the insurable interest of former spouses by ordering one or both former spouses to maintain a life insurance policy for the other former spouse's benefit. When this happens, the court order restricts the insured former spouse from changing a beneficial designation on an existing policy from the other former spouse to a third person.[10]

Example 8.4: This example illustrates the obligatory nature of the policyholder to pay insurance premiums. During marriage to Langston, Natoma obtains a term life insurance policy from ABC Life Inc. on her own life for $100,000 of coverage. Natoma names her mother, Minerva, as the beneficiary on the policy. Each year, Natoma pays the policy premium with community property funds. In the California community property system, term life insurance proceeds are characterized by the last premium rule. The last premium rule holds that the character of the last

---

[8] Cal. Fam.Code § 902 and 903.

[9] *Tyre v. Aetna Life Ins. Co.*, 54 Cal. 2d 399, 6 Cal. Rptr. 13, 353 P.2d 725 (Cal. 1960) (in bank).

[10] *Phoenix Mut. Life Ins. Co. v. Birkelund*, 29 Cal. 2d 352, 175 P.2d 5 (Cal. 1946) (in bank).

premium payment determines the character of any insurance proceeds that may pay out during that term. If Natoma should die in a term that was paid for with community property, Minerva will be entitled to $50,000 — as Natoma's beneficial designee — and Langston will be entitled to the other $50,000 by virtue of owning the community property funds that paid the premium.

Example 8.5: This example illustrates the difference between beneficial and equitable claims to the policy proceeds. Natoma and Langston marry. During marriage, Natoma has a life insurance on her own life. Natoma pays the policy premiums with her earnings. Natoma names her mother, Minerva, as the sole beneficial designee on her life insurance. At Natoma's death, ABC Life Inc. pays out $100,000 in insurance proceeds: Minerva is entitled by contract to $50,000 of the proceeds subject to Langston's equitable claim in his one-half community property share ($50,000). Langston's equitable claim arises from his community property ownership of the funds that were used to pay the life insurance premiums.

Example 8.6: This example illustrates how a P.O.D. designation is a mere expectancy up until the death of the insured. Natoma and Langston are married. Natoma has a life insurance policy that she pays for with community property funds. In the first term of the policy, Natoma names her mother, Minerva, as the beneficiary. In the second term of the policy, Natoma changes the beneficial designation from Minerva to her friend, Marina. In the third term of the policy, Natoma removes Marina as beneficial designee and names her spouse, Langston. In that same term, Natoma dies. Langston is entitled to all (100%) of the life insurance proceeds: one-half (50%) by Natoma's beneficial designation, and the other one-half (50%) by equitable ownership of the community property funds that paid the last policy premium. Minerva (as Natoma's mother) had an insurable interest in Natoma's life, but Marina (as Natoma's friend) did not. Nevertheless, since the rule is that a beneficial designee need not have an insurable interest in the insured's life, either could be named a designee at Natoma's discretion. However, beneficial designations are also ambulatory. Therefore, once Natoma removed Minerva and subsequently Marina as beneficial designee, Minerva and Marina respectively lost any expectancy interest in the insurance proceeds. Meanwhile, Langston gained an expectancy interest in Natoma's one-half of any insurance proceeds upon being named beneficial designee. Langston's expectancy vested upon Natoma's death.

The above examples illustrate five basic points about a community property life insurance policy. One, during life, each spouse has an insurable interest in his or her own life as well as in the other spouse's life. Two, either spouse (as a policy owner) has the right to name a policy beneficiary, absent an agreement restricting that power; however, that power extends only to either spouse's one-half interest in the face value of the policy. Three, beneficial designees take subject to competing equitable claims, such as the community property claims of a surviving spouse. Four, the insurance company must promptly deliver the proceeds to the named beneficial designee or else pay interest.[11] Five, In the event of competing claims, an insurance company may (and typically does) deposit the proceeds with a court pending a final resolution as to ownership. After the date of the deposit with the

[11] *See, e.g., Jacobs. v. Farmers' Mut. Fire Ins.*, 5 Cal. App. 2d 1, 41 P.2d 960 (Cal. App. Ct., 3d Dist. 1935).

court, the insurance company may not be required to pay interest on the policy.[12]

[A] Premium Payments

During marriage, when the insured spouse designates a nonspousal beneficiary on a life insurance that designation constitutes a gift of the premium payment to the beneficiary.

Either spouse has absolute disposition over community personal property under § 1100(a). Premium payments take the form of cash, which brings them under this broad grant of authority.

However, § 1100(b) prohibits a spouse from making a unilateral gift of community personal property to a third party **"without the written consent of the other spouse."** A gift **"mutually given by both spouses to third parties . . . ."** is not avoidable under § 1100(b). Term insurance premium amounts are typically not out of proportion to other community assets. Plus term life insurance has no value carried over from term to term. Hence gifts of premium payments are rarely litigated. Even so, § 1100(b) allows the noninsured spouse to avoid such a gift unless it was mutually given by both spouses.

If avoidance occurs during marriage, the noninsured spouse is entitled to one hundred percent (100%) of the gift wrongfully transferred during marriage. If the gift of premium payments is made during or after a dissolution proceeding, the noninsured spouse is entitled to fifty percent (50%) of the gift. The ownership of the term insurance proceeds, as opposed to the premium payments, (only) becomes an issue upon the occurrence of the peril insured against, which is to say the death of the insured spouse.

One spouse's co-signature on the other spouse's nonspousal beneficial designation provides (only) written consent to the other spouse's beneficial designation. Hence, a nonspousal beneficial designation made with the consent of the noninsured spouse becomes a gift *of the policy premiums*. It is not a gift of the proceeds, unless the consent form is also a valid transmutation.[13] One spouse can dispose of the entirety (100%) of community property life insurance proceeds upon the insured's death only by an enforceable agreement or a valid transmutation.

A beneficial designation is revocable until the death of the insured. Therefore, when the noninsured spouse is removed or added as a beneficial designee to a community property policy, § 1100(e) imposes a fiduciary obligation on the policy owner to provide notice to the noninsured spouse of that change. This is especially the case during a period of separation or pending dissolution since § 1100(e) requires spouses to inform each other of changes in existence, characterization and valuation of community property **"until such time as the assets and liabilities have been divided by the parties or by the court."**

After dissolution, absent an agreement otherwise, the community property retains an interest in the life insurance policy up until the point at which the

---

[12] Couch on Insurance §§ 74:249, 179:19 (3d ed. 1994).

[13] *See Estate of MacDonald*, 51 Cal. 3d 262, 272 Cal. Rptr. 153, 794 P.2d 911 (Cal. 1990) (in bank).

premiums are paid entirely with individual (separate) property funds. Only at that point, do equitable rights arising from community property premium payments expire.

***Example** 8.7:* This example illustrates how the act of naming of a nonspousal beneficiary on a community property policy constitutes a gift of the premium payments. During marriage to Langston, Natoma buys a term life insurance policy from ABC Life Inc. for $100,000 of coverage. Each year, ABC Life Inc. sends Natoma a bill for the $500 premium; each year, Natoma pays that bill. In year 1 through 5 of the policy's existence, Natoma names her mother, Minerva, as the sole beneficial designee on the life insurance. In year 6 of the policy's existence, Natoma changes the beneficial designation to her spouse, Langston. Langston and Natoma have no plans to dissolve their marriage. However, when Langston finds out that Natoma's life insurance contract named Minerva as the beneficial designee for five insurance terms, he seeks to recover $2,500 ($500 × 5 payments) from Natoma's separate property estate. In a dispute between Langston (who represents the community property estate) and Natoma's separate property estate, Langston prevails in the amount of $2,500. The $2,500 represents Natoma's gift of community personal property made, during marriage, without Langston's written consent or after the fact ratification. The amount recoverable is $2,500 (rather than $1,250) because these parties are still married. During marriage, each spouse enjoys an undivided right to the whole of the community property.

***Example** 8.8:* This example illustrates how the act of naming of a nonspousal beneficiary on a community property policy might be discussed in a dissolution proceeding. Same as Example 8.7 except that the question about Natoma's gift of life insurance premiums comes up during a dissolution proceeding. Langston seeks one-half (50%) of the value of Natoma's unauthorized gift of premium payments to Minerva. In a dissolution dispute between Langston and Natoma, Langston prevails in the amount of his one-half community property interest in the policy premiums ($1,250).

[B] The Policy

The issue of whether to characterize a term life insurance policy has received disparate treatment at the appellate level. Generally, a term life insurance is not divisible upon dissolution absent special circumstances. But given the different outcomes in the different districts, it's fair to say that the issue is unsettled.

In 1983, in *Marriage of Lorenz*, the Second District Court of Appeal held that a term life insurance policy without cash value is not property subject to division at dissolution.[14] In 1985, in *Marriage of Gonzalez*, the Fourth District Court of Appeal held that a term life insurance policy could be valued for purposes of division at dissolution, notwithstanding its lack of cash surrender value. The *Gonzalez* court suggested factors that a court might consider in valuing — and thus dividing — a term life insurance policy, especially given the insured spouse's diminished insurability due to age and health.[15] In 1987, the First District Court of

[14] *Marriage of Lorenz*, 146 Cal. App. 3d 464, 194 Cal. Rptr. 237 (Cal. App. Ct., 2d Dist. 1983).

[15] *Marriage of Gonzalez*, 168 Cal. App. 3d 1021, 214 Cal. Rptr. 634 (Cal. App. Ct., 4th Dist. 1985).

Appeal held in *Marriage of Logan* that a term life insurance policy is divisible property, but only when the insured becomes uninsurable — i.e. not able to obtain an individual life insurance.[16] In 1992, the Third District Court of Appeal, in *Marriage of Spengler*, a group term life insurance case, took the view in dictum that a term life insurance policy could be divisible property, but only if the insured becomes uninsurable during a term in which premiums are paid *with community property funds*.[17] In 1996, In *Marriage of Havins* the Fourth District Court of Appeal disagreed with the rationale in *Marriage of Spengler* about group term life insurance policy.[18]

In *Spengler*, the record showed that at the time that his marriage to first wife, Barbara dissolved, Daniel, was uninsurable because of a cancer diagnosis. Barbara and Daniel negotiated a marriage settlement agreement in which Barbara was to receive one-half of Daniel's life insurance proceeds. That settlement — later formalized as a judgment — omitted any mention of Daniel's *group* life insurance policy, which was part of his employment package. Daniel subsequently married Rose, whom he named as his sole beneficiary on the group life insurance policy. Upon Daniel's death, the group life policy was paid to Rose in accordance with the contract. Barbara sued Rose to recover one-half of the proceeds. Specifically, Barbara argued that the group life insurance policy was included in the marriage settlement agreement even though Daniel failed to disclose its existence. The trial court agreed with Barbara. Rose appealed. The court of appeal reversed. The Third District Court of Appeal held that the group life insurance policy in question was not divisible property of the Barbara-Daniel marriage because it was not an individual term life insurance. The court of appeal reasoned that because Daniel did not have an enforceable right to renew the group life insurance, he didn't own it, as such, and therefore it was not covered by the Barbara-Daniel marriage settlement agreement. In dicta, the court stated: "As a matter of law, the renewal right aspect of an employment-related group term life insurance policy is not property subject to division in marital dissolution where the employee has no enforceable right to renewal."[19]

Daniel's group life insurance policy was categorized as a fringe benefit of his employment. The employee group was large enough so that when Daniel became terminally ill, he nevertheless remained insurable under the policy. Daniel's ability to obtain life insurance was based on his employer's at-will decision to continue offering the group life insurance benefit to its employees, not on his health. The relevance of this distinction was that Daniel had the right to name Rose as his beneficial designee, notwithstanding his marriage settlement agreement with Barbara. The court explained its decision on equitable grounds: The community of

---

[16] *Estate of Logan*, 191 Cal. App. 3d 319, 236 Cal. Rptr. 368 (Cal. App. Ct., 1st Dist. 1987).

[17] *Marriage of Spengler*, 5 Cal. App. 4th 288, 6 Cal. Rptr. 2d 764 (Cal. App. Ct., 3d Dist. 1992).

[18] Group term insurance refers to the way that the insurance is sold. Group life insurance is sold to a group of associated individuals, such as employees, without a qualifying medical exam. Often an employer who offers group insurance pays a portion of the premium or the group administration costs. This makes the group insurance term life insurance policy affordable especially for employees who are not otherwise insurable.

[19] *Marriage of Spengler*, *supra*, at 299.

Daniel and Barbara received full benefit of its bargain for the contract terms that were paid for with community property funds. There is no carry over right from the days of the prior marriage.

Marriage of Havins disagreed with *Spengler's* view that an employer group insurance policy is a fringe at-will employment benefit.[20] In *Havins*, the employee was a retiree with a vested — enforceable — right to renew his *health* insurance plan so long as he continued to pay the policy premiums. The court in *Havins* recognized that a vested right to insurance may be subject to valuation; and this, in turn, would make it divisible at dissolution. However, *Havins* then went on to apply the last premium rule to hold that the policy had become a separate property policy after the parties' dissolution.

If a court decides to exercise its discretion to characterize a term life insurance policy as divisible at dissolution — a questionable outcome in light of the above line of cases — *Gonzalez* sets out possible factors that might be used to determine the replacement value of that policy. Those factors include but are certainly not limited to: the face value of the premium (typically $0 for a term life insurance); the amount of premium; the insured's life expectancy; the possibility of converting the term life insurance policy to a whole life policy; and replacement costs. *Estate of Logan* dismissed these factors. *Logan* instead recommended looking at the actuarial present value of the proceeds payable under the policy, considering the shortened life expectancy from whatever caused the uninsurability.[21]

Perhaps California law is settling toward the approach that an individual term life insurance *policy* — as opposed to the proceeds — is not a divisible community property asset during the lifetime of the insured unless the insured becomes uninsurable in a term that is paid for with community property funds. Perhaps not. As for group insurance policies, the important question is whether the policy is a fringe at-will benefit of employment, as it was deemed in *Spengler*, or whether it is a vested right, as it was for the retiree in *Havins*.

Example 8.9: This illustrates how an individual term life insurance is most likely treated at dissolution. Natoma and Langston terminate their marriage. At that time, both are healthy, insurable, and employable. Natoma is the policyholder on a $100,000 term life insurance policy from ABC Life Inc. on her life. During marriage, Natoma paid the policy premiums with community property funds. At dissolution, the individual term life insurance policy is not property subject to division.

Example 8.10: This illustrates how a group term life insurance is most likely treated once separate property pays the insurance premium payment after dissolution. Natoma and Langston terminate their marriage. At that time, both are healthy, insurable, and employable. Natoma owns a $100,000 term life insurance policy from ABC Life Inc. on her life. During marriage, Natoma paid the premiums with community property funds. At dissolution, this group term life insurance policy is not property subject to division. After dissolution, Natoma eventually will

---

[20] *Marriage of Havins*, 43 Cal. App. 4th 414, 50 Cal. Rptr. 2d 763 (Cal. App. Ct., 4th Dist. 1996).

[21] *Logan, supra*, at 326, n8.

pay the premium with individual (separate) property. When this happens, Natoma acquires the right to name a beneficiary for the entirety of the proceeds.

[C] The Proceeds

The mere fact of divorce may not necessarily defeat a former spouse's contract rights to the proceeds. If a former spouse is named a beneficial designee, that former spouse is entitled to the proceeds by the terms of the insurance contract, perhaps even as against a later-in-time surviving spouse. The rationale is that an insured person who continues to name a former spouse as a beneficial designee is presumed to have made a gift of the proceeds to that former spouse. Upon the occurrence of the peril insured against, the insurer is obligated to pay the former spouse, unless that former spouse surrendered his or her right by agreement. Surrender can occur by property settlement agreement, court order, or a divestiture statute related to divorce or domestic violence.

California has a divestiture statute for nonprobate transfers made to a former spouse. That statute applies in cases where there is no record of domestic violence. It is based on the Uniform Probate Code, and it turns on the legal definition of the phrase "*surviving spouse*."[22]

The California divestiture statute, found at Cal. Prob. Code § 5600, provides:

> **[A] nonprobate transfer to the transferor's former spouse, in an instrument executed by the transferor before or during the marriage, fails if, at the time of the transferor's death, the former spouse is not the transferor's surviving spouse as defined in Section 78, as a result of the dissolution or annulment of the marriage. A judgment of legal separation that does not terminate the status of husband and wife is not a dissolution for purposes of this section.**

Cal. Prob. Code § 78 defines the qualifying term **"surviving spouse"** in the negative. " **'Surviving spouse' does not include any of the following:**

> **(a) A person whose marriage to the decedent has been dissolved or annulled, unless, by virtue of a subsequent marriage, the person is married to the decedent at the time of death.**
>
> **(b) A person who obtains or consents to a final decree or judgment of dissolution of marriage from the decedent or a final decree or judgment of annulment of their marriage . . .**
>
> **(c) A person who, following a decree or judgment of dissolution or annulment of marriage obtained by the decedent, participates in a marriage ceremony with a third person.**
>
> **(d) A person who was a party to a valid proceeding concluded by an order purporting to terminate all marital property rights.**

---

[22] *McDaniel*, *supra* (affirming there is a consequential distinction between a legal spouse and a surviving spouse), following *Estate of Lahey*, 76 Cal. App. 4th 1056, 91 Cal. Rptr. 2d 30 (Cal. App. Ct., 1st Dist. 1999).

Cal. Prob. Code § 5600 only applies to a beneficial designation naming a former spouse, and then only if that designation was made before or during the marriage. Exceptions are at § 5600(b)(1) and (2):

> **(1) The nonprobate transfer is not subject to revocation by the transferor at the time of the transferor's death.**
>
> **(2) There is clear and convincing evidence that the transferor intended to preserve the nonprobate transfer to the former spouse.**

Life Ins. Co. v. Ortiz, a federal court case applying California law in an interpleader action involving life insurance proceeds, illustrates.[23] In *Ortiz*, the insured was Jerry Ortiz, a peace officer killed in the line of duty. Just months before he was killed, Jerry had dissolved his marriage with Gloria and married Graciela. At that time, Jerry's nearly $500,000 life insurance policy named his former spouse, Gloria, as beneficial designee, not his surviving spouse, Graciela. The evidence showed that the property settlement in Jerry's and Gloria's marriage did not explicitly cover Jerry's life insurance policy. For that reason, Jerry's lawyer several times stressed after the divorce the importance of removing former spouse Gloria's name as beneficial designee on the life insurance policy. Jerry indicated that he understood his lawyer's instructions. The evidence showed that Jerry had two children with Gloria. It also showed that in the four or so months between the dissolution of his former marriage, his subsequent marriage to Graciela, and his death, Jerry took no action to change the beneficial designation on his life insurance policy from Gloria to Graciela.

The trial court directed that Jerry's life insurance proceeds be paid to his probate estate for distribution to his surviving spouse — Graciela — and his minor children with Gloria. Gloria appealed. The federal court of appeal reversed. It remanded on the ground that the evidence was clear and convincing that Jerry intended to maintain Gloria as his beneficial designee, notwithstanding the dissolution of their marriage. As a result the insurance proceeds were ordered delivered to Gloria, who took by contractual right, subject to any equitable claims of the insured's surviving spouse, Graciela. Judge Kozinski filed a vigorous dissent.

The question of who should take the proceeds is an important one. First, proceeds help survivors carry on financially after the death of a loved one. Second, only proper payment can discharge the insurer's liability. Third, the insurer is obligated by contract to pay the full policy amount to the contract beneficiary subject to any existing equitable claims. The community property interests of a surviving spouse are existing equitable claims. Both the insurer and the contract beneficiary to whom the proceeds were (mis)delivered are liable to the equitable claimant in the event of misdelivery.

---

[23] *Life Ins. Co. v. Ortiz*, 535 F.3d 990 (9th Cir. 2008). *See also McDaniel*, *supra* (affirming that the Probate Code distinguishes, in Cal. Prob. Code § 78, between a legal spouse and the surviving spouse in a case where the insured died between the time that the petition for dissolution was filed and the final judgment is granted), following *Estate of Lahey*, *supra* (holding that a judgment for legal separation that terminates the community property estate but not the parties' marital status nevertheless extinguishes the separated spouse's status as a surviving spouse under Cal. Prob. Code § 78).

Example 8.11: This example illustrates an application of the California divestiture statute, which is based on the Uniform Probate Code. After a final judgment of dissolution, Natoma neglects to change the beneficial designation on her life insurance policy from her former spouse, Langston, to her current spouse Clay. At Natoma's death, Cal. Prob. Code § 5600 automatically revokes Natoma's beneficial designation to Langston upon dissolution of that marriage. The two Probate Code exceptions to this rule are: (a) Natoma is under court order not to change the beneficiary designation naming Langston; or (b) there is clear and convincing evidence that Natoma intended to preserve Langston's expectancy interest in the policy. No evidence of Natoma's intent to protect Langston's expectancy exists here: Thus Langston is removed as Natoma's beneficial designee by operation of law. Natoma's life insurance proceeds are deliverable to Natoma's alternate beneficial designee or, if she didn't name an alternate, to her intestate heirs.

Example 8.12: This example illustrates California case law interpreting the divestiture statute.[24] Same as Example 8.11 except that Natoma dies in a motorcycle accident the day after the issuance of a judgment of legal separation in which Natoma and Langston reached *"a final division of their property, released all claims, including those based on any contract expectancy, and waived rights of spousal support."* At Natoma's death, Langston is (still) the named beneficiary on Natoma's ABC Life Ins. policy. In a contest between Langston — Natoma's legal spouse — and Minerva — Natoma's mother and sole intestate heir — Minerva should take anywhere between one-half and all of the proceeds depending on the character of the last premium. The rationale is that even though Natoma's and Langston's marriage still existed, the judgment of legal separation represented a final termination of their community property estate. Hence, at Natoma's death, Langston was Natoma's legal spouse, but he was not her *surviving spouse* for purposes of Cal. Prob. Code § 78, the definition of which determines the application of Cal. Prob. Code § 5600. Therefore, absent additional evidence, Natoma's beneficial designation of Langston fails.

§ 8.04 WHOLE LIFE INSURANCE

A whole life insurance policy — sometimes called a cash-value policy — has two components: A life insurance component and a savings component. Each time the policyholder pays a whole life premium, part of the premium pays for the life insurance and the other part of the premium goes toward the savings plan that is part of the insurance product. The savings portion of the life insurance premium accumulates on a tax-deferred basis so long as the policy is in force. Savings are invested by the insurance company on behalf of the policyholder, and not otherwise subject to the control of the policyholder. The policyholder can access the savings, however, by taking a loan against the policy or by surrendering the policy. A whole life policy is valued at its cash surrender value, a figure typically quoted in the policy contract. If the insured becomes uninsurable during a term when the premium was paid for with community property funds, the value of the policy may be measured

---

[24] *Lahey, supra; McDaniel, supra.*

differently, as the savings component is still a recoverable asset.[25]

Upon the death of the insured, a beneficial designee has a contractual right to both the amount of coverage stated in the insurance contract and to any accumulated savings. There are many different types of cash-value life insurance policies. Every policy is governed by its contract terms.

At dissolution — a point at which both spouse are still alive — the savings component of a whole life insurance policy is subject to characterization and division. Apportionment is permitted.

Where relevant, savings are apportioned by the basic tracing formula.

The community property percentage is calculated by dividing the savings that trace back to community property premium payments by the total savings component. Each spouse owns a one-half interest in the community property savings component of the policy at dissolution.

The separate property percentage is calculated by dividing the savings that trace back to a separate property premium payment by the total savings component.

The California Supreme Court held in *Marriage of Valli* that the ownership of a whole life insurance purchased during marriage with community property funds is community property, notwithstanding that only one spouse is named as the policyholder.[26] In *Valli*, the trial court characterized the premium payments so as to characterize the policy as entirely community property. The court of appeal reversed. The California Supreme Court granted review and superseded the Second District Court of Appeal opinion in *Valli*.[27]

In *Valli*, the $3.75 million whole life insurance policy named wife Randy as the policyholder. It insured husband Frankie's life. It named Randy as the sole beneficial designee. It had a savings component of over $300,000. The trial court settled the question of the policy's ownership by ordering Frankie to pay Randy her one-half of the savings component, but otherwise giving the policy to Frankie. Randy appealed. She argued that when Frankie purchased the whole life policy from a third party in Randy's name only, he implicitly transmuted the policy under § 852(a) from community property to Randy's separate property. Alternatively, she argued that the evidence code form of title presumption superseded the Family Code general community property presumption.

On May 15, 2014, the California Supreme Court unanimously rejected Randy's implicit transmutation argument. The court upheld the trial court's method of characterizing the policy in line with the premium payments. However it remanded the case for a reconsideration of how to divide the policy consistent with the equality principle (50-50 division).

Remand was necessary because the trial court erred when it limited Randy's community property interest to the savings component of the policy. In this case,

---

[25] *Marriage of Gonzalez, supra.*

[26] *Marriage of Valli*, 58 Cal. 4th 1396, 171 Cal. Rptr. 3d 454, 324 P.3d 274 (Cal. 2014).

[27] *Id.*

the policy was still in force, it had been paid for, and it had established Randy's right to an insurable interest in Frankie's life. Once Randy and Frankie dissolved their marriage, Randy was no longer eligible to purchase a new policy on her former spouse's life. She only had the existing policy. Therefore, when the trial court determined that the policy belonged to Frankie, Randy was divested of two assets. The first was her insurable interest in Frankie's life — a valuable right. The second was her right to name a beneficial designee on the existing policy — a related and also valuable right.

A concurring opinion was filed. It rejected Randy's alternate argument that the form of title presumption found in Cal. Evid.Code § 662 supersedes the § 760 general community property presumption whenever title to property is taken in one spouse's name with the other's consent. The concurring opinion emphatically stated that marriage is a partnership. Thus property bought with partnership funds is partnership property notwithstanding the form of title in which the property is taken. The unnamed spouse retains an equitable interest in all partnership (i.e., community) property. This principle, the court wrote, has been the basic principle of California community property law since statehood.

§ 8.05 SUMMARY

California community property law seeks to balance the insured spouse's right to dispose of property freely at death — by naming a beneficial designee on a life insurance policy — with the surviving spouse's equitable interest in life insurance proceeds.

Generally, a family relationship creates no beneficial rights to insurance proceeds. Instead, beneficial rights are expressly created by contract, not by the law of wills or intestacy. For that reason, during marriage, an insured spouse has the right to name a beneficiary of his or her choice, and the right to change a beneficial designation up until incapacity, death, or a court order preventing a change.

In a period during which a nonspousal beneficiary is named, premium payments made with community property constitute a gift of community personal property to the named beneficial designee. The noninsured spouse can consent to or ratify such a gift, or withhold consent. If consent to the gift is withheld, the nonconsenting spouse can recover 100% of the premiums paid while the third party was named as beneficial designee (if the claim is made during marriage) or 50% of the premiums (if the claim is made at marriage's end). These important rights can be contracted away by use of a premarital contract, a transmutation agreement, or a property settlement agreement.

A noninsured spouse has a community property right in a community property life insurance on the insured spouse's life. In the case of a community property policy, if the insured names the other spouse as beneficiary, then the surviving spouse's rights to the decedent insured's one-half of the proceeds derive from contract law. By comparison, the surviving spouse' rights to the other one-half of the proceeds derive from ownership of the community property premiums that purchased the term period. In the case where an insured names a non-spousal beneficial designee, the nonspousal beneficiary takes one-half of the proceeds by contract right while the surviving spouse takes the other half by community property right.

Returning to the language of § 1100(a), the insured has the right to manage and control community personal property in all matters not testamentary. The naming of a life insurance beneficiary is a testamentary matter. Even though the insured is free to dispose of life insurance proceeds by beneficial designation, or even to change a beneficial designation during marriage, § 1100(a) restricts the insured from disposing of more than his or her one-half interest of any community property proceeds. Additionally, § 1100(e) imposes a duty on the policy owner to notify a spouse about any changes in a community property insurance during marriage, and certainly in a dissolution proceeding.

Proceeds pay out upon the death of the insured. The first step in resolving a dispute over the character of life insurance proceeds is to determine the character of the policy.

According to the last premium rule, if the last contract premium was paid with community property funds, the proceeds are community property. If the last contract premium was paid with separate property, the proceeds are separate property. If the last premium was paid partly with community property and partly with separate property funds, the proceeds are proportionally owned, by application of the tracing principle. In the case of proportionally owned proceeds, the noninsured surviving spouse owns an equitable one-half interest (only) in the proceeds that trace back to community property premium payments.

When the insured dies, the insurer becomes obligated to pay the proceeds to the beneficial designee. A nonspousal beneficiary may waive (disclaim) his or her rights to the proceeds in favor of a surviving spouse, but waivers are rare, and they require clear evidence in the form of specific contract language. Similarly, the noninsured spouse may consent, on the policy itself, to the insured spouse's non-spousal beneficial designation. However, consent to name a nonspousal beneficial designee, without more, does not constitute a transmutation of a community property interest in the insurance proceeds. A valid transmutation requires a written express declaration that was made voluntarily by the spouse whose interest in the property is adversely affected. These issues are discussed in Chapter 10. Therefore, unless the nonspousal contract beneficiary waives his or her interest in the proceeds in favor of the surviving spouse, or the surviving spouse transmutes his or her equitable interest in the proceeds in favor of the contract beneficial designee, the insurer is obligated, as a debtor to pay: (1) any beneficial designee who has a contract right to the proceeds; and (2) a surviving spouse who has an equitable right to one-half of the community property proceeds.

Generally, nonprobate transfers are revoked upon the termination of the marriage, unless a court order provides otherwise or there is clear and convincing evidence of the decedent's intent to preserve the former spouse's expectancy interest in the life insurance proceeds.

Chapter 9

WORK LIFE: FROM TRAINING TO RETIREMENT

Pensions and retirement benefits are deferred earnings for services rendered by an employee to an employer; they are not employer gratuities.

When deferred earnings are earned during a period of marriage, they are properly characterized as community property under § 760. California law defines retirement benefits as deferred earnings.

Retirement benefits can include a wide array of assets. Defined benefit plans and defined contribution plans are certainly deferred earnings. But so too are employee stock options, enhanced early retirement benefits, severance pay, partnership profit distributions, and business gifts. In short, any form of deferred compensation is a benefit that an employee receives for services rendered to an employer. Therefore, if the benefit is acquired during marriage it is community property in character.

Deferred compensation benefits are characterized by the employee's marital status at the time of employment, not by whether the benefits are vested or contingent, matured or not.[1]

This chapter starts with education and moves through to retirement benefits.

§ 9.01 INCOME ENHANCING DEGREES AND LICENSES

The question of how to address the so-called career threshold dissolution was hotly debated in the 1970s and 1980s, before women started entering professional degree programs in significant numbers.

The career threshold situation occurs when (1) a spouse enters into an educational or training program that promises to substantially enhance that person's future income; (2) that spouse completes the training or education; (3) soon after doing so the marriage dissolves; and (4) at the time of dissolution, the spouses have no or few assets other than the human capital that the student spouse's degree or training represents.

Some states, like New York, treat an income-enhancing degree as property by monetizing what that degree could be worth over the student spouse's working career. These states recognize that just as the student spouse has a property interest in the education, so too does the non-student spouse who contributed to that education, often at the cost of lost opportunities. Thus, in some states, whether

---

[1] *Marriage of Brown*, 15 Cal. 3d 838, 842, 845, 126 Cal. Rptr. 633, 634–37, 544 P.2d 561 (1976) (in bank); *Marriage of Lehman* 18 Cal. 4th 169, 74 Cal. Rptr. 2d 825, 955 P.2d 451 (1998); *Marriage of Sonne*, 48 Cal. 4th 118, 124, 105 Cal. Rtpr. 3d 414, 419, 225 P.3d 546 (Cal. 2010); *Marriage of Green*, 56 Cal. 4th 1130, 158 Cal. Rptr. 3d 247, 302 P.3d 562 (Cal. 2013).

a spouse contributes to a career, a career potential, or an education, upon dissolution he or she has a statutory right to claim a proportional share of the educated spouse's projected (future) earnings over that person's projected (future) career. A successful claim results in judicial recognition of the claimant's equitable property right in the education. Any award based on such a right is not discretionary alimony; rather, it is a proportional share of ownership.

California takes a different approach.

[A] Property Outside of the California Community Property System

In California, a person's education or training is a form of personal property; *but it is not property subject to division at dissolution.* By authority of § 2641, an income enhancing degree, license, or training is outside of the community property system. So too are the future earnings that might derive from such a degree, except insofar as they are used to determine spousal support.

When a marriage dissolves, (only) the educated spouse walks away from the marriage with a property right to the human capital that his or her income enhancing degree represents. Neither the non-student spouse, as an individual, nor the community estate, as a partnership, acquires a property right — equitable or otherwise — in one spouse's education. A former spouse does not obtain a property right to a theoretically determined future income stream that an education acquired during marriage might produce.

Example 9.1: This example illustrates the basic property principles of the California approach. Bay and Sutro are married. During marriage Bay earns a law degree. Shortly thereafter Bay and Sutro file a petition for dissolution. In this case, the law degree is Bay's personal property, and as such it is not subject to division upon dissolution. Sutro has no property right to Bay's law degree, equitable or otherwise. However, Bay's law degree may factor into a discretionary determination of spousal support.

[B] The Community Reimbursement for Direct Contributions to Education

Under § 2641 one spouse's education, degree, license, and so forth are items of value outside of the California community property system. Rather than permitting the nonstudent spouse to obtain a property right in the student spouse's education, the California Family Code permits the nonstudent spouse to claim:

> (1) On behalf of the community, a § 2641 reimbursement, with interest, for provable direct contributions made to the student spouse's education; and
>
> (2) On behalf of him or herself, a § 4320 discretionary spousal support determination that factors in the degree and on all general contributions that the community made to the acquisition of the student spouse's degree.

The community's reimbursement is mandated by § 2641(b)(1), which provides: **"The community shall be reimbursed for community contributions to education or training of a party that substantially enhances the earning capacity of the party."** This provision is understood as a "limitation . . . intended to restrict litigation by requiring that the education or training must demonstrably enhance earning capacity"; it is also part of an overall policy "to redress economic inequity" between the spouses.[2] The § 2641 reimbursement is the community's exclusive remedy, absent **"an express written agreement of the parties to the contrary."**[3]

The issue of substantial enhancement is a matter of fact for the trial court. In *Marriage of Graham*, husband Jeffrey, a police officer, became a law student, during marriage, at Western State University College of Law in 1994. The community paid $12,000 for Jeffrey's tuition. In 1999, Jeffrey filed a petition of dissolution. At the time of trial in 2000, Jeffrey had one semester remaining in order to graduate. He had no plans to take the California Bar exam, but he did expect to continue his work as a police officer, making $4,400 per month. Wife Katherine sought a community reimbursement for the $12,000 in tuition payments that the community had paid for Jeffrey's law school tuition. Jeffrey contested the reimbursement. He testified that he went to law school to "further his education, but did not necessarily have any plans to become an attorney."[4] He explained that he was not a serious student during college (he partied and played football), and so he decided to go to law school to make up for lost educational opportunities, not to enhance his income. Additionally, Jeffrey pointed out that he worked as a police officer before, during, and after law school; and had he focused exclusively on his job rather than on pursuing a legal education while working, he might have actually enhanced his work earnings more than he did by going to law school. The trial court denied the § 2641 reimbursement on the ground that it found "no substantive enhanced earning capacity" resulting from Jeffrey's education.[5] Katherine appealed; she urged the court of appeal to adopt a rule that a law degree is a per se substantial enhancement of earning capacity for purposes of § 2641. In affirming the trial court's denial of the reimbursement, the court of appeal concluded its discussion of § 2641 with "this is a perfect case to demonstrate the fallacy of [Katherine's] proposed rule."[6]

Example 9.2: This example illustrates how § 2641 acts as a limitation on litigation. Bay and Sutro get married just after they graduate from college: both are computer programmers. During marriage, Bay decides to leave a high paying IT job to earn a law degree. Just after admission to the California Bar, Bay is hired by a national law firm at a top salary for new attorney hires. Bay's pre-law school salary was $150,000 per year; Bay's post-law school salary will be $150,000 per year. Subsequently, Bay and Sutro file a petition for dissolution. Sutro seeks a reimbursement for the $100,000 in tuition payments that were made by the community

---

[2] *Marriage of Graham*, 109 Cal. App. 4th 1321, 1325, 135 Cal. Rptr. 2d 685, 688 (Cal. App. Ct., 4th Dist. 2003), citing Cal. Law Revision. Com., 29D West's Ann. Fam. Code foll. 2641 (1994).

[3] Cal. Fam. Code § 2641(e) (operative Jan. 1, 1994).

[4] *Graham*, *supra*, at 1325.

[5] *Id.* at 1324.

[6] *Id.* at 1325.

toward Bay's law school education. Bay argues against the reimbursement, saying that law school was (merely) a way to make up for a misspent undergraduate career. In this case, relying on *Graham*, the trial court has discretion to deny the reimbursement: Bay was making as much before law school as after; and Bay's law school education has not resulted in a demonstrably enhanced earning capacity for purposes of the § 2641 reimbursement. Nor is it certain that Bay's law degree will result in enhanced earnings over time.

Example 9.3: This example illustrates how § 2641 redresses economic inequity. Bay and Sutro get married just after they graduate from college: both are art majors. During marriage, Bay decides to earn a law degree. Just after admission to the California Bar, Bay is hired by a national law firm at a top salary for new attorney hires. Bay's pre-law school salary was $10,000 per year; Bay's post-law school salary will be $150,000 per year. Bay and Sutro petition for dissolution. Sutro seeks a reimbursement for $12,000 in tuition payments that were made by the community toward Bay's law school education. Bay argues against the reimbursement, saying law school was meant to make up for a misspent youth, not to enhance Bay's earning capacity. In this case, notwithstanding *Graham* and notwithstanding Bay's motivations for earning a law degree, the trial court should exercise its discretion in favor of awarding the § 2641 reimbursement to the community. The reason is that Bay's pre-law school/ post-law school earnings are substantially different. Therefore, as a matter of fact, Bay's law school education resulted in a demonstrably enhanced earning capacity for purposes of determining a § 2641 reimbursement. Additionally, the purpose of the reimbursement is to prevent economic inequity between the spouses in cases where they have no assets to divide at dissolution.

While other reimbursements due to the contributing party are made without interest, as in the case of the general reimbursement provision found at § 2640, the community estate's reimbursement for contributions to education, per § 2641(b)(1) is **"[w]ith interest at the legal rate, accruing from the end of the calendar year in which the contributions were made."**

Contributions to training or education are defined under § 2641(a). **"Contributions . . ."** means **"[p]ayments made with community or quasi community property for education or training or for the repayment of a loan incurred for education or training, whether the payments were made while the parties were resident in this state or resident outside this state."** The phrase **"[p]ayments . . . for education or training"** has been interpreted to mean payments for direct expenses of education, such as tuition, fees, books, and so forth.[7] Indirect contributions to family expenses during a period in which an education is pursued are not reimbursable under § 2641. Instead, community to contributions to general family expenses are factored into the § 4320(b) discretionary determination of spousal support for the non-student spouse.[8]

Community contributions to **"a loan incurred for education or training"** are reimbursable under § 2641. No case delimits the meaning of the phrase **"a loan**

---

[7] *Marriage of Watt*, 214 Cal. App. 3d 340, 262 Cal. Rptr. 783 (Cal. App. Ct., 1st Dist. 1989).

[8] Cal. Fam. Code § 4320(b).

incurred for education or training " However, given that § 2641 reimbursements are limited to direct educational expenses, it's plausible that any reimbursement for payments to a loan incurred for education or training is similarly limited to designated student loans. Outstanding **"educational loans shall be assigned"** at dissolution to the student spouse by application of § 2627. The term **"educational loans"** is not defined in either § 2641 or § 2627.

Marriage of Weiner raised the issue of whether the § 2641 reimbursement covers all educational costs paid with community contributions, even those that occurred (long) before the marriage.[9] In that case, the non-student spouse claimed a community reimbursement for community contributions made to the principal payment of medical school loans that were incurred by husband prior to marriage. The trial court granted the reimbursement. The husband appealed. The court of appeal affirmed, but remanded the issue of how much of a reimbursement was due.

The court of appeal reasoned:

> Our conclusion the statute was intended to cover all educational costs paid with community funds, even when, as here, the education occurred before the marriage, is consistent with the history and intent of the statute. Before enactment of . . . the predecessor to section 2641, spouses had no means of directly recouping the cost or value of one spouse's education and training, even though the community may have contributed considerable financial support to the education or training. . . . [Section 2641] remedies this injustice and serves the state interest in equitable dissolution of the marital partnership by providing for a reimbursement to the community for expenditures made in acquisition of the student spouse's education or training [10]

Chief among the potential inequities to the nonstudent spouse is that, regardless of when the education occurred, "the trained spouse can expect a continuing benefit from his or her education whereas, following dissolution, the other member of the community will receive no future benefit from the community's payment of the prior educational expenses."[11] For that reason, the § 2641 phrase " . . . **repayment of a loan incurred for education or training . . .**" extends the community's right of reimbursement to the repayment of student loans that were incurred before the marriage.

Example 9.4: This example illustrates how community contributions to student loans incurred prior to marriage may be included within the definition of the § 2641 reimbursement, assuming all other qualifications are met. Bay graduates from law school in 2000 with $100,000 of educational debt. In 2004, Bay and Sutro marry. Bay and Sutro dedicate themselves to repaying Bay's student debt. In 2007, Bay and Sutro petition for dissolution. Bay still owes $50,000 in student debt at that time. In this example, the community reduced the principal obligation on Bay's student loan in the amount of $50,000. As such, under § 2641, the community is entitled to a

---

[9] *Weiner v. Weiner*, 105 Cal. App. 4th 235, 240, 129 Cal. Rptr. 2d 288 (Cal. App. Ct., 4th Dist. 2003).

[10] *Id.* at 240.

[11] *Id.*

$50,000 reimbursement, with interest. The reimbursement is divisible: Sutro is entitled to $25,000 of the reimbursement, with interest; and Bay the other $25,000 with interest.

The community reimbursement is mandatorily offset in three situations, as set forth in § 2641(c):

- the community has already substantially benefited from the education, most specifically as demonstrated by property accumulations;
- the spouses exchanged educational opportunities: one spouse went to school supported by the community, and then the other spouse did the same;
- the education was provided by the community as a way of enabling the student spouse to become self-supporting.

With respect to the first balancing factor, § 2641(c)(1) employs a rebuttable presumption affecting the burden of proof. If the community contributions were made **"less than 10 years before the commencement of the proceeding"** the presumption is that the community has not substantially benefited from the education or training. But if the community contributions were made **"more than 10 years before the commencement of the proceeding"** the presumption is that the community has substantially benefited from the education or training.

§ 9.02 CELEBRITY IDENTITY

Goodwill is community property. But talent — without more — is personal to its holder and therefore outside of the community property system.[12]

Celebrity identity is not the same as raw talent. Rather, celebrity identity is a form of intellectual personal property created by labor, developed by labor, and protected by labor. Labor is a community asset under § 760.

Celebrity identity is subject to the exclusive exploitation of the celebrity who develops it. Profits from celebrity identity are measured by factors that signal the celebrity's development and control of his or her celebrity image. Profits may flow from contracts, derivative contracts, licensing agreements, cease and desist communications, law suits, and any and all others forms of conduct that signal the celebrity's intention to possess and control his or her intellectual property (i.e., the celebrity identity).

Celebrity identity is recognized and protected by Cal. Civ. Code § 3344, which authorizes damages for the knowing use of another's name, signature, photograph or likeness , and — by case law[13] — identity for a commercial purpose, without prior consent. Damages listed under CC § 3344 include lost revenues.

Because celebrity identity is protected by statute, one unanswered question is whether it is divisible upon divorce in its own right, or only by reference to

[12] *Marriage of McTiernan and Dubrow*, 133 Cal. App. 4th 1090, 35 Cal. Rptr. 3d 287 (Cal. App. Ct., 2d Dist. 2005), rev. den., Jan. 25, 2006.

[13] *White v. Samsung Electronics America, Inc.*, 989 F.2d 1512 (Cal. App. Ct., 9th Cir. 1993).

derivative contracts and licenses. If celebrity identity is divisible upon divorce, then the time period in which it was developed will determine its characterization. If it was developed while the parties were married, then that celebrity asset is onerously acquired community property. If it was developed while the parties were unmarried or during the period from separation to divorce, then that celebrity identity would be initially characterized as separate property. Under this approach, commingling could perhaps occur through the use of community property resources or uncompensated labor to develop what was an initially separate property celebrity identity.

The courts have not yet decided whether celebrity identity is subject to division upon dissolution. However, § 4320(b) requires that a court shall factor the existence and any income from celebrity identity into the discretionary determination of spousal support.

§ 9.03 WORK ISSUES

Property onerously acquired during marriage is community property. This includes property acquired during marriage through labor, talent, industry, judgment, development, ingenuity, and so forth. As discussed in Part II, Chapters 2 and 3, the concept of onerously acquired property is contrasted to that of lucratively acquired property. Onerous property is acquired through effort. Lucrative property is acquired by gift or windfall.

Work related compensation is onerously acquired. During periods of employment, a certain percentage of an employee's compensation is distributed in the tax year in which it is earned, in the form of annual salary or wages. The remaining percentage of the employee's compensation in any given tax year is set aside, which is to say deferred. Deferred compensation either is held in the employer's general account — on the promise of the employee's future participation in a defined benefits plan — or is deposited into an employee-managed tax deferred account like, for example, an IRA account, a 401(k) account, or a 403(b) account. Deferred compensation is earned far in advance of the time that the employee can exercise the right to withdraw it without penalty. Nevertheless, the character of deferred compensation is properly determined by the employee's status (single or married) during the period in which the deferred compensation was earned.[14]

When deferred earnings — including pension benefits — are earned entirely during a period when the employee is married, benefits are entirely community property.

Example 9.5: This example illustrates a defined pension plan that is entirely community property. Bay and Sutro marry in 2000. At that time, Bay begins her career as a lawyer at a firm that offers a defined pension plan. Shortly thereafter, Bay and Sutro divorce. In this case, whatever pension benefits Bay may be entitled to (whether contingent or vested) are community property in nature. At dissolution, Sutro is entitled to a one-half community property interest in Bay's pension benefits.

---

[14] *Brown, supra,* and its progeny, especially *Marriage of Drapeau,* 93 Cal. App. 4th 1086, 114 Cal. Rptr. 2d 6 (Cal. App. Ct., 1st Dist. 2001) and *Green, supra.*

Apportionment is permitted and indeed required when deferred employment compensation is earned over the span of periods when the employee spouse's status transitions from single to married, or vice versa. These transitional periods can occur before and during marriage; during a period of living separate and apart; or during marriage and a period while living separate and apart that resolves back into marriage.[15] Apportionment must "reasonably and fairly represent" the contributions that the employee spouse's separate property estate and the community estate made to its acquisition.[16] A high degree of arithmetic complication can arise in any given case. This complication is not the result of the apportionment rule so much as it is the result of the myriad factors that employers can or might use to determine an employee's eligibility to the defined benefit plan that the employer offers.

[A] Defined Benefit Plans

Defined benefit plans do not contemplate keeping an individual account for the employee. In other words, the pension is *not* the result of an actual sum certain deposited by the employee over the period of his or her employment.

Instead, pension rights are computed based on a formula that is determined entirely by the employer. One employer might use a formula that includes a length of service factor, a salary factor, and an age factor, for example. A different employer may use a point system. These systems represent how the employer will arrive at the employee's ultimate pension benefit, once the employee's right to the pension matures.

A pension right is divisible at dissolution whether it is contingent, vested, or mature.[17] A contingent right is uncertain; it will not survive the discharge or voluntary termination of the employee. If and when an employee meets certain vesting conditions that are within his or her control, the pension right vests. Typically these conditions have to do with the duration of the employment.

A vested pension right is far more durable than a contingent right primarily because a vested right survives the discharge or voluntary termination of the employee. However, a vested pension right may or may not be mature. A vested pension right matures only when all conditions precedent that are within the employee's control are met. At that time, the employee is eligible to withdraw income — as determined by the employer's formula — from the employer's general pension fund.

Pension plans earned entirely during the marriage belong to the community estate. Pension plans earned partly during a period when the employee is married and partly during a period when the employee is single are subject to apportionment.

A large number of pension plans use time to calculate an employee's right of withdrawal from the general pension fund. The basis for apportionment of these plans is left up to the trial court's discretion. For that reason, California law refers

---

[15] *Green*, *supra*, at 1142.

[16] *Marriage of Poppe*, 97 Cal. App. 3d 1, 11, 158 Cal. Rptr. 500 (Cal. App. Ct., 4th Dist. 1979).

[17] *Brown*, *supra*.

generally to apportionment by the time rule.[18] The time rule apportions defined pension benefits as community or separate depending on the ratio of time worked during marriage divided by the entire time employed, versus the time worked while single divided by the entire time employed.[19] The time rule is not, however, the only way to apportion defined pension benefits.

A time based apportionment formula is fair when the employer uses time as a factor for determining an employee's pension eligibility rights. But other methods for determining eligibility may and must sometimes be used. *Marriage of Gray* held that the time rule is appropriate (only) when the amount of the retirement benefits is "substantially related" to the number of years employed.[20] *Poppe* illustrates.

In *Poppe*, the employed spouse's pension was based on points earned for various activities voluntarily undertaken by the employee during employment, not on years served. The trial court used the time formula to apportion the pension. The non-employee spouse appealed. On appeal, the court of appeal reversed and remanded with a strong suggestion that the trial court apportion the defined benefit plan on the basis of points earned rather than on the basis of years served.[21]

Marriage of Green is the most recent California Supreme Court case on the subject.[22] In *Green*, the husband's pension rights were attributable to employment before and during marriage. Pre-marriage the husband's pension was based on military service. During marriage the husband's pension benefit was based on employment as a state firefighter. Under state law, husband was able to consolidate his pensions under the same fiduciary [CalPERs]. As a result, the husband obtained the right to purchase four additional years' worth of his pre-marital military pension. The husband exercised that right during marriage by using community property funds to purchase four years of additional retirement credit for that part of his pension attributable to his pre-marital military service. The trial court apportioned husband's pension using the time rule: The trial court characterized the husband's pension rights earned prior to marriage (including the additional four years that the husband purchased during marriage) as husband's separate property; the pension rights earned during marriage were characterized as community property; and the husband was ordered to reimburse the community for its contributions to the purchase of the four year credit for the pre-marital military service portion of the pension. The trial court order also required that the wife be reimbursed one-half of the amount of money the community used to obtain the four extra years of service, plus interest. Wife appealed on the ground that she was entitled to the pension benefits from the purchased four year credit, not just to a reimbursement for the community funds that husband used to purchase those benefits. The court of appeal reversed. The California Supreme Court upheld the trial court's outcome on the rationale that the right to purchase the four year credit

[18] Cal. Fam. Code § 2610.

[19] *Poppe, supra*, at 8.

[20] *Marriage of Gray*, 155 Cal. App. 4th 504, 509, 66 Cal. Rptr. 3d 87 (Cal. App. Ct., 6th Dist. 2007).

[21] *Poppe, supra.*

[22] *Green, supra.*

was made possible "not due to what the community contributed — part of the installment payments — but to what the husband brought to the community — his military service."[23]

The policy underlying *Green* supports fairness between the parties. It also retains and further encourages efficient arithmetic outcomes in an area that can quickly spiral into numeric complexity. In *Green*, the rule stated was taken from earlier cases: The trial court has discretion to determine the apportionment method "so long as the result is reasonable and fairly represents the relative contributions of the community and separate estates."[24]

Example 9.6: This example illustrates the time rule of apportionment. Bay begins her career as a lawyer at a firm that offers defined pension benefits in 2000. Bay and Sutro marry in 2002. They seek dissolution in 2010. Bay voluntarily terminates her employment in 2010. Bay's employer determines pension eligibility rights on the basis of time. Applying the time rule, Bay's pension is apportioned between Bay's separate property estate in the amount of 20% (i.e., 2 years out of 10 years used to calculate Bay's pension was earned while Bay was single) and 80% community property (i.e., 8 years earned out of the 10 years used to calculate Bay's pension was earned while Bay was married to Sutro). The community property portion of Bay's pension is divisible: Sutro is entitled to a one-half share of 80% of Bay's defined pension benefits.

Example 9.7: This example illustrates the rule of apportionment based on a different factor. Bay begins her career as a lawyer at a firm that offers defined pension benefits in 2000. Bay and Sutro marry in 2002. They seek dissolution in 2010. Bay voluntarily terminates her employment at that time. In this example, Bay's employer determines pension eligibility rights using a point based calculation. Apportioning Bay's pension should be by reference to the point system. Assume that Bay earned 2 points out of 10 total while she was single. She earned 8 points out of 10 total while she was married to Sutro. Using a point system, Bay's pension rights are 20% her separate property (2 points earned while single divided by 10 points total while employed) and 80% community property (8 points earned while married to Sutro divided by 10 points total while employed). The community property portion of the defined pension benefit is divisible: Sutro is entitled to a one-half of 80% of Bay's defined pension benefits.

In each of the above examples, whatever pension benefits Bay may be entitled to (whether contingent or vested) are community property in character if they were earned during marriage. Sutro is entitled to an accounting, and ultimately entitled to a one-half interest in Bay's community property pension benefits.

[B] Defined Contribution Plans

Defined contribution plans are individual accounts funded by and controlled by the employee. The defined contribution amount is dependent, either in whole or part, on actual sum certain deposits that are made by the employee over the period

---

23 *Green, supra*, at 1139.

24 *Green, supra*, at 1142.

of his or her employment. Moreover, defined contribution plans are either held by the employer in the employee's name, which is to say out of the employer's general investment fund. Or, more typically, they are held by a financial institution in the employee's name and subject to the employee's right of access. Early withdrawals are typically subject to tax penalties.

Defined contribution plan accumulations are analyzed as if they were bank accounts. Importantly, tax-deferred and tax-protected contribution plans have not, to date, been treated like taxable stock or investment accounts. Defined contribution plans represent tax deferred earnings held in an account with a tax-deferred (e.g., a 401(k)) or a future tax-exempt (e.g., Roth IRA) status, depending on the account. Taxable investment accounts, by contrast, are apportioned by reference to the separate property business rules, as was decided by *Beam*.[25] The distinction in tax status between the two accounts justifies shielding defined contribution plans from the separate property business apportionment rules discussed in Chapter 7.

§ 9.04 SUMMARY

Education or training is not property subject to division upon dissolution. Community contributions to the *direct* expenses of one spouse's education are reimbursed to the community, with interest. Direct expenses of education include cash contributions and the principal repayment of educational loans, whether the loans are incurred before or during the marriage. Community contributions to *general* expenses of living, by comparison, factor into a determination of discretionary spousal support. General expenses include rent, transportation, medical care, and all other family expenses that support the student spouse but do not go directly to that student spouse's education.

Income earned from celebrity falls within the balancing factors for determining spousal support.

Compensation earned during marriage is community property, whether it is distributed in the tax year earned or deferred. This is the case no matter the form that the distributed or deferred compensation takes. And it is the case regardless of whether the deferred compensation is contingent, vested or matured.

Deferred compensation is characterized depending on the employee's marital status. Deferred compensation earned while single is separate property. Deferred compensation earned while married is community property. Apportionment is typically, but not necessarily, by the time rule. However, the trial court has discretion to determine the apportionment method so long as the result is reasonable and fair.

---

[25] *Beam, supra.*

Part IV

DUTIES, RIGHTS, AND LIABILITIES

Chapter 10

MANAGEMENT AND CONTROL OF COMMUNITY PROPERTY

Ownership of property gives a person the right and the obligation to manage and control that property. Ownership includes every permutation of the right to use, transfer, and exclude others from using the property. Property related liabilities also stem from an owner's rights to manage and control the property.

Either spouse has the right to manage and control community personal property. This right is subject to the other spouse's right to avoid a gift, a low-value transfer, or the transfer of certain family items without written consent.

Either spouse has the right to manage and control community real property. This right is subject to the requirement of joinder for certain leases, sales, conveyances and encumbrances.

Both spouses have a quasi-fiduciary duty to the other spouse that includes a duty of loyalty, good faith and fair dealing, and care, as measured by the business judgment rule. Duties to disclose may also arise as to any records that a spouse or the spouses keep.

§ 10.01 MANAGEMENT AND CONTROL: A BRIEF TIMELINE

Prior to 1975, California followed a male management system that gave a husband the legal right to manage and control all community property relative to a wife.[1] A wife was permitted to protect her community property earnings and personal injury recoveries from her husband's premarital creditors, as discussed in Chapter 12.

In 1974, the Legislature adopted equal management and control legislation. Effective January 1, 1975, either spouse gained the legal right to manage and control community property. The use of the word *either* rather than both signals that the California legislation was intended to recognize that either spouse, even acting alone, has equal, present, and existing rights to manage and control all community personal property acquired during marriage. Texas, by comparison, uses a dual management system that gives a spouse control over the community property that he or she earns unless and until there is commingling, at which point the spouses become dual managers of the commingled community property.

---

[1] Jo Carrillo, *The M Word: From Partial Coverture to Skills-Based Fiduciary Duties in Marriage*, 22 Hastings Women's L.J. 257 (2011).

The California legislation on the management and control of community property states the rights and liabilities of the spouses, in relation to each other. This legislation:

- Distinguishes between community personal and community real property;
- Places the spouses into a confidential relationship by operation of law;
- Recognizes the existence of partnership fiduciary duties between the spouses;
- Employs a presumption of undue influence in transactions between the spouses that result in one spouse taking any unfair advantage over the other spouse; and
- Provides a statutory cause of action (with enumerated remedies) to a spouse whose interest in community property was, is, or will be impaired.

§ 10.02 COMMUNITY PERSONAL PROPERTY

Personal property can create the bulk of a person's or a couple's net worth.

Personal property can be titled, but often it is not. It can be fixed (permanently attached) to real property, but often it is not. If it is fixed, it can be removed. Depending on the asset, personal property can be movable, concealable and transferable. Personal property is subject to valuation uncertainty, since there may or may not be a reliable used market against which to compare the value of any specific item on any given day. The absence of comparable sales can lead to speculative valuations, made unreliable by emotional factors that might cloud one (or both) party's judgment. For example, a family heirloom may have an emotional value that is far higher than what a willing buyer would pay for it. Another example: Trade tools may be how one spouse makes a living, but trade tools are only worth their price on the used personal property market (i.e., a garage sale, Craig's list, or possibly e-bay). The value of an item, after all, is not the seller's asking price; it is the buyer's purchase price. If an item has not yet been sold, its fair market value is what a hypothetical willing buyer would pay for it.

As personal as personal property can be, it also can be impersonal. Accounts, for example, hold electronic impulses that represent sums on deposit. Cash is impersonal. Shares of stock are impersonal. Professional licenses are personal, but still impersonal in the sense that they allow their holder to practice a profession, which in turn equates to earning capacity, which in turn can result in wages and deferred compensation. A car is personal, but not in the sense that jewelry is personal. A car is personalized while it is in use, but only a rare car plausibly might be considered personal in the sense that, say, jewelry is personal. Moreover, for many car owners, the car is an asset that is periodically traded in for a newer version. An investment in art may or may not be personal. However, for art to function as an investment, it must be a possession that the owner is willing to part with in order to realize a capital gain. For items like these, notwithstanding the fact there may be a comparable market against which to measure the value of the asset on any given date, disputes can arise between the spouses. Concerns about valuation may be raised. So too might concerns about management and control.

Personal property can be tangible or intangible. A copyright, a patent, a trademark, all of these are intangible rights that give rise to an income stream that, when acquired during marriage, is community personal property. Intellectual property is the right to exclude others from use of whatever is protected. The right to exclusive use is coupled with the exclusive right to exploit the intellectual property. Similarly, an employment contract is an obligation which, if performed, gives rise to an income stream. When one spouse secures a contract of employment during marriage, realized and deferred earnings from that are contract community property. So too is the bargained for exchange that the contract represents.

So what is community *personal* property? The California Civil Code defines personal property as everything that isn't real property.[2] Here is a noninclusive and very short alphabetized list of personal property. Some of the entries on the list can be defined as obligations, but for now focus on the possibilities latent in the phrase *personal property*. Keep in mind that not all of these assets are necessarily property divisible at dissolution:

> Accounts, animals, appliances, art, boats, bonds, businesses, business good will, cars, cash, clothing, collectibles, computer equipment, contract rights, credit histories, credit scores, data, debts, deferred earnings, electronics, emails, employment contracts, fixtures, furniture, income streams, instruments, insurance policies, intellectual property, investment accounts, issues, life insurance contracts, loans, motor cars, necklaces, physical copies of books, physical (tangible) manifestations of intellectual property, prototypes, records, realized real estate equity, rents, personal injury awards, personal injury claims, professional licenses, profits, retirement accounts, securities, shares of stock, sums on deposit in an account, registered trademarks, taxable investment accounts, tax deferred accounts, tax refunds, texts, trade tools, xylophones, yachts, and zithers.

Noticeably absent from the above list is a leasehold interest in real property. Under § 700 **"a leasehold interest in real property is real property, not personal property"** for purposes of rights and obligations during marriage.

[A] Equal Management and Control

Section 1100(a) is one of the most important sections in the Family Code.

Section 1100(a) provides that **"[e]ither spouse has the management and control of the community personal property . . . with like absolute power of disposition, other than testamentary, as the spouse has of the separate estate of the spouse."**

This broad grant of authority extends to all personal property acquired during the marriage. It also extends to all commingled property that the community has or may have an interest in. Personal property acquired during the marriage, whether acquired before or after the legal transition to equal management is covered by § 1100(a). So too is community and commingled personal property in

[2] Cal. Civ. Code § 663 (**"Every kind of property that is not real is personal."**).

the form of a bank account, an investment account, a business, credit proceeds, deferred compensation, and so forth.

The § 1100(a) grant of authority applies to all lifetime dispositions that are not testamentary in nature. Executing a will is a matter testamentary in nature. So too is naming a life insurance pay-on-death beneficiary. Testamentary matters are excluded from the broad grant of authority of § 1100(a) because a spouse only has the power to dispose of his or her one-half of a community property asset at death.

There are some limitations on the § 1100(a) absolute power of disposition.

Section 1100(b) prohibits a spouse from making unilateral gifts or low-value transfers of community personal property **"[w]ithout the written consent of the other spouse."** This limitation does not apply to **"[g]ifts mutually given by both spouses to third parties and gifts given by one spouse to the other spouse."** Gifts ratified after the fact fall under the category of gifts mutually given. **"[G]ifts given by one spouse to the other spouse . . ."** are governed by transmutation law, as discussed in Chapter 14. Section 1100(b) covers any category of community personal property, tangible or intangible; however it is limited to unilateral gifts and dispositions of **"[l]ess than fair and reasonable value . . . ."**

Transfers made by one spouse in violation of § 1100(b) are avoidable at the option of the nonconsenting spouse absent evidence of ratification.[3]

Transactions can be ratified after the fact, or even posthumously.

Mutually consented to gifts or transfers otherwise restricted under § 1100(b) or (c) are not avoidable by either spouse.

The age of an item is probably the most relevant bit of information for assessing fair (used personal property) market value. The phrase "used personal property market" means a consignment shop, a flea market, a garage sale, Craig's list, and so forth. Purchase price is not relevant to assessing the fair and reasonable (used market) value of an item; nor is replacement cost.

Example 10.1: This example illustrates how one spouse, acting alone, can manage and control community personal property as if it were his or her separate property. Without Noe's knowledge or consent, Castro uses community property cash to buy a snowboard, a down coat, and ski lift tickets for a winter vacation. All of Castro's transactions are authorized under § 1100(a). The rationale is that either spouse can act **"with like absolute power of disposition"** over community personal property. Under this rule, Castro can make decisions about the use of community property cash as if it were Castro's own separate property. None of Castro's purchases are avoidable by Noe.

Example 10.2: This example illustrates how either spouse acting alone can transfer community personal property to a third party. Noe and Castro own a piano. While Castro is away on vacation, Noe sells the piano to neighbor Truett for $1. By the authority of § 1100(a), Noe has the authority to transfer title to the piano to a third party, but this transfer is voidable by Castro on two grounds: first, it is a low-value transfer and second, it is a transfer of a family furnishing.

---

[3] *Spreckels v. Spreckels*, 172 Cal. 775, 158 P. 537 (Cal. 1916) (in bank).

Additionally, because Noe did not obtain Castro's written consent, avoidance is at Castro's election: Castro can consent to the transfer, seek a remedy against Noe's separate property estate, or sue Truett for return of the piano in exchange for the sale proceeds.

Example 10.3: This example illustrates how one spouse can ratify the management decisions of the other spouse. Noe sells the piano to neighbor Truett for $50. Castro uses the piano sale proceeds to buy a used saxophone. In this example, Noe had the authority to transfer title of the piano to a third party. Noe did not have Castro's written consent to make the sale, which makes the piano sale voidable at Castro's option. However, because Castro subsequently used the piano sale proceeds to purchase something else (the saxophone), Castro ratified Noe's low-value sale of the piano.

Example 10.4: This problem illustrates management and control rights relative to a gift made by one spouse to a third party without the other spouse's written consent. Noe gives sibling Taylor a gift of $14,000 community property cash. Noe has absolute power of disposition over community personal property. But unless Noe obtains Castro's written consent to make the gift, Castro has the right to avoid that gift.

Example 10.5: This example shows how § 1100(b) protects a spouse's undivided one-half share in community personal property during marriage. Noe makes a $14,000 community property cash gift to sibling Taylor without Castro's written consent. Castro seeks to avoid the gift during marriage. Noe has authority to make a gift under § 1100(a), but since the gift was made without Castro's consent, Castro has the right to avoid the gift under § 1100(b). Because the parties are still married, and because community property is owned in undivided one-half interests, Castro's right to avoid Noe's gift extends to the entire $14,000.

Example 10.6: This example shows how § 1100(b) protects a spouse's undivided one-half share in community personal property upon dissolution. Same facts as Example 10.5 except that Castro now seeks to avoid the gift in a dissolution proceeding. In this context, Castro can prevail in avoiding his own one-half community property share of Noe's gift to Truett. Castro is entitled to $7,000.

Example 10.7: This example shows how § 1100(b) protects a spouse's undivided one-half share in community personal property when a marriage ends by the death of a spouse. Same as Example 10.5 except that Castro seeks to avoid the gift after Noe's death. Castro is entitled to his own one-half community property share of the gift ($7,000) as against either Noe's estate or as against Noe's inter vivos donee Taylor.[4]

Example 10.8: This example illustrates that a gift unilaterally made by one spouse without the other spouse's written consent can be ratified by the nonconsenting spouse. Noe makes a gift of $14,000 cash to sibling Taylor. The gift is made without Castro's consent. When Taylor drops by to express thanks, Castro listens in on the conversation. Castro subsequently sends Taylor a text expressing relief that Castro and Noe could help Taylor out. By sending the text to Taylor,

---

[4] *Fields v. Michael*, 91 Cal. App. 2d 443, 205 P.2d 402 (Cal. App. Ct., 2d Dist. 1949).

Castro ratifies Noe's gift, thus making it a gift mutually given. Castro can no longer avoid the gift on § 1100(b) grounds.

Example 10.9: This example illustrates posthumous ratification. Same as Example 10.8 except that Castro dies leaving a valid will that expressly ratifies Noe's gift of community property cash to Taylor. The $14,000 gift is mutually given.

Example 10.10: This example illustrates evidence from which an inference of posthumous ratification can be drawn. Same as Example 10.9 except that Castro's will gifting structure implicitly affirms Noe's gift to Taylor. Here again, upon Castro's death, Castro's will is evidence of Castro's posthumous ratification of Noe's gift of community property. An inference can be drawn that the $14,000 gift is mutually given.

As noted above, § 1100(c) applies to unilateral dispositions of certain types of tangible community personal property made for fair market value. Thus, under § 1100(c): **"a spouse may not sell, convey, or encumber community personal property used as the family dwelling, or the furniture, furnishings, or fittings of the home, or the clothing or wearing apparel of the other spouse or minor children which is community personal property, without the written consent of the other spouse."** Transactions can be ratified after the fact. Mutually consented to transfers are not avoidable by either spouse. The age of an item is probably the most relevant bit of information for assessing fair (used personal property) market value. As with § 1100(b), the term used personal property market means a consignment shop, a flea market, a garage sale, Craig's list, and so forth. Purchase price is not relevant to assessing the fair and reasonable (used market) value of an item; nor is replacement cost.

Example 10.11: This example illustrates how fair market value and less than fair market value are ordinarily calculated for a used item. Castro, acting alone, holds a garage sale. Castro sells the family's dining room table for $5 without Noe's consent. Noe establishes that the dining room table has a market value on the used personal property market of $100. In this case, by selling the dining room table for $5, Castro's transaction disposes of a community personal property for less than its fair and reasonable value on the open market ($100). Castro has the § 1100(a) authority to make the sale, Noe has the corollary right to avoid the sale, either under the **"less than fair and reasonable value"** clause of § 1100(b) or under the **"furniture, furnishings, or fittings of the home"** clause of § 1100(c).

Example 10.12: This example illustrates how garage sale value is fair market value for a used item. Same as Example 10.11 except that Castro sell the family's dining table for $95 without Noe's consent. Noe establishes that the dining room table has a market value on the used personal property market of $100. Castro's transaction disposes of a community personal property for its fair and reasonable value on the open market ($100/$95). Thus Castro has the § 1100(a) authority to make the sale. But now Noe only has the right to avoid the sale under the § 1100(c) **"furniture, furnishings, or fittings of the home"** clause. Because the table was sold at market value, it is not included within the gift or **"less than fair and reasonable value"** limitation of § 1100(b).

Example 10.13: This example illustrates how trade tools may fall under the § 1100(c) limitation. Same as Example 10.12 except that Castro sells Noe's trade tools for their fair (garage sale) market value. Assume that Noe earns a living as a welder.[5] On these facts, Castro appears to have the § 1100(a) authority to sell Noe's trade tools. In turn, Noe has the right to avoid such a sale. Noe's right has its source not in § 1100(b) — since the trade tools were sold for fair market value. Rather Noe's right has its source in § 1100(c): **"furniture, furnishings, or fittings of the home, or the clothing or wearing apparel of the other spouse . . ."** clause. The legal argument for including Noe's trade tools under this provision is that they are a tangible part of Noe's work uniform, and as such they constitute Noe's clothing. The counter argument is that welding tools are not common necessaries, as contemplated by § 1100(c).

Another limitation on the absolute power of disposition of either spouse over community personal property appears at § 1100(d). That section recognizes the right of one spouse to exercise **"primary management and control"** in conducting a business that is **"all or substantially all of the personal property."** Primary management and control is not the same as sole management and control. A spouse with primary control may act alone in managing the business, so long as that spouse **"shall give prior written notice to the other spouse of any sale, lease, exchange, encumbrance, or other disposition of all or substantially all of the personal property used in the operation of the business . . . ."** Remedies for the breach of § 1100(d) **"are only as specified in Section 1101."**

[B] Disclosure Obligations

As to fiduciary duties, § 1100(e) governs the disclosure that one spouse owes to the other spouse with respect to the character, existence and valuation of community personal property. When a spouse acts alone in managing **"[c]ommunity assets and liabilities . . ."** that spouse is subject to the **"general rules governing fiduciary relationships, which control the actions of persons having relationships of personal confidence as specified in Section 721 . . . ."** These duties arise during the existence of the community, and they last **"until such time as the assets and liabilities have been divided by the parties of the court."**

The significance of § 1100(e) is that it incorporates § 721(b) by reference, thus confirming that for purposes of community personal property management the spousal relationship is a confidential relationship by operation of law. That confidential relationship gives rise to quasi-fiduciary duties related to the management and control of community assets and liabilities. The phrase "community assets and liabilities" is broader than the phrase "community property.

The spouses owe each other a *quasi* fiduciary duty rather than a fiduciary duty because the § 721(b) duty is not the same high standard to which a professional trustee is held. The § 721(b) duty is more in the nature of the duty that a business partner owes another business partner.

---

[5] *Austin v. Austin*, 190 Cal. App. 2d 45, 11 Cal. Rptr. 593 (Cal. App. Ct., 2d Dist. 1961).

Two examples illustrate the *quasi*-fiduciary nature of a spouse's duty under § 1100(e): A spouse need not account to the other spouse on a quarterly basis, as a professional trustee must. A spouse need not follow modern portfolio theory in managing community property investments, as a professional trustee must. A spouse's duty of care is measured by the business judgment rule, which is a standard far lower than the one to which a professional trustee is held.[6] In the trade tool example, a trustee — assuming an equally broad grant of authority in the trust instrument — can transmute trade tools into cash without a beneficiary's consent, but a business partner cannot. Thus if Noe, the welder from Example 10.13, showed up at her place of business only to learn that her business partner had sold her trade tools, she'd have a cause of action against the partner, just as she would have one against her spouse.

The duty is quasi-*fiduciary* because, in a single transaction or a pattern or series of transactions a spouse who acts alone owes the other spouse a heightened duty of care with respect to the: (1) characterization, (2) existence, and (3) valuation of community property assets and liabilities. By this heightened duty of care, a spouse who acts alone in a transaction must disclose all material facts about the transaction to the other spouse, as well as provide access, at all times, to all financial records and books kept regarding the transaction. Access should be sufficient to allow the other spouse to inspect and copy the records.

The § 721(b) provision expressly discusses the parameters of disclosure required under § 1100(e) (the community personal property provision into which § 721(b) is incorporated):

> **Each spouse shall act with respect to the other spouse in the management and control of the *community assets and liabilities* in accordance with the general rules governing fiduciary relationships which control the actions of persons having relationships of personal confidence as specified in Section 721, until such time as the assets and liabilities have been divided by the parties or by a court.[7] This duty includes the obligation to make full disclosure to the other spouse of all material facts and information regarding the existence, characterization, and valuation of all assets in which the community has or may have an interest and debts for which the community is or may be liable . . . .**

This § 1100(e) language indicates that it applies generally to either spouse who acts with respect to community personal property; and that § 721(b) applies as well. Case law interprets § 1100(e) to mean that the most recent version of 721(b) applies.[8] The most recently amended version of § 721(b) incorporates the most recently amended version of the Revised Uniform Partnership Act [RUPA].

---

6 *Marriage of Duffy*, 91 Cal. App. 4th 923, 111 Cal. Rptr. 2d 160 (Cal. App. Ct., 2d Dist. 2001) (superseded by § 721(b)).

7 This section, along with the amended **"community assets and liabilities"** language became operative in 1993. The 1992 enactment and the 1993 amendment became operative on the same date: January 1, 1994.

8 *Marriage of Walker*, 138 Cal. App. 4th 1408, 42 Cal. Rptr. 3d 325 (Cal. App. Ct., 1st Dist. 2006).

RUPA holds spouses to the same standards as business partners generally with respect to access, true and full information, and holding in trust for the community any benefit or profit received while engaged in the management and control of community personal property. Under § 721(b)(1)–(3), which incorporates RUPA by reference:[9]

- Either spouse has **"access at all times to any books kept regarding a transaction for the purposes of inspection and copying."**
- Either spouse must render **"upon request"** accurate and full information affecting any transaction that concerns the community property;
- Either spouse holds **"as a trustee any benefit or profit derived from any transaction by one spouse without the consent of the other spouse which concerns the community property."**

Therefore, under § 1100(e), each spouse has a duty **"[t]o provide equal access to all information, records, and books that pertain to the value and character of** [community] **assets and debts, upon request."**

The phrase **"upon request"** has created ambiguity as to whether an acting spouse has a duty to disclose as a matter of course or whether the duty to disclose is (only) triggered by the other spouse's request for information. In other words, is the duty to disclose proactively triggered by a spouse's management of the property? Or, is the duty to disclose reactively triggered by the nonacting spouse's request for information from the managing spouse?

The relationship between formal discovery and § 1100e) pushes toward answering this question in favor of a more (rather than a less) proactive and exacting disclosure requirement during marriage and up until assets have been divided by the court.[10]

In *Marriage of Feldman,* husband, Aaron, represented to wife, Elena, that he was renting his post-separation residence. So, when Elena stumbled upon evidence that Aaron was paying real estate taxes on that post-separation "rental," she had her attorney make a formal discovery inquiry into the character or possible character of the rental. Aaron responded that he was renting the property from one of his separate property LLC business entities, an entity that Elena suspected was being partially capitalized with community property funds. Aaron argued that he had no duty to disclose matters relating to his separate property; and thus he had no duty to disclose information about the LLC or its holdings. Elena countered that disclosure was necessary to determine if the community property had an interest in the LLC or its holdings. Elena requested $250,000 in sanctions, $140,000 in attorney's fees, and $750,000 in conditional sanctions cancelable upon Aaron's full

---

[9] Cal. Corp. Code, Chapter 5, Uniform Partnership Act of 1994.

[10] During a dissolution or legal separation proceeding, § 2100 states a policy to avoid dissipation of the community estate before distribution. To promote that policy, § 2100(c) requires:

> **[f]ull and accurate disclosure of all assets and liabilities in which one or both parties have or may have an interest must be made in the early stages of a proceeding for dissolution of marriage or legal separation of the parties, regardless of the characterization as community or separate, together with a disclosure of all income and expenses of the parties.**

compliance with his § 1100(e) disclosure duties. The trial court found that Aaron breached his § 1100(e) duty to make full disclosure of all material facts related to the possible capitalization of a LLC entity with community property funds, and to the subsequent purchase of a residence through that LLC. Sanctions of $250,000 were granted against Aaron for disclosure noncompliance, with an additional $140,000 granted for Elena's attorney's fees. Aaron appealed. The court of appeal affirmed; it held that the trial court did not abuse its discretion in concluding that Aaron's "lack of candor" was part of a pattern of nondisclosure that warranted the imposition of sanctions, even without proof of injury to Elena. The harm to Elena occurred, the court explained, when Aaron failed to meet his § 1100(e) duties as to the disputed asset. Without disclosure, Elena could not determine if the property was or could be community property. Thus sanctions were based on Aaron's intention to circumvent the disclosure process, and — by extension — to frustrate the policy of promoting settlement at dissolution.

Section 1100(e) is understood to require the parties to voluntarily disclose all information about community assets and liabilities, including proportionally and potentially owned ones. Voluntary disclosure during the continuance of the marriage, at least in theory, can reduce the necessity, cost, and emotional toll of formal discovery in the event the marriage ends. Formal discovery can be an expensive and drawn out phase of a legal separation or dissolution proceeding. Not all parties are forthcoming; and even cooperative parties are not always as forthcoming as they could be. Therefore, one's spouse's failure to meet his or her § 1100(e) duties constitutes a harm to the other spouse for which there are numerous discretionary remedies.[11] Moreover, the unlawful withholding of evidence of income and assets closes the door to that party's rights of appeal on related issues: After a trial court exercises its discretion, the nondisclosing party cannot later complain that a related order is not based on the evidence that he or she refused to disclose in the first place.[12]

[C] Impairment Claims and Remedies

A spouse who has proof of the other spouse's breach of fiduciary duty has a claim for impairment, as delineated by § 1101(a): **"A spouse has a claim against the other spouse for any breach of the fiduciary duty that results in impairment to the claimant spouse's present undivided one-half interest in the community estate, including , but not limited to, a single transaction or a pattern or series of transactions, which transaction or transactions have caused or will cause a detrimental impact to the claimant spouse's undivided one-half interest in the community estate."**

The claim applies to property that is or may be community property, whether tangible or intangible, real or personal. It applies to one transaction or multiple transactions. It applies to a series of sequential transactions. It applies to a pattern of transactions that emerges only in hindsight from seemingly unrelated events. It

---

11 Cal. Fam. Code § 271, § 2030; *see also Marriage of Feldman*, 153 Cal. App. 4th 1470, 1489, 64 Cal. Rptr. 3d 29 (Cal. App. Ct., 4th Dist. 2007).

12 *Marriage of Hofer*, 208 Cal. App. 4th 454, 145 Cal. Rptr. 3d 697 (Cal. App. Ct., 2d Dist. 2012).

applies to a past, present, or future transaction.

Remedies under § 1101(g) sound in ordinary negligence.

Remedies under § 1101(h) are punitive in nature **"when the breach falls within the ambit of Section 3294 of the Civil Code . . . ."** Cal Civ. Code § 3294 provides: **"In an action for the breach of an obligation not arising from contract, where it is proven by clear and convincing evidence that the defendant has been guilty of oppression, fraud, or malice, the plaintiff, in addition to the actual damages, may recover damages for the sake of example and by way of punishing the defendant."**

An impairment settlement is the recovering spouse's separate property per the language of 1101(g) and (h), both of which provide that the award against one spouse is an award to the other spouse.

A judgment for impairment may be collectable from an insurance contract that insures the impaired asset. A comprehensive general liability clause in a home owner's insurance policy, a title insurance policy, a car insurance policy, an umbrella insurance policy, or (in case of death) a life insurance policy, also may be a source of satisfaction absent an excluding event. Coverage will depend, of course, in part upon the terms and limitations of the policy. However, as a matter of law, intentional torts are excluded from liability insurance contracts, including homeowner's insurance contracts.[13]

If insurance is not available to satisfy the impairment judgment, the impaired spouse can reach the impairing spouse's separate property. Where the impaired spouse has no separate property or available insurance, § 1101 (g) and (h) expressly authorize a court to award to the impaired spouse the impairing spouse's one-half interest in any or all community property. This can be done by conveyance, reconveyance, resulting trust, constructive trust, equitable lien, and so

---

[13] Cal. Ins. Code § 533 provides that: **"An insurer is not liable for a loss caused by the wilful act of the insured; but he is not exonerated by the negligence of the insured, or of the insured's agents or others."**

The first enactment of Cal. Ins. Code § 533 first appeared in the 1872 Civil Code as § 2629 and in the Insurance Code as § 533 in 1935, where it has remained unamended, notwithstanding changes in insurance products. Under Cal. Ins. Code § 533 a contract that directly or indirectly exempts a person from responsibility for intentional torts is against public policy and thus unenforceable. Civil Code § 1668 also states this policy. Cal. Ins. Code § 533 is implied in every insurance contract; it is the equivalent of an exclusionary clause in the contract itself. *Nuffer v. Insurance Co. of North America*, 236 Cal. App. 2d, 349, 356, 45 Cal. Rtpr. 918 (Cal. App. Ct., 4th Dist. 1965), distinguished by *Hartford Fire Insurance Co. v. Sup. Court*, 142 Cal. App. 3d 406, 191 Cal. Rptr. 37 (Cal. App. Ct., 2d Dist 1983).

In *Evans v. Pacific Indemnity Co.*, 49 Cal. App. 3d 537, 122 Cal. Rptr. 680, 682 (Cal. App. Ct., 3d Dist 1975), spouses contracted for a comprehensive liability policy to protect them in the management of their Butte County bar. Husband got into a bar fight at the bar; he was successfully sued for assault and battery. The prevailing plaintiff sought to satisfy the judgment with the comprehensive liability policy. The insurer refused to pay. The prevailing plaintiff sued the insurance company. The trial court, citing Cal. Ins. Code § 533, held that the general comprehensive liability policy could not be used to satisfy an intentional tort judgment. On appeal, the trial court decision was affirmed.

Evans is distinguished by *Century Sur. Co. v. Polisso*, 139 Cal. App. 4th 922, 43 Cal. Rptr. 3d 468 (Cal. App. Ct., 3d Dist. 2006), which is called into doubt by *Wilson v. 21st Century Ins. Co.*, 42 Cal. 4th 713, 68 Cal. Rptr. 3d 746 , 171 P.3d 1082 (Cal. 2007), which is distinguished by an unpublished case.

on. Debts may be assigned as part of the process.

More generally, tort law is available and often necessary to address all of the proximate harm (personal, emotional, and financial) that can result from a single transaction, a series of transactions, or a pattern of transactions that form the basis of an impairment claim. *See* Chapter 11.

Recoveries for a § 1101(a) claim are the claimant spouse's separate property.[14]

§ 10.03 COMMUNITY REAL PROPERTY

Community real property is an important asset in many a community property portfolio. Thus California law requires that both parties join in any consequential transaction regarding community property real estate. This requirement is commonly referred to as the *joinder* requirement. A nonconsenting party has a limited period of time to avoid the specific instrument that he or she did not join in executing.

[A] The Joinder Requirement

Equal management of real property is governed by § 1102, which provides: **"[E]ither spouse has the management and control of the community real property . . . but both spouses, either personally or by a duly authorized agent, must join in executing any instrument by which that community real property or any interest therein is leased for a longer period than one year, or is sold, conveyed, or encumbered."** Joinder protects the community property interest in real estate while also protecting third parties who enter into a real estate transaction with a married person. Spouses are not required to join in real estate transactions between themselves, but they are required, when transmuting property between themselves, to do so by written express declaration without taking any unfair advantage of the other.[15] Transmutations are discussed in Chapter 14.

[B] Avoidance

The § 1102(d) avoidance remedy is a fairly narrow one: It is limited to **"[a]ny instrument"** — as opposed to any title or transaction — **"[a]ffecting any property standing of record in the name of either spouse alone, executed by the spouse alone . . . ."** Additionally, the avoidance remedy is time sensitive. The spouse who seeks to avoid an instrument under § 1102(d) must commence the

---

[14] However, if that award is commingled with community property, the award — assuming it has been deposited into an account — is governed by the presumption for sums on deposit. This would be the case, for example, where a cash award is received by one spouse, and deposited into an account with community property. Unless the tort award sums on deposit remain traceable or the parties have entered into an agreement, extrinsic from the account deposit agreement, that the award is not to be characterized as community property, overtime the award can get transmuted into community by operation of law. Several legal theories rationalize this outcome: The § 5305 special presumption for sums on deposit, the § 852(d) transmutation by operation of law provision, and the doctrine of confusion.

[15] Cal. Fam. Code § 852(a) and § 721(b).

action within "[o]ne year from the filing for record of that instrument in the recorder's office in the county in which the land is situated." From that point on, the nonjoining spouse's action to avoid expires. An exception exists under § 1102(c)(1) for any instrument executed solely by the husband before the January 1, 1975.

Third parties are protected by § 1102(c)(2), so long as they accepted the disputed instrument "[i]n good faith without knowledge of the marriage relation. . ."

A spouse is no longer precluded "[f]rom encumbering his or her interest in community real property in order to pay reasonable attorney's fees in order to retain or maintain legal counsel . . ." for a dissolution, nullity, or legal separation proceeding. This clarification, found at § 1102(e), reverses the holding in *Droeger*.[16] It went into effect on January 1, 1994.

[C] The House on Halm Avenue: The Limits of a § 1102 Avoidance Remedy

Lezine v. Security Pacific Financial Services, Inc. illustrates a series of transactions that resulted in an impairment of wife Gloria's community real and personal property interest, past, present, and future.[17] *Lezine* also illustrates the difference between avoiding an instrument and avoiding a transaction. Under § 1102, a nonjoining spouse only has the limited right to avoid an instrument.

In *Lezine*, husband, Henry, forged wife, Gloria's, name on a quitclaim deed to the title of the family house on Halm Avenue. The quitclaim deed purported to divest Gloria of her interest in the family home. Gloria's signature was falsely notarized. Henry recorded the fraudulent deed. He then used it to obtain a mortgage ($240,000), secured by a deed of trust on the Halm Avenue house in favor of Lender #1. Lender #1 advanced a portion of the loan proceeds to repay a previous mortgage on the property, as well as to repay other community property debts. Lender #1 then delivered the remainder to Henry, in cash, as extracted home equity. Henry used the cash proceeds for his own purposes. Two months later, Henry used the fraudulent deed again — this time to originate a $100,000 home equity line of credit on the Halm Avenue house. This debt was secured by a deed of trust in favor of Lender #2. Henry withdrew cash from Lender #2's line of credit for his own purposes. During marriage, Henry withdrew approximately $193,700 of home equity from the Halm Avenue house in the form of cash.

Gloria had no knowledge of Henry's activities. But, when she found out, she immediately filed a petition for dissolution. The petition was filed on June 5, 1990; and Gloria also sought to cancel the deeds of trust that the lenders had filed as contract liens on the family's Halm Avenue house. On June 16, 1991, a bifurcated judgment dissolved Gloria's and Henry's marriage; at that time, the court reserved

---

[16] *Droeger v. Friedman, Sloan & Ross*, 54 Cal. 3d 26, 283 Cal. Rptr. 584, 812 P.2d 931 (Cal. 1991) (in bank) (superseded in part by § 1102(e)).

[17] *Lezine v. Security Pacific Financial Services, Inc.*, 14 Cal. 4th 56, 58 Cal. Rptr. 2d 76, 925 P.2d 1002 (Cal. 1996) (in bank).

jurisdiction over property matters. On March 6, 1992, the trial court avoided Lender #1's and Lender #2's deed of trust on (what is now) § 1102 grounds; the trial court also ruled in favor of each lenders' cross-complaints for an equitable lien on the Halm Avenue property. Additionally, the trial court awarded a money judgment against Henry personally in favor of the lenders, in the amount of $390,308.[18] On April 2 1992, the lenders recorded abstracts of their respective money judgments against Henry as judgment liens on the Halm Avenue house, which was still community property. On July 1, 1992, the court awarded the Halm Avenue house to Gloria as her sole and separate property, subject to the lenders' equitable liens. At that time, no mention was made of the lenders' judgment liens. Gloria was aware of and accepted the lenders' equitable liens on her (now separate) Halm Avenue property; she was not aware of the lenders' judgment liens.

Shortly thereafter Gloria tried to refinance the Halm Avenue house so that she could pay off the equitable liens on title. Gloria found out at that point about the lenders' judgment liens on her title. On December 11, 1992, Gloria moved to clarify the July 1, 1992 dissolution judgment. She contended that the trial court judgment made her title subject to equitable liens, not to judgment liens. She asked the court to cancel the March 6, 1992 money judgments on § 1102 grounds. The trial court did so, citing *Droeger* for the proposition that joinder for those liens was required since the house was still community real property held in undivided concurrent interests, and thus not divisible until dissolution.[19] In the meantime, Henry defaulted on his (now) personal liability; he became judgment proof. Lender #1 appealed.

The court of appeal reversed the trial court on the ground that § 1102 gave the trial court the authority to avoid the instrument for which joinder was lacking: thus, Gloria could avoid the security interests that Henry obtained without Gloria's signature, but not the March 6, 1992 money judgments that the lenders had obtained against Henry and (lawfully) filed as judgment liens against the Halm Avenue house through the judicial process. The California Supreme Court granted review and affirmed.

After *Lezine*, when an instrument is executed in exchange for consideration, but without joinder, a court has the authority to avoid (only) the instrument for which joinder is lacking. This is a precise avoidance remedy of § 1102. In *Lezine*, the scope of § 1102 authorized the trial court to avoid the security interests that Henry wrongfully gave to the lenders, but not the money judgments that the lenders obtained by suing Henry. Given that Henry became judgment proof after the dissolution — i.e., he had no assets for the lender to collect — canceling the money judgments would have effectively canceled Henry's debt. But Henry, as the contract debtor, had taken possession of the lenders' loan proceeds during marriage. Were the court to cancel the money judgment it would be forgiving the debt.

According to the state Supreme Court's rationale, § 1102 authorizes a court to cancel an instrument for which joinder is absent, but it doesn't authorize a court to

[18] The amounts were: $302,528 in favor of the first lender and $87,780 in favor of the second lender.

[19] *Droeger, supra.*

cancel a debt. Importantly, the fact that Henry misspent the loan proceeds did not automatically transmute those proceeds into Henry's separate obligation. Nor did Henry's use of the proceeds without Gloria's knowledge relieve the community of liability, weigh in favor of canceling the debt, or otherwise preclude the lenders from securing their money judgments on community real property.

The upshot is that § 1102 is limited to the avoidance of the instrument for which joinder is absent. It is also limited to certain instruments: **"[b]oth spouses, either personally or by a duly authorized agent, must join in executing any instrument by which that community real property or any interest therein is leased for a longer period than one year, or is sold, conveyed, or encumbered."** A security interest is an encumbrance; a deed is a conveyance; and a transfer of title for consideration is a sale. Absent joinder, any of these instruments are avoidable by the non-joining spouse. By comparison, a lender's money judgment filed as a lien on a community property title is not avoidable under § 1102, even if the loan proceeds were misspent by the debtor spouse.

Upon obtaining a judgment against a spouse, a lender has the legal right to secure that judgment against any available real property. Section 1102 does not preclude or otherwise frustrate a lender from asserting any legal rights that it may have to secure an unsecured debt. In *Lezine*, Henry's fraud was against both Gloria and the lenders. This left the trial court with the task of balancing the rights of an innocent spouse against the rights of innocent encumbrancers. Application of § 1102 properly allowed Gloria to avoid the security interest (the instrument for which joinder was lacking), but it was not a basis upon which to cancel the money judgment that was filed on the Halm Avenue residence as a lien.

Commentators denounced the state Supreme Court decision and the lenders in support of innocent Gloria, who was left to either pay her ex-husband's fraudulently obtained debt or else lose the house that the trial court had assigned to her as a remedy for Henry's pattern of financial abuse. Moreover, the nearly $200,000 of monetized home equity that Henry gained possession of as a result of fraud against Gloria and against two lenders was gone. Henry was in default and judgment proof. And Gloria was left to pay for Henry's debt, either from the sale of her house or from other funds.

In an inflexible lenders-versus-Gloria binary, it's obvious that there was no good solution. It's also obvious that Henry did more than simply fail to get Gloria's joinder as was required by § 1102. And it's equally obvious that Gloria's § 1102 remedy was far from sufficient to address the harm that Henry caused to her personally and to the community property estate as an entity.

Henry breached basic notions of good faith, fair dealing and loyalty in relation to his spouse Gloria by engaging in a pattern of financial abuse. He disturbed Gloria's peace, which is grounds for a finding of abuse under the Domestic Violence Prevention Act [DVPA], discussed in Chapter 11. He engaged in tortious behavior, giving rise to multiple statutory and common law claims against him. And to the extent that he did so with criminal intent, he was culpable on that basis as well.

For all of these reasons, it would have been imperative for Gloria to obtain exclusive rights to manage and control the community real and personal property during the continuation of her marriage. But to do so, her attorney would have had to have known to file a DVPA petition, as discussed in Chapter 11.

§ 10.04 RIGHTS AND OBLIGATIONS RELATED TO ANY AND ALL COMMUNITY PROPERTY

A spouse has a quasi-fiduciary duty as to all community property, real and personal, and to all property that the community has or may have an interest in. A spouse's duty in a transaction with the other spouse is found at § 721(b), a provision that incorporates the Revised Uniform Partnership Act by reference.

[A] Section 721(b): Transactions With Each Other and Third Parties

Section 721(a) applies to both community personal property and to community real property: **"Subject to subdivision (b), either husband or wife may enter into any transaction with the other, or with any other person, respecting property, which either might if unmarried."**

Subdivision (b) provides: "**[i]n transactions between themselves, a husband and wife are subject to the general rules governing fiduciary relationships which control the actions of persons occupying confidential relations with each other.**"

The confidential relationship recognized by § 721(b):

> **[I]mposes a duty of the highest good faith and fair dealing on each spouse, and neither shall take any unfair advantage of the other. This confidential relationship is a fiduciary relationship subject to the same rights and duties of nomarital business partners, as provided in Sections 16403, 16404, and 16503 of the Corporations Code, including, *but not limited to*, the following:**
>
> > **(1) Providing each spouse access at all times to any books kept regarding a transaction for the purposes of inspecting and copying.**
> >
> > **(2) Rending upon request, true and full information of all things affecting any transaction which concerns the community property. Nothing in this section is intended to impose a duty for either spouse to keep detailed books and records of community property transactions.**
> >
> > **(3) Accounting to the spouse, and holding as a trustee any benefit or profit derived from any transaction by one spouse without the consent of the other spouse which concerns the community property.**

(Italics added.)

[B] The Statutory Duty of the Highest Good Faith and Fair Dealing

The § 721(b) phrase **"a duty of the highest good faith and fair dealing"** includes a duty of loyalty, a duty of good faith and fair dealing, and a duty of care (as measured by the business judgment rule).[20] This duty is both recognized by case law and by the incorporation of § 721(b) of Cal. Corp. Code § 16403(a), which provides that a partner owes **"fiduciary duties . . . to the partnership"** of loyalty, care, good faith, and fair dealing.

The duty of loyalty includes all of the following under Cal. Corp. Code § 16403(b):

> **(1) To account to the partnership and hold as trustee for it any property, profit, or benefit derived by the partner in the conduct and winding up of the partnership business or derived from a use by the partner of partnership property or information, including the appropriation of partnership opportunity.**
>
> **(2) To refrain from dealing with the partnership in the conduct or winding up of the partnership business as or on behalf of a party have an interest adverse to the partnership.**
>
> **(3) To refrain from competing with the partnership in the conduct of the partnership business before the dissolution of the partnership.**

The duty of loyalty requires not that a spouse act as a trustee, but rather that a spouse *account* to the other spouse as a trustee for any property, profit, or benefit that he or she derived from not accounting, from the use of community property or information, from acting as a party with an adverse interest to the community estate, from competing with the community estate, and so forth. In lay terms, the duty of loyalty is a commitment by a spouse not to take any unfair advantage of the other spouse, and this includes unfair advantages that may come from commingling property, not keeping records, treating the community estate as an adverse party, competing with the community estate for purchase opportunities, and so on.

Statutorily, the duty of care is **"limited to refraining from engaging in grossly negligent or reckless conduct, intentional misconduct, or a knowing violation of the law."**[21] Judicially, the duty of care exists as measured by the business judgment rule, which *Marriage of Duffy* defined using the above language from Cal. Corp. Code 16404(c).[22]

Duties are not necessarily breached when one spouse furthers his or her own interest.[23] A spouse can amend or revoke a premarital contract, or benefit from a transmutation, or commingle separate property sums on deposit and keep specialized records, purchase an asset from a commingled account, and so forth. However,

---

[20] *Duffy, supra.*

[21] Cal. Corp. Code § 16404(c).

[22] *Duffy, supra.*

[23] Cal. Corp. Code § 16404(e).

in any transaction in which one spouse obtains any unfair advantage over the other spouse, § 721(b) permits a presumption of undue influence to be raised in favor of the adversely affected spouse. The definition of **"any unfair advantage"** is discussed in Chapter 14. Rebuttal is by the benefitted spouse who must show that the nonacting spouse consented to the transaction after disclosure was made.

Finally, these duties exist through the partnership, through dissolution, and beyond, at least with respect to the period during which the partnership was in existence.[24]

Example 10.14: This example illustrates guarding against the appropriation of a community property opportunity in the case of a stock purchase made from a commingled account. Castro commingles separate property sums on deposit with community property sums on deposit in Account 123. Castro keeps specialized records sufficient to meet the CAMPAL and *See v. See* standards, as discussed in Chapter 5. On a certain date, after careful study, Castro decides to use separate property funds to purchase shares of ABC stock for his separate property estate. On that same date, Castro discloses to Noe that ABC is a start-up internet company, and that there are sufficient separate property sums *and* sufficient community property sums on deposit to make the ABC stock purchase on the proposed date. Castro transfers possession of the account ledger to Noe for inspection, which is an act of disclosure. Based on Noe's understanding of the entries, Noe voluntarily consents to Castro's separate property purchase of the ABC stock. On the date of purchase, Castro also declares an intention to buy the ABC stock with separate property, as is required by *Hicks-Mix*, which is discussed in Chapter 5. Castro's written declaration is separate from the account register itself. On these facts, Castro has rebutted the CAMPAL presumption, rebutted the general presumption as to the ABC shares of stock that were purchased with net separate property sums on deposit, and likely complied with applicable § 721(b) duties. The shares of stock belong entirely to Castro's separate property estate.

Example 10.15: This example illustrates the difference between the legal duty to keep records and the need to keep records. Same as in Example 10.14 except that Castro does not keep records. The first spouse to commingle has a legal duty to keep records for purposes of rebutting a community property presumption. But there is no positive requirement that the commingling spouse keep records of net character deposits. In the absence of account records that show net character deposits, all sums on deposit are presumptively community property under CAMPAL. Without evidence to rebut the CAMPAL presumption as to sums on deposit in the account, a spouse does not have the legal basis to make a separate property claim to the sums on deposit or to the assets purchased from the commingled account. The shares of stock are entirely community property.

Example 10.16: This example illustrates a breach of the duty of loyalty. Same as in Example 10.14 except that on the date of the stock purchase, Castro does not declare a written intention to purchase the ABC stock with his net separate property sums on deposit in Account 123. Instead, Castro deducts the stock purchase from the community property sums on deposit with the intention of

[24] Cal. Corp. Code § 16405.

altering the ledger entries to make it appear as if his separate property made the purchase *if* the ABC stock appreciates in value. Several years later, when the ABC stock does in fact appreciate in value and divorce is looming, Castro backdates the ledger entries to reflect that the stock purchase was made with Castro's net separate property deposits. Castro also backdates a written declaration of intent to support his separate property claim. In this transaction between the spouses, Castro has breached his § 721(b) duties of loyalty, good faith and fair dealing. Castro has a duty to account to Noe: Castro can do this by correcting the account records and by accounting for any property, profit, or benefit that was derived by Castro from the use of community property sums to purchase ABC stock. If there were profits, Castro holds them in trust for the community. In any event, the shares of ABC stock are entirely community property; and Castro is liable, at the very least, for an accounting, for breach of trust (for profits received), and for impairment of a community property interest in the sums on deposit in the account.

The duty of good faith has been defined as honesty in fact, the absence of malice, "and the absence of design to defraud or to seek an unconscionable advantage."[25] The duty of good faith is measured by whether the acting spouse disclosed the existence of an asset, kept adequate records to account for the appropriation of a community opportunity, provided access to existing records, or otherwise refrained from acting adversely to the interests of the community estate in the transaction in question.

Example 10.17: This example illustrates what sort of profit might be obtained by the appropriation of a community opportunity. Same facts as 10.16 except that on the date that Castro purchases the ABC shares of stock with community property deposits from Account 123, he also purchases XYZ stock with separate property from an established separate property source. Assume that had Castro made the ABC stock purchase with net separate property sums on deposit in Account 123, he would have had insufficient separate property funds to make the XYZ stock purchase. By using community property, Castro enhanced the buying power of his separate property funds at the expense of the community estate. This is a breach of § 721(b) in the sense that Castro appropriated a community property buying opportunity for himself, he took advantage of the community property estate by making an excessive withdrawal, he manipulated Noe's trust in allowing him to purchase appreciable assets from the a commingled account, he backdated records so as deceive Noe and thereby gain profits at the expense of the community, and depending on the emotional context underlying the transaction, he may also face liability on other grounds, such as those discussed in Chapter 11.

Example 10.18: This example illustrates the duty of good faith in a transaction between spouses. In order to impress a friend, Castro invests all of the family's savings in one high-risk biotechnology startup company with questionable potential. Castro tells Noe that the investment is a guaranteed winner. Noe has no experience with securities investments. In this transaction, Castro has arguably breached his duty of good faith to Noe under § 712(b). Specifically, Castro has misrepresented the risk level of the investment to Noe in a way that allowed him to take unconscionable advantage of Noe's lack of knowledge and experience in the matter.

---

[25] *Duffy, supra.*

Example 10.19: This example illustrates the low standard of the duty of care in a transaction between spouses. After a semester of formal study on the topic of startup investments, Castro invests all of the family's savings in one high-risk biotechnology startup company with solid potential. Castro explains to Noe that the risk is high, but so is the potential reward. Based on the accurate information Castro provides to Noe about the investment opportunity, Noe consents to take the risk. Eventually the biotechnology company goes bankrupt. In this case, Castro obviously made a losing investment, but the community property's loss was not caused by a breach of Castro's duty of care under § 712(b) as it incorporates Cal. Corp. Code § 16404. Castro's (losing) decision cost the community estate its savings, but the decision to invest was made after careful study, not out of gross negligence, recklessness, intentional misconduct, or a knowing violation of the law.

[C] Disclosure

Section § 721(b)(1) expressly states the quasi-fiduciary duty includes **"providing each spouse access at all times to any books kept regarding a transaction for the purposes of inspection and copying."** This language presupposes that books — transaction records — are maintained in written paper or electronic form. And indeed this requirement is confirmed in Corporations Code § 16403, which provides:

> **(a) A partnership shall keep its books and records, if any, in writing or in any form capable of being converted into clearly legible tangible form, at its chief executive office.**
>
> **(b) A partnership shall provide partners and their agents and attorneys access to its books and records. It shall provide former partners and their agents and attorneys access to books and records pertaining to the period during which they were partners. . . .**
>
> **(c) Each partner and the partnership shall furnish to a partner . . . both of the following, which may be transmitted by electronic transmission by the partnership. . .**
>
>> **(1) Without demand, any information concerning the partnership's business and affairs reasonably required for the proper exercise of the partner's rights and duties under the partnership agreement . . . ; and**
>>
>> **(2) On demand, any information concerning the partnership's business and affairs, except to the extent the demand or the information demanded is unreasonable or otherwise improper under the circumstance.**

Financial records are useful to rebut the general community property presumption. They are necessary to prove a reimbursement under § 2640. *Specialized* financial records are required to rebut the special Cal. Prob. Code § 5305(a) community property presumption as to sums on deposit in an account, and the general community property presumption as to purchases from a commingled account. Financial records can take any useful form, except for in the case of purchases from a commingled bank account. In that situation, specialized records must be kept in accordance with the decision in *See v. See*, which is consistent with Cal. Prob. Code § 5305(a).

Otherwise, § 721(b)(2) expressly provides: **"Nothing in this section is intended to impose a duty for either spouse to keep detailed books and records of community property transactions."** Nor is there a requirement as to how books must be kept as a general matter. As noted above, the § 721(b) duties are quasi-fiduciary in the sense that the statute itself does not create mandatory record keeping requirements. Nevertheless, keeping records in the ordinary course of the continuance of the marriage allows a spouse to meet his or her duties under § 1100(e) and under § 721(b). This makes it more likely that a spouse can then meet any demands for disclosure in the context of legal separation, dissolution or probate.[26]

§ 10.05 SUMMARY

Either spouse has the right to manage and control community property.

With respect to community personal property, either spouse has the legal right to manage the property as if it were that spouse's separate property. The right is phrased as one of absolute power of disposition, but the right is limited. A spouse may not make gifts or low value transfers of community personal property without the other spouse's written consent or after the fact ratification. Nor may a spouse make market value transfers of certain tangible items of community personal property — clothing, furniture, fixtures, and other like items — without the other spouse's written consent or ratification. The nonconsenting spouse has the right to avoid such a transfer.

With respect to community real property, either spouse can act, but joinder is required for enumerated transactions involving leases of over a year, sales, conveyances and encumbrances. A spouse who does not join in executing an consequential instrument has a right to avoid that instrument.

With respect to any and all community property, a spouse may enter into any transaction with the other spouse, as he or she could with a third party. However, due to the confidential nature of the marital relationship, a spouse has general fiduciary duties to the other spouse in transactions between themselves. The confidential relationship gives rise to additional fiduciary duties that include providing access to existing records, a duty of loyalty, a duty of good faith and fair dealing, a duty of care as measured by the business judgment rule, and disclosure duties.

---

[26] Cal. Fam. Code § 721(b), incorporating Cal. Corp. Code § 15405.

Chapter 11

DOMESTIC VIOLENCE

The Family Code has long authorized interspousal claims for property and contract matters. Where there are no specific Family Code provisions in place, general principles of law protect the spouses in their ownership and contract rights relative to each other, as well as in their rights to personhood.

The doctrine of spousal tort immunity was adopted in California in 1909, and abolished for intentional and negligent torts in 1962.

In 1993, California adopted the Domestic Violence Prevention Act [DVPA] as Division 10 of the Family Code. The DVPA governs the issuance of restraining orders intended to prevent domestic violence. Domestic violence restraining orders can be initiated by a peace officer or a party. Party initiated petitions for restraining another person can be brought through the DVPA or in a separation, dissolution, or nullity proceeding. DVPA restraining orders are not limited to adults in a voluntary sexual or dating relationship; however, for purposes of this chapter, civil restraining orders will be discussed within that framework. DVPA restraining orders have a direct impact on the parties' rights to manage and control community property, if married or RDPs, or partnership property, for nonmarried cohabitants. Successful restraining orders will enhance one party's management and control of property and restrict the restrained party's rights to that same property.

Effective Jan. 1, 2010, the Judicial Council adopted rule 10.464 of the California Rules of Courts to provide for education on domestic violence for judges, commissioners, and referees. This rule applies to judicial officers who hear matters in criminal, family, juvenile delinquency, juvenile dependency, or probate court.

A number of torts not recognized at common law are authorized by the California Civil Code. The policy behind codifying individual torts, at least in the domestic relationship context, is intended to avoid any return — intentional or otherwise — to the spousal tort immunity doctrine.

§ 11.01 HISTORICAL BASES AND GENERAL PROCEDURE FOR INTERSPOUSAL TORT CLAIMS

The Spanish *ganancial* system permitted spouses to protect or enforce their rights against each other. The rationale was that husband and wife were separate legal entities, notwithstanding the marriage. De Funiak and Vaughn locate a possible earliest authorization for interspousal recoveries in the 13th century Spanish law known as Las Seite Partidas, Part 3, Title 2, Law 5. Las Seite Partidas provided that spouses should not sue each other, "but that one might sue the other when unjustly deprived of any property by the other and its return or reparation therefore was sought."[1] This provision applied to suits to protect property, as it suggests, but it also recognized that the wife could bring a civil suit for harms to her person. If she recovered, any damages would be her separate property.

The common law system, by contrast, followed the doctrine of interspousal immunity, a doctrine that prohibited tort actions between spouses. Today, the doctrine has been abolished in most if not all U.S. jurisdictions. Abolishing the doctrine of interspousal tort immunity implicated the confidential marital communications privilege, a privilege that even 17th century common law commentators recognized.[2] The confidential marital communications privilege was justified by the rationale that it prevented "discord and dissention" in the marriage, it prevented law suits between spouses, and it prevented spouses from being required by law to communicate about sensitive topics.[3] Opponents of the confidential marital communications privilege criticized these points as mere sentiment.[4]

The common law and its rationales have permeated all community property systems. For that reason, the doctrine of interspousal immunity found its way into the jurisprudence of the community property law states. Louisiana held truest to its civil law origins, but even judicial precedent in Louisiana eventually provided that a wife could sue her husband's insurer, but not her husband.[5] In Arizona, it appears that the doctrine of spousal immunity may be retained for intentional tort cases based on domestic abuse.[6] Nevada and New Mexico, two other examples, historically disallowed one spouse to sue the other unless a statute authorized the claim.[7]

California adopted the doctrine of spousal immunity in *Peters v. Peters*, a 1909 case involving a husband who brought a civil suit against his wife for assault and battery.[8] The factual basis for the husband's claim was that the wife shot him without justification. The husband was seriously injured, yet the verdict and judgment were in favor of the wife. The husband moved for a new trial; his motion was denied. The plaintiff-husband appealed. His appeal was denied on the ground that "the verdict against the husband is harmless because he has no right to maintain the action [against his wife] at all."[9] The court reasoned that the state Code related solely to property and contract rights, and thus to interpret it as authorizing the assault and battery claim would be to "make a departure from the common law so radical, and so opposed to its general policy, as the authorization of a suit by the husband or wife against the other for injuries to the person or

---

1 DE FUNIAK & VAUGHN, PRINCIPLES OF COMMUNITY PROPERTY, *supra* Chapter 1, at § 151, n98.

2 Edward J. Imwinkelried, *Spousal Relationship, in* THE NEW WIGMORE: A TREATISE ON EVIDENCE: EVIDENTIARY PRIVILEGES § 6.21 (2013), citing COKE, A COMMENTARY UPON LITTLETON § 6b (1628) and J. WIGMORE, EVIDENCE, § 2227, at 2112 (McNaughton rev. 1961).

3 Imwinkelreid, *supra*, at § 6.21, citing Richard A. Posner, *An Economic Approach to the Law of Evidence*, 51 Stan. L. Rev. 1477 (1999).

4 Imwinkelreid, *supra*, at § 6.21, citing CHARLES A. WRIGHT & KENNETH W. GRAHAM, JR., FEDERAL PRACTICE AND PROCEDURE: EVIDENCE § 5572, at 482 (1989).

5 *Burke v. Mass. Bonding & Ins. Co.*, 19 So. 2d 647 (La. App. 1944).

6 *Windauer v. O'Connor*, 107 Ariz. 267, 485 P.2d 1157 (S.Ct. 1971).

7 *See Romero v. Romero*, 58 N.M. 201, 269 P.2d 748 (S.Ct. 1954), overruled by *Maestas*, *supra*.

8 *Peters*, *supra*.

9 *Id.*

character."[10] The *Peters* court's concern with the common law was obviously misplaced since California has been a community property jurisdiction since the state's inception.

In 1962, the California Supreme Court abolished the doctrine of spousal immunity for intentional and negligent torts. In *Self v. Self*, one spouse sued the other for assault and battery, just as the injured husband in *Peters* had done.[11] The *Self* court rejected the instrumentalist view of the spousal tort immunity doctrine, as well as the *Peters v. Peters* rationale. *Self* announced the rule that one spouse may sue another for an intentional tort, even in the absence of a statute authorizing the suit. In *Klein v. Klein*, spousal immunity was abolished in negligence cases.[12]

In a lawsuit involving a married person, the related question of the marital confidential communication privilege may arise. Generally, a spouse has a privilege not to disclose confidential marital communications made by the other spouse. This includes not being required to testify against a spouse in a criminal proceeding, and not being called as an adverse witness against a spouse.

Specifically, Cal. Evid. Code § 980 provides that **"a spouse (or his guardian or conservator . . .) whether or not a party, has a privilege during the marital relationship and afterwards to refuse to disclose, and to prevent another from disclosing, a communication if he claims the privilege and the communication was made in confidence between him and the other spouse while they were husband and wife."** Likewise, in a criminal proceeding or any other proceeding brought by a third party against a spouse, **"a married person has a privilege not to testify against his [or her] spouse in any proceeding."** And, a married person **"has a privilege not to be called as a witness by an adverse party to that proceeding without the prior express consent of the spouse having the privilege under this section unless the party calling the spouse does so in good faith without knowledge of the marital relationship."**

Wyoming — a common law jurisdiction — adopted a marital confidential communication privilege similar to Cal. Evid. Code § 980.[13] *Curran v. Pasek*, a case widely cited in the treatise literature, is instructive.[14] In *Curran*, a physician shared confidential marital communications with his spouse about his daily marijuana use. When the physician committed suicide, marijuana was found in his possession. During the suicide investigation, the surviving spouse commented to the sheriff about her deceased husband's marijuana use. Later, in a medical malpractice case against the deceased physician, a witness in federal court subpoenaed the physician's surviving spouse. The physician's personal representative moved to quash the subpoena. The U.S. Magistrate for the District of Wyoming denied the motion. The personal representative appealed to the U.S. District Court.

---

[10] *Id.* at 36.

[11] *Self, supra.*

[12] *Klein, supra.*

[13] Wyo. Stat. Ann. § 1-12-101(a) (1988). This privilege does not exist when one spouse is convicted of a crime against the other, as provided in Wyo. Stat. Ann. § 1-12-104 (1988).

[14] *Curran v. Pasek*, 886 P.2d 272 (Wyo. 1994).

The U.S. District Court asked the Wyoming Supreme Court to clarify the relationship between the codified confidential marital communication privilege and the codified privilege of spousal immunity. The court answered that the confidential marital communication privilege survives the death of either spouse; and it is available to both spouses. But the confidential marital communication privilege must first be or have been waived by the party-spouse against whom the confidential marital communication will be used. Only then is the non-party spouse free to testify. *Rogers v. State* subsequently held that no marital privilege exists for either spouse when one is alleged to have committed a crime against the other spouse, and in fact one spouse can compel the other to testify.[15]

Parallel principles hold in California. Only if and when the party-spouse has waived the marital confidential communication privilege may the non-party spouse elect to assert or waive the privilege of spousal immunity.

An exception exists when one spouse sues the other spouse. Cal. Evid. Code § 984 provides that: **"there is no privilege under this article in: (a) A proceeding brought by or on behalf of one spouse against the other spouse."**

That rule is clear enough. But what happens in a criminal proceeding in which one spouse is accused of a crime against the other? And what happens if the criminal proceeding might be the basis for a later civil tort claim by one spouse against the other?

Cal. Evid. Code § 972 provides:

> [a] **married person does not have a privilege under this article in: . . . a criminal proceeding in which one spouse is charged with:**
>
> **(1) A crime against the person or property of the other spouse or . . . cohabitant of either, whether committed before or during marriage.**
>
> **(2) A crime against the person or property of a third person committed in the course of committing a crime against the person or property of the other spouse, whether committed before or during marriage.**
>
> **(3) Bigamy.**
>
> **(4) Specified criminal acts that occurred prior to marriage.**
>
> **(5) Actions to enforce child or spousal support, so long as property and debts of the marriage have not been adjudicated.**

California appears to be leading the way in developing case law on domestic torts. So far, three claim categories emerge from the statutes and case law:

- Domestic violence protective orders and monetary awards;
- Interspousal torts, statutory and common law; and
- Community property impairment claims — discussed in Chapter 10.

---

[15] *Rogers v. State*, 189 P.3d 265 (Wyo. 2008).

Interspousal tort claims may be pursued during marriage, independent of a dissolution proceeding, or consolidated with a pending dissolution. They may also be pursued after a final judgment of dissolution. Authority for consolidation comes from Cal. Civ. Proc. Code § 1048. It rests on judicial discretion, in actions involving a "**[c]ommon question of law or fact . . . pending before the court**" to "**order a joint hearing or trial of any of all the matters in issue in actions . . . .**" The statutory rationale is to "**[a]void unnecessary costs or delays.**" However, California Rules of Court 5.104 does not permit a tort action to be joined with or pleaded in a dissolution action.

A three year statute of limitations applies to domestic abuse actions, as set forth in Cal. Civ. Proc. Code § 340.15. The action must be commenced either "**within three years from the date of the last act of domestic violence**" or "**within three years from the date the plaintiff discovers or reasonably should have discovered that an injury of illness resulted from an act of domestic violence by the defendant against the plaintiff.**"

Cal. Civ. Proc. Code § 340.15 was the subject of *Pugliese v. Superior Court*, where the court held that the continuing tort doctrine applied to the tort of domestic violence; and that the battered spouse was permitted to recover damages for acts of domestic violence that occurred more than three years prior to the battered party's civil complaint.[16] In *Pugliese*, the plaintiff, arguing domestic abuse over a period of 15 years, was permitted to recover damages for all acts of domestic violence that occurred during the marriage, *subject to proof of a continuous course of abusive conduct*. After *Pugliese*, any suit related to continuing abuse must be filed within three years of the last act of domestic violence.[17]

Any recovery obtained by an injured spouse from the other spouse is characterized upon receipt as the separate property of that person under § 781(c). To meet the tort liability, the tortfeasor spouse's separate property (if any) is marshaled first, pursuant to § 782, which provides: the community property "**[m]ay not be used to discharge the liability of the tortfeasor spouse to the injured spouse . . .** [unless] **the injured spouse gives written consent thereto after the occurrence of the injury.**" And § 782(c) clarifies that the above provision does not affect the right to indemnity provided by an insurance to discharge the tortfeasor spouse's liability.

For an act of domestic violence perpetrated by one spouse against the other, if there is no reachable separate property, a court has discretion in a pending legal separation or dissolution proceeding to enforce a judgment for civil damages against the tortfeasor spouse's one-half share of the community property. The discretionary authority to grant such relief appears at § 2603.5.

For a negligent tort, a judgment may be satisfied from a general comprehensive liability policy.[18] Insurers are not prohibited from seeking indemnification under § 782(c).

---

16 *Pugliese, supra.*

17 *Id.*

18 *See* Chapter 10, n11.

§ 11.02 DOMESTIC VIOLENCE PROTECTIVE ORDERS AND MONETARY CLAIMS

California adopted the Prevention of Domestic Violence Act, which may be cited as the Domestic Violence Prevention Act [DVPA], as Division 10 of the Family Code in 1993. The DVPA consolidates the former Family Law Act, the Domestic Violence Prevention Act, and the Uniform Parentage Act. The DVPA appears at §§ 6200–6409.[19] The DVPA governs the issuance of restraining orders intended to prevent domestic violence. Petitions for restraining orders may be issued in a DVPA proceeding or in a dissolution, nullity, or legal separation proceeding.[20] Approved mandatory and optional forms are available through the California Judicial Council.

During the continuance of the marriage, a DVPA restraining order can have a direct impact on one or both spouses' rights of management and control of community property, real or personal.

For purposes of the DVPA, **"domestic violence"** is defined by §6211 as abuse that has or could be perpetrated against a *spouse* or *former spouse*, or cohabitant or former cohabitant. This definition is drawn from the definition of domestic violence in Cal. Penal Code § 13700. A cohabitant is defined by § 6209 as a person who regularly resides in the same household as the plaintiff. Persons in an *engagement or dating relationship*, including in a *romantic or romantically friendly relationship*; co-parents; a child of a party or a child who is the subject of a paternity action; or any other person related to the plaintiff by consanguinity or affinity to the second degree. Affinity is defined at § 6205 as **"the connection existing in consequence of marriage between each of the married persons and the blood relatives of the other."** Household means "those who dwell under the same roof and compose a family, also a social unit comprised of those living together in the same dwelling."[21]

Where there is domestic violence, a civil emergency protective order [EPO] can be requested by a peace officer, based on DVPA § 6251 grounds.[22] The standard of proof for an EPO, also under § 6251, is that there is an immediate and present danger of abuse, abduction or stalking. Protective orders are for the purpose of preventing future acts of abuse, abduction, or stalking. Generally, an EPO is more restrictive of the restrained person than is a party-initiated restraining or protective order: Firearms and ammunition are automatically prohibited, and immediate exclusion from the residence can be ordered if the respondent lives with the petitioner.[23]

An EPO may not be issued solely on allegations of financial abuse.[24]

---

[19] For an element-by-element discussion of DVPA issues, see, e.g., Cherri N. Allison et al., Domestic Violence Remedies in California Family Law Cases (2007).

[20] *See* Cal. Fam. Code §§ 2045 (ex parte protective orders), 2047 (protective orders; restraining orders; mutual protective orders, 2049 (protective orders included in judgments; restraining orders).

[21] *O'Kane v. Irvine*, 47 Cal. App. 4th 207, 209, 212, 54 Cal. Rptr. 2d 549 (Cal. App. Ct., 1st Dist. 1996).

[22] Cal. Fam. Code §§ 6261, 6240.

[23] Cal. Fam. Code §§ 6389, 6321.

[24] Cal. Fam. Code § 6250(d).

[A] The DVPA Temporary Restraining Order

A party may initiate the DVPA protection process by petitioning for a temporary restraining order [TRO] against another person. An ex parte TRO may be issued on the same day as filed on proof of a past act or acts of abuse; again, with the purpose of preventing future acts of abuse.[25] No statute requires that the past act(s) of abuse have occurred within a specific time frame, which leaves it to the judge to exercise discretion to grant or deny a TRO, depending on the individual facts of the case. A TRO is valid until the date of the hearing, which is not later than 21 days from the date of the order or 25 days if good cause is shown to the court.[26] A TRO can be issued without notice to the other party; but a copy of the TRO and hearing notice must be served on the responding party.

Generally, § 241 provides: ***"Except as provided in Section 6300,* an** [ex parte order] **may not be granted without notice to the respondent unless it appears from the facts shown by the affidavit in support of the application for the order, or in the application for the order that great or irreparable injury would result to the applicant before the matter can be heard on notice."**[27] However, the "great or irreparable injury" standard for no notice under § 241 does not apply to ex parte orders issued under § 6300. Instead, under § 6300 ex parte petitions are considered for **"reasonable proof of a past act or acts of abuse."**

In a DVPA hearing, the court has broad discretion to grant or deny the petition for a protective order; but that discretion "is not unfettered" insofar as "a DVPA restraining order must be based on a finding that the party being restrained committed one or more acts of domestic abuse."[28] At the petition hearing, the standard is this: A court may exercise its discretion to issue a temporary restraining order if there is evidence, as required by the statute, of **"reasonable proof of a past act or acts of abuse"**; an order denying the petition must include the reasons for denying the petition.[29] A court of appeal applies the substantial evidence standard of review.[30]

"Abuse" is defined in § 6203 as any of the following:

- Intentionally or recklessly causing bodily injury;
- Sexual assault;
- Stalking;
- Placing a person in **"reasonable apprehension of imminent serious bodily injury to that person or to another"**; or

---

[25] Cal. Fam. Code § 6300.

[26] Cal. Fam. Code § 242(a).

[27] Cal. Fam. Code § 241; *see also* Cal. Fam. Code § 240 et. seq.

[28] *S.M. v. E.P.*, 184 Cal. App. 4th 1249, 1264, 1267, 109 Cal. Rptr. 3d 792 (Cal. App. Ct., 4th Dist. 2010) (trial court 's restraining order reversed on appeal where the trial court issued a DVPA restraining order but found that restrained party had not committed an act of domestic abuse.)

[29] Cal. Fam. Code §§ 6300, 6320.5 (which codifies *Nakamura v. Parker*, 156 Cal. App. 4th 327, 67 Cal. Rptr. 3d 286 (Cal. App. Ct., 1st Dist. 2007)).

[30] *Sabbah v. Sabbah*, 151 Cal. App. 4th 818, 822, 60 Cal. Rptr. 3d 175 (Cal. App. Ct., 4th Dist. 2007).

- Engaging in any behavior that is or could be enjoined pursuant to § 6320, the code section on ex parte orders enjoining contact. This code provision enjoins **"disturbing the peace of the other party,"** discussed in § 11.02[D]. This phrase is broad enough to reach financial abuse.

Thus, a trial court has discretion, under § 6320, to issue **"an ex parte order enjoining a party from molesting, attacking, striking, stalking, threatening, sexually assaulting, battering, . . . harassing,** [or] **telephoning"** another party. This list includes but is not limited to **"annoying telephone calls . . . destroying personal property, contacting, either directly or indirectly by mail or otherwise, coming within a specified distance of, or disturbing the peace of the other party."** Annoying telephone calls are described at length in Cal. Penal Code § 653m, where they are listed as a misdemeanor criminal offense. Annoying phone calls include contact by telephone or **"by means of an electronic communication device"** such as texting, e-mailing, or by other medium including the Internet. Under § 6320(b), restraining orders can extend to **"the exclusive care, possession, or control of any animal owned, possessed, leased, kept, or held by either the petitioner or the respondent or a minor child residing"** in the family dwelling. Effective July 1, 2014, § 6320(a) is amended to include as grounds for the granting of an ex parte order **"credibly impersonating"** and **"falsely personating"** the petitioning party.

Mutual restraining orders may be issued, but they are subject to additional requirements, as set forth in § 6305. Both parties must personally appear, both parties must present written evidence of past abuse or domestic violence, and the court must make **"detailed findings of fact indicating that both parties acted primarily as aggressors and that neither party acted primarily in self defense."**

In *J.J. v. M.F.*, the appellate court held that the trial court's issuance of a mutual restraining order was an abuse of discretion where a mother [J.J.] pushed the father [M.F.] during an altercation while protecting her son.[31] On appeal, M.F. contested the issuance of the TRO against him on the ground that there was no record of past abuse on his part. J.J. contested the mutual nature of the TRO for the same reason. The trial court determined that there was a past history of abuse by M.F. against J.J; as well as by J.J. against M.F. Past acts of abuse by M.F. against J.J. were well documented. M.F. had "pushed [J.J.] out of the car, pushed her through a glass door, and sent her threatening text messages saying he was going to 'f — ' her up, among other things."[32] As for J.J.'s conduct, the trial court specifically found that J.J. made repeated calls to M.F.'s phone, and pushed M.F. on the night in question. A mutual restraining order was issued on the basis of these findings. J.J. appealed.

The court of appeal affirmed that M.F. had a history of past abuse. The court next analyzed the issue of whether J.J.'s repeated phone calls to M.F. could be the basis for the mutual restraining order. The issue turned on whether J.J.'s phone calls were made with the intent to harass. On the night of the altercation, J.J. made numerous (approximately 20) missed phone calls on M.F.'s cell phone after he

---

[31] *J.J. v. M.F.*, 223 Cal. App. 4th 968, 167 Cal. Rptr. 3d 670 (Cal. App. Ct., 2d Dist. 2014).

[32] *Id.* at 973.

dropped off their child at J.J.'s grandmother's home. The evidence showed that J.J.'s intention was to reach M.F. so that he could turn around and retrieve their child's jacket. The child was sick, the night was cold, and the child had only one jacket to wear to daycare the next day. The reviewing court concluded that J.J. made the phone calls in good faith. Therefore, J.J.'s repeated phone calls were not a proper basis for issuing a restraining order against her.

Next, the court of appeal found that substantial evidence did not support a finding that J.J. acted primarily as an aggressor and not in self-defense when she pushed M.F. On the issue of whether J.J.'s act of pushing M.F. was an act of past abuse upon which a DVPA restraining order could be based, the court concluded: "Given this dispute, his history of physical abuse, and his threats to harm her, [J.J.] reasonably believed [M.F.] might do her harm when he came at her and yelled to her to hand over their son. The force she used to push him away was not excessive, as neither he nor she said he was harmed by the push." Even so, J.J. had a right to use **"any necessary force . . . to protect the person or property of** [herself] **or of a child,"** under Cal. Civ. Code § 50.

TROs can retrain a number of activities such as:[33]

- Personal conduct, including the management and control of property;
- Protection of animals;
- Stay-away orders;
- Residence exclusion[34] where **"the court determines, regardless of which party holds legal or equitable title or is the lessee of the dwelling"** that a showing has been made of all three conditions following:
  - o **". . . the party who will stay in the dwelling has a right under color of law to possession of the premises."**
  - o **"That the party to be excluded has assaulted or threatens to assault the other party . . . ."**
  - o **"That physical or emotional harm would otherwise result to the other party . . ."**
- Other restraints necessary to effectuate the court's order;
- Prohibiting public address disclosure;
- Temporary custody and visitation of minor child;
- Prohibitions from taking action to locate a protected party;
- Firearm possession and ownership;
- Ammunition possession, custody, control.

As to firearms and ammunition possession, federal law and California law coexist, and both can apply to a given situation. Federal law does not preempt California statutory law unless there is a direct and positive conflict between the

---

[33] Judges Guide to Domestic Violence Cases, F. 2.23 Reference Chart: Temporary Restraining Order.

[34] Cal. Fam. Code § 6321.

federal provision and the state law such that the two cannot be reconciled or consistently stand together.[35]

Procedures for obtaining domestic violence ex parte hearings are listed on county court websites. Forms are available in multiple languages.

[B] Intersection of DVPA Protective Orders and Property Management and Control

Protective orders, including those issued ex parte, can directly impact a spouse's right to management and control of community property.

An ex parte order can be issued specific to the management and control of real or personal property. If so, § 6324 provides that the order may determine **"the temporary use, possession, and control of real or personal property of the parties and the payment of any liens or encumbrances coming due during the period the order is in effect."** An ex parte order may also determine or restrain a married person's or a registered domestic partner's access to and management rights over community property, quasi-community property, quasi-marital property, and commingled separate property.

Additionally, the express language of § 2045, which applies during the pendency of the proceeding, gives a court authority to restrain either spouse's powers of disposition over community personal property (§ 1101) and community real property (§ 1102) including but not limited to:

> **[t]ransferring, encumbering, hypothecating, concealing, or in any way disposing of any property, real or personal, whether community, quasi-community, or separate, except in the usual course of business or for the necessities of life, and if the order is directed against a party, requiring that party to notify the other party of any proposed extraordinary expenditures and to account to the court for all extraordinary expenditures.**

Abuse under the DVPA is broadly defined to connect past acts of abuse with current threats for the purpose of preventing future acts. Restraining orders (in theory) ensure a period of separation between the parties. Abuse often involves physical contact, but non-physical acts can also form the basis for an ex parte domestic violence restraining order specific to real and personal property. Thus, for example, fear of imminent offensive contact, imminent apprehension of offensive sexual battery, and imminent apprehension of any conduct, including financial abuse, that disturbs the peace and calm of the threatened spouse can provide a factual basis for petitioning for a domestic violence restraining order. Such an order may and likely will result in a residence exclusion provision, which is a judicial determination about who has the exclusive right to remain in the dwelling, and who has liability for rent or mortgage payments. It can also determine future access to available financial resources.

---

[35] *See* 18 U.S.C. § 927; *Helmer v. Miller*, 19 Cal. App. 4th 1565, 1572, 25 Cal. Rptr. 2d 8 (Cal. App. Ct., 4th Dist. 1993); Cal. Penal Code § 298000(a).

Under § 6321, a court may issue an order "**excluding a party from the family dwelling . . . regardless of which party holds legal or equitable title or is the lessee of the dwelling.**" But under § 6301, the right to bring a petition continues even if the petitioner should decide to vacate the family dwelling.[36]

In the marriage context, once a domestic violence restraining order is obtained, §§ 1100(e) and 2040(d)(2) require that either spouse continue to meet Family Code fiduciary duties as to community property until service of a reciprocal temporary restraining order to the contrary is issued. A domestic violence restraining order will specifically describe the way or ways in which the restrained spouse's legal rights to manage and control specific assets are altered for the period during which the TRO is in effect.

The DVPA recognizes that financial constraints make victims of domestic abuse more likely to stay in abusive relationships and circumstances. Through § 2045, it also implicitly recognizes that financial control may be key to seeking safety. Therefore, in addition to community property determinations, spousal and child support may be ordered as part of the restraining order process. To aid the court in this matter an Income and Expense Declaration and a Property Declaration must be filed and served. These declarations should be current, meaning completed within the last three months, and specific. The forms for such declarations require disclosure of and as to accounts (all of which are subject to CAMPAL, as discussed in Chapter 5).

At dissolution, in setting spousal support under § 4320, "**[a]ny history of domestic violence**" may be considered by the court. Additionally, case law holds that there is a rebuttable presumption *against* ordering spousal support for a spouse who has been convicted of domestic violence.[37] A finding of domestic violence can affect the restrained party's child custody rights.

[C] Property Destruction During an Altercation

While § 1100(a) confers on either spouse absolute powers of disposition over community personal property, this power does not include within it the right to vandalize the community property. *People v. Wallace* is a criminal case on point. In *Wallace*, the court affirmed that the intentional destruction of separate or community property by a spouse inside the marital home is within the scope of felony vandalism.[38]

Wallace involved a situation where one spouse returned home to find the criminal defendant-spouse smoking crack cocaine. An altercation ensued, during which the defendant-spouse intentionally destroyed commingled real property and community personal property. The defendant was charged with felony vandalism. His defense was that a married person cannot be guilty of vandalizing property

---

[36] Cal. Fam. Code § 6301.

[37] *Marriage of Cauley*, 138 Cal. App. 4th 1100, 41 Cal. Rptr. 3d 902 (Cal. App. Ct., 6th Dist. 2006).

[38] *People v. Wallace*, 123 Cal. App. 4th 144, 19 Cal. Rptr. 3d 790 (Cal. App. Ct., 5th Dist. 2004) (destruction of community real and personal property took place inside the family home).

inside of a marital home because "a person's home is his or her castle."[39] The court of appeal rejected the defendant's argument, as it had been requested to do by the California Attorney General citing the rationale that "the criminal law protects each owner's interest in community property against nonconsensual damage by the other." The court went on to say that the essence of the crime of vandalism, in the context of marriage, lies in the prohibited physical acts that are taken by one spouse against the other spouse's property, as well as against the other spouse's *ownership interest in the community property*. This rationale applies when the victim and defendant are community property owners of the vandalized property. And it applies whether the vandalism takes place inside or outside of the family home.[40]

DVPA monetary relief is discretionary. Its purpose is to prevent future acts of abuse, not to address proximate harm caused by past acts of abuse. Past harm is addressed either by a civil tort claim or by a criminal proceeding.

The main difference between the DVPA and a tort claim lies in the relief obtainable. Tort recoveries can include general, specific and punitive damages: These include damages for pain and suffering. The DVPA, by contrast, allows monetary awards, spousal support, and child support. Monetary awards are restitutionary under § 6342: When a TRO is issued, restitution is given for lost earnings and out-of-pocket expenses related to the factual findings upon which the TRO was granted. When the TRO is denied, the respondent is owed restitution by the petitioner for out-of-pocket expenses related to responding to the TRO. Any public or private entities that are brought into the matter are due restitution; so too is any batterer's program that the respondent have been assigned to.

To reiterate, monetary awards under the DVPA are limited to: the abused spouse's immediate costs in applying for the restraining order, including any legal fees; compensation for lost earnings; out-of-pocket family expenses such as medical care, temporary housing and transportation; child support; and, under § 6341, necessary spousal support.

In conclusion, abuse is traditionally understood as an act of physical violence or the threat of physical violence by one spouse against the other spouse's person. The DVPA relies on this definition, but then expands it in important ways. Thus, upon proof of a past act or acts of domestic violence, a temporary restraining order may be granted ex parte to enjoin the respondent. The respondent is restrained so as to address direct acts of abuse as well as to enjoin acts that disturb or agitate the other person, or that destroy that person's peace.

DVPA proceedings examine the current situation for purposes of affecting the future. This makes the DVPA process as fluid as the circumstances that give rise to the need for seeking protection in the first place. So for example, intentionally breaking a physical lock or boundary can provide a factual basis for domestic violence restraining order, it can lead to a protective order excluding a party from

---

[39] *Id.*

[40] *People v. Kahanic*, 196 Cal. App. 3d 461, 241 Cal. Rptr 722 (Cal. App. Ct., 5th Dist. 1987) (destruction of property took place outside of the home).

the family dwelling, it can lead to a related DVPA monetary award, *and* it can give rise to a tort claim or a criminal charge.

Example 11.1: This example illustrates the fact-sensitive nature of the DVPA restraining order process. The spouses are amicably living physically separate and apart. The *spouses have no history of domestic violence.* Both have access to the dwelling for purposes of co-parenting their children. One day, one spouse returns to the dwelling to find the other spouse installing a deadbolt lock on the front door. (The removal of a lock constitutes breaking a lock; and it can give rise to a trespass claim depending on the circumstances.) The nonresident spouse explains that there was a burglary next door so it seemed important to install a deadbolt lock, since the landlord would not. At that time, the nonresident spouse hands the resident spouse all of the keys, including duplicate keys, to the deadbolt lock and leaves. The resident spouse responds with gratitude for installing a deadbolt lock. This is not a factual scenario that could (or should) give rise to a restraining order against the party who broke the original lock.

Example 11.2: This example also illustrates the fact-sensitive nature of the domestic violence petition process. When the spouses separate, the respondent has one past act of abuse in their history. The spouse who signed the lease leaves the family dwelling, the other remains. One day, the resident spouse returns home to find the other spouse installing a deadbolt lock on the front door of the family dwelling. The resident spouse becomes angry and fearful. The nonresident spouse responds by shouting: "I need to keep an eye on you, and plus the lease is in my name, so I'll give you one key and keep the duplicates!" The nonresident spouse throws a key at the resident spouse, and then storms off, in possession of the duplicate keys, with a threatening, "I'll be back!" The resident spouse petitions for a DVPA order excluding the nonresident spouse from the dwelling. On these facts, given the respondent's past act of domestic violence, the breaking of a lock, the retention of duplicate keys, the assault, the implied threat of future harm, and the disturbance of the petitioner's peace, a court would be well within its discretionary rights to issue a DVPA restraining order against the respondent, notwithstanding the fact that the nonresident's name is on the lease.

Examples 11.1 and 11.2 are qualitatively different for purposes of the DVPA. In Example 11.1, there is no past history of abuse, there is no present altercation, there is no discernible fear of imminent or future harm on either spouse's part; the nonresident spouse's act of installing a deadbolt lock on the family apartment is regarded by the other spouse as helpful, not as a trespass. Moreover, in Example 11.1, the nonresident spouse relinquishes possession of all original and duplicate keys to the resident spouse in an act of recognition that the resident spouse has exclusive control over the dwelling.

In Example 11.2, by contrast, there is a past act of abuse. Under the DVPA, one or more past acts of abuse justify the court's exercise of discretion to issue a TRO. In Example 11.2, in addition to a past act of domestic abuse, there is present conduct involving trespass, vandalism, and verbal assault. These actions on the part of the respondent leave the petitioner surprised, upset, angry, and reasonably fearful about the respondent's current and possibly future trespass, vandalism, assault, and battery, not to mention stalking and other related worries that breach the petitioner's peace. The respondent has broken a physical lock, trespassed onto the petitioner's premises, installed a deadbolt lock, retained the duplicate keys of that deadbolt lock, implicitly threatened the resident spouse with surveillance, expressed anger in an assaultive way, and implied future physical threats. All of these actions, particularly in light of the parties' history of domestic violence, compel that the resident spouse's petition for a protective order be granted notwithstanding the fact of the lease.

[D] Disturbing the Peace

Stalking is one possible basis for DVPA relief, either in the form of an EPO or a TRO initiated by the petitioner.

The California civil jury instruction for stalking under Cal. Civ. Code § 1708.7 defines **"harass"** to mean **"[a] knowing and willful course of conduct directed at a specific person which seriously alarms, annoys, torments or terrorizes the person, and which serves no legitimate purpose. The course of conduct must be such as would cause a reasonable person to suffer substantial emotional distress, and must actually cause substantial emotional distress to the person."**[41]

Emotional and mental abuse are each a basis for a restraining order. "Peace," as the court of appeal noted in *Marriage of Nadkarni*, discussed below, has to do with "'freedom from anxiety, disturbance (emotional, mental or spiritual), or inner conflict . . . . Thus, the plain meaning of the phrase 'disturbing the peace of the other party' in section 6320 may be properly understood as conduct that destroys the mental or emotional calm of the other party."[42]

An annoying phone call for purposes of the Penal Code is a misdemeanor offense that extends to any annoying electronic contact. Contact is typically directed at a person, but it also can be contact with third parties *about* a person. The use of a third person's electronic device to establish the annoying contact is a misdemeanor offense, even if the annoying telephone call did not come from the abuser's own electronic device. An annoying call can include obscene language, threats to the person, or threats to property. Obscenity is defined by its common dictionary meaning.[43] Contact may occur through a conversation; however, annoying telephone contact need not result in a conversation.

Initiating electronic contact can form the basis of a DVPA restraining order. Phone (or electronic device) tag can be the basis for an annoying phone call as well. This is because the Penal Code explicitly covers situations where the abusive party did not initiate the phone call in which person-to-person contact was actually or eventually made. Thus, given the Penal Code definition, calling and leaving a message to return a call may be the basis of DVPA relief if — when the return call

---

[41] California Civil Jury Instructions, BAJI 7.58, Stalking (Spring 2013).

[42] *Marriage of Nadkarni*, 173 Cal. App. 4th 1483, 93 Cal. Rptr. 3d 723 (Cal. App. Ct., 6th Dist. 2009).

[43] *People v. Hernandez*, 231 Cal. App. 3d 1376, 1384, 283 Cal. Rptr. 81 (Cal. App. Ct., 2d Dist. 1991) (holding that Penal Code § 653m does not violate the U.S. Constitution, 1st Amendment, and upholding trial court instruction to the jury defining obscene in its common usage as "offensive to one's feelings, or to prevailing notions of modesty or decency; lewd").

is made — the contact escalates into an annoying phone call.

Disturbing the mental and emotional calm of the other party is a form of abuse, even if the disturbance does not arise from actual physical contact, injury, or assault. This is relevant information for purposes of restraining financial conduct as a form of abuse.

Marriage of Nadkarni is the case on point.[44]

In *Nadkarni,* the parties obtained their final dissolution judgment in 2005, after which they remained involved in a child custody dispute. In 2007, the former husband accessed his former wife's e-mail account without her permission. By so doing he obtained copies of his former wife's e-mails, including some between his former wife and her business associates and attorney. The former husband copied the illegally obtained e-mails as attachments to documents that he then presented to the trial court in the child custody matter. He testified that he understood that the e-mails were illegally obtained, but that he had accessed his former wife's electronic communications for the safety of his children. He also claimed that he had no intention of sharing the e-mails with any persons not involved in the child custody proceedings. The former wife petitioned for a restraining order under DVPA. Petitioner alleged that the respondent's behavior constituted abuse under § 6203, which incorporates the § 6320 definition of abuse as including **"disturbing the peace of the other party."** The trial court granted a TRO prohibiting the respondent from accessing her e-mails; all other related conduct was also restrained. The responded filed a motion to show cause. At the show cause hearing the trial court dismissed the DVPA restraining order on the ground that the DVPA definition of abuse required a disturbance of the peace to be physical in nature. The petitioner appealed on this issue.

The court of appeal reversed. It ruled that the DVPA expressly authorizes a restraining order to enjoin **"disturbing the peace of the other party."** The petitioner's application for a restraining order was based on allegations that the respondent had disturbed her mental and emotional calm by accessing, reading, and publicly disclosing the password-protected content of her e-mails and confidential e-mails; "that respondent's behavior had resulted in shock and embarrassment to the petitioner"; that the respondent's veiled threats about limiting (or not) the publication of the illegally obtained e-mails led the petitioner to fear for the destruction of her business relationships; and that the petitioner was in fear for her safety. The court of appeal agreed with the trial court that no physical abuse was involved. Nevertheless the court of appeal interpreted the respondent's conduct as "conduct of destroying the mental and emotional calm of his former wife." As such, the respondent's act of accessing the petitioner's password protected e-mail without her permission fell under the § 6320 prohibition on **"disturbing the peace of the other party."**

Nadkarni affirms that the DVPA definition of abuse includes nonphysical acts that disturb the peace of the petitioner. Thus nonphysical acts of domestic abuse

[44] *Nadkarni, supra,* at 1497.

can be the basis for a TRO.[45]

Burquet v. Brumbaugh further clarifies the definition of non-physical abuse laid out *Nadkarni*.[46]

In *Burquet*, petitioner applied for a domestic violence ex parte restraining order against a former dating partner. Petitioner showed that she had terminated the relationship, but that the respondent could not accept that fact. Respondent repeatedly contacted petitioner between June and October of 2012, despite her requests that he not do so. In these communications, respondent persisted with inappropriate sexual innuendos and pleas "beseeching her to renew their intimate relationship."[47] Whenever the petitioner asked the respondent to stop contacting her, he responded with anger. The respondent finally stopped seeking physical contact, but he persisted in contacting the petitioner with e-mail and text messages. Several months later, the respondent showed up on the petitioner's porch unannounced and uninvited. The petitioner asked the respondent to leave. She testified: "He got angry. He started saying in a very — in a loud voice 'I love you, I don't know, I'm sorry.'"[48] The petitioner also testified that she felt frightened. She asked the respondent to leave, but he paced around the porch for about 10 minutes and then called her and "asked her not to be scared, but she was scared because he was angry." Respondent had a history of past acts of abuse toward the petitioner: On two prior occasions, he had expressed anger with physical force directed against the petitioner. The trial court exercised its discretion in favor of granting a TRO. After the hearing, the court later granted the TRO on the ground that the respondent had disturbed the petitioner's peace and tranquility. The trial court relied on *Nadkarni*.[49] Respondent appealed.

Nadkarni defined abuse, for purposes of § 6320, in such a way that "the requisite abuse need not be actual physical injury or assault."[50] Respondent challenged this legal definition. He argued that the correct definition for disturbing the peace should be taken from Cal. Penal Code § 415: "[T]he disruption of public order by acts that are themselves violent or that tend to incite violence." Under the Penal Code definition of disturbance of the peace, the respondent argued, there was insufficient evidence to support a finding that respondent had disturbed the peace, and as a consequence insufficient evidence to grant a DVPA restraining order against him.

The court of appeal rejected the respondent's legal theory. Instead, it affirmed the trial court's decision to grant the restraining order based on the *Nadkarni* interpretation of **"disturbing the peace of the other party"** under § 6320. The court of appeal explained that "the plain meaning of the phrase 'disturbing the peace of the other party' in section § 6320 may be properly understood as conduct that destroys the mental or emotional calm of the other party." The DVPA

[45] *Nadkarni*, *supra*, at 1496–98.

[46] *Burquet v. Brumbaugh*, 223 Cal. App. 4th 1140, 167 Cal. Rptr. 3d 664 (Cal. App. Ct., 2d Dist. 2014).

[47] *Burquet*, *supra*, at 1142.

[48] *Id.*

[49] *Nadkarni*, *supra*, at 1495.

[50] *Id.*

definition of disturbing the peace may be physical, but it need not be. A broad interpretation of disturbing the peace as including physical and nonphysical disturbances, the court said, comports with the Legislative history of the DVPA as it was enacted in 1993. Thus the DVPA definition of disturbing the peace is broader than the Penal Code definition of that same term.

Electronic realities have increased the likelihood of nonphysical domestic abuse, especially related to family or individual finances. But where is the line between stalking and searching?

Whether an electronic search of information about another person is legal or not depends upon the parties' expectations of privacy, as well as on whether there has been a past invasion of privacy. For example, information obtained from a Google search is legally obtained and admissible. Thus, Google searches can be the basis for determining issues about the management and control of community real or personal property. Any information about assets discovered in another state from a Google search, to give another example, is legally obtained and admissible in a court proceeding. Once admitted, that evidence can then be used to bring dissolution of the asset under the court's jurisdiction as quasi-community property. Wrongful manipulation of public search engines, however, can be the basis for a DVPA petition to enjoin stalking.

Searches of public company websites, including posted biographical and work-related information are legal. The spouse who is not employed by the company is legally within his or her rights to conduct a search of public company websites to determine, from public (non password-protected) information, what sort of deferred compensation or insurance benefits the employed spouse is or may be entitled to. A spouse may be able to glean from the other spouse's biographical puffery on a company website, or from a spouse's posted resume, whether undisclosed businesses, benefits, prizes, or other rewards have or will be acquired.

Searches of a spouse's computer browsing history are legal, but only if the search is made on a computer that is not password-protected. Observing a spouse's cell phone screen is legal, so long as the phone was not password-protected when the information was observed. Public pages of social network sites are searchable, so long as password-protected information is not accessed without the other spouse's permission. Photos — on any public website or social media site — that tag a spouse can be particularly useful by the other spouse to determine lapses in disclosure related to asset ownership or spousal support. For example, when one spouse threatens to drain community property bank accounts and is then tagged in a photo enjoying a separate vacation, or an undisclosed purchase like a new car, or new clothing, or a pied-à-terre, that electronic information is admissible in court and may — *if there is a history of abuse* — be the basis for a TRO. Moreover, the information may come from the spouse's social media site or from the sites of any person or persons linked to the surveilled spouse.

Stalking can be a series of physical acts, but electronic devices can also be used to stalk (i.e., to willfully, maliciously, and repeatedly follow another or harass another so as to cause fear or pose a threat). Secretly installing phone-locator GPS software to track the other spouse's physical movements, for example, is an electronic form of stalking. As such, it is abusive, tortious, and possibly criminal.

Likewise, secretly switching out a GPS device for the purpose of surveilling the other spouse is a form of stalking. Smartphones on a private account cannot be accessed, without prior permission; to do so may be a form of stalking, as well as a possible DVPA disturbance of peace. A smartphone that is one of several on a family account in the investigating spouse's name or in both spouses' names might be generally searchable by the account owner. But once the search crosses the line into obtaining password-protected information, it can become the basis for DVPA relief under § 6320, as well as the basis for a civil tort claim.

Accessing a spouse's *password-protected* electronic information, wherever that information is found (smartphone, hard drive, e-mail, facebook page, social media site, and so forth), is possible grounds for DVPA relief, a tort claim, and criminal liability.

Likewise, when one spouse installs keystroke software on a home computer to monitor the other spouse's password-protected activity, the evidence obtained is illegal and inadmissible because it derives from stalking. Importantly, however, the flipside is likely not true: Information obtained against the spouse who installed the keystroke software is admissible because it does not derive from stalking: A person cannot disturb his or her own peace for purposes of § 6320.

Upon a finding of abuse, the abused spouse can seek a DVPA TRO; a DVPA restitutionary monetary award to address the costs related to obtaining the restraining order; court costs; and necessary child and spousal support. Civil tort relief may also be available. Any money received or to be received that exceeds family expenses (for a DVPA claim) is the TRO petitioner's separate property under § 781(c). So too is a tort remedy. *See* Chapter 3.

Moreover, in a case involving domestic abuse, any monetary claims and tort damages that an injured spouse receives from the other spouse falls under the § 2603.5 definition of **"civil damages for an act of domestic violence by one spouse perpetrated against the other spouse."** Such a claim can be enforced against the perpetrator's one-half of the community property if a proceeding for dissolution of marriage or legal separation is pending and a final judgment has not yet been entered.

Example 11.3: This example illustrates the preventive and restitutionary nature of a DVPA monetary award. One spouse strikes the other in the face, resulting in injury. As a result, the injured spouse must take a medical leave of absence from work. Past acts of abuse are proved. Assume the DVPA petitioner is granted a restraining order against the respondent. The restraining order is intended to prevent future offensive contact; it can be phrased so as to exclude the respondent from the dwelling. Additionally, the petitioner is entitled to any monetary claims related to obtaining the restraining order, including attorney's fees, court costs, and necessary spousal and child support. Any part of the DVPA monetary award that does not go to family expenses is characterized as the petitioner's separate property.

§ 11.03 RELATED WRONGS: RESTRAINING ORDERS, TORTS, AND CRIMES

Cal. Civ. Code § 1708 states the general principle. **"Every person is bound, without contract, to abstain from injuring the person or property of another, or infringing upon any of his or her rights."** One spouse's common law or civil tort claim arises from the other spouse's tortious conduct, whether that conduct is directed toward the plaintiff's person, the plaintiff's identity, or the community property.

Interspousal torts are an important component of community property law. Potential tort causes of action must be considered by an attorney who is aware that his or her client has experienced, is experiencing, or is under imminent threat of experiencing domestic abuse.

Obviously, there are multiple potential common law and statutory civil tort actions. A (truly) non-exhaustive list might include: assault; battery; conversion; defamation; destruction of personal property; disparagement of title; false imprisonment; false light; fraud; fraudulent concealment of profits;[51] harmful or offensive contact; interference with business opportunity; harm to an animal; damages to personal property; imminent fear of harm; intentional infliction of emotional distress; intentional interference with contractual relations; interference with the payment of child support obligations, intentional interference with prospective economic relations; liability to a bystander, such as when one spouse observes the abuse of a child, or — as is all too common — the abuse of a companion animal;[52] loss of use of real property; malicious prosecution; negligent infliction of emotional distress; negligent transmission of HIV; negligent transmission of an STD; offensive contact; property torts and crimes; slander; sexual assault; sexual battery; trespass to chattels; trespass to land; unauthorized use of name, signature, photograph or likeness for commercial purposes; vandalism; wrongful detention of personal property.

Intentional tortious conduct can give rise to a number of legal claims. Vandalism — the intentional destruction of property — can be the basis for a tort claim as well as the physical basis of misdemeanor or felony crime under the Penal Code. Misdemeanor vandalism is **"malicious mischief"** under Cal. Penal Code § 11172(a); **"felony vandalism"** under Cal. Penal Code § 594 involves the intentional destruction of property.

Furthermore, a spouse can deprive the other spouse of property without destroying the property. Intent to permanently deprive one's spouse of property can result in a criminal charge of theft. For example, given certain facts, depriving a spouse of a vehicle can be the basis of a DVPA claim, a civil claim for conversion, and vehicle theft under Cal. Veh. Code § 10851.

---

[51] *Roddenberry v. Roddenberry*, 44 Cal. App. 4th 634, 51 Cal. Rptr. 2d 907 (Cal. App. Ct., 2d Dist. 1996) (trial court judgment awarded the plaintiff-wife "one-half the profit participation payments from Star Trek I" on the marital settlement agreement, without offset; and $900,000 of jury awarded punitive damages on a fraudulent concealment of profits claim. The court of appeal upheld the trial court judgment).

[52] Exemplary damages are available for harms to animals.

False reports of child abuse are related to slander and defamation, giving rise to a claim for damages under Cal. Penal Code § 11172 (knowingly making a false report of child abuse) and cumulative sanctions under § 3027.

Assault and battery are general claims, but they apply to any permutation of current, estranged, and former intimate partners under Cal. Penal Code § 273.5.

The unauthorized use of name, signature, photograph or likeness for commercial purposes gives rise to liability for damages, lost net profits, attorney's fees, and costs under Cal. Civ. Code § 3344.

Misrepresentations about love, sexual attraction, and affection are not actionable. California has an established public policy against litigating promises (contracts) of love and marriage, as codified in Cal. Civ. Code § 43.5. Notwithstanding this policy, material misrepresentations about love, sexual attraction, communicable diseases, pregnancy, sexually transmitted diseases, intent to act monogamously, and so forth may, depending on the circumstances, constitute grounds for fraud, sexual battery, and other civil tort claims. Fraudulent claims of love, affection, or sexual attraction also may (1) serve as the basis for an annulment action, if they go to obtaining consent for the marriage (as discussed in Chapter 15) or (2) result in a tort recovery.

Fraud can be the basis of a tort claim or a criminal charge.

Fraud can be the basis for challenging the enforceability of a premarital contract, a marital contract, and the validity of a transmutation.[53] Fraud can determine relief for an impairment of community property.[54] Fraudulent transfers of assets by transmutation can be the basis for a creditor to avoid a transfer under the UFTA, as discussed in Chapter 12.

Failure to disclose the diagnosis of a sexually transmitted or communicable disease may constitute fraud and thus can give rise to civil tort damages.

The California Supreme Court recognized the tort of *negligent* transmission of HIV in *John B. v. Superior Court*.[55] *John B.* was filed as a compilation of common law tort claims brought by one spouse against the other for damages related to the intentional and negligent infliction of emotional distress, fraud, and negligence. The plaintiff alleged that the defendant had infected her with the HIV virus while deceiving the plaintiff into believing that she had brought HIV to the marriage. The California Supreme Court recognized the plaintiff's allegation — *negligent* transmission of HIV — as the basis upon which the case could proceed.[56]

The preliminary issue in *John B.* was whether plaintiff could discover information about the defendant's premarital and marital sexual history, including the addresses and phone numbers of the defendant's sexual partners. Plaintiff's goal was to determine whether John B. brought HIV to the marriage.

---

[53] Cal. Fam. Code § 1615(c)(4), (5).

[54] Cal. Fam. Code § 1101(a),(g)

[55] *John B. v. Superior Court*, 38 Cal. 4th 1177, 45 Cal. Rptr. 3d 316, 137 P.3d 153 (Cal. 2006).

[56] *Id.* at 1190–1203.

The Supreme Court considered the plaintiff's wide ranging discovery request, but eventually ruled in such a way as to narrow the time-frame. In doing so, the court clarified the elements of a claim for *negligent* transmission of HIV as: (1) The defendant was infected with HIV and knew or should have known that he or she was infected; (2) the plaintiff and defendant were in a relationship that, at least as far as the plaintiff was concerned, was contemplated as a sexually exclusive one; (3) the defendant insisted on having unprotected relations with others; (4) the defendant represented to the plaintiff that he or she was disease free; (5) the plaintiff relied on the defendant's representation for purposes of engaging in unprotected sexual relations with the defendant; and (6) the sexual activity was the cause of plaintiff becoming infected with HIV, which led to damages.

It is unclear whether element number 2 (the plaintiff and defendant were in a relationship that, at least as far as the plaintiff was concerned, was contemplated as a sexually exclusive one) is a necessary element of the claim. The uncertainty arises from Justice Baxter's rationale that society has an "overriding policy of preventing the spread of sexually transmitted diseases (*see* Cal. Health & Safety Code § 120290), especially HIV (*see, e.g.*, Cal. Health & Safety Code § 120291), which would be enhanced by imposing a duty of care on those who have reason to know they are infected with HIV."[57]

In setting out the elements for the negligent transmission of HIV, Justice Baxter kept carefully to the facts of the case. Thus, what is clear after Justice Baxter's opinion in *John B.* is that a tort claim arises when one person negligently infects another with HIV. What is unclear after *John B.*, is whether a plaintiff can allege negligent transmission of HIV if he or she is having sexual relations in a non-exclusive relationship; if he or she is having a sexual relationships with someone who has not represented him or herself as disease free; or if he or she has a partner who has protected (rather than unprotected) sex outside of the relationship.

The defense to the tort of negligent transmission of HIV is that the plaintiff knew or should have inferred that the condition existed or was highly probable.

Finally, with respect to alleging harm in the context of a marriage or intimate relationship, differences in burdens of proof may be strategically relevant. The burden of proof in a tort case is generally lower (preponderance of the evidence) than it is in a DVPA TRO hearing (reasonable proof of a past act or acts of abuse) than it is in a criminal matter (beyond a reasonable doubt). In a DVPA or tort claim, one spouse is suing the other, who is ostensibly personally liable to the prevailing petitioner. In a criminal matter by comparison, the criminal defendant's marital status may (and probably will) expose the community estate to liability for fees related to the defendant-spouse's legal representation, bail, incarceration, restitution, court ordered treatment program, and so forth. A criminal conviction may also lead to criminal forfeiture of assets that the innocent spouse believed to be community property.[58]

---

[57] *Id.* at 1190, 1192, citing Lawrence O. Gostin & James G. Hodge, Jr., *Piercing the Veil of Secrecy in HIV/AIDS and Other Sexually Transmitted Diseases: Theories of Privacy, and Disclosure in Partner Notification*, 5 Duke J. Gender L. & Policy 9, 40 (1998).

[58] *See U.S. v. Hooper*, 229 F.3d 818 (9th Cir. 2000) (federal criminal forfeiture statute applies to

Intentional torts are excluded from a homeowner insurance policy as a matter of public policy. As discussed previously, *Evans v. Pacific Indemnity Co.* held that Cal. Civ. Code § 533 is part of every homeowner's insurance contract in the state.[59]

DVPA monetary and tort relief may be satisfied from jointly owned property. If so, one spouse can carve a settlement out of property with a conveyance, a reconveyance, an equitable lien, the avoidance of contractual liens, and so forth.

For example, in the 2002 settlement entitled *Jane Doe v. John Roe*, a Los Angeles Superior Court approved a tort settlement between former nonmarried cohabitants in a case alleging assault and battery.[60] Plaintiff alleged that the intentional torts occurred when the defendant: (1) threw a glass table at the plaintiff, thereby cutting her feet; (2) stalked, threatened, and harassed her, thereby causing emotional distress; and (3) filed, without plaintiff's knowledge, a lien in the form of a second deed of trust against their joint tenancy condo, thereby causing plaintiff emotional distress. Plaintiff claimed $2,200 in past medical expenses and $25,000 in lost earnings. She settled for $5,000 on the assault and battery claim, and clear title to the joint tenancy condo, plus attorney's fees. Eventually, the settlement was satisfied with the joint tenancy property. The plaintiff accepted $40,000 (from the defendant's equity in the joint tenancy condo), a deed conveying defendant's interest in the condo to plaintiff; the avoidance of the deed of trust lien on plaintiff's property; and a reconveyance from the deed of trust holder (who was a relative of the defendant). Title to the condo was cleared in plaintiff's name only.

To conclude, a person who commits a tortious act of domestic violence upon another is statutorily liable to the injured person for damages, including but not limited to general damages, special damages, and punitive damages. An injured party is also entitled to equitable relief, an injunction, costs, and any other relief that the court deems proper, including reasonable attorney's fees. The Family Code defines damages arising from domestic violence tort recoveries as the prevailing plaintiff-spouse's separate property.

Sometimes parties remain married after one spouse obtains a domestic violence recovery against the other. A tort award in the form of cash is the prevailing plaintiff-spouse's separate property, but it can be commingled with community property, as discussed in Part III. This would be the case, for example, where a tort judgment or settlement is received by one spouse and subsequently deposited into an account during the continuance of the marriage. Unless the tort award or settlement sums on deposit remain traceable, or the parties have entered into an agreement — extrinsic from the account deposit agreement — that the award sums are not to be characterized as community property, over time those sums can be transmuted to community property. Several theories rationalize this outcome: the § 5305 special presumption for sums on deposit, the § 852(d) transmutation by

---

"innocent spouses" so that community estate forfeits proceeds of crime committed by one spouse, or property purchased with those proceeds).

[59] *Evans, supra.*

[60] *Former Condo Co-Habitants Settle Battery/Partition Claims*, Cal. Jury Verdicts Weekly, Nov. 4, 2002, at 5.

operation of law provision, and the doctrine of confusion.

§ 11.04 COMMUNITY PROPERTY IMPAIRMENT CLAIMS AND RECOVERIES

Impairment claims address harms to the claimant's undivided one-half community property interest that result from a single transaction, a series of transactions, or a pattern of transactions on the part of one spouse against the other spouse. A claim of deliberate misappropriation may be dealt with in a dissolution proceeding, under § 2602, or as a management issue under § 1100 (management of community personal property), § 1102 (community real property), and § 1101(a) (impairment of community property), as discussed in Chapter 10.

The difference may be that § 2602 calls for an unequal division of the community estate to reimburse the wronged party for his or her loss.[61] Whereas, under the management and control provisions, deliberate misappropriation — what one case called "calculated thievery"[62] — refers to impairment by malice, oppression, and fraud. All are grounds upon which an aggrieved spouse may petition for a DVPA restraining order and a related monetary award, file a civil tort claim, file an impairment of community property claim, and possibly bring criminal charges.

As with a tort claim, a successful impairment claim may be collectable from an insurance contract insuring the asset. If insurance is not available to satisfy the judgment, the impairing spouse's separate property, if any, is reachable by the impaired spouse. Where the impairing spouse has no separate property § 1101(g) and (h) allow for a court to award to the impaired spouse — by conveyance, reconveyance, resulting trust, constructive trust, equitable lien, and so on — the impairing spouse's one-half interest in any or all community property asset. Debts may be assigned as part of the process.

Impairing community property frequently causes financial chaos. Returning to damages, a tort claim is often available and necessary to address all of the proximate harm (personal, emotional, and financial) that can result from a single act of impairment or a pattern or series of impairments. The remedies of § 1101(g) and (h) — the Family Code impairment remedies — are useful, but limited. They provide for comparatively less recovery than a tort action might.

§ 11.05 REMEDIES FOR CONVICTION FOR ATTEMPTED MURDER OF A SPOUSE, WRONGFUL DEATH, AND HOMICIDE

Family Code § 782.5 provides that a spouse who is "**convicted of the attempted murder of the other spouse**" or of "**soliciting the murder of the other spouse**" forfeits any community property interest in the "**retirement and pension benefits**

---

[61] *Marriage of Stephenson*, 162 Cal. App. 3d 1057, 209 Cal. Rptr. 383 (Cal. App. Ct., 2d Dist. 1984); *Marriage of Lister*, 152 Cal. App. 3d 411, 199 Cal. Rptr. 321 (Cal. App. Ct., 2d Dist. 1984); *McTiernan & Dubrow, supra.*

[62] *Marriage of Schultz*, 105 Cal. App. 3d 846, 855, 164 Cal. Rptr. 653 (Cal. App. Ct., 2d Dist. 1980).

of the injured spouse." The victim's retirement benefits leave the marriage as the victim spouse's property, notwithstanding any community property interest in them.

A statutory tort for the wrongful death of certain family members is found at Cal. Civ. Proc. Code § 377.60. Spouses and domestic partners are covered under Cal. Civ.Pro § 377.60(a), but nonmarried cohabitants are not. Parents have a separate cause of action for the wrongful death of a child under § 377.60(a)–(c). Children are also entitled to recover. In *Reiser v. Reiser*, two children sued their father for the death of their mother. The jury found for the children in the amount of $60 million against their father who was convicted of first-degree murder of their mother.[63] Wrongful death actions must generally be brought within two years of the person's death per Cal. Civ. Code § 335.1. A wrongful death recovery against a spouse or former spouse is defined by the Family Code as the recovering spouse's separate property.

A person who **"feloniously and intentionally causes the decedent's death,"** including a spouse, RDP, or unmarried cohabitant is barred from receiving any property under Cal. Prob. Code § 250. The slayer is not entitled to property under a will or trust of the decedent, powers of appointment conferred by a will or trust, or any nomination of the killer as an executor, administrator, trustee, guardian, conservator, or custodian. Nor is the slayer entitled to any of the decedent's property by intestate succession. Instead, the property of the decedent passes as if the slayer had predeceased the decedent. In the case of bank accounts, tracing may be required to determine the decedent's share. The slain spouse's estate is entitled full credit for prior separate property contributions to the property; and, if necessary, the court can impose a constructive trust on the slayer in favor of the slain spouse's estate.

When a joint tenant **"feloniously and intentionally kills another joint tenant,"** that act severs the joint tenancy **"so that the share of the decedent passes as the decedent's property and the killer has no rights by survivorship."** Cal. Prob.Code § 251. This probate provision applies to assets titled in joint tenancy. This provision is currently out of date because it does not explicitly cover community property with the right of survivorship titles. Strong policy reasons suggest that the statute should be updated.

If a named beneficiary of a bond, life insurance, or other contractual arrangement **"feloniously and intentionally kills the principal obligee or the person upon whose life the policy is issued,"** the named beneficiary is not entitled to any benefit on the bond or contract. Instead the proceeds become payable **"as though the slayer had predeceased the decedent"** under Cal. Prob. Code § 252.[64] Generally, the statute is meant to prevent a slayer from benefitting from the crime,

[63] *Reiser and Reiser*, No. RG08406864, Superior Court of Alameda County, Alameda, Ca., July 17, 2012 (defendant's charges were reduced to second-degree murder in exchange for him revealing the location of the victim's buried body).

[64] *People v. Rodriguez*, 58 Cal. 4th 587, 168 Cal. Rptr. 3d 380, 319 P.3d 151 (Cal. 2014) (criminal defendant was convicted of first degree murder and sentenced to death for administering poison, and for murder for financial gain; the spouse obtained life insurance on her husband, named herself sole beneficiary, and murdered husband to obtain the proceeds).

but the statute is limited by California case law to felonious and intentional acts, not to manslaughter or accidents. Notwithstanding the California cases, there is at least one federal case holding that insurance proceeds may not pass to a beneficial designee who caused the death of the insured; exceptions exist for insanity, accidental killing, and self-defense.[65]

Finally, California has a catch-all provision that applies to **"any case not described in Section 250, 251, or 252,"** the code sections discussed above. Under Cal. Prob. Code § 253, if one person feloniously and intentionally kills another, **"any acquisition of property, interest, or benefit by the killer as a result of the killing of the decedent shall be treated in accordance with the principles** [set forth in the Bars to Succession part of the Probate Code]."

"A final judgment of conviction of felonious and intentional killing is conclusive" to effect a change in the order of devise or succession for any of the above statutes, according to Cal. Prob. Code § 254. Where there is no final judgment, the court has the discretion to decide by a preponderance of the evidence whether the killing was felonious and intentional for purposes of affecting a change to the order of devise or succession. The burden of proof is on the party who seeks to establish that the killing was felonious and intentional.

§ 11.06 SUMMARY

California abolished the spousal tort immunity doctrine for intentional and negligent torts in 1962. The state passed the DVPA in 1993. Spouses can thus sue each other for DVPA monetary claims, common law torts, statutory torts, and for impairment of a community property interest.

Ordinarily either spouse has management and control of the community property. The DVPA permits a court to issue a restraining order, on an ex parte basis, that grants to one spouse the exclusive authority to manage and control the community property for the duration of the order.

A cause of action that arises during the marriage on the part of one spouse against the other is the separate property of the injured spouse.

---

[65] *Shoemaker v. Shoemaker*, 263 F.2d 931, 932 (Cal. App. Ct., 6th Cir. 1959).

Chapter 12

GENERAL PRINCIPLES OF COMMUNITY PROPERTY LIABILITY

Under the civil law, the matrimonial regime was a net community property estate defined as community assets minus community liabilities. At divorce, the parties divided the net community estate. In the traditional civil law system, the community could be a debtor/obligor.

Common law states follow different general principles of liability. In these states, separate property ownership is the norm, while marital property — as for example property held in joint tenancy or tenancy by the entirety (in states where that title form is available) — is an optional method of holding family wealth. In a minority of common law states, married couples have the option of using the joint tenancy or — alternatively — the tenancy by the entireties title form. The latter form provides the spouses with rights of survivorship relative to each other, some protections against unilateral conveyance, and some protection from the reach of one spouse's creditors, at least up until divorce or the death of the last spouse to survive.[1] At divorce, debts are assigned as "liabilities" to one or both spouses.

California grafted common law principles onto the community property system. Today, California law on the issue of liabilities can be considered a hybrid managerial approach. One or both spouses — not the community estate as an entity — is a debtor/obligor. Either spouse has the legal right to manage and control the community property, as discussed in Chapter 10. Therefore, either spouse, acting alone, can obligate the community estate to the claims of a creditor. A creditor can reach the community property for all debts of either spouse, whether incurred before, during, or sometimes after separation. A creditor can reach the separate property of the obligor spouse. In some cases, a creditor can reach the separate property of the non-obligor spouse. The estates subject to the claims of a creditor are marshaled depending on when and for what purposes the debt in question was incurred.

One systemic policy rationale for California's approach is to protect the rights of creditors and, in so doing, to protect the spouses' access to credit and other financial products. Another policy rationale is to better define legal familial support obligations, particularly in cases of separation, dissolution, and remarriage.

---

[1] *See Sawada v. Endo*, 57 Haw. 608, 561 P.2d 1291 (1977).

§ 12.01 GENERAL PRINCIPLES

The general liability principles followed in California have their origin in the common law approach. The "community property estate" holds the assets that are acquired by the spouses during marriage by onerous means. Debts are "liabilities" that arise from contract, tort, or other obligations. Rather than calculate a net community property estate at divorce, debts are assigned to one or both spouses at the end of the marriage. At dissolution, assets are assigned either by agreement or on an asset-by-asset basis; debts are assigned to one or both spouses.

During marriage, liabilities that are retired — i.e., bills that are paid — are factored into an analysis as family expenses. Family expenses are properly deductible first from the community property, second from the separate property of the spouse who incurred the obligation (the obligor spouse), and third from the separate property of the other spouse (the non-obligor spouse).

At marriage's end, unpaid liabilities like the mortgage, any credit cards that maintain a balance, and educational loans, to give just a few examples are assigned to one or both spouses, depending on when the debt was incurred and which of the spouses incurred the debt. Debts can be paid from the sale proceeds of a securing asset, or with post-marital income.

California uses a timing method to assess the order of liability between the community estate and the spouses' respective separate property estates. Details are discussed below, but to provide a preview to community property liability: The community estate is liable for a debt incurred by either spouse before or during marriage. The community property, if any, is liable for debts incurred during a period of separation for the support of either or both spouses. The community property is liable for one or both spouses' tort obligations to a third party, if incurred from the date of marriage to the date of separation. Spouses may also be personally liable on a debt incurred before or during marriage, or after separation.

During a legal separation or dissolution, the Family Code provisions on the division of property in a marital action control the assignment of debts.

Under § 902, a **"debt"** is statutorily defined as **"[a]n obligation incurred by a married person before or during marriage, whether based on contract, tort, or otherwise."** The spouse who is personally obligated to pay the debt is the obligor. The spouse who does not have personal liability for the debt is the non-obligor.

Under § 903, the type of obligation determines when the debt is incurred.

A contract debt is incurred **"[a]t the time a contract is made."** This is true even if the performance on the contract extends after the parties are separated.[2]

A tort debt is incurred **"[a]t the time the tort occurs."**

In all other cases, the debt is incurred, **"[a]t the time the obligation arises."**

The general rule of community property liability is found at § 910: **"Except as otherwise provided by statute, the community estate is liable for a debt**

[2] *Marriage of Feldner*, 40 Cal. App. 4th 617, 47 Cal. Rptr. 2d 312 (Cal. App. Ct., 4th Dist. 1995).

incurred by either spouse before or during marriage, regardless of which spouse has the management and control of the property and regardless of whether one or both spouses are parties to the debt or to a judgment for the debt."

The introductory clause of § 910 makes clear that the community estate is liable for all debts absent an express statutory exception or an enforceable written agreement between the parties. An included debt can be satisfied from any and all community property sources, including a source that is under the primary management and control of one spouse. Sums on deposit in a sole bank account, a community property trust, a conservatorship, or a community property business are all potentially reachable by creditors to satisfy the debts of one or both spouses.

The general rule expressed in § 910 holds the community estate liable for debts incurred by either spouse before or during marriage. That general rule does not apply to debts incurred while the spouses are living separate and apart; nor does it apply to debts incurred after a judgment of legal separation, the signing of an enforceable marital settlement agreement, or a judgment of dissolution.[3] Therefore, the phrase **"during marriage"** refers to a time when the spouses are married persons living together in a confidential relationship.

[A] Basic Terms and Concepts

A *creditor* is a person or entity who has a claim against a debtor.[4] The term creditor can include an assignee of an original creditor.[5] In the California context of marriage, one or both spouses can be a debtor to a creditor. The community estate itself is not the debtor.

A *claim* is the creditor's right to a payment. A creditor need not reduce a claim to judgment. The right to payment can arise from contract, tort, or any other obligation. It can be reduced to a judgment or not, fixed or variable, liquidated or nonliquidated, contingent or vested, matured or unmatured, disputed or undisputed, legal, equitable, secured, or unsecured.[6] In the context of marriage, the creditor's claim can be against the debtor. In California, while community estate is not a debtor, the community property is generally liable for the claims of each spouse's premarital and marital creditors.

California follows the Uniform Fraudulent Transfer Act (UFTA), as set forth in Cal. Civ. Code §§ 3439–3439.12. The UFTA has a federal counterpart in Bankruptcy Code § 548 (11 U.S.C. §§ 101–1330). A bankruptcy trustee may bring an action under the UFTA.[7] Creditors with UFTA claims arising out of allegedly

---

[3] Cal. Fam. Code §§ 902, 910; *Lezine, supra*, at 63–64; *Litke O'Farrell, LLC v. Tipton*, 204 Cal. App. 4th 1178, 139 Cal. Rptr. 3d 548 (Cal. App. Ct., 1st Dist. 2012).

[4] Cal. Civ. Code § 3439.01(c).

[5] Id..

[6] Cal. Civ. Code § 3439.01(b).

[7] 11 U.S.C. §§ 546(a); *In Re Mahoney, Trocki & Assoc. Inc.*, 111 B.R. 914, 916–20 (Bankr. S.D. Cal. 1990).

fraudulent transactions have equal standing with other creditors.[8]

A *transfer* is of possession and control to an asset. One or both spouse cannot make a transfer with the actual intent to hinder, delay or defraud creditors, as determined by the debtor's state of mind. The burden is on the creditor to prove fraud by a preponderance of the evidence.[9] The transferee is defined by whether he or she has dominion or control over the asset transferred. A claim may be satisfied by the transfer of an asset made by the debtor to the creditor; or a payment of a claim may be hindered by the transfer of an asset by the debtor to another party, not the creditor.

An *asset* available to a creditor, in the context of marriage, includes but is not limited to:

- Property to the extent it is not encumbered by a valid lien;[10]
- Property to the extent it is generally exempt under nonbankruptcy law, meaning the law of the state or federal law that is not part of the federal Bankruptcy Code.[11]
- An interest in property held in tenancy by the entireties, when the creditor's claim is not just against one of the married tenants. California does not permit tenancy by the entireties, but may recognize its function.[12]
- Property under the legal management and control of either spouse, even if held in a sole bank account, a revocable trust, or a community property business: this is by application of the controlling *Grolemund* principle.[13]
- One spouse's transmutation to the other spouse, made with the intent to hinder, delay or defraud the transmuting spouse's creditors: § 851.

In the absence of fraud, a debtor may decide to pay or prefer one creditor over another, even if the transfer will frustrate the nonpreferred creditor's attempts to collect on its debt.[14] A debtor incurs debts beyond his or her ability to pay them when the debtor's cash flow projections at the time the debt is undertaken are insufficient to meet the debt. A debtor becomes insolvent if and when the sum of the debtor's debts is greater than all of the debtors assets.[15]

Under *Grolemund,* since both spouses have the legal right to manage and control the community property, either spouse can obligate the community property to the claims of creditors. A creditor can reach any property over which the debtor (obligor) has the legal right to manage and control.

---

[8] Cal. Civ. Code § 3439.04(a)

[9] *Liodas v. Sahadi,* 19 Cal. 3d 278, 291–293, 137 Cal. Rptr. 635, 562 P.2d 316 (Cal. 1977).

[10] Cal. Civ. Code §§ 3439.01(a)(1), 3439.01(f), (h), (j) (defining "lien," "property," and "valid lien").

[11] Cal. Civ. Code § 3439.01(a)(1); Cal. Civ. Proc. Code §§ 703.101–704.995 (describing exempt property).

[12] *Sawada, supra.*

[13] *Grolemund v. Cafferata,* 17 Cal. 2d 679, 111 P.2d. 641 (Cal. 1941).

[14] Cal. Civ. Code § 3432; *Wyzard v. Goller,* 23 Cal. App. 4th 1183, 1187–1190, 28 Cal. Rptr. 2d 608 (Cal. App. Ct., 2d Dist. 1994) (applying the UFTA).

[15] Cal. Civ. Code § 3439.02(a).

The Family Code uses the phrase *obligor* rather than debtor. In a dissolution proceeding, the debts will be assigned as obligations. A dissolution proceeding is separate and distinct from a bankruptcy proceeding.

[B] Contract Liabilities

A contract liability is incurred when the contract is made. If made during marriage, the community estate, the obligor's separate property estate, and the non-obligor's separate property estate are all liable for any contract debt that was incurred by one or both spouses during marriage for necessaries of life.

A contract creditor can reach the community property estate even if the non-obligor spouse was not made a party to the contract debt for purposes of enforcing a judgment. As the obligor's spouse, the non-obligor spouse is personally liable for the obligor's contract debt. As a spouse, he or she is also entitled to any insurance benefits that may arise from such a contract.[16]

[C] Tort Liabilities

A tort liability is incurred when the tort occurs. For a tort that occurs during marriage, if both spouses are tortfeasors, then the community property and separate property estates of both spouses are liable for that obligation. If the tort is the obligation of one spouse, then the community property and the separate property of the tortfeasor are liable. The non-tortfeasor spouse's separate property is not liable except in cases where he or she would be liable if the marriage did not exist.[17]

A tort creditor can reach the community property notwithstanding the fact that only one spouse was adjudged the tortfeasor.[18] This is the case whether (or not) the tortfeasor spouse was or was not acting for the community benefit at the time the tort occurred. When the tortfeasor was not acting for the community benefit when the tort occurred, the question is not *whether* the injured party can use the community property to satisfy the tort claim, it's *when* the tort creditor can reach the community estate.

California follows a marshaling approach set out in § 1000(b)(1) and (2). Tort creditors can reach the community property first if the tort was committed while the tortfeasor spouse was **"[p]erforming an activity for the benefit of the community."**[19] But if the tortfeasor spouse's liability **"[i]s not based upon an act or omission which occurred while the married person was performing an activity for the benefit of the community"**[20] then tort creditors must exhaust the tortfeasor spouse's separate property before they can satisfy the claim against any available community property.

---

[16] *Century Surety Co., supra.*

[17] Cal. Fam. Code § 1000(a).

[18] Cal. Fam. Code § 1000(b).

[19] Cal. Fam. Code § 1000(b)(1).

[20] Cal. Fam. Code § 1000(b)(2).

Most acts or omissions that lead to tort liability can be cast, in § 1000(b) terms, as **"an activity for the benefit of the community"** unless they involve domestic violence, gross negligence, or criminal activity. But even here, if the nontortfeasor spouse ratifies the tortfeasor's tortious activity, the resulting obligation becomes one for which the community is liable. In Arizona, for example, a wife shouted encouragement to her husband in a bar fight; and even though the husband's act was not initially for the benefit of the community, the wife's encouragement ratified his tortious act for purposes of assessing community property liability. Mutual combat is a breach of peace.[21] The majority rule is that when parties engage in mutual combat in anger — as the two bar patrons did — each is civilly liable to the other for any physical injury inflicted by him or her during the combat; voluntary agreement to engage in combat is not a defense. By extension, when the wife gave mutual support to her combatant husband, the bar fight crossed the line from being an activity not for the benefit of the community to one with a community purpose. Under § 1000, the effect of the transition would place the community property in first position for purposes of satisfying any resulting tort obligation.

In Washington, by comparison, a married couple hosted a party on their sail boat. After the party, unbeknownst to the wife, the husband raped a guest.[22] In order to reach the community property assets, the tort judgment creditor argued that the party itself was the community activity that led to the tort because it was held on community property (the boat) and paid for with community property. The wife (successfully) argued that the husband's criminal conduct was the act that gave rise to the tort. Different jurisdictions have different rules, but the point is that the § 1000(b) phrase **"for the benefit of the community"** is a question of fact that depends on what happened. It is also a practical question answered by which estate (community or separate) the tort victim seeks to reach first.

The phrase **"for the benefit of the community"** also includes obligations arising from judgments and settlement costs owed to insurers. For example, in *Axis Surplus Ins. Co. v. Reinoso*, a lessor spouse was adjudged liable to his tenants for claims arising from safe and unsanitary apartment conditions.[23] The court held that the non-lessor spouse was jointly and severally liable for the torts of her husband since she was a co-owner of the community property real estate. The insurer was permitted to reach the community property to recover settlement costs expended in the lessor spouse's defense.

[D] Other Obligations

A general obligation is one that does not arise from contract or tort. The general rule of community property liability expressed in § 910 covers all other obligations incurred before and during marriage as well. Obligations are discussed in more detail below.

---

[21] *Howe v. Haught*, 11 Ariz. App. 98, 462 P.2d 395 (Cal. 1969).

[22] *de Elche v. Jacobsen*, 95 Wash.2d 237, 622 P.2d 835 (S.Ct. 1980) (in bank).

[23] *Axis Surplus Ins. Co. v. Reinoso*, 208 Cal. App. 4th 181, 145 Cal. Rptr. 3d 128 (Cal. App. Ct., 2d Dist. 2012).

Family expenses of the current marrage are support obligations. The community property is liable for any necessaries of life incurred from the date of the marriage to its end, whether those expenses arise from contract, tort or other obligations. The rationale is that either spouse has the legal right to manage and control the community property; and thus under *Grolemund*, a creditor that provides necessaries of life to the family has the right to reach the entirety of the community property. Here the rationale is that spouses have mutual obligations of support: If the community property is insufficient to meet those obligations, then separate property must be used. Either spouse's separate property is liable for necessaries of life, with a reimbursement available only if community property was available on the date that the family expense was satisfied with separate property.

The general rule of § 910 extends to premarital and extramarital support obligations as well. These include:

- Premarital child support obligations;
- Extramarital child support obligations;
- Spousal support obligations for a former spouse; and
- Parental support obligations for an indigent parent or parents.

Example 12.1: This example illustrates the general rule of community property liability during marriage for contract liabilities. During marriage Haight, who is a culinary arts student, becomes upset when he loses his minimum wage job. To get back at Ashbury for crashing the family car, Haight buys a $2,000 used car with a $2,000 car loan from ABC Finance. Haight's contract debt was incurred for the purpose of buying a car, which in most California cities would fall in the necessaries of life category. Assuming the price of the car is in Haight and Ashbury's financial budget, if Haight defaults on the ABC Finance loan, ABC Finance can reach: (1) all available sources of community property, (2) Haight's separate property, and (3) Ashbury's separate property. In other words, Haight incurred the contract debt, which makes him personally liable on the contract, the community property is liable under § 910, and Ashbury is personally liable on the contract under decisional law (the joint and several liability rationale) and the necessaries of life doctrine set forth in § 914(a)(1), as discussed in § 12.03 below.

Example 12.2: This example illustrates how the necessaries of life doctrine might protect the non-obligor spouse from personal liability. Same as Example 12.1 except that Haight buys a $50,000 sports car with a $50,000 car loan from ABC Finance. In this example, Haight lost his job and the family needs transportation. Haight is personally liable on the contract since Haight signed it. The community property is liable on the contract since the contract was made during marriage. But Ashbury can contest personal liability under § 914(a)(1) if she can show that *this* $50,000 car falls outside of the necessaries of life category for the family.[24]

Example 12.3: During marriage, Haight decides to "grow the family funds" at a casino roulette table. Once in the casino, Haight negligently injures Truett. Truett sues Haight for negligence and wins a judgment. Here, Haight is the tortfeasor, so he is personally liable for the tort obligation. The community is also liable because

---

[24] Cal. Fam. Code § 771. Ashbury's post-separation earnings are defined as separate property.

the tort occurred during the marriage. Ashbury, however, is not personally liable to Truett. Which assets Truett can use to satisfy the tort judgment depends upon whether Haight was — or was not — performing an activity for the benefit of the community under § 1000(b)(1) and (2) at the time that the tort occurred. If yes, then Truett can reach the community property assets first. If no, then Truett must satisfy the tort judgment from Haight's separate property assets before turning to the community property assets.

§ 12.02 SUPPORT OBLIGATIONS

The community property is liable for the support obligations related to the current marriage. The community property is also liable for extramarital support obligations that arose before or during the current marriage.

[A] Child and Spousal Support Obligations

The community estate is liable for obligations under § 910. Under § 915(a), **"[a] child support or spousal support obligation of a married person that does not arise out of the marriage shall be treated as a debt incurred before marriage . . . ."** However, § 915(b) exempts the community property if the obligor spouse has nonexempt separate property available to satisfy the support obligation; it reimburses the community property if community funds are applied to satisfy a support obligation **"[a]t a time when nonexempt separate income of the person is available but is not applied . . . ."**

Notwithstanding the above exemption, § 915(c) authorizes a court to take into account the earnings of both spouses in setting an extramarital support obligation that **"does not arise of the marriage"** but that was nevertheless incurred during the marriage.

Example 12.4: This example illustrates the general rule that the community property is liable for support obligations that do not arise out of the marriage. Haight and Ashbury marry. Ashbury has child and spousal support obligations from her prior marriage to Truett. Ashbury has no available separate property with which to satisfy those obligations. Therefore, the Ashbury-Haight community property is liable for Ashbury's obligations under § 915(a) which refers back to the general rule expressed in § 910. Since Ashbury has no separate property to meet her premarital support obligations, the community property is not eligible for a § 915(b) exemption.

Example 12.5: This example illustrates the community estate's right of reimbursement. Same as Example 12.4 except that Ashbury does have available separate property. In this case, the Haight-Ashbury community property is eligible for the § 915(b) exemption. And in the event that any Haight-Ashbury community property is used to satisfy Ashbury's premarital support obligation, the community estate is entitled to reimbursement under 915(b). Reimbursement is restitutionary, not punitive.

Example 12.6: This example illustrates the general rule that the community property is liable for a support obligation that does not arise from the marriage but that was nevertheless incurred during the marriage. During marriage to Ashbury, Haight has a child with Paige. Haight earns $100,000 per year. Ashbury earns $200,000 per year. Paige has limited earnings. In this case, Haight incurs an extramarital child support obligation during the marriage. That obligation is payable to Paige on behalf of Haight's child. Support is determined by reference to the Haight-Ashbury community property: In this case support should be set after consideration of all community property sources, including Haight and Ashbury's annual combined income of $300,000.

[B] Parental Support Obligations

A little known fact of California law is that § 4400 recognizes a duty on the part of adult child to support an indigent parent or parents: "**[a]n adult child shall, to the extent of his or her ability, support a parent who is in need and unable to maintain himself or herself by work.**" Neglect of this duty is a misdemeanor under the Penal Code § 270(c).

A person's duty to support an indigent parent is similar and different from a child or spousal support obligation. The duty to support a parent is similar in the sense that one's obligation to support an indigent parent is not optional under California law, notwithstanding the absence of a court order. The obligation to support a parent is different in the sense that the law does not recognize a right of reimbursement for the community estate in the case of a parental support duty while it does in the case of child and spousal support obligations. Thus, even if the obligor spouse had separate property funds at hand when community property is applied to a parental support obligation, the community estate is not statutorily entitled to a reimbursement.

In *Marriage of Leni*, the husband applied community funds to support his indigent and ailing mother.[25] During the dissolution proceeding, the wife sought reimbursement from the husband on behalf of the community estate. She argued that husband's support of his mother was an unauthorized gift of community personal property made without her written consent. The trial court ordered the husband to reimburse the community. The husband appealed. The court of appeal held that the trial court erred in ordering the reimbursement. The court of appeal discussed the case in terms of § 4400 and Pen.Code § 270(c) — neither of which discuss a right of reimbursement as compared to § 910 and § 915, which expressly allow for reimbursements to the community property.

A parental support obligation is incurred when the parent can no longer support him or herself through work. The obligation is formalized when a parent or county, on behalf of the parent, brings an action against the adult child to enforce the duty of support.[26]

Section 4404 provides that:

> **[I]n determining the amount to be ordered for support, the court shall consider the following circumstances of each party:**

---

[25] *Marriage of Leni*, 144 Cal. App. 4th 1087, 50 Cal. Rptr. 3d 886 (Cal. App. Ct., 3d Dist. 2006).

[26] Cal. Fam. Code § 4403.

(a) **Earning capacity and needs.**

(b) **Obligations and assets.**

(c) **Age and health.**

(d) **Standard of living.**

(e) **Other factors the court deems just and equitable.**

An adult child may be relieved from the duty to support an indigent parent for equitable or statutory reasons.

Statutory grounds for relief are found at § 4410. Relief requires a court order finding all of the following:

(a) **The child was abandoned by the parent when the child was a minor.**

(b) **The abandonment continued for a period of two or more years before the time the child attained the age of 18 years.**

(c) **During the period of abandonment the parent was physically and mentally able to provide support for the child.**

An adult child must formally petition an order relieving the child of legal obligations of support for the parent.[27] After a hearing on the matter, the court decides whether to issue the order. An order of relief exempts the child from liability for obligations related to the **"[s]upport, care, maintenance, and the like of a parent,"** and from any obligation to **"[r]eimburse the state or a local public agency for furnishing the support, care, maintenance, or the like of a parent."**[28]

Example 12.7: This example involves a parental support obligation incurred during the marriage. Haight's parent, Frederick, becomes indigent during Haight's marriage to Ashbury. Haight rents an apartment for Frederick. Ashbury contends that the community property is not liable for Frederick's support. In this case, the Haight-Ashbury community property is liable for Frederick's support under § 4400, § 903 (which recognizes the obligation as one incurred during marriage), and § 910 (which holds the community estate liable for debts incurred during marriage).

Example 12.8: This example involves a parental support obligation incurred before the marriage. Same as 12.7 except that Frederick becomes indigent before Haight and Ashbury marry. For the same reasons stated in Example 12.7, the Haight-Ashbury community property is liable for Haight's support obligation to Frederick, notwithstanding the fact that the obligation was incurred before marriage.

Example 12.9: This example illustrates the grounds upon which an order relieving an adult child of the legal obligation of parental support may be granted. Assume Haight was abandoned by his father, Frederick, when Haight was 5-years old. After Haight and Ashbury achieved financial success, Frederick — who is still

---

[27] Cal. Fam. Code §§ 4410–14.

[28] Cal. Fam. Code § 4414(a)(1), (2).

indigent — located Haight on facebook. Frederick files a petition for support from Haight. In this case, Haight has a § 4400 legal duty to support Frederick. However, § 4410 permits Haight to file a petition for relief from that duty. Haight must file in the county where Frederick resides, and on the ground that Frederick abandoned Haight from the age of 5 on, even though, during that period, Frederick was physically and mentally able to care for Haight. If Haight's petition is granted, he will be relieved from any legal obligation to support Frederick, as will the Haight-Ashbury community estate.

Example 12.10: This example illustrates the potential for difficult questions of fact that may arise in a proceeding to relieve an adult child from parental support obligations. Haight was abandoned by his father Frederick when Haight was 15-years old. At the time, Haight was difficult to control and drug dependent, and he voluntarily left the family home. Frederick had a life threatening condition that limited his mobility. After Haight and Ashbury achieve financial success, indigent Frederick finds Haight on facebook. Frederick files a petition for support from Haight. In this case, Haight has a § 4400 legal duty to support Frederick. But, as in Example 12.9, § 4410 permits Haight to file a petition for relief from that legal duty. Haight's petition alleges that Frederick abandoned Haight from the age of 15 on even though he (Frederick) was physically and mentally able to care for Haight. This is by no means a clear case. Haight must show that Frederick was physically and mentally able to care for Haight at a time when Haight voluntarily left home and was difficult to control. Additionally, given Haight's financial success, the equities may now be in favor of ordering Haight to support Frederick as a matter of law.

§ 12.03 EXEMPTIONS FOR THE NON-OBLIGOR SPOUSE

Exemptions may be available to remove one spouse's assets from the reach of the other spouse's creditors.

[A] Community Property Earnings

During marriage, the community estate is liable for either spouse's premarital obligations. However, a non-obligor spouse may take action to exempt his or her community property earnings from the obligor spouse's non-revolving premarital debt.

To exercise the § 911 exemption, the non-obligor spouse must continuously meet the following two elements.

- The non-obligor spouse must hold his or her community property earnings **"[i]n a deposit account"** in his or her name only — in other words, the earnings must be in a sole account to which the obligor spouse **"[h]as no right of withdrawal"**; and
- The non-obligor must keep those community property earnings **"[u]ncommingled with other property in the community estate, except property insignificant in amount."**

The rationale for the exemption is intent driven: The exemption comes into play when the non-obligor spouse removes his or her community property earnings from the non-obligor's day-to-day management and control. Only compliance with § 911 invokes the exemption; and then only as to the non-obligor spouse's earnings; and then only as to the obligor spouse's premarital creditors. Otherwise, under *Grolemund* and the general rule of § 910, there is no principled reason to shield community property (including the non-obligor's earnings) from the reach of an obligor spouse's premarital creditors. Community property, after all, is property over which either spouse has like power of absolute disposition.[29]

The § 911 earnings shield remains in place only so long as the non-obligor spouse continuously meets and maintains the necessary elements. By the express terms of § 911, de minimus commingling of exempt community property with other sources of community property is not sufficient to cast doubt upon the non-obligor's intention to invoke the § 911 exemption, but substantial commingling is. Therefore, at the point that the non-obligor's intention becomes muddied by the act of commingling § 911 exempt and nonexempt community property, the § 911 exemption is no longer available. At that point, the obligor spouse's premarital creditors can once again satisfy a premarital liability with any and all available community property, including the non-obligor spouse's community property earnings.

A couple of caveats:

- Segregated earnings may not be shielded through changes in form: The obligor spouse's premarital creditors can satisfy a debt with any purchase made with § 911 exempt community property earnings.
- The § 911 exemption does not protect the non-obligor's earnings against the obligor's premarital revolving debt (i.e., credit cards).

Example 12.11: This example illustrates the how the § 911 exemption works to protect the non-obligor's community property earnings from the obligor spouse's premarital creditors. Haight and Ashbury plan to marry. Ashbury knows that Haight has premarital debts related to a business that Haight once owned. In order to protect her earnings, Ashbury opens a deposit account in her name only; Haight has no access or right of withdrawal to Ashbury's account. Ashbury deposits her community property earnings into that account. Ashbury has successfully removed her earnings from the reach of Haight's premarital creditors.

Example 12.12: This example illustrates how the § 911 exemption drops once the obligor spouse gains (informal) access to the account. During marriage, even though Haight's name is not on Ashbury's sole account, Ashbury authorizes a debit card in Haight's name. By authorizing the debt card, Ashbury is no longer eligible for the § 911 exemption because a debit card gives Haight rights of withdrawal in Ashbury's sole account. Once Haight obtains the debit card to Ashbury's account, Haight's premarital creditors can satisfy their claims against Ashbury's community property earnings on deposit in the account.

---

[29] Cal. Fam. Code § 1101(a).

Example 12.13: This example illustrates how the § 911 exemption drops once the obligor spouse gains the right of access to the account. During marriage, Haight sues Ashbury to compel the addition of Haight's name to Ashbury's § 911 account. Once Haight's name is added to what was once Ashbury's sole account, Haight has the right of access (which includes the right of withdrawal) to the account. Haight's premarital creditors can thereafter reach Ashbury's community property earnings on deposit in the account.

Example 12.14: This example illustrates how the § 911 remains in place even if insubstantial commingling occurs. During marriage, and to her dismay, Ashbury discovers that she deposited into her sole account one of Haight's salary checks, in the amount of $100. Ashbury's account holds $15,000. Here, Ashbury has commingled exempt § 911 community property earnings with nonexempt community property earnings (the $100 obtained from Haight). A question of fact is raised on the issue of whether commingling $100 of nonexempt sums in an account that holds $15,000 of exempt sums on deposit is enough to cancel the§ 911 exemption. In this case, Ashbury's earnings likely remain exempt from the reach of Haight's premarital creditors.

Example 12.15: This example illustrates how the § 911 drops if substantial commingling occurs. Same as Example 12.14 except that Ashbury deposits into her sole account $1,000 of Haight's earnings, every month, from January to December. In this case, Ashbury commingles deposits of $12,000 of nonexempt community property into an account that has $15,000 of exempt sums on deposit. Because 80% (nearly half) of the sums on deposit are nonexempt funds, Ashbury's act of commingling is substantial enough to cast doubt on Ashbury's intention to invoke the § 911 exemption. Once Ashbury's intention to keep her earnings exempt under § 911 becomes unclear, Haight's premarital creditors can reach all of the sums on deposit in Ashbury's account.

Example 12.16: This example illustrates how the § 911 exemption does not apply to revolving debt. Prior to marriage, Haight maintains a balance of $2,000 on a credit card. Ashbury sets up a § 911 account into which she deposits her community property earnings. Haight continues to use his credit card during marriage, for groceries and gas. In this case, the credit card obligation was one of Haight's premarital debts; but once Haight allowed the credit card account to carry a balance past the date of the marriage, the credit card debt transformed from a premarital debt into a contract obligation incurred during marriage. Credit card debt is revolving debt; it incurs interest debt daily, with a new balance reported and billed each cycle. Thus, by function of timing, the credit card contract debt becomes a support obligation of the marriage. Haight, as obligor, is personally liable on the debt. The community property is liable on the debt under § 910 because it was incurred during marriage. And, notwithstanding Ashbury's compliance with § 911, Ashbury is personally liable on the debt since it is used to purchase necessaries of life during the marriage.

[B] Separate Property

The non-obligor spouse's separate property is not liable for debts incurred by the other spouse during marriage, but there are many exceptions to this rule.

The general rule is stated in § 913(a): **"The separate property of a married person is liable for a debt incurred by the person before or during marriage."** And under § 913(b), **"[t]he separate property of a married person is not liable for a debt incurred by the person's spouse before or during marriage."** This general rule exempts the non-obligor's separate property from the premarital and marital debts of the obligor.

However, § 720 and the family expense presumption recognize family support obligations as debts payable from the community estate. Moreover, case law requires that separate property be used to support the family, without reimbursement, whenever community funds are exhausted. For that reason, despite the general rule of § 913, a non-obligor spouse's separate property is liable for a wide range of debts that are incurred by the obligor spouse before and during marriage. This liability survives the death of the obligor spouse.

Even in a dissolution proceeding, the non-obligor's separate property can be liable for certain of the obligor's post-separation debts, with liability based in part on who incurred the dept and on the needs and the abilities of the spouses to pay the debt at the time it is incurred.[30] Indeed, in light of the spouses' mutual duty of and right to support, the non-obligor spouse remains potentially liable for the other spouse's debt until such time as that debt is assigned to the obligor spouse by an enforceable marital settlement, a judgment of legal separation, or a final judgment of dissolution.

[C] Exceptions: The Necessaries Doctrine

Exceptions to § 913 appear in § 914(a)(1) and (2):

> **Notwithstanding Section 913, a married person is personally liable for the following debts incurred by the person's spouse during marriage:**
>
> > **(1) A debt incurred for necessaries of life of the person's spouse while the spouses are living together.**
> >
> > **(2) Except as provided by Section 4302, a debt incurred for common necessaries of life of the person's spouse while the spouses are living separately.**

The necessaries doctrine governs during marriage. The two spouses and their community property are all liable for a contract debt incurred by the obligor spouse for necessaries of life; the community property and the tortfeasor spouse's separate property are liable for a tort obligation incurred during marriage; and the community estate and the obligor spouse are liable for obligations incurred before and during marriage such as premarital and extramarital support obligations and parental support obligations. Section 4302 provides: **"A person is not liable for support of the person's spouse when the person is living separate from the spouse by agreement unless support is stipulated in the agreement."**

---

[30] Cal. Fam. Code § 2623.

A family's standard of living goes into the determination of what is or isn't a support obligation of the current marriage.

For example, spouses living in a high income community may have family expenses that are common to other residents in that community. Expenses, for example, related to food, shelter, transportation, clothing, cars, furnishings, fixtures, and so forth. But that same family's *actual* standard of living may be far lower or higher than other families in the community, depending on how frugal (or not) the family is.[31]

One family on a street in an affluent residential area may own or have rights to vacation houses, cars, horses, boats, club memberships, times shares; they may opt for elective medical care, elective surgeries, international travel, private schools for their children; they may lease luxury cars; they may keep their home stylishly renovated; and forth. In the event of separation, when this spendthrift family dismantles their community estate, it may become apparent that their lifestyle was dependent upon one high-earning spouse's income. If so, this family may have little in the way of measurable community assets (i.e., savings) to draw on for support during periods of separation.

In that same neighborhood may be a different family. The spouses in this lower spending family have the same income as the higher spending family, but they lead a modest lifestyle. They have little in the way of debt or prestige consumer items, but they may have a considerable amount of banked community property assets — i.e., savings and other available financial resources. During a period of separation, this family will have community property assets sufficient to draw upon for the support of one or both spouses.

These two sets of spouses live in the same community, but due to their actual spending habits they have different standards of living. More to the point, they have different levels of wealth and savings to draw on if they separate. The living standard for the spendthrift spouses depends upon one spouse's income; therefore, during a period of separation, that spouse's income is what becomes available to maintain the family standard of living and to support the other spouse. By contrast, the frugal spouses have access to earnings and community property accumulations (savings) that can be drawn on for support during a period of separation. As a result, the frugal family can draw on community property resources to meet their mutual obligations of support during a period of separation, while the spendthrift family must rely on earnings, which after separation are characterized as the separate property of the earning spouse, not as community property.

During a dissolution proceeding, debts are allocated and assigned depending upon such factors as the timing of the debt, the reason for the debt, and the ability of the obligor spouse to pay the debt.

[1] Necessaries of Life During Marriage

During the continuance of the marriage, the necessaries of life doctrine set forth in § 914(a)(1) controls:

---

[31] *See, e.g.*, Thomas J. Stanley & William D. Danko, The Millionaire Next Door (2d ed. 2010).

(a) Notwithstanding Section 913, a married person is personally liable for the following debts incurred by the person's spouse during marriage:

(1) A debt incurred for necessaries of life of the person's spouse while the spouses are living together.

This provision does not require that a couple use community funds before they use separate property funds to pay for necessaries of life. This becomes evident in light of § 914(b), which gives non-obligor's separate property a right of reimbursement **"[i]f separate is . . . applied at a time when nonexempt property in the community estate or separate property of the person's spouse is available but is not applied to the satisfaction of the debt, the married person is entitled to reimbursement to the extent such property was available."**

The non-obligor's right of reimbursement is consistent with the family expense presumption. Under that presumption, the community is liable for family expenses because those expenses are obligations of support for the current marriage. Only if and when community funds are exhausted, does separate property become liable for family expenses without reimbursement, absent an agreement otherwise. This outcome is also rationalized by the § 720 support obligation. By comparison, § 914(b) gives the non-obligor's separate property a right of reimbursement if community property assets could have been used but weren't. The non-obligor's § 914(b) reimbursement is restitutionary, not punitive.

Debts for necessaries of life and common necessaries of life can be incurred in a myriad of ways involving contracts, torts and other obligations.

During marriage, as discussed above, contract creditors can satisfy debts incurred for **"necessaries of life"** from the community property estate, and both spouses' separate property estates. But during periods of separation, while contract creditors can continue to reach a married person's separate property, they can only reach one-half of the community property for a debt incurred by the obligor spouse, and then only for common necessaries of life.

[2] Common Necessaries of Life During Separation

After separation the common necessaries of life doctrine is set forth in § 914(a)(2):

(a) Notwithstanding Section 913, a married person is personally liable for the following debts incurred by the person's spouse during marriage:

(2) Except as provided by Section 4302, a debt incurred for common necessaries of life of the person's spouse while the spouses are living separately.

The non-obligor's separate property is exempt from the reach of creditors unless the debt is for the obligor's **"common necessaries of life."** Then, only if there is no available community property, can creditors reach the non-obligor's separate property estate for expenses that were incurred by the obligor spouse for common necessaries of life. In other words, the non-obligor's separate property only becomes liable if the community property and the obligor's separate property cannot meet his or her basic living expenses. And even then, the non-obligor may be entitled to a reimbursement from either the community estate or the obligor's separate property, if and as funds in those estates become available.

The term *necessaries* is a relative term whose "meaning must be ascertained by reference to the context, and to the objects and purposes of the statute in which it is found."[32] The concept of necessaries derives from exemption statutes for debtors — statutes that are interpreted by the longstanding policy that encourages a liberal construction of exemption statutes in favor of the debtor, and a strict construction of statutes that limit exemptions. Against this backdrop, during marriage, the *necessaries of life doctrine* (standard of living expenses) limits the non-obligor spouse from invoking an exemption for his or her separate property for expenses related to spousal support. The *common necessaries of life doctrine* (basic living expenses), on the other hand, encourages that exemption.

During a period of separation, absent a court order otherwise, the non-obligor spouse is personally liable (only) for the other spouse's common necessaries of life. In the early case of *Los Angeles Finance Co. v. Flores*, the husband's purchase of a gold wrist watch for his wife was deemed not a common necessary exempt from the claims of creditors. In reaching this holding the court distinguished between "necessaries of life" and "common necessaries of life." Necessaries of life are expenses "necessary to the particular debtor considering all the circumstances — his station in life, his particular type of employment, etc. . . . while 'common necessaries of life' means those things which are commonly required by persons for the sustenance of life regardless of their employment or status."[33] The court went on to say that statutes enacted to exempt property from execution — in this case the non-obligor's separate property — are enacted for "the benevolent purpose of saving debtors and their families from want by reason of misfortune or improvidence; whereas statutes that limit exemptions are to be liberally construed" out of fairness to creditors.[34]

Therefore, during separation, the word "common" places a serious limitation on the concept of necessaries of life. Common necessaries of life are basic living expenses, not standard of living expenses. Common necessaries include clothing, food, and shelter. In another important early case, *Evans v. Noonan*, the court held that medical services are common necessaries of life. To hold otherwise, the court said:

> . . . [W]ould appeal to our minds as barbaric both in its conception and conclusion. . . . *Common necessaries of life* [are] such things as are proper and requisite for the sustenance of man. With equal certainty these include, besides food, clothing and shelter such medical attentions in cases of illness as are absolutely requisite to relieve physical suffering and pain and to

---

[32] *San Diego & Coronado Ferry Co. v. Railroad Com.*, 210 Cal. 504, 512, 292 P. 640 (Cal. 1930) (in bank).

[33] *Los Angeles Finance Co. v. Flores*, 110 Cal. App. 2d. Supp. 850, 856, 243 P.2d 139 (Cal. App. Ct., 2d Dist. 1952).

[34] *Id.* at 854.

> overcome or conquer disease, if by such attentions it can be done.[35]

(Italics in the original.)

Liability continues up until the time of division as provided by § 916(a)(2):

> **The separate property owned by a married person at the time of the division and the property received by the person in the division is not liable for the debt incurred by the person's spouse before or during marriage, and the person is not personally laible for the debt, unless the debt was assigned for payment by the person in the division of the property. Nothing in this paragraph affects the liability of property for the satisfaction of a lien on the property.**

In a recent case, the court of appeal held that the date that an enforceable marriage settlement agreement is signed constitutes the division of community property for purposes § 916(b)(2). On that date, the nondebtor's (formerly) community property interest becomes separate property exempt from the liabilities that the other spouse incurred before or during marriage, including for necessaries of life, and through separation, including for common necessaries.[36]

Finally, a secured debt that gets assigned to a party is that party's personal debt. However, as in *Lezine*, the property that secures that debt can be used to satisfy the creditor's claim in the event of default by the debtor.[37]

Example 12.17: This example illustrates the concept of necessaries of life. Haight and Ashbury are both high-earning physicians. Due to their busy work schedules, they find it necessary to employ a full time housekeeper. During their marriage, the housekeeper's salary (a contract debt) falls into the category of necessaries of life.

Example 12.18: This example illustrates the concept of common necessaries of life during separation. Haight and Ashbury are both high-earning physicians. When they separate, Haight is so distraught that he can no longer support himself by work. The spouses have no community property savings that Haight can draw on for support during the period of separation. Haight rents an apartment. He fires the housekeeper that he and Ashbury employed during the marriage; he immediately rehires that person to provide domestic services in his apartment. Eventually, Haight owes the housekeeper $1,500 in back pay. Ashbury knows that Haight's rent is a common necessary of life, as is his clothing, food, and medical care. However, Ashbury refuses to pay the contract debt for housekeeping. The housekeeper sues Ashbury for breach of contract. The housekeeper contends that the contract debt for housekeeping is included within the category of common necessaries of life during Haight's separation from Ashbury given that housekeeping was a necessaries of life expense during their marriage.[38] In the housekeeper's suit against

---

[35] *Evans v. Noonan*, 20 Cal. App. 288, 292, 293, 128 P. 794 (Cal. App. Ct., 3d Dist. 1912) (reviewing court cases from other jurisdictions).

[36] Cal. Fam. Code § 916(a)(2), interpreted by *Litke O'Farrell, supra.*

[37] *Lezine, supra.*

[38] *Wisnom v. McCarthy*, 48 Cal. App. 697, 192 P. 337 (Cal. App. Ct., 1st Dist. 1920).

Ashbury, Ashbury prevails. Haight is the obligor on the housekeeping contract, not Ashbury — so Haight is personally liable on that contract. Haight has no separate property, and there is no community property. Even so, Ashbury's separate property — which would include her post-separation earnings and accumulations — is not reachable by Haight's contract creditor in this case because housekeeping services are not *common* necessaries of life.

Finally, a debt for necessaries of life, even if obtained during marriage, can be assigned to the obligor spouse as his or her personal debt either in an enforceable marriage settlement agreement or by a court order or judgment. For example:

- A debt incurred during marriage but in anticipation of separation was held to be the obligor's personal debt;[39]
- A contract debt for attorney's fees related to one spouse's criminal defense was held to be the defendant-spouse's personal debt;[40]
- A contract debt advanced to the obligor spouse in fraud of the community was held to be the obligor's personal debt even though the debt was incurred during marriage and some of the fraudulently obtained loan proceeds were applied to a community property mortgage;[41]
- A contract to hire a private investigator during marriage so as to assist in a dissolution proceeding was assigned to the obligor spouse a personal debt;[42] and
- Hospital debt incurred by the obligor while the parties were still married but living separate and apart was assigned to the obligor as a personal debt.[43]

§ 12.04 SUMMARY

From the date of the marriage on, the community property is liable for the premarital and marital debts of both spouses. This is because either spouse has management and control of the community property.

Some exemptions exist. For example, during the marriage, a non-obligor spouse can exempt his or her community property earnings from the premarital debts of the obligor spouse. Also, a non-obligor spouse is liable only for the other spouse's contract debts for common necessaries of life during a period of separation, not for standard of living expenses, and then only if the obligor cannot meet those obligations him or herself. Additionally, a tort judgment or other obligation against one spouse is not generally satisfiable against the separate property of the other spouse.

---

39 *Mahone*, 123 Cal. App. 3d 17, 176 Cal. Rptr. 274 (Cal. App. Ct., 2d Dist. 1981).

40 *Marriage of Stitt*, 147 Cal. App. 3d 579, 195 Cal. Rptr. 172 (Cal. App. Ct., 5th Dist. 1983).

41 *Lezine, supra.*

42 *Marriage of Munguia*, 146 Cal. App. 3d 853, 195 Cal. Rptr. 199 (Cal. App. Ct., 1st Dist. 1983).

43 *CMRE Financial Services, Inc. v. Parton*, 184 Cal. App. 4th 263, 109 Cal. Rptr. 3d 139, (Cal. App. Ct., 4th Dist. 2010) (rev. denied).

California marshals the estates from which a creditor can satisfy a claim depending on whether the debt was incurred for a family purpose (or not).

Liability to third parties intersects with support obligations. During marriage, the spouses have mutual duties of support. These duties commence on the date of the marriage; they extend through the marriage until separation. During marriage, the community property and the spouses' separate property estates are liable for necessaries of life. From separation to the final judgment of dissolution, a non-obligor remains potentially liable (only) for the other spouse's common necessaries.

In the dissolution proceeding, the debts are confirmed to one or both spouses.

Part V

CONTRACTS BETWEEN PROSPECTIVE SPOUSES, SPOUSES, AND NONMARRIED COHABITANTS

Chapter 13

PREMARITAL AGREEMENTS

Agreements between married persons come in several forms.

A *premarital contract* — sometimes called a prenuptial or ante nuptial agreement — is an agreement made between prospective spouses in contemplation of marriage. A *marital agreement* is an agreement made during marriage: Some marital agreements are executed for the first time during marriage, while others amend or revoke a premarital contract. A *marriage settlement agreement* is an agreement between spouses to dissolve and divide the community estate at the termination of a marriage. For purposes of premarital and marital agreements, registered domestic partners have the same rights and obligations as spouses. This chapter refers to premarital agreements as applied to spouses, but only for the sake of brevity.

Different agreements are governed by different Family Code provisions. Therefore, it is important to distinguish premarital agreements, amendments and revocations from other marital agreements, such as transmutations.

The chapter starts with a general overview of the premarital contracting. From there it moves to the following specific issues: spousal support, disclosure, voluntariness, and equitable remedies.

The contract modification principle is one of the cornerstone principles of the community property system.

§ 13.01 PREMARITAL AGREEMENTS: AN OVERVIEW

The Spanish *ganancial* system allowed prospective spouses to "contract away the community edifice."[1] In the historic *ganancial* system, unlike in the historic common law system, the wife retained her legal identity during marriage. This meant that in the *ganancial* system prospective spouses had the legal capacity to enter into a premarital contract that would take effect on the date of marriage and become enforceable in the event that the marriage terminated. Consideration came in the form of mutual consent. Undue influence, duress, deceit or fraud made the contract unenforceable for lack of consideration. In accordance with the contract modification principle, spouses could change some or nearly all of the *ganancial* system rules. Therefore, absent a premarital agreement, the spouses were presumed to have accepted the default terms of the applicable community property law. A court had discretion to order post-dissolution spousal support.

---

[1] William Q. de Funiak & Michael J. Vaughn, Principles of Community Property (2d ed. 1971).

Following the *ganancial* system, California law also permitted prospective spouses to enter into premarital contracts.[2] Parties could validly contract as to property owned by them before marriage and to property (including earnings) that they expected to acquire during marriage. Historically, as to spousal support obligations, the majority view in the U.S. was that the husband had a duty to support the wife during and after marriage in accordance with his financial ability. In that same male management era, a California husband's support obligation was also understood to exist during the lifetime of the parties.[3] The wife had a corollary duty to support her husband. But whereas the husband's duty was not limited, the wife's duty existed only if the parties were living together, the husband had no separate property, there was no community property or quasi community property, and the husband was unable, from infirmity, to support himself.[4] Moreover, the wife's duty only came into existence if the husband had not abandoned or "deserted the wife."[5]

In *Marriage of Higgason*, a 73 year old woman with substantial wealth married a 48 year old man who had no assets other than his earnings of $2 an hour plus tips. Prior to their 1969 marriage, the parties signed a contract in which each waived "all right for contribution to the support, maintenance and expenses of the other party."[6] When the parties separated, the husband sought support from the wife for necessary living expenses. The trial court declined to give the husband spousal support, citing the premarital contract. Eventually, the California Supreme Court heard the case. It ordered the trial court to exercise its discretion with respect to the husband's post-separation and post-dissolution spousal support petitions. The California Supreme Court confirmed the law of that time: Spousal support waivers were against California public policy, and thus unenforceable as a matter of law.[7]

In 1975 California transitioned to an equal management regime. In 1985, California adopted its version of the model Uniform Premarital Agreement Act (UPAA 1983).[8] The CPAA 1985 went into effect on January 1, 1986. It was reenacted in 1994 as part of the Cal. Fam. Code §§1600 through 1617. In 2001, the Legislature added provisions to the CPAA 1985. The CPAA 2001 legislation became effective January 1, 2002.

The law on premarital agreements has changed considerably since the decision in *Higgason*. Today, there are three legal regimes to consider depending on when the premarital contract at issue was executed or amended: (1) the pre-CPAA law, most of which is decisional; (2) the CPAA 1985; and (3) the current CPAA 2001. Contracts executed (or amended) before January 1, 1986 are governed by the pre-CPAA law. The CPAA 1985 governs contracts executed (or amended) on or

---

[2] *Pereira, supra*, Chapter 7.

[3] *Marriage of Higgason*, 10 Cal. 3d 476, 110 Cal. Rptr. 897, 516 P.2d 289 (1973) (in bank), citing 54 Harv. L. Rev. 473, 478 (1941).

[4] *Id.* at 487–88 (in bank), citing Cal. Civ. Code § 5132 (1970).

[5] *Marriage of Higgason, supra*, at 487.

[6] *Id.* at 479.

[7] *Id.*

[8] National Conference of Commissioners on Uniform State Laws.

between January 1, 1986 and December 31, 2001. The CPAA 2001 governs contracts executed (or amended) on or after January 1, 2002.

Generally, amendments to the Family Code apply retroactively. Questions about CPAA retroactivity arise, however, because the CPAA 1985 includes a non-retroactivity clause, but the CPAA 2001 does not.[9] The omission of a non-retroactivity clause from the CPAA 2001 has raised the issue of whether the Legislature intended the 2001 amendments — specifically§ 1612(c) and § 1615(c) — to apply retroactively. In 2011, a court of appeal held in *Marriage of Howell* that CPAA 2001 § 1612(c) imposes additional duties on prospective spouses, and as such is a non-retroactive material change to the prior legislation (CPAA 1985).[10] In *Marriage of Hill and Dittmer*, CPAA 2001 § 1615 was held non-retroactive; again the rationale was that the amended version of § 1615 imposed additional duties on prospective spouses.[11]

Today, the CPAA 2001, as it appears in the Family Code, governs all premarital contracts entered into on or after January 1, 2002. Generally, **"the property rights"** of spouses **"prescribed by statute may be altered by a premarital agreement or other marital property agreement"** both by case law and by the authority of § 1500. Even so, during marriage, basic duties to support one's spouse cannot be waived by premarital or marital contract.[12] Otherwise, prospective spouses may alter one, some or nearly all of the community property laws by contract.

Premarital and marital contracts that meet CPAA 2001 formality and consent requirements are nonconclusively presumed to be enforceable. The presumption of enforceability is rebuttable if the party against whom enforcement is sought can show either that the contract was unconscionable when it was signed, or that it was the product of coercion. Unconscionability and involuntariness are discussed in § 13.05.

As with the historic *ganancial* system, marital property is excluded from the general property rules of the Civil Code. It is governed instead by the Family Code, the policy of which is to create equality of interest between the spouses in property matters. The default rules of the Family Code apply only in the absence of an enforceable premarital agreement.

Contrary to popular understanding, *prospective* spouses cannot owe each other obligations stemming from community property ownership. This is because the community estate does not exist until the date of marriage. Prospective spouses can own property jointly before marriage, but they own that property as individuals, not as a marital community; and therefore that property comes to the marriage as

---

[9] Cal. Fam. Code § 4(c).

[10] *Marriage of Howell*, 195 Cal. App. 4th 1062, 126 Cal. Rptr. 3d 539 (Cal. App. Ct., 4th Dist. 2011), distinguishing *Marriage of Fellows*, 39 Cal. 4th 179, 46 Cal. Rptr. 3d 49, 138 P.3d 200 (Cal. 2006) (in bank); *see also Marriage of Melissa*, 212 Cal. App. 4th 598, 151 Cal. Rptr. 3d 608 (Cal. App. Ct., 4th Dist. 2012); *In re Marriage of Facter*, 212 Cal. App. 4th 967, 152 Cal. Rptr. 3d 79 (Cal. App. Ct., 1st Dist. 2013).

[11] *Marriage of Hill and Dittmer*, 202 Cal. App. 4th 1046, 136 Cal. Rptr. 3d 700 (Cal. App. Ct., 2d Dist. 2011).

[12] *Higgason, supra*; *Borelli v. Brusseau*, 12 Cal. App. 4th 647, 16 Cal. Rptr. 2d 16 (Cal. App. Ct., 1st Dist. 1993).

concurrently owned separate property. At marriage, the community has a zero balance in its asset column. The balance changes for better or worse during marriage.

Premarital agreements specifically determine the rights of the parties in relation to each other. They can also determine the rights of a third party donee or transferee who has notice of the agreement. General rules of actual, inquiry, and record notice apply to third parties. For real property, record notice is given when a premarital agreement is recorded in the County Recorder's Office of each county in which the real property affected by the agreement is situated.

§ 13.02 FORMALITIES

Prospective spouses can use a premarital contract to enter into a binding legal agreement about their property rights and obligations during marriage.

CPAA § 1611 sets forth the basic formalities for premarital contracts.

[A] The Writing Requirement

All premarital agreements and other marital property agreements **"shall be in writing and signed by both parties,"** not just the party to be charged.[13] Under the CPAA, only prospective spouses can execute a premarital contract, not their relatives. The CPAA has no provision for contract signature by proxy or agent. Thus a premarital agreement that is signed by parents, proxies, matchmakers, or any other cultural agents who are clothed by tradition or culture with indicia of authority to contract marriage on behalf of the prospective spouses does not meet the basic § 1611 formalities.[14] This is a clear departure from any traditional understanding of the premarital contract as one in which the parties' parents, elders, or cultural agents have the indicia of authority to negotiate contracts on the prospective spouses' behalf.

Consideration is not a required element for enforceability.

If a marriage is later deemed void, the agreement that would otherwise have been a premarital agreement may be enforceable, but **"only to the extent necessary to avoid an inequitable result."**[15] Parties often contract around this provision with a clause that links the validity of the contract to the occurrence and validity of the marriage (e.g., "*If we do not marry this contract is null and void. If one or both of us obtains a judgment of nullity, this contract is void.*")

In California, prospective spouses are not (yet) in a confidential relationship as a matter of law. Instead, they are legal strangers negotiating a quasi-commercial contract. From this position, prospective spouses negotiate over what (they hope) will occur in the context of their upcoming marriage, but they do so from outside the quasi-fiduciary structure discussed in Chapter 10. What protects the

---

[13] Cal. Fam. Code § 1611

[14] *See Marriage of Noghrey*, 169 Cal. App. 3d 326, 215 Cal. Rptr. 153 (Cal. App. Ct., 6th Dist. 1985).

[15] Cal. Fam. Code § 1616.

prospective spouses against allegations of each other's coercion, then, is careful compliance with the CPAA 2001 provisions on formalities and consent.[16]

As one reads this chapter, keep this guiding principle in mind: A fair contract is more likely to be enforceable in the event of dissolution than is an unfair contract.

Example 13.1: This example illustrates the relationship between CPAA § 1611 compliance and enforceability. Harrison and Winona want to marry. They orally agree that all of their earnings will remain their separate property during marriage. This agreement fails to meet the basic formalities of the CPAA. The contract is unenforceable.

Example 13.2: This example also illustrates the relationship between CPAA § 1611 compliance and enforceability. Harrison and Winona want to marry. They agree in writing that all of their earnings will remain their separate property during marriage. Both sign a written agreement to that effect. This agreement meets the basic formalities of the CPAA, notwithstanding the lack of consideration. The contract is potentially enforceable.

[B] Permissible Subject Matter

CPAA § 1612(a)-(7) expressly permits prospective spouses to contract over a broad range of topics such as:

- the parties' rights and obligations over property acquired by either (or both) before or during marriage, including property in other jurisdictions;
- how property will be managed and controlled;
- how property will be disposed of in the event of separation, dissolution, or the death of a spouse;
- how property will be disposed of in the event of a contingency such as an inheritance, a windfall, the success (or failure) of a business, and so forth;
- testamentary and trust matters;
- life insurance matters;
- choice of law matters, whether secular or religious;
- and, in accordance with § 1612(a)(7), **"any other matter, including their personal rights and obligations, not in violation of public policy or a statute imposing a criminal penalty"** at the time that the contract is executed. This statutory clause implicitly authorizes spousal support waivers. It appears in both the CPAA 1985 and CPAA 2001.

[1] Property Terms

"Property" is defined under CPAA § 1610(b) to mean: **"An interest present or future, legal or equitable, vested or contingent, in real or personal property, including income and earnings."**

---

[16] In some other states prospective spouses are in a confidential relationship to each other as of the date of their engagement.

Premarital and marital contract debts, tort liabilities, and other obligations are payable by the community estate. Moreover, these types of liabilities (past, present, and future) are readily quantifiable, and thus (easily) the subject of a premarital agreement. So too are clauses that define debts in relation to family purpose.

Some common property-related themes of premarital contracting include but certainly are not limited to:

- Inventorying all assets and liabilities;
- Valuing assets as of the date of marriage;
- Agreements about:
  - o property acquired by inter vivos gift during the marriage, including engagement and wedding gifts;
  - o the management and control of community property;
  - o the acquisition and control of separate property during the marriage;
  - o the purchase, maintenance, and disposition of insurance, including home, liability, disability, umbrella, and life insurance;
  - o compensation for the use of labor in a separate property business;
  - o choice of law at dissolution;
  - o liability for premarital debts;
  - o liability for debts incurred by one or both spouses during marriage or periods of physical separation;
- The disposition of property in the event of dissolution or death;
- Post-dissolution spousal support.

Choice of law provisions are permitted under § 1612(a)(6). Pursuant to this clause, parties may opt for different rules within the community property system, such as particular tracing methods, different apportionment methods, and so forth. Parties may contract for the law of another state. Parties may incorporate the law of another jurisdiction (civil or religious) into their premarital contract. Choice of law provisions are permitted, subject to legal and constitutional limitations.[17]

[2] Non-Quantifiable Terms

Non-quantifiable contract terms appear in premarital contracts as what are sometimes referred to as "lifestyle" terms. Lifestyle terms — such as who will do the housework, whether any children of the marriage will be allowed to engage in a given activity, or what kind of car the parties will drive — are more likely to be regarded as unenforceable at divorce since there is no evident (monetizable) remedy for their breach.

Likewise under § 1612(a)(7) courts will not enforce premarital contract terms that **"violate public policy or a statute imposing a criminal penalty."** A contract term that requires one spouse to convert to the other spouse's religion, for example,

---

[17] *See Marriage of Shaban*, 88 Cal. App. 4th 398, 105 Cal. Rptr. 2d 863 (Cal. App. Ct., 4th Dist. 2001).

can be challenged as an impairment of constitutional rights.[18] A contract term that requires sexual performance in exchange for financial support or that exacts promises about sexual behavior, or that promises money in exchange for virginity is likewise subject to challenge on public policy grounds. Such terms raise vexing questions about the role of the courts in defining private sexual activity. Moreover, enforcing contract language about the definition of sex has legal consequence. First, it gives rise to precedent about the meaning of the word sex. Second, any such precedent runs the risk of returning fault to the dissolution equation. Third, to the degree that a contract clause governing sexual conduct may be a proxy for adherence to a religious view, it is also subject to challenge.

Promises of a sum-certain lump sum settlement on divorce (inconsistently) have been held unenforceable for promoting divorce.[19]

Therapy and anger management clauses appear to be non-quantifiable, but they clearly can have implications for the control and management of property. During marriage, either spouse has absolute power of disposition over community property, modified by quasi-fiduciary duties. For that reason, altercations that result in the intentional or negligent destruction of community property are actionable on several grounds, no matter whether the destructive act occurred inside or outside the home. When one spouse wrongfully destroys community property, the other spouse's community property rights in that property are impaired. An affected spouse can seek a restraining order, sue for civil tort, or file a criminal complaint against the other spouse.

Furthermore, the Domestic Violence Prevention Act (DVPA), which appears at §§ 6200–6409, permits one spouse to apply for an ex-parte order to alter or cancel the other (abusive) spouse's rights to manage and control community property during the marriage.[20] An anger management clause in a premarital contract can allow the prospective spouses to agree on how abusive behavior will be defined in the context of their upcoming marriage, and on how abusive incidents will be documented. If one spouse applies for an ex parte restraining order, this jointly compiled record (at least initially) will serve as the basis for a court order that grants one spouse the exclusive control of property, at least until a hearing can be scheduled. Domestic violence issues are discussed in Chapter 11.

[C] Amendments and Revocations

Under CPAA § 1614, **"After marriage, a premarital agreement may be amended or revoked."** However, any and all such amendments or revocations must comply with CPAA § 1614, which also requires a subsequent **"written agreement signed by the parties."**

Amendments and revocations must comply with the same formalities as the original premarital contract. Additionally, because the parties are married, § 721(b) fiduciary duties come into play. *See* Chapter 10.

---

[18] *Marriage of Weiss*, 42 Cal. App. 4th 106, 49 Cal. Rptr. 2d 339 (Cal. App. Ct., 2d Dist. 1996).

[19] *Pereira*, supra; *Noghrey*, *supra*.

[20] Cherri N. Allison et al., Domestic Violence Remedies in California Family Law Cases (2007)

In the original premarital contract, parties can agree about events that might trigger amendment or revocation. Or, they can agree to a date after which the premarital agreement automatically becomes ineffective (i.e., "*Upon our tenth wedding anniversary, this agreement will no longer be effective.*")

[D] Stale Premarital Contracts and Contract Terms

Under §1617, during marriage: **"Any statute of limitations"** for **"a claim for relief under a premarital agreement is tolled,"** even though **"equitable defenses limiting the time for enforcement, including laches and estoppel are available to either party."**

Premarital contracts can become so stale that the passage of time constitutes a form of conduct. When this happens, one party may have an equitable defense to the contract under § 1617. California has no cases directly on point. However, recent cases from this and other jurisdictions illustrate when equitable defenses might arise. Generally, they would arise when the spouses develop expectations during the continuance of their marriage that are so different from the expectations upon which their premarital contract was based that the failure to update is itself conduct that gives rise to an equitable contract defense. Life changes can render even the fairest contract term unfair over time. In light of this reality, the CPAA seeks to uphold the prospective spouses' contract rights, while also, under § 1617, preserving the parties' equitable remedies.

CPAA 2001 § 1617 is adopted from UPAA § 8: the latter provision explains that tolling any statute of limitations on a premarital contract claim during marriage is a necessary way to prevent compelling the spouses to litigate contract issues. Spouses are not required to sue each other during the continuance of the marriage, but neither can they sit on their rights. The flip side of § 1617 is that either party has an implied duty to address changed circumstances during the marriage. If a premarital contract has become stale, amendment is likely required. By amending the contract to better reflect updated family realities, the party who expects to enforce the contract in a (potential) future dissolution or probate proceeding diminishes the risk that the contract may be deemed unenforceable. Likewise, the party against whom (a future) enforcement might be sought must take proactive steps to protect his or her rights so to minimize the opposite risk that a stale term may be deemed enforceable. Thus, the benefit to the community property system of tolling any statute of limitations during the marriage under § 1617 appears to be balanced against an implicit recognition that the spouses have a duty to amend or revoke a premarital contract if circumstances change.

In *Marriage of Melissa*, Raymond and Roberta were married in 1985. Although *Melissa* was not brought under § 1617, the case illustrates how a contract might become unconscionably stale. In 1985, Raymond and Roberta signed a premarital agreement waiving post-dissolution spousal support. Raymond and Roberta subsequently had a child, R., who was born with a mental disability. R. also suffered from Fragile-X syndrome and autism. In 1997, Raymond and Roberta (orally) agreed that Roberta would stop working full time to care for R. Roberta cared for R. up until a 2009 dissolution proceeding was filed. A year into the dissolution proceeding, Raymond sought to enforce the 1985 premarital contract against Roberta.[21] This California case was decided on different grounds, but the fact pattern is a good example of how circumstances and expectations can change radically over the course of a marriage.

On one hand, the CPAA § 1614 requires that all amendments to premarital contracts be in writing. But on the other hand, when Robert and Roberta's expectations about Roberta's ability to earn income changed suddenly and radically at R.'s birth, a § 1617 issue arose. Was Raymond estopped from enforcing the original contract against Roberta given that (1) R. needed home care; (2) Raymond consented to and encouraged Roberta to quit her paying job so that she could care for R. full time; (3) Raymond financially benefitted from Roberta's decade-long home care of R; and (4) Raymond did nothing in that decade to amend or otherwise update the original 1985 premarital contract in which Roberta had waived post-dissolution spousal support rights?[22]

A New Jersey case, *Rogers v. Gordon*, addresses the § 1617 equitable remedies issue head on.[23] In *Rogers*, a premarital agreement was executed in 1981. At the time they married, the parties were of disparate educational backgrounds: Ricki Rogers was a recent Princeton graduate; Richard Gordon was an occasional community college student who was employed by the U.S. Postal Service. At marriage, Ricki and Richard had no assets, but Ricki had every expectation of inheriting a substantial estate from her father. For that reason, she and Richard signed a premarital agreement that contained an alimony waiver clause, and a property clause restricting the definition of property that would be subject to equitable division in the event of a divorce. In 1987 — just six years after the original premarital agreement was signed — New Jersey enacted the UPAA. In response to that legal transition, Ricki requested that Richard sign a declaration affirming that he had executed the 1981 premarital contract.[24] He did so.

In 2005, Ricki filed for divorce. She moved to enforce the 1981 premarital contract. Richard countered, in part, on grounds that the premarital contract was unconscionable given that the parties were in very different circumstances at the end of their marriage than they had been at its beginning. Over the course of a quarter century, the couple had gone from owning nothing to (Ricki) owning substantial assets; Ricki came into ownership of what was once her father's company and she drew a salary of $578,000 from that company. Richard, meanwhile, had quit his secure federal job, with pension benefits, to work as an at-will employee at Ricki's company. Richard made $63,000 per year during marriage. His job skills were unique to Ricki's company, and he suspected that Ricki would fire him once the divorce was final. Richard petitioned for alimony to avoid having to apply for public assistance after the divorce. An extensive trial record was compiled on Ricki's contract enforceability motion. The trial court held that the entire 1981 premarital contract was unenforceable due to change of circumstances.

---

21 *Melissa, supra.*

22 *Id.*

23 *Rogers v. Gordon*, 404 N.J. Super. 213, 961 A.2d 11 (S. Ct. 2008).

24 The UPAA requires that amendments be in writing and signed by both parties. A declaration by one party does not meet this requirement.

Interlocutory appeals and cross-appeals followed. Eventually, the New Jersey Supreme Court severed the alimony waiver, but otherwise enforced the 1981 contract. The court based its decision on several factors, the most relevant of which was that Richard affirmed the 1981 premarital contract in 1987, in response to New Jersey's adoption of the UPAA.

Rogers was decided by pre-UPAA law, notwithstanding Richard's declared affirmation of the contract in 1987. Ricki — the party who sought to enforce the contract — did not sit on her rights in 1987 when she learned that about New Jersey's adoption of the UPAA, but neither did she follow the UPAA formalities for amending a premarital contract. Instead, Ricki asked Richard to affirm the premarital contract by a unilateral declaration made without the benefit of independent counsel.

Rogers raises several issues about the scope of § 1617. Does § 1617 impose a duty on the parties to update a premarital contract when conditions change during the continuance of the marriage? If it does, aren't such amendments and revocations required to be in writing and signed by both parties under the UPAA? And, what should be the consequences under the UPAA of a non-UPAA compliant amendment or revocation?

These issues gravitate around the question of what role amendments play in the UPAA. The need — as opposed to the desire — for amendments can arise, for example, as it did in *Marriage of Melissa* when a special-needs child is born, or as it did in *Rogers v. Gordon* when one spouse gives up a secure job, with retirement benefits, in order to assist the other spouse with a family business.

In these situations, § 1617 appears to implicitly obligate the parties to address any major change in their circumstances. But it is not (yet) clear which party bears the legal burden of seeking updates. Given that premarital contracts are often mutual on many terms, both parties have an interest in keeping a premarital contract updated, as neither party knows — until the dissolution or probate proceeding — which of them will seek to enforce the contract.

One important function of §1617 is to toll statutes of limitations during the continuance of the marriage while also preserving equitable defenses for the party against whom enforcement might be sought. Arguably contract formation defenses are not contemplated by § 1617: This is because a premarital contract that does not comply with basic CPAA formalities will almost certainly be held unenforceable.

However, where a party seeks to enforce an otherwise valid but stale premarital contract, the party who seeks to enforce the contract can and should expect that the party against whom enforcement is sought will raise equitable defenses under § 1617. Additionally, permitting a premarital contract to go unconscionably stale during the continuance of a marriage may be alleged as a violation of the benefitted spouse's fiduciary duty in relation to the adversely affected spouse.

§ 13.03 STATUTORY SUBJECT MATTER LIMITATIONS

The CPAA lists three categorical subject matter limitations on the prospective spouses' right to contract. They are discussed in order of their appearance in the statute.

[A] Provisions in Violation of Public Policy

Parties are prohibited as a matter of public policy from contracting in any way that adversely affects child support. For this reason, § 1612(b) makes clear that: **"The right of a child to support may not be adversely affected by a premarital agreement."** Child support waivers, child custody agreements, child visitation agreements — none of these issues can be settled by the enforcement of a contract at the end of the marriage. To the contrary, all require an updated assessment of the best interests of the child.

More generally, § 1612(a)(7) prohibits parties from contracting in violation of public policy. Terms that violate public policy are unenforceable. Such terms include, but certainly are not limited to:

- Any contract term that attempts to waive spousal support *during* marriage;
- Any contract term that attempts to waive the duty of good faith and fair dealing during marriage;
- Any contract term whose enforcement would be unconstitutional;
- Any contract term that promotes dissolution, as determined by the contract language itself;
- Any post-dissolution spousal support provision that is unconscionable at the end of the marriage.

Finally, § 1612(a)(7) also provides that parties may not contract **"in violation of . . . a statute imposing a criminal penalty."** Here the test for enforceability is whether the contract term was in violation of a statute that imposed a criminal penalty as of the contract execution date. Given the large number of property related offenses in the Criminal Code, this restriction may cover a large amount of legal territory.

[B] Spousal Support Provisions

The *ganancial* system permitted prospective spouses to waive post-divorce spousal support by contract. California law, by contrast, did not. Prior to the adoption of the UPAA, California law held that spousal support waivers were per se unenforceable. *Marriage of Higgason*, affirmed this rule in 1973 by a unanimous decision of the California Supreme Court.[25] In 2000, the California Supreme Court altered the bright-line rule of *Higgason* in *Marriage of Pendleton and Fireman* when it held that spousal support waivers are not per se unenforceable. Instead, their enforceability depends upon the parties' circumstances at the time that the

[25] *Higgason, supra.*

premarital contract is executed. In response to *Marriage of Pendleton and Fireman*, the Legislature added § 1612(c) to the CPAA in 2001. CPAA 2001 § 1612(c) treats as presumptively enforceable any spousal support provision executed on or after January 1, 2002 that was executed with the assistance of independent counsel *and* that is not unconscionable at enforcement (i.e., at termination of marriage by dissolution or death).

To summarize, the *Higgason* ban on post-dissolution spousal support waivers has been superseded by CPAA § 1612(a)(7). The *Pendleton and Fireman* rule that (only) the parties' circumstances at contract execution determine whether a post-dissolution spousal support waiver is upheld at enforcement has been superseded by § 1612(c). *Higgason* continues to stand for the rule that spousal support obligations and rights are not gender specific, and it continues to be discussed in relation to what level of mental capacity is necessary to file a petition for dissolution.[26]

[1] Spousal Support During Marriage

During marriage, spouses contract toward each other obligations of mutual respect, fidelity, and support. The duty of support is found at § 720. The duty to give and receive support is a core element of the marriage contract as well as of the community property system. The duty to give and receive support is recognized by the statutory law, by spousal liability rules, by case law, and by the CPAA 2001. *See* Chapters 10, 11, and 12.

The § 720 support obligation is reflected in § 1620, which provides that **"husband and wife cannot, by a contract with each other, alter their legal relations, except as to property."** In *Mathiasen*, an unpublished case, the parties' agreement to split expenses on an equal basis was held unenforceable.[27] In *Borelli v. Brusseau*, wife, Hildegard, sued her deceased spouse Michael's estate for specific performance on what appeared to be an orally amended 1980 premarital agreement. During the marriage Michael had heart problems, and eventually suffered a stroke. As a result, Michael and Hildegard agreed that Hildegard would care for Michael at home in exchange for Michael's promise to bequeath property to Hildegard.[28] Hildegard performed her end of the bargain; Michael did not.

Hildegard sued Michael's estate. The estate demurred on the ground that a promise of support is not consideration for a contract between spouses. The trial court granted the demurrer. The court of appeal sustained; it reasoned that apart from community property rights that arise from the marriage itself, a spouse is not entitled to compensation for providing support to the other spouse. A dissent expressed skepticism about whether the general duty of spousal support includes within it a more specific duty to provide home nursing care to a spouse who is near death. The very fact that such a dissent was published foretells that the scope of the

---

[26] *Marriage of Straczynski*, 189 Cal. App. 4th 531, 116 Cal. Rptr. 3d 938 (Cal. App. Ct., 4th Dist. 2010) (discusses *Higgason, supra*, at length in a case where a spouse alleges that the other has dementia).

[27] *Marriage of Mathiasen*, 219 Cal. App. 3d 1428, 268 Cal. Rptr. 895 (Cal. App. Ct., 6th Dist. 1990) (rev. denied (unpublished)).

[28] *Borelli, supra*.

duty of spousal support, especially in cases of grave illness, may be open to interpretation in light of changing times.[29]

The duty to give and receive spousal support is reflected in debt liability statutes. Either spouse is liable to third party creditors for the other's necessaries of life (i.e., standard of living expenses) during marriage. Likewise, either spouse is potentially liable to third party creditors for the other spouse's common necessaries of life (i.e., basic living expenses) during periods of physical separation.

Generally, the spousal support obligation ends when the marriage ends unless a court orders one spouse to provide post-dissolution spousal support to the other.

[2] Spousal Support After Dissolution

The Spanish *ganancial* system allowed for spousal support in theory, but not always in fact. Louisiana, a state that hews most closely to its civil law roots, once allowed post-divorce spousal support to be paid out of property holdings only, but not out of post-divorce earnings. This is no longer the rule in Louisiana today. All the same, when this law was in effect, it shielded an earning spouse's post-dissolution income from the claims of a former spouse.

Today, a court has discretion to order one party to support the other for a certain period of time after the final judgment of dissolution. The amount of support is determined by statutorily provide metrics. Resulting financial rights and obligations are by court order. Post-dissolution spousal support may be paid out of the supporting party's accumulated property or post-divorce income.

§ 13.04 POST-DISSOLUTION SPOUSAL SUPPORT WAIVERS: LEGAL TRANSITIONS

The *ganancial* rule allowed spouses to waive spousal support. But this rule was contrary to a long line of California precedent.

[A] *Marriage of Higgason*: The Pre-CPAA 1985 Standard

The CPAA 1985 was adopted against the backdrop of *Higgason*.

The CPAA 1985 appeared to be consistent with the ban on spousal support waivers, since the CPAA 1985 was based on the model UPAA 1983 statute. Specifically, CPAA 1985 included the § 1612(a)(7) clause providing that parties may contract over "**[a]ny matter, including personal rights and obligations, not in violation of public policy,**" but it omitted any express language that could be construed as allowing spousal support waivers. Predictably, litigation ensued over how to interpret the CPAA 1985.

---

[29] *Straczynski, supra.*

[B] *Marriage of Pendleton & Fireman*: The CPAA 1985 Standard

The defining case of the CPAA 1985 period (Jan. 1, 1986 to Dec. 31, 2001) was *Marriage of Pendleton & Fireman*.[30] In that case, Barry and Candace, with the help of separate and independent counsel, signed a premarital contract with reciprocal spousal support waivers. The premarital contract was executed in 1991; thus it was governed by CPAA 1985. At the time, Barry and Candace were relatively equal in terms of education and finances. Barry and Candace did not amend or revoke their original premarital contract before their separation in 1995. In 1996, Candace filed a petition for dissolution and sought spousal support. At dissolution, each spouse had a net worth of approximately $ 2.5 million. Together, they maintained a lifestyle in the $30,000 per month range, paid for primarily from Barry's business enterprises. When Barry sought to enforce the premarital contract, Candace responded that spousal support waivers were per se unconscionable under the rule in *Higgason*. If not, she argued, the enforcement of the premarital contract spousal support waiver would significantly lower her post-dissolution standard of living. She would be required to live on a net income of $4,233 per month.

The trial court ordered Barry to support Candace in the amount of $8,500 per month on the theory that the spousal support waiver was unenforceable as a matter of law. The court of appeal reversed, citing *Higgason*. The California Supreme Court reviewed the question of the relationship between CAPP 1985 and *Higgason*: The court hold that premarital waivers of spousal support are not per se unenforceable between intelligent, well-educated persons, each of whom appears to be self-sufficient in property and earning ability, and both of whom have the advice of counsel . . . *at the time they execute the waiver*."[31] (Italics added.) Justice Kennard dissented: She pointed out that the Legislature was fully aware of California's ban on contractual spousal support waivers when it enacted CPAA 1985.[32]

[C] The CPAA 2001 Standard

In response to *Marriage of Pendleton & Fireman* the Legislature amended the CPAA 1985 to include § 1612(c), effective January 1, 2002. Today, for premarital contracts that are executed on or after January 1, 2002, parties may agree to waive post-divorce spousal support by premarital contract. Authorization for the waiver is found in § 1612(a)(7). A premarital agreement spousal support waiver will be scrutinized at two points in time, by standards expressly set forth in § 1612(c).

The standards of § 1612(c) are straightforward.

---

[30] *Marriage of Pendleton and Fireman*, 24 Cal. 4th 39, 99 Cal. Rptr. 2d 278, 5 P.3d 839 (Cal. 2000) (in bank).

[31] *Pendleton and Fireman, supra.*

[32] *Id.*

[1] Represented by Independent Counsel at Execution

A party who waives spousal support must be represented by separate and independent counsel for purposes of the premarital contract. Otherwise the spousal support provision is unenforceable as to that party.

[2] Not Unconscionable at Enforcement

Later, at enforcement, the party against whom enforcement is sought — even if represented by counsel at the execution phase — can present evidence that the spousal support waiver is unconscionable and thus unenforceable as a matter of public policy. Unenforceable spousal support waivers are severable from an otherwise (possibly) enforceable premarital contract.[33]

The word "unconscionability" is used twice in the CPAA 2001: once in § 1612(c) and again in § 1615.[34] The § 1612(c) definition of unconscionability is the only definition relevant at this juncture. Unconscionability for purposes of § 1612(c) means that the enforcement of the spousal support waiver will leave the party against whom enforcement is sought eligible for public assistance. This definition is consistent with the model UPAA definition.

Unenforceable spousal support provisions are severable from the contract as a matter of law. The formalities argument for severability turns on § 1611, which holds that a premarital contract is enforceable without consideration. The fairness argument turns on § 1612(c), which together with § 1612(a)(7), recognizes that an unconscionable spousal support waiver violates public policy.

Two comparative examples help clarify the remedy of severance. In Louisiana, succession rights are considered a matter of public interest, and spousal support a matter of private right. A contract term that alters the established order of intestate succession is severed from an otherwise enforceable contract, whereas an unconscionable spousal support waiver is rescinded so as to restore the status quo ante between the parties. In New Mexico a court of appeals has held that an unenforceable spousal support waiver makes the entire premarital contract unenforceable on the ground that the offending waiver might have been used as consideration for other terms in the contract.[35]

By comparison, California statutory law, case law, and public policy all support the remedy of severance — not rescission or contract unenforceability — for a spousal support provision found unconscionable at enforcement.[36] The rationale is that prospective spouses have the right to alter property rights by contract, but the public interest trumps that right. Thus, when a court has a choice to order a former spouse to pay spousal support, on one hand, or to enforce a premarital contract spousal support provision that would leave the party against whom enforcement is sought eligible for public assistance, on the other hand, the choice is clear under

---

33 *See, e.g.*, *Facter*, *supra*.

34 The Cal. Fam. Code § 1615 definition by comparison relates to a two-pronged understanding of consent that turns on disclosure and consent.

35 *Rivera v. Rivera*, 149 N.M. 66, 243 P.3d 1148 (Ct. App. 2010).

36 *Facter*, *supra*.

§ 1612(c). The court must exercise its discretion in favor the public interest.

This result is consistent with the underlying policy of the community property system. At the end of a marriage, current normative understanding dictates that the financial responsibility to support a former spouse who is less financially secure should fall on the former spouse who is (relatively) more financially secure before it falls on the public. An unconscionable spousal support waiver that results in the reversal of that outcome is severable because it violates public policy. Consideration is no longer required for a premarital contract. Hence the offending spousal support waiver can be severed from an otherwise enforceable premarital contract, even if the parties do not include a severance term in the original contract. The rationale of rescission – used in the Louisiana example above — is irrelevant in California.

Even if a spousal support provision is enforceable under § 1612(c), it might be subject to challenge on § 1615(c)(5) grounds. This is especially the case when the parties have a documented history of abuse on or near the date of contract execution. In light of such a history, a court has the discretion to hold the entire premarital contract unenforceable. This returns the party against whom enforcement is sought to the general protections of the Family Code; it also prevents unjust enrichment of the party who seeks enforcement of the spousal support provision.

Therefore, a spouse against whom a spousal support waiver clause is sought has at least three layers of CPAA protection:

- The presence of a separate and independent attorney when the contract is signed, as is required by § 1612(c);
- A strong public interest in favor of requiring a former spouse to pay spousal support before the state is required to do so — this is reflected in the § 1612(c) definition of unconscionability; and
- A broad grant of discretion that permits a judge to consider any factor relevant to the issue of voluntariness — this appears in § 1615(c)(5).

Example 13.3: This example illustrates the relationship between independent counsel at execution and the enforceability of a spousal support waiver. Harrison and Winona sign a premarital agreement that includes a spousal support waiver. When the contract is signed, Winona is not represented by counsel. At enforcement, the spousal support waiver is unenforceable as applied to Winona and hence severable from the contract.

Example 13.4: This is an example of a spousal support waiver that was enforceable when it was executed, but that became unconscionable over time. Same as Example 13.3 except that Winona is represented by counsel when the contract is signed. At that time, both parties are high school teachers. Ten years later, when the Harrison and Winona seek dissolution, Harrison is the CEO of a Fortune 500 company, while Winona is the family homemaker. Harrison seeks to enforce the spousal support waiver against Winona, who establishes that without spousal support she will be left destitute. Under § 1612(c), the spousal support waiver is unconscionable, and hence severable from the contract.

§ 13.05 GENERAL CONTRACT ENFORCEABILITY: DISCLOSURE AND CONSENT

An enforceable premarital contract is one that is based on fair disclosure and entered into voluntarily.

Coercion in the area of premarital contracting is more often than not subtle. This is because, despite any alleged coercion, the marriage has occurred and the premarital contract is presumptively enforceable. Furthermore, as a practical matter, a dispute about whether a contract was the product of coercion *when it was signed* does not come up until one party seeks to enforce the contract against the other party. Enforcement typically happens at dissolution, when the parties have already made the decision to terminate their marriage.

When a contract proponent produces a contract that meets § 1611 formalities, the burden of proof shifts to the contract opponent to prove that the contract (as a document) is either unconscionable or involuntary. The CPAA refers to the contract opponent as **"the party against whom enforcement is sought."**

Unconscionability for purposes of § 1615(a)(2) is a question of law that relates to fair disclosure.[37] Voluntariness for purposes of § 1615(a)(1) is a question of fact.

[A] Consent: Disclosure/Unconscionability

Unconscionability is defined in terms of disclosure under §1615(a). This definition of unconsionability is different than the definition contemplated by § 1612(c). Under § 1615(a), a contract is unconscionable as a matter of law if **"before execution of the agreement, all of the following applied to that party":**

- the party against whom enforcement is sought was not provided with a **"fair, reasonable, and full disclosure of the property or financial obligations of the other party,"** and
- that party **"did not voluntarily and expressly waive, in writing, any right to disclosure . . . beyond the disclosure provided,"** and
- that party **"did not have, or reasonably could not have had, an adequate knowledge of the property or financial obligations of the other party."**

[B] Consent: Voluntariness/Coercion

In 2001, effective 2002, the Legislature added § 1615(c) in response to *Marriage of Bonds*.[38] The policy underlying the CPAA is to facilitate the enforceability of premarital agreements, even though the § 1615(c) requirements are framed in the negative, "as though all intendments weigh against finding compliance in the usual case." The negative framing of § 1615 recognizes that all premarital contracts are subject to legal challenge, especially in light of the broad grant of discretion that the CPAA gives to a trial court judge under § 1615(c)(5). Indeed, it is more likely

---

[37] Cal. Fam. Code § 1615(b).

[38] *Marriage of Bonds*, 24 Cal. 4th 1, 99 Cal. Rptr. 2d 252, 5 P.3d 815 (2000).

than not that a premarital contract should and will be challenged at enforcement. For that reason, both parties' share an interest in building a solid record of fairness and voluntariness at the time that a premarital contract is signed.

Under § 1615(c), a premarital agreement is the product of coercion,

> **"[u]nless the court finds in writing or on the record all of the following":**
>
> - **"The party against whom enforcement is sought was represented by independent legal counsel at the time of signing the agreement . . ."** or else that party waived the right to representation in writing; and
> - The party against whom contract enforcement is sought had **"not less than seven calendar days between the time that party was first presented with the agreement and advised to seek independent legal counsel and the time the agreement was signed."**
> - There is no evidence of **"[d]uress, fraud, or undue influence, and the parties did not lack capacity to enter into the agreement."**[39] and
> - There are no other factors that the court deems relevant to the question of voluntariness.

Section 1615(c) clearly places the burden of legal proof of coercion on **"the party against whom enforcement is sought,"** even if that party turns out to be the financially less secure spouse. In *Marriage of Bonds*, 23 year-old Sun and 23-year old Barry executed a premarital contract in 1988.[40] At that time, each party waived any interest in the earnings and acquisitions of the other party during the marriage. Sun testified that at contract execution she had limited English proficiency skills, and that she signed the contract without the benefit of independent counsel. Barry, on the other hand, was represented by multiple professionals. Moreover, Barry had an annual salary of $105,000 at the start of the marriage, and multiple millions of dollars per year at its end. Sun had no earnings during the marriage. At dissolution, Barry sought to enforce the premarital contract. Sun argued against contract enforcement. She contended that Barry should have the burden of proof, and that the court should apply a strict scrutiny standard to the premarital contract since she was unrepresented by counsel when the contract was signed, whereas Barry was fully represented.

---

[39] *Marriage of Stevenot*, 154 Cal. App. 3d 1051, 1073, n.6, 202 Cal. Rptr. 116 (Cal. App. Ct., 1st Dist. 1984) (defining duress as "more than mere threats or puffing; a party must be shown to have intentionally used threats or pressure *to induce action or nonaction* to the other party's detriment" (italics added)); *Marriage of Meagher and Maleki*, 131 Cal. App. 4th 1, 9, 31 Cal. Rptr. 3d 663 (Cal. App. Ct., 1st Dist. 2005) (reversing a trial court order granting annulment to a wife whose husband made premarital misrepresentations about his financial status; the husband's misrepresentations were not enough to get a judgment of nullity on the grounds of fraud, but had they been made to induce a premarital agreement, those misrepresentations could have formed the basis for unenforceability of the contract on grounds of fraud).

[40] *Bonds, supra.*

The trial court enforced the contract on the ground that Barry and Sun were not in a confidential relationship at execution, and that the CPAA 1985 placed the burden of proof on **"the party against whom enforcement was sought"** — in this case Sun, not Barry. Sun appealed. In a split decision, the majority opinion of the court of appeal reversed the trial court judgment and directed a retrial on the issue of voluntariness. That opinion stressed the following facts: Sun lacked independent counsel; she did not waive counsel; she had limited English language skills; she was unsophisticated in business matters; it was not made clear to her that Barry's lawyers were not her lawyers; and she received no explanation of the legal consequences of the contract. Instead, she testified that she was told that there would be no marriage if she didn't sign the contract. According to the court of appeal, these facts called for strict judicial scrutiny, with a dissent voting instead for trial court discretion in any given case. Barry appealed.

In a lengthy decision that discusses the difference between commercial contracts and contracts between intimate partners, the California Supreme Court held that the CPAA burden of proof does not shift away from the party against whom enforcement is sought, even if that party was not represented by counsel at the execution phase, and even if that party did not (formally) waive the right to counsel in writing. In the end, the Supreme Court determined, Sun may have made an unfortunate decision, but she made it voluntarily unless and until she could prove otherwise.

In response to *Bonds*, the Legislature added § 1615(c) to the CPAA in 2001.

Section 1615(c)(1)–(3) links voluntariness to the presence of separate and independent counsel at execution, as established by the sufficiency of the parties' records. Best practices require that both parties be represented by their own counsel at execution. But, if only one party is represented by counsel, the contract may still be enforceable. This will depend upon the sufficiency of the record that the party who seeks to enforce the contract compiles. CPAA 1985 § 1615(c) requires that there be evidence in the record that the unrepresented **"party against whom enforcement is sought . . . was fully informed of the terms and basic effect of the agreement as well as the rights and obligations he or she was giving up by signing the agreement, and was proficient in the language in which the explanation of the party's rights was conducted and in which the agreement was written."** The unrepresented party against whom enforcement is sought also must sign a declaration that he or she received the above information. That declaration must state who provided the information. All explanations must be memorialized in writing.

On the issue of language proficiency, the CPAA represents best practices in protecting prospective spouses who are not proficient in English. To step into the commercial sphere for a moment: In commercial contracting Cal. Civ. Code § 1632, protects the rights of consumers who speak one of five protected language groups: Spanish, Chinese, Tagalog, Vietnamese, and Korean. No other language groups are protected under the Civil Code at this time. The CPAA, by contrast, expands language protection for prospective spouses whose language of facility is in *any* language other than English. To ensure voluntariness, § 1615(c) requires that all CPAA required documents be translated into the prospective spouse's language of proficiency. Until a court holds otherwise, the contract and all explanations made by one spouse's attorney to the other unrepresented party must be translated.

Example 13.5: This is an example of how translated documents are required when a party is unrepresented by counsel and proficient in a language other than English. Harrison is unrepresented by counsel. Winona's counsel explains the contract to Harrison in Cantonese. The explanation is memorialized in Cantonese. Harrison signs a declaration, in Cantonese, that Winona's attorney provided; it contains the information required by § 1615(c). Because Harrison lacks an attorney, under § 1615(c)(3), Harrison must be fully informed of the basic terms and effect of the agreement as well as the rights and obligations Harrison was giving up by signing the agreement. The **"explanation of** [Harrison's] **rights and obligations"** must be **"memorialized in writing"** and delivered to Harrison prior to the signing of the premarital agreement. In turn, Harrison must **"execute a document declaring that** [he] **received the information . . . and indicating who provided that information."** In this example, contract enforceability is at risk because of Harrison's decision not to hire counsel. Winona's attorney can mitigate that risk by creating the documentary record required by § 1615(c)(1)–(3) to help establish Harrison's voluntary execution of the contract. Key to this record will be proof that Harrison received the required documents in his language of proficiency.

Example 13.6: This is an example of how language proficiency is related to understanding, and, hence, to voluntary agreement. Harrison's language of proficiency is Cantonese. Winona is proficient in Cantonese and in English. Harrison and Winona are in the process of negotiating a premarital contract. Each is represented by separate and independent counsel. Harrison's attorney requests that the contract document itself be translated into Cantonese. Winona's attorney disagrees. In this case, best practice suggests that the contract be translated into Cantonese. If Harrison were unrepresented by counsel, Harrison would be entitled to all necessary documents in Cantonese, including the contract, as discussed in Example 13.5. There is no similar CPAA provision that the contract itself shall be in a party's language of proficiency when that party is represented by counsel. But, given the importance that § 1615(c) places on understanding as proof of voluntariness, at least two factors suggest that, even if Harrison is represented by counsel, the agreement should be translated into Harrison's language of proficiency. The first is that § 1615(c)(3) requires that the agreement be written in an unrepresented party's language of proficiency. The second is that the contract is more predictably enforceable if Harrison receives contract documents in Cantonese. Therefore, it is in Winona's best interest to provide Harrison with a premarital agreement translated into Cantonese.

Example 13.7: This is an example of how translation issues can compromise voluntary consent. Same as 13.5 except that Winona's attorney asks Harrison's 11 year old child to explain the contract to Harrison, by way of an oral translation. The child, unfamiliar with legal terms, tells Harrison, It doesn't mean anything during marriage. You just sign it."[41] This explanation is not memorialized. Harrison executes a document declaring that Harrison's child provided information about the contract. In this example, Harrison's voluntary consent to the contract is called into

[41] *See In re Nelson's Estate*, 224 Cal. App. 2d 138, 36 Cal. Rptr. 352 (Cal. App. Ct., 1st Dist. 1964).

question because Harrison's child is not the appropriate party to explain Harrison's legal rights. Winona's attorney has failed to take all necessary steps under § 1615(c) to protect the enforceability of the contract.

[C] Other Factors

Additional statutory pressures against finding compliance in the usual case appear at §§ 1615(c)(4) and (5).

Section 1615(c)(4) requires evidence that: **"The agreement and the writings executed pursuant to paragraphs (1) and (3) were not executed under duress, fraud, or undue influence, and the parties did not lack capacity to enter into the agreement."**

Section 1615(c)(5) gives a court broad discretion to consider **"any other factors [that] the court deems relevant."** Taken as a whole, § 1615(c)(5) accomplishes two somewhat competing goals. It addresses the underlying policy of furthering the enforceability of premarital contracts, and it acknowledges the importance of judicial discretion in a dissolution proceeding. Premarital contracts are not like commercial contracts for purposes of how they are negotiated, established, or enforced. Subtle and blatant coercion is expected in commercial contracting, whereas that same degree of coercion in the context of a premarital contract would call the enforceability of the contract into question. In part this is because marriage is a "highly regulated institution of undisputed social value, and there are many limitations on the ability of persons to contract with respect to it, or to vary its statutory terms, that have nothing to do with maximizing the satisfaction of the parties or carrying out their intent."[42]

Thus, the regulatory grid of the family law makes it necessary for a court to consider subtle coercion as the (future) basis upon which a premarital contract might be challenged, even if that same evidence would not support a contract rescission claim in the commercial context. As *Bonds* made clear, the status quo ante of the spouses cannot be restored at divorce. Nor are damages contemplated for the breach of the marital contract. Whatever the reason a trial court deems a premarital contract unenforceable, the result is that the parties are returned to the default rules of community property law. Section § 1615(c)(5) allows for this result.

On the other hand, either party to a marriage has the right to contract away or otherwise alter the community property edifice. This is known as the contract modification principle of community property law. By this principle, the parties have a right to determine their individual rights in marriage, by use of a premarital agreement that is signed before marriage, effective during marriage, and enforceable at the end of the marriage. If and when enforced, the premarital agreement will prevail over the default statutory rules that would otherwise apply.

More generally, § 1615 links the CPAA to the Domestic Violence Prevention Act provisions of the Family Code (DVPA), which appear at §§ 6200–6409. Premarital contracts are typically enforced (if at all) when a marriage ends by divorce or death. Every premarital contract must be fairly disclosed and voluntarily entered

[42] *Bonds, supra.*

into. Documented incidents of abuse, or tortious or illegal conduct by one party against the other before or near the date of execution, can be the basis for arguing (or holding) that the abused party's voluntariness was compromised.

Example 13.8: This problem illustrates the contractual modification principle of community property law. Harrison and Winona sign a premarital agreement that reads: "*All income earned during marriage and all purchases made with that income will be characterized as the separate property of the earning spouse.*" Harrison and Winona marry. Winona earns income during the marriage, Harrison does not. All purchases during marriage are made with Winona's earnings. At the end of the marriage, Winona seeks to enforce the premarital agreement against Harrison. An enforced premarital contract will trump the ordinary community property rules by making all of the property that was acquired during marriage, with Winona's earnings, Winona's separate property. On the other hand, an unenforceable premarital contract will return Harrison to the default protections of the community property rules.

Example 13.9: This example illustrates the importance of fair disclosure. Harrison and Winona are in the process of negotiating a premarital agreement. Harrison requests, though counsel, all paper and electronic records of Winona's separate property business earnings and obligations. Winona, through counsel, complies with that request as to Winona's one business: Winona'sStuff LLC. Winona has satisfied the disclosure requirement. If all other disclosures are in order, the contract is presumptively enforceable.

Example 13.10: This example illustrates the importance of full disclosure. Harrison requests, though counsel, all paper and electronic records of Winona's separate property earnings and obligations. Winona, through counsel, declines to comply with that request. Under § 1615(a)(2): Harrison has the right to disclosure; Harrison has invoked (not waived) that right; and without Winona's disclosure Harrison cannot reasonably obtain **"knowledge of the property or financial obligations"** of Winona'sStuff LCC, given Winona's use of the LLC form. In this case, even if all other disclosures are in order, Winona's lack of disclosure about Winona'sStuff LLC makes the premarital contract unconscionable and, therefore, unenforceable as against Harrison.

Example 13.11: This is an example of how the party who fails to disclose cannot use that failure as a shield against enforcement. Same as Example 13.10, except that, after fully disclosing his information, Harrison seeks to enforce the premarital contract against Winona, who has not fully disclosed. Winona's failure to disclose cannot shield her from having the contract enforced against her. The rationale is § 1615(a)(2)(A)–(C), which provide that a contract is not enforceable **"if the party against whom enforcement is sought proves"** that the other party did not provide disclosure. Here, *Winona*, the party against whom enforcement is sought, has not disclosed information about Winona'sStuff LLC. Harrison has. Winona's disclosure lapse cannot shield her from contract liability.

Example 13.12: This is an example of how a documented history of abuse can create grounds with which to challenge an otherwise enforceable contract. Winona behaved in an abusive manner toward Harrison during their dating relationship, their engagement, and their marriage; and Harrison has the records to prove it.

Winona seeks to enforce a premarital contract against Harrison, citing full compliance with § 1615 disclosure requirements, and the presence of separate and independent counsel who established a record of voluntariness at execution for purposes of § 1615(c)(1)–(4). Despite Winona's evidence, Harrison's proof of domestic violence is relevant under § 1615(c)(5); this catch-all provision gives a court discretion to deem a premarital contract unenforceable for **"any other factors the court deems relevant."** The presence of counsel at execution weighs against a finding of undue influence, but the documented incidents of abuse weigh in favor of a finding of undue influence. Indeed Harrison's evidence of domestic abuse, which apparently covers dates on or near the contract execution date, suggests that Harrison's voluntary execution of the contract was compromised. Therefore, it is well within a trial court's discretion, citing § 1615(c)(5), to find that Harrison's rights and obligations as to Winona should be determined by the Family Code rather than by the premarital contract.

Section 1615(a) provides that **"a premarital agreement is not enforceable if the party against whom enforcement is sought proves the party — did not execute the agreement voluntarily"** as defined by a finding in the record of **"all"** § 1615(c)((1)–(5) elements. As in Example 13.12, a party can establish a record as to presumptive voluntariness, but the other party can rebut that presumption with evidence of corroborated domestic abuse that took place on or near the contract execution date.

To reiterate, spousal support provisions clearly are given two levels of scrutiny, as discussed above. They are scrutinized at execution for the presence of separate and independent counsel. They are scrutinized again at enforcement for unconscionability. Unenforceable spousal support waivers are severed from the contract.

The enforceability of an entire premarital contract — not just of a support provision — is determined by § 1615, which reads as if a premarital contract gets only one level of temporal scrutiny, namely at the date of execution. Once a contract is presented for enforcement, § 1615(a)(1) and (2) provide that it is up to **"the party against whom enforcement is sought"** to prove either that **"that party did not execute the agreement voluntarily"** or **"the agreement was unconscionable when it was executed."** Both of these provisions specifically direct the court's attention to period in which the contract is signed.

But once focused on that period, the court has § 1615(c)(5) discretion to consider **"any other factors"** it deems **"relevant"** to the question of voluntariness at execution. Voluntariness is, therefore, not defined only in terms of the presence or absence of independent counsel. To be sure, the presence or absence of independent counsel is scrutinized under § 1615(c)(1)–(4). But when circumstances warrant, the totality of the circumstances give a court a broad grant of discretion under § 1615(c)(5). For that reason, in any given case, the term voluntariness is ultimately defined by the court's discretionary sense of things. Upon proof of abuse, coercion, or undue influence at the contract execution phase, a court clearly has discretion to use hindsight to reanalyze the other events that surrounded the contract's execution, notwithstanding the parties' compliance with § 1611 formalities. The possibility that a court might exercise its broad grant of

§ 1615(c)(5) discretion gives the party against whom enforcement of the contract is sought an opportunity to look back at the relationship to perhaps better understand if and how the presence of subtle coercion at the contract execution phase might have compromised his or her consent.

§ 13.06 AMENDMENTS AND REVOCATIONS

The CPAA § 1614 applies to **"a premarital agreement or other marital property agreement."** A premarital contract may be amended or revoked during marriage, but § 1614 requires that this be done **"only by a written agreement signed by the parties."** As with the underlying contract, amendments and revocations are enforceable without consideration. They are subject to the § 1612(c) and § 1615 parameters discussed above.

A premarital contract may contain milestones that trigger the need to amend or revoke the original contract. Some examples of trigger clauses include but are not limited to the following. The parties might agree to a sunset clause that after a certain number of years they will revoke the premarital agreement. The parties might agree that after the birth of a child each spouse is obligated to purchase a life insurance policy in a certain amount that names the other party as a pay on death (P.O.D.) beneficiary. The parties might agree that in the event of a job change their premarital contract must be updated. Or the parties may agree about a process by which they can fairly create a written record of abusive incidents.

Amendments and revocations are marital contracts negotiated during marriage, and such they are governed by:

- The CPAA on issues of
    - o Spousal support waivers,
    - o Fair disclosure,
    - o Voluntariness, and
    - o The availability of general equitable defenses.
- General fiduciary duties imposed by § 721(b) on spouses in transactions between themselves;
- Fiduciary duties related to the management and control of community personal property under§ 1100(e); and
- Issues related to the management of **"a business or an interest in a business that is all or substantially all community personal property"** under §1101(d).

Other specific Family Code sections may also be implicated, depending on the type of property involved. These Family Code sections come into effect because the marriage itself puts the spouses in a confidential relationship as a matter of law. Generally, § 721(b) provides that **"[i]n transactions between themselves"** the parties (now the spouses) are subject to **"the general rules governing fiduciary relationships which control the actions of persons occupying confidential relations with each other."** A presumption of undue influence is raised in favor of the disadvantaged spouse who introduces evidence that the other spouse obtained

"any unfair advantage of the other." Rebuttal requires that the advantaged spouse show that the transaction was fair and voluntarily entered into. Fiduciary duties are discussed more generally in Chapter 10. Therefore, as discussed above, the failure to update an obviously stale premarital contract may itself be a breach of fiduciary duty during the continuance of the marriage.

§ 13.07 MARITAL CONTRACTS

Marital agreements are entered into during marriage, at a time when the parties are in a confidential relationship as a matter of law. The formalities of premarital contracting — including amendments and revocations — are set forth in the CPAA. A contract is only governed by the CPAA during the marriage if it amends or revokes a previously enforceable premarital contract.

Not all marital contracts are governed by the CPAA. Some marital contracts are entered into for the first time during the marriage, as discussed in Chapter 14.

Even so, the enforceability of any and all contracts entered into during marriage — whether to amend or revoke a premarital agreement or otherwise — is subject to § 721(b). Upon marriage, § 721(b) holds spouses to a quasi-fiduciary duty in **"transactions between themselves,"** whether those transactions involve community personal property or community real property, gifts or bargained for exchanges, uncommingled community property, commingled property, or separate property that impacts the community estate.

Marriage of Burkle is an instructive case involving spouses who physically separated but then decided to reunite.[43] To step back a bit, generally, when spouses are living separate and apart, their earnings and accumulations are separate property. Notwithstanding this important change, the spouses continue to be in a confidential relationship, with quasi-fiduciary duties. Their duties to each other last until an enforceable marriage settlement agreement is reached or a final order of dissolution is granted.

During a period of physical separation, Ronald and Janet Burkle executed a reconciliation agreement. The agreement provided that when Ronald and Janet resumed living together as spouses, Ronald would have sole management and control over the schedule of community property assets. In exchange, Janet would receive annual million-dollar payments, as her separate property. In the event of dissolution, Ronald was to get all of the community property listed on the schedule and any property derived from that property. Janet was to receive her share of the community property valued as of the date of contract execution; plus she would leave the marriage with her accumulated separate property. Each spouse retained a team of separate and independent counsel for purposes of negotiating the reconciliation agreement. The teams of counsel appear to have carefully followed the contracting formalities of the CPAA as a model, even though they were not bound to do so. (The contract was not an amendment to a premarital contract; it can perhaps best be labeled a transmutation agreement.) Each spouse disclosed to the

---

[43] *Marriage of Burkle*, 139 Cal. App. 4th 712, 43 Cal. Rptr. 3d 181 (Cal. App. Ct., 2d Dist. 2006) (reh'g den., rev. den.).

other, and no record of domestic abuse was admitted.

Four years after execution, Janet filed for dissolution. She challenged the enforceability of the reconciliation agreement on § 721(b) grounds. Janet argued that the fact that Ronald was walking away from the marriage with significantly more wealth than she was, meant that Ronald had gained **"any unfair advantage"** over her in the contract negotiation process. Janet argued that § 721(b) compelled the judge to raise a presumption of undue influence in her favor. The trial court declined to do so. Instead, the trial court left it to Janet, as the party against whom enforcement was sought, to prove that the contract was unconscionable or otherwise not voluntarily entered into. When Janet did not carry that burden, the trial court found that the reconciliation contract was presumptively enforceable, as the product of a bargained for exchange, negotiated with fair disclosure, and entered into with the assistance of separate and independent counsel. The court explained that the mere fact that one spouse negotiates for an outcome that results in a financial gain over time is not evidence of **"any unfair advantage"** under § 721(b). Janet appealed.

The court of appeal affirmed the trial court. In interpreting § 721(b), the court of appeal said that in a contractual exchange between spouses, § 721(b) obligates either spouse to a fiduciary duty that requires that **"neither shall take any unfair advantage of the other."** If one spouse presents evidence that the other took any unfair advantage of the marital relationship in order to secure a gain, then a presumption of undue influence may be raised. But, evidence that one spouse came out ahead in a negotiated outcome, without more, does not constitute **"any unfair advantage of the other"** under § 721(b). Rather, **"any unfair advantage of the other"** means that the wrongful spouse took advantage "of the confidence reposed" in him or her and in the marriage "for the purpose of gaining an unreasonable advantage over the mate."[44]

§ 13.08 SUMMARY

Premarital agreements and amended premarital agreements are regulated by the Family Code.

A premarital agreement is negotiated while the parties — spouses or registered domestic partners — are not yet married and thus not yet in a confidential relationship. And yet, when they contract over the rights and obligations of marriage, they walk a fine line between trading future gains against future obligations in relation to a trusting prospective spouse. Depending on its actual terms, a premarital contract can seriously deviate from popular notions of romantic love. Indeed, the historical case law is replete with examples of prospective spouses who acted as if their freedom of contract rights allowed them to obtain any unfair advantage over their future spouse. It is against this historical backdrop that the CPAA was enacted and amended. The CPAA seeks to set forth clear formalities and standards for proving as well as testing the fairness and voluntariness of any contract between intimate partners.

---

[44] *Burkle*, *supra*, at 731, citing *Saslow*, *supra*, at 863–64.

A premarital contract is executed before marriage. It becomes effective upon marriage. It is typically enforced (or not) when the marriage ends. Indeed it is only at marriage's end that the parties know for certain whether the specific terms of the premarital contract will (or will not) trump the general terms of the community property law. Every premarital contract presented for enforcement is measured against the standards of the CPAA. Those standards balance principles of voluntariness and disclosure against each spouse's freedom of contract rights.

The default community property system extends an array of substantive protections to married persons and registered domestic partners. For that reason, when parties wish to alter those default rules by contract, the CPAA formalities and standards must be followed: CPAA formalities and standards are not optional. And yet, even when CPAA formalities are followed, enforceability is never certain. Lapses in disclosure, subtle coercion, changes in circumstance, or any other factors that concern a judge at the time of enforcement can weigh against contract enforceability. The CPAA gives a trial court judge a broad grant of discretion to assess the situation as it presents itself in a legal separation or dissolution proceeding. An unenforceable contract term or contract returns the party against whom enforcement was sought to the protections of the community property system.

Therefore, premarital contracts are predictably challenged at enforcement on any number of potential grounds. This leaves the party who sought enforcement to perhaps seek a remedy against the attorney who helped him or her negotiate the contract in the first place.

During marriage, spouses can enter into marital contracts. They can amend or revoke existing premarital contracts. If they do, the CPAA will govern the enforceability of those contracts, but so too will § 721(b). Spouses might also enter into reconciliation contracts during periods of separation; it has not yet been determined with specificity whether the CPAA governs reconciliation contracts as well. Once married, agreements between spouses continue to require mutuality of consent. If one spouse alleges that the other gained *any* unfair benefit from an agreement or from a transaction by manipulating the other spouse or the marital relationship, a presumption of undue influence arises in favor of the spouse who was adversely affected by the agreement. The presumption assigns the burden of proof to the party who was beneficially affected by the agreement to show that the agreement was entered into voluntarily and with full and fair disclosure by adversely affected spouse.

One of the animating principles of the California community property system is that prospective spouses may contract over their property rights within that system. Any such agreement must meet statutory formalities, and it must be voluntarily entered into. Even when the parties meet these Family Code requirements, they retain equitable defenses that can limit the time for enforcement of the agreement. Finally, judges have a broad grant of discretion to assess any fact that may have compromised the voluntariness of the spouse against whom contract enforcement is sought.

Chapter 14

TRANSMUTATION

A transmutation is a change in the character of property that takes place during marriage. Spouses can change the character of property from separate to community, community to separate, or from the separate property of one spouse to the separate property of the other spouse.[1] In California, spouses may freely transmute property during marriage. Other states, like Texas, are more restrictive.

§ 14.01 THE STATUTORY FRAMEWORK

A transmutation can be made either by a transfer of title or by an agreement between the spouses. When a transmutation is made by transfer, the effective date of the transmutation is the date on which the transfer document is signed. When a transmutation is made by agreement, the effective date of transmutation is the date on which the contract is executed. In the latter case, the spouse who is adversely affected by the transmutation assumes executory duties as of the date of the contract to transfer title to the transmuted asset.

[A] Statutory Authority

The spouses have Family Code authority to transmute property during marriage. That grant of authority appears in § 850, § 721, and§ 1500.

A specific grant of authority for transmutations appears at §850:

> **[M]arried persons may by *agreement or transfer* with or without consideration do any of the following:**
>
> **(a) Transmute community property to separate property of either spouse.**
>
> **(b) Transmute separate property of either spouse to community property.**
>
> **(c) Transmute separate property of one spouse to separate property of the other spouse.**

(Italics added.)

Transmutation formalities are set forth in § 852(a). Formalities require, to be valid, that a transmutation be **"made in writing by an express declaration that is made, joined in, consented to, or accepted by the spouse whose interest in the property is adversely affected."**

---

[1] Cal. Fam. Code § 850 et. seq.

The general rule permitting transactions between spouses appears at § 721(a): **"[e]ither** [spouse] **may enter into any transaction with the other . . . respecting property, which either might if unmarried."** Additionally, under § 721(b), **"[i]n transactions between themselves,** [spouses] **are subject to the general rules governing fiduciary relationships which control the actions of persons occupying confidential relations with each other."** This confidential relationship **"[i]mposes a duty of the highest good faith and fair dealing on each spouse, and neither shall take any unfair advantage of the other."**

The general rule regarding the contractual modification principle appears at § 1500: **"the property rights of the** [spouses] **prescribed by statute may be altered by a premarital agreement or other marital property agreement."** Transmutations that occur as an amendment or revocation to an enforceable premarital agreement fall within the parameters of both § 852(a) and CPAA 2001 § 1614; as such they may be subject to CPAA § 1615 provisions discussed in Chapter 13. The rationale for this is discussed in *Marriage of Bonds*, which distinguishes between bargained for exchanges in the marketplace and bargained for exchanges in the context of intimate relationship.[2] In this context then, amended or revoked premarital contracts that involve transmutation agreements must be **"[b]y a written agreement signed by the parties"** under § 1614; additionally, they must be § 852(a) compliant. Additionally, because the spouses are in a confidential relationship by virtue of their marriage, each is held to fiduciary duties as set forth in § 721(b). *See* Chapter 13.

[B] Transmutation by Transfer or by Agreement

A transmutation can be gratuitous or the product of a bargained for exchange. Gratuitous transmutations occur when one spouse makes a gift or a low value transfer to the other, regardless of the adversely affected spouse's motivation. A transaction by bargained for exchange is based on legal consideration.

The purpose and legal effect of a transmutation is to alter the rights of the spouses in relation to each other with respect to the transmuted property. Thus the consequence of a transmutation is that one spouse walks away beneficially affected from the transaction (i.e., richer in terms of net worth relative to the other spouse), while the other walks away adversely affected (i.e., poorer in terms of net worth relative to the other spouse).

A transmutation may affect the rights of a third party, a donee, or a transferee. Good faith purchasers are protected by § 852(b), which provides: **"[a] transmutation of real property is not effective as to third parties without notice thereof unless recorded."** For personal property, a transmutation need not be recorded, but it is subject to the laws that govern fraudulent transactions.[3]

Recently, the California Supreme Court explicitly rejected the theory that § 852(a) formalities contain an implicit exemption for purchases made by a spouse from a third party and titled in the other spouse's name only. In *Marriage of Valli*,

---

2 *Bonds, supra.*

3 The Uniform Fraudulent Transfer Act appears at Cal. Civ. Code §§ 3439–3439.12

the state supreme court ruled that when a spouse uses community property funds to buy an item from a third party, by application of the tracing principle that item is community property, regardless of whether title was taken in one name only. Either spouse can later transmute his or her one-half interest in the item into the other spouse's separate property. But that spouse must comply with the express declaration requirements of § 852(a) to do so.

A transmutation by transfer typically involves a deed that complies with general Civil Code deed requirements. Such a deed must be § 852(a) and § 721(b) compliant.

Example 14.1: This example illustrates how a deed transfer can change the character of an asset. Olive owned an apartment building before marriage. During marriage, Olive used a deed to convey the apartment building from "Olive" to "Olive and Franklin as community property." The deed effects a valid transmutation, assuming there is no evidence that Franklin took any unfair advantage of Olive in the transaction.

A transmutation by agreement is, by definition, a marital agreement.

Precedent holds that once § 852(a) formalities are established, the validity of a transmutation, whether by transfer or by agreement, also depends on compliance with § 721(b).[4] To this end, if the adversely affected spouse produces evidence of **"any unfair advantage"** taken by the beneficially affected spouse, then a presumption of undue influence arises in favor of the adversely affected spouse.[5] The presumption is rebutted by proof that the transmutation was made with mutual consent, which is to say voluntarily and in light of any necessary information.

§ 14.02 VALIDITY

Oral transmutations were valid in California prior to January 1, 1985. In 1984 the Legislature enacted non-retroactive legislation that governs all transmutations made on or after January 1, 1985. Today that legislation appears at Cal. Fam. Code §§ 850–853.

The formalities for a valid transmutation appear at § 852(a).

[A] The Express Declaration

Under § 852(a), a transmutation must be **"made in writing by an express declaration that is made, joined in, consented to, or accepted by the spouse whose interest in the property is adversely affected."**[6] Some interspousal gifts are exempt from § 852(a) formalities under § 852(c), as discussed below.

---

[4] *Marriage of Holtemann*, 166 Cal. App. 4th 1166, 83 Cal. Rptr. 3d 385 (Cal. App. Ct., 2d Dist. 2008); *Marriage of Lund*, 174 Cal. App. 4th 40, 94 Cal. Rptr. 3d 84 (Cal. App. Ct., 4th Dist. 2009).

[5] *Marriage of Burkle, supra.*

[6] Interspousal gifts are exempt from Cal. Prob. Code § 852(a) formalities under § Cal. Prob. Code § 852(c), which is discussed below.

No particular type of document or wording is necessary to effect a valid transmutation. Any written document will do. What matters is that the transmutation serve as written proof of the adversely affected spouse's express declaration to change the character of the asset(s) in dispute. The written express declaration changes an asset's character once made. The express declaration requirement is not (merely) a statute of frauds.[7]

A transmutation need not be signed by both parties. For example, a transmutation by deed from sole to community property is an effective transfer that only the adversely affected grantor-spouse signs. A transmutation by agreement, on the other hand, precisely because it is an agreement, does appear in a written instrument that is signed by both spouses. Moreover, § 852(a) formalities, require that a written express declaration be made, joined in, consented to, or accepted by the adversely affected spouse, thus necessitating the adversely affected spouse's signature on contract documents that purport to include transmutation agreements. Additionally, when a titled asset is transmuted by agreement, record title to that asset must be (eventually) changed to comply with the terms of the agreement. Thus, for titled assets, a transmutation by agreement will necessarily be followed by a supporting deed transfer.

Transmutation disputes typically arise at divorce or at the death of one spouse when the benefited spouse discovers that the title change process was or was not completed. In this case, the adversely affected party (or his or her executor) argues that the agreement was not a valid transmutation as to the disputed asset or assets. The beneficially affected party demands specific performance of what he or she argues was a valid transmutation. Specific performance takes the form of a characterization determination followed by a conveyance or a transfer of the asset or assets in question.

For purposes of § 852(a) the **"spouse whose interest in the property is adversely affected"** is the party whose net worth stands to be diminished by the change in the character or ownership of the property in question. The spouse who is beneficially affected by the transaction is the spouse whose net worth stands to be enhanced. In a negotiated bargained for exchange, each spouse is beneficially and adversely affected overall; but in terms of the allegedly transmuted asset, only one spouse is adversely or beneficially affected specifically in terms of net worth. Therefore, in a transmutation agreement that lists mutually transmuted multiple assets or groups of assets, each spouse must transmute by express declaration those assets that will leave him or her worse off than he or she was before the transmutation.[8]

The definition of **"express declaration"** comes from case law. In *Estate of MacDonald*, when spouse Margery learned that she had a life threatening disease, she and her spouse, Robert, engaged in estate planning with the assistance of counsel.[9] As part of that effort, Margery liquidated her one-half interest in the community property with the intention of leaving that one-half to her children from

---

[7] *Marriage of Benson*, 36 Cal. 4th 1096, 32 Cal. Rptr. 3d 471, 116 P.3d 1152 (Cal. 2005).

[8] *Marriage of Starkman*, 129 Cal. App. 4th 659, 28 Cal. Rptr. 3d 639 (Cal. App. Ct., 2d Dist. 2005).

[9] *Estate of MacDonald*, 51 Cal. 3d 262, 272 Cal. Rptr. 153, 794 P.2d 911 (1990) (in bank).

a prior marriage. In exchange, Robert changed the P.O.D. designations on three of his retirement accounts from Margery to his children by a prior marriage. As part of the process of changing Robert's beneficial designations, Margery signed a (standard) financial institution consent form indicating that she consented to Robert's P.O.D. changes. That same form did not expressly declare, however, that Margery intended to transmute her one-half of the community property sums on deposit in the accounts that were affected by Robert's P.O.D. change.

At Margery's death, her child petitioned to establish Margery's community property interest in Robert's IRA accounts. The trial court found that Margery transmuted her community property interest in Robert's IRA accounts when she signed the P.O.D. consent forms. Margery's child appealed. Eventually the California Supreme Court held that the beneficial consent forms that Margery signed, without more, were not substantial evidence of her intent to transmute her interest in Robert's retirement funds. The court reasoned that providing one's consent to a beneficial designation is not an express declaration for purposes of § 852(a).

The California Supreme Court went on to say that a valid express declaration is an unambiguous statement of (present) intent to change the character of the asset in question. An express declaration must be clear on its face. In Margery's case, her signature on the P.O.D. consent forms merely gave the financial institution authority to settle Robert's IRA funds with the named non-spousal P.O.D. beneficiaries. It did not give Robert Margery's one-half community property share in the retirement funds. As the court put it, the policy behind § 852(a) is "to create a writing requirement which enables courts to validate transmutations without resort to extrinsic evidence and, thus, without encouraging perjury and the proliferation of litigation."[10]

Estate of Bibb applied *Estate of MacDonald* in a case involving two alleged transmutations by transfer.[11] The first transfer concerned an apartment building that husband Everett owned before his marriage to Evelyn. The second transfer concerned a Rolls Royce that Everett purchased prior to marriage. Everett and Evelyn were married in 1992. In 1994, Everett applied for a $225,000 refinance loan for the apartment building. The lender declined to extend the loan to Everett, but it agreed to lend to Everett and Evelyn, based on Evelyn's good credit history. As part of the refinancing process, Everett signed a grant deed conveying the apartment building from himself to himself and Evelyn, "his wife as joint tenants."[12] Evelyn subsequently signed the note that was secured by a deed of trust on the apartment building. Also during the marriage, Everett reregistered the Rolls Royce in the names of "Everett or Evelyn."[13] When Everett died in 1995, Evelyn terminated the joint tenancy and took title to the apartment building in her name alone. She also reregistered the Rolls Royce in her name alone. And she filed a petition for probate of Everett's estate. Everett's adult son responded with a

---

10 *Benson, supra.*

11 *Estate of Bibb*, 87 Cal. App. 4th 461, 104 Cal. Rptr. 2d 415 (Cal. App. Ct., 1st Dist. 2001).

12 *Id.*.

13 *Id.*

petition to establish the estate's ownership of the apartment building and the Rolls Royce under the rule in *Estate of MacDonald.* The trial court denied that petition. Everett's son appealed.

The question for the court of appeal was whether the trial court had correctly determined that Everett had transmuted the apartment building and the Rolls Royce. The court analyzed the grant deed for the real estate and the DMV registration record for the Rolls Royce in light of the § 852(a) express declaration requirement. As to the apartment building, the court of appeal upheld the trial court's decision that the grant deed was an effective transmutation. The rationale was that the word "grant," being the historical and legal word for transferring interests in real property, left no doubt that Everett intended to change the ownership of the apartment building when he signed the deed from his separate property to his and Evelyn's joint tenancy property. As to the Rolls Royce, the court of appeal reversed the trial court's judgment to hold that the DMV registration record not an effective transmutation. The court of appeal pointed to the absence of an § 852(a) compliant express declaration on the DMV registration printout that Evelyn introduced into evidence. The Rolls Royce was thus separate property belonging to Everett's probate estate.

A transmutation by transfer is often a matter of an asset-by-asset change in character. Whereas a transmutation by agreement may involve a single asset, a group of assets, or an entire estate. This remains the rule despite the holding in *Marriage of Starkman*, where a court of appeal affirmed that the transfer of stock dividends into a community property revocable trust account was not a transmutation of that property, absent an asset-specific express declaration.

In *Marriage of Starkman*, husband Christopher (heir to the United Parcel Service) transferred all of his separate property into The Starkman Family Revocable Trust, which he managed with wife Christine.[14] When Christopher and Christine separated, Christopher exercised his right to revoke the Trust pursuant to its terms.[15] As part of an interlocutory characterization proceeding, the trial court determined that the disputed stock assets were Christopher's separate property. Christine appealed on the ground that the stock assets were transmuted from Christopher's separate property into community property by the Trust document. In support of her position, Christine presented the stock brokerage forms, a general assignment, and the Trust Document: She argued that the court had a duty to construe these documents together.[16] The court rejected Christine's argument. Instead, it affirmed the *Marriage of MacDonald* no-extrinsic-evidence rule for purposes of establishing an § 852(a) express declaration. Only the Trust Document, the court said, was relevant to the issue of whether Christopher transmuted separate property stock into community property stock.

---

[14] *Starkman, supra.*

[15] *Id.* at 665 (rejecting Christine's contention that Christopher breached a § 721(b) fiduciary duty by disputing the characterization or asserted transmutation of the stock dividends).

[16] *Id.* at 663 (Christine cited Cal. Civ. Code §1642 which provides that agreements made by the same parties as to the same transaction must be construed together).

Christine subsequently directed the court's attention to the Trust Document. She argued that Paragraph 2.03 was an § 852(a) compliant express declaration of the stock assets. Paragraph 2.03 read: "Settlors agree that any property transferred by either of them to the Trust . . . is the community property of both of them unless such property is identified as the separate property of either Settlor. If either Settlor claims that a portion of the Trust Estate is separate property, the Settlor making such a claim agrees to indemnify the Trust and Trustee from all costs and liability incurred in establishing or defending such claim." Paragraph 2.03 also provided that the "[s]ettlors declare that any community property transferred to the Trust shall retain its character as such, notwithstanding the transfer to the trust."[17] The court of appeal rejected Christine's argument. Instead, it labeled Paragraph 2.03 a "vacuum cleaner clause" not specific enough to be an express declaration of the identifiable stock assets that were in dispute.

Marriage of Starkman makes clear that an express declaration does not simply mean one or more documents signed by the adversely affected party. Rather, an express declaration is evidence of the adversely affected party's specific intent to affect a present transfer of identifiable property. To quote a now often-cited phrase, "a party does not slip into a transmutation by accident."[18]

Marriage of Holtemann distinguishes *Starkman*.[19] In *Marriage of Holtemann*, during his three year marriage to wife Barbara, husband Frank transmuted the entirety of his separate property estate to community property with a single express declaration. This occurred when Frank asked an estate attorney to draw up some documents that would eliminate the need for probate and minimize taxes in the event of his death. Frank's estate documents included a trust and a document titled "Transmutation of Husband's Separate Property to Community Property." The document labeled a transmutation read: "Property described in Exhibit A (including any future rents, issues, profits, and proceeds of that property) *is hereby transmuted* from [Frank's] separate property to the community property of both parties." [Italics added.] Both parties signed the trust document as well as the "Transmutation of Husband's Separate Property to Community Property." Shortly thereafter, Frank revoked the trust, thinking that by doing so he would also revoke the transmutation agreement. Barbara filed a petition for dissolution. She inventoried the property described in Exhibit A of the transmutation document as community property. Frank disputed that characterization on the theory that he had revoked the transmutation document. The trial court rejected Frank's argument. It determined that the transmutation agreement took effect once Frank signed it, and it remained in effect, notwithstanding Frank's subsequent revocation of the trust. Frank appealed.

Relying on *Marriage of Starkman*, Frank argued that the transmutation agreement was but one document in a larger (now revoked) estate plan. The court of appeal rejected this view. In doing so it distinguished *Marriage of Starkman* on

---

[17] *Id.* at 662.

[18] *Id.* at 664, citing *Marriage of Koester*, 73 Cal. App. 4th 1032, 1037, n5, 87 Cal. Rptr. 2d 76 (Cal. App. Ct., 4th Dist. 1999).

[19] *Holtemann, supra.*

its facts. In *Marriage of Starkman* the alleged express declaration in the trust was vague. In *Marriage of Holtemann*, the transmutation agreement was, as the court put it, "such a clear expression, in the form of an express agreement to transmute property transferred into a trust established for the same purpose." On the basis of the clarity of the express declaration, the court of appeal determined that the transmutation agreement that Frank signed was valid because it met the requirements of § 852(a).

Frank attempted to persuade the court that Barbara obtained an unfair advantage under the transmutation contract and thus a presumption of undue influence was in order. In Frank's view, the estate planning attorney represented him and Barbara, not just him; and, therefore, that attorney should have added an express disclaimer to the transmutation. However, as the court pointed out, the evidence showed that the estate planning attorney advised Frank of the consequences of signing the transmutation in a separate letter. The attorney also suggested that Frank obtain separate counsel for purposes of the transmutation. Based on this record, the court of appeal found that Barbara had not taken any unfair advantage of Frank. Therefore, once Frank signed the transmutation document, he changed the character of his separate property to community property. The case was remanded to determine the amount of Frank's § 2640 statutory reimbursement, without interest, for his separate property contributions to the community property estate.

Marriage of Lund followed. In that case, husband Earl began to plan his estate.[20] As part of several estate planning documents, a 5-page document titled "Agreement to Establish Interest in the Property of Earl E. Lund Jr. and Anne (Kathryn) Lund" [the Agreement] was prepared by an estate planning attorney who represented both spouses. The agreement recited that "it is the intention of the parties . . . to fix and establish their respective interest in all property now owned by them . . . at the date of marriage the Husband owned property, real or otherwise of substantial value and the [W]ife had assets of de minimus value; and the Husband, for estate planning purposes desires to convert said separate property into community property." The express declaration appeared in section B of the Agreement, which read: "COMMUNITY PROPERTY . . . All property, real and personal, of the parties hereto, whether title thereto is held in the names of one or the other of the parties or both of the parties as joint tenants or otherwise, is the community property of the parties hereto, each having a present, existing, and equal interest therein." On the day that the estate planning documents were signed, Kathryn, who had not previously reviewed the documents, spent 20 minutes in the attorney's office.

Shortly thereafter Earl and Kathryn sought dissolution. At that point, Earl and Kathryn disagreed as to the meaning of the Agreement. Kathryn argued that the Agreement transmuted all of Earl's separate property into community property. Earl argued that the Agreement was (merely) an estate planning document that was intended to become effective only upon the death of one of the spouses. On appeal, the court found that the Agreement contained an § 852(a) compliant express declaration, notwithstanding that it was part of an estate plan meant to

---

20 *Lund, supra.*

take effect at Earl's death. Still, because the transmutation was gratuitous, a presumption of undue influence was raised on Earl's behalf. At trial, Kathryn attempted to rebut that presumption with a clause from Agreement that read: "I have carefully read and understand all of the provisions of the foregoing Agreement and approve of and agree to all the terms hereof." The trial court rejected the rebuttal. Kathryn appealed. The court of appeal reversed. It held that Earl's attestation of the relatively simple 5-page Agreement was substantial evidence of his consent to the transmutation transaction.

Marriage of Lico, an unpublished case, challenged the line of precedent that separates the issue of formalities (§ 852(a)) from the issue of validity (§ 721(b)). Doctrinally, *Lico* raised this question: assuming § 852(a) is more specific a statute than § 721(b), is § 852(a) compliance sufficient evidence of voluntariness for purposes of § 721(b)? Wife Beth Ann appealed a trial court judgment finding that the § 721(b) presumption of undue influence was unrebutted. Beth Ann relied on *Estate of Cover* for the proposition that mutual consent means full and fair disclosure *or* advice of counsel, but not both.[21] *Estate of Cover* was unlikely precedent for three reasons. First, *Cover* arose in an era when the husband had exclusive rights of management and control over community property; since then the law has shifted to equal management. Second, *Cover* was decided in 1922 when oral and implied transmutations were valid; since then only written express declarations of transmutations are recognized as valid. And third, *Cover* was an estate case, whereas *Marriage of Lico* was a divorce case for which both parties were available to testify. Beth Ann petitioned to the California Supreme Court. That petition was denied; hence for a valid transmutation the current policy continues to require both an § 852(a) compliant express declaration and a §721(b) finding of consent and disclosure.

A transmutation agreement can be a key part of estate planning. And yet when it is, a single fact can turn the analysis in favor or against finding a valid transmutation.

At least one general lesson from *Starkman, Holtemann, Lund,* and *Lico* is that a valid transmutation affects a change in the character of identifiable property as of the transmutation execution date. There is no precedent in support of a conditional transmutation. In the above cases, the parties' motivations for executing the transmutation as part of an estate plan was to influence tax outcomes in the event that one spouse were to predecease the other. But when the marriage ended by divorce, while the estate plan could be revoked, the transmutation — because it was valid as of the date of its execution — could not be revoked or otherwise avoided except with a subsequent reverse-transmutation.

The important point here is that even when a valid transmutation is part of a revocable estate plan, the character of the transmuted assets changes on the date that the transmutation agreement is signed.

The Legislature has addressed the difference between a transmutation and an estate plan in § 853(a), which provides that "**[a] statement in a will of the character of property is not admissible as evidence of a transmutation of the**

---

[21] *Estate of Cover*, 188 Cal. 133, 204 P. 583 (Cal. 1922) (in bank).

property in a proceeding commenced before the death of the person who made the will." Unlike a transmutation, a will is an ambulatory document. As such, one spouse's declaration in a will is conditional, future-tense, and subject to change; at least as long as the testator retains testamentary capacity. During the testator's lifetime, a will clause creates no legally enforceable property interest: it is a mere expectancy, at best, not a change of title. A valid will passes title to the named beneficiary only at the testator's death. A valid transmutation, by contrast, passes title once the express declaration is made, joined in, consented to, or accepted by the spouse whose interest in the property is adversely affected. For these reasons, § 853(a) distinguishes a statement in the will of a living testator from an § 852(a) express declaration. A statement in a will only becomes admissible as evidence of a transmutation upon the death of the testator.

For nonprobate transfers, **"A written joinder or written consent to a nonprobate transfer of community property on death that satisfies Section 852 is a transmutation."** Chapter 2 of the Probate Code governs the validity of non-probate transfers. However § 850 et seq. and the Family Code governs the validity of the transmutation.

A revocable trust may or may not be an effective written express declaration, depending on whether the trust document meets § 852(a) formalities as to identifiable assets.[22] Unlike a will, a revocable trust is effective once it is settled. But unlike a transmutation, a revocable trust gives the settlor the right to revoke the trust in accordance with its terms. Most assets can be commingled in a trust without losing their character: Therefore, if a trust does not meet the § 852(a) express declaration requirements as to an identifiable asset, then that asset can go into and out of the trust without being transmuted. An exception is made for sums on deposit, discussed in the California Multiple-Party Accounts Law materials in Chapter 5.

Example 14.2: This example illustrates how oral transmutations are no longer valid under California law. Olive and Franklin orally agree that Olive will transfer to Franklin a percentage of separate property real estate in exchange for a percentage of Franklin's community property interest in some securities. This agreement does not meet § 852(a) statutory formalities. The transmutation attempt is invalid.

Example 14.3: Here is an example of a written transmutation based on a bargained for exchange. Olive transfers to Franklin separate property securities in ABC Corp. in exchange for cash. The transfer is made by a written document that reads "I, Olive, hereby transfer to Franklin, as Franklin's separate property, 100 shares of ABC Corp. in exchange for their fair market value in cash." Both parties sign the document after full disclosure is made about the exchange. Each is represented by separate and independent counsel. This transmutation meets § 852(a) express declaration formalities, it is based on a bargained for exchange, and its effect is to change the character of the identified shares of stock. Olive has an executory duty to transfer the 100 shares of ABC stock to Franklin as his separate property.

---

[22] *Starkman, supra.*

Example 14.4: This is an example of a gratuitous transfer — a gift. Same as 14.13 except that Olive writes "I will give Franklin 100 shares of ABC Corp. stock at the end of this tax year." Only Olive signs the document. This written document does not contain an express declaration as is required by § 852(a). Olive's intent is to transfer the shares in the future ("I will transfer"), not to transfer the shares as of the date of her signature. The § 852(a) noncompliant transmutation is void.

[B] Validity

Transmutation formalities are only prerequisites to validity. In other words, no transmutation attempt is valid without meeting the § 852(a) express declaration formalities. But what of a transmutation that complies with those formalities. Is such a transmutation valid simply because it meets statutory formalities, or is it subject to challenge on other grounds?

To date, the validity of an § 852(a) compliant transmutation is decided by § 721(b), which provides that during marriage, **"in transactions between themselves,"** spouses are **"held to the general rules governing fiduciary relationships which control the actions of persons occupying confidential relations with each other."** The effect of § 721(b) is that amendments, revocations, marital property agreements, and transmutations executed or made during marriage must comply with the general rules that govern fiduciary relationships. Under § 721(b) this includes **"a duty of the highest good faith, and fair dealing,"** as well as the duty that **"neither** [spouse] **shall take any unfair advantage of the other."** Relatively recent amendments to § 721(b) incorporate sections of the Revised Uniform Partnership Act (RUPA) by reference, **"including but not limited to"** duties related to providing access to any books kept, requests for disclosure, and accounting by one spouse, to the other, for benefits or profits derived **"from any transaction by one spouse without the consent of the other spouse which concerns the community property."** *See* § 721(b)(1)–(3)

Indeed, mutual consent is one of the essential elements of a contract between non-fiduciaries. All the more reason why consent is required for a transmutation agreement between spouses, who are fiduciaries for purposes of transactions between one another. Consent must be voluntarily given, which is to say that an § 852(a) express declaration must be freely made. The concept of mutuality means that the consent freely given is communicated by each party to the other. But mutuality also means that the parties "all agree upon the same thing in the same sense."[23] This question has come up in community property law in relation to the characterization of common law joint titles at dissolution. In that area, the courts have long defined mutual consent to arise from words, deeds and circumstances surrounding the transaction, which is to say from outward expressions and communications that actually occur between the parties. A party may argue that his or her unexpressed understanding or intention should be (or not) evidence of mutual consent. In the divorce context, this argument is rejected, as it should be. Unexpressed intentions or unilaterally held beliefs are not evidence of an agreement or of consent given or denied.

---

[23] BAJI, *supra* Chapter 11, 10.60, Mutual Consent.

Rather, consent requires two elements: voluntariness (consent freely given) and full and fair disclosure (agreeing on the same thing in the same sense). Moreover, in relation to transactions between themselves, the Legislature has consistently relied on the two-pronged legal definition of consent. Under § 852(a), an express declaration must be **"made, joined in, *consented to*, or accepted by the spouse whose interest in the property is adversely affected."** (Italics added.) Under § 721(b)(3), the spousal confidential relationship includes, among other duties, **"Accounting to the spouse, and holding as a trustee, any benefit or profit derived from any transaction by one spouse *without the consent* of the other spouse which concerns the community property."** (Italics added.) Consent is used in the civil tort area as well. It plays an especially important role in identifying acts of abuse or domestic violence. The two-pronged definition of consent is used to establish liability for community property impairment and mismanagement claims under § 1101(a) and § 1100.

The CPAA 2001§ 1615, in tandem with *Marriage of Bonds*, adopts the two-pronged definition of consent as applied to contracts between intimate partners.[24] A premarital agreement — or an amendment or revocation of that agreement executed during marriage — is not enforceable if the party against whom enforcement is sought proves either: **"That the party did not execute the agreement voluntarily"** or **"the agreement was unconscionable when it was executed."** To defeat a premarital contract on § 1615 grounds, the contract opponent need only prove that one element was absent. Since the definition of consent requires evidence of its two constitutive elements — consent must be freely given and it must be based on full and fair disclosure — the absence of one element indicates that consent was not mutual, whether due to duress, menace, fraud, undue influence, mistake, or any other factor. The reason why mutual consent is lacking in any given case might go to the question of assessing damages, but the fact that consent is lacking makes the alleged contract (or transmutation) unenforceable.

Burkle complicates the definition of bargained for exchange, not the definition of mutual consent.[25] Under § 721(b) when one spouse takes **"any unfair advantage of the other"** in a transaction, then that spouse's wrongful action compromises the other spouse's ability to give his or her mutual consent to that transaction. In *Burkle*, the court explained that **"any unfair advantage"** is established when the spouse who was adversely affected by the transaction can show that the spouse who was beneficially affected by that same transaction manipulated the other spouse or the marriage in order to secure an ill gotten gain. **"Any unfair advantage"** does not mean that one spouse got the better of a deal with the other spouse. It means that one spouse breached the trust of the other spouse so as to get the better of a deal in the transaction.

For that reason, when any unfair advantage is established, the burden of proof shifts to the spouse who was beneficially affected by the transaction. If the transaction is specifically a transmutation agreement, the beneficially affected

[24] *Bonds, supra.*

[25] *Burkle, supra.*

spouse can rebut the presumption of undue influence with evidence that the transmutation was based on mutual consent. In the contract context, mutual consent means that both parties freely agreed to the transaction, based on the disclosures that each made to the other. In the transmutation arena, it means that the adversely affected spouse voluntarily agreed to transmute property based on full and fair information about the legal consequences of such a decision in terms of the adversely affected party's net worth.

In other words, once the presumption of undue influence is raised, it's up to the beneficially affected spouse to show — stated negatively — that he or she did not lie, steal, cheat, or manipulate the other's trust in order to secure the other spouse's consent to the transmutation. He or she did not secretly appropriate, obtain, or retain an advantage over the adversely affected spouse. He or she did not take advantage of the other spouse's confidence or trust in order to secure a material advantage. He or she did not take any unfair advantage of the other's weakness of mind, or lack of education, knowledge, or experience. He or she did not take any unfair advantage of the other's necessities, distress, or duress, or otherwise deceive or comfort the other spouse in order to unfairly gain a material advantage. He or she did not induce the other spouse to part with property or to otherwise alter his or her position with respect to the character of that property. He or she did not manipulate the other spouse into assuming a risk or accepting a liability. All of the above goes to consent.

But consent is determined not just by voluntariness. It also requires a showing that the parties were agreeing to the same thing in the same sense. For this element, the spouse who is beneficially affected by a transmutation must show that he or she made no false statements or representations, that no information was concealed or suppressed, that no breach of trust occurred with respect to profits or benefits obtained, and so forth.

Both of these elements — voluntariness and disclosure — bring us to the present day reliance on § 721(b) for assessing the validity of an § 852(a) compliant transmutation document. Section 721(b) delves into the duties of a confidential partner — a fiduciary — in securing consent. It also delves into disclosure matters by requiring that available books be open and available for inspection, existing records be rendered upon request, and profits and benefits be accounted for in trust.

The presence of separate and independent counsel goes a long way toward quelling any of the above suspicions about any given transmutation agreement. Evidence that the disadvantaged party was represented by separate and independent counsel will establish mutual consent as to the transaction. At least in theory, the presence of separate and independent counsel levels the playing field. But even in the premarital agreement context, separate and independent counsel is not necessarily required for a contract to be enforceable. Under CPAA 2001 § 1615 — the Family Code provision most directly on point — if one party has counsel and the other doesn't, the represented party must document his or her counsel's efforts to explain the basic consequences of the agreement to the unrepresented party. And that explanation must be made in a manner and in a language that the unrepresented party will understand. The parties, in other words, must agree to the same thing in the same sense, even if only one is represented by counsel.

Where both parties lack counsel, or where they have counsel for, say, estate planning purposes but not for divorce planning purposes, then the presumption of undue influence can be an important protection for the disadvantaged party, especially in the case of a gratuitous transaction. Section 721(b) protects the spouse who is adversely affected by presuming the transmutation invalid until evidence of voluntariness and consent is produced. Section 721(b) also protects the spouse who succeeds in rebutting its presumption of undue influence by shielding him or her from future liability for any number of civil tort claims and criminal charges related to the transmutation.

Currently for purposes of § 721(b), whether one spouse has obtained **"any unfair advantage over the other"** in a transmutation agreement is a question of fact.

For bargained for exchanges, *Burkle* held that evidence that one spouse walked away from the transmutation agreement poorer is not necessarily evidence of unfair advantage sufficient to raise the presumption of undue influence. The presumption is properly raised only if there is proof that the benefited spouse took any unfair advantage of the other spouse. Even so, as *Burkle* also illustrates, even the most carefully orchestrated bargained for exchange can raise issues later in time about whether subtle coercion compromised consent at the contract execution phase.

For gratuitous exchanges or exchanges for less than market value, the presumption of undue influence is raised in favor of the adversely affected spouse as a matter of course. The rationale is that the beneficially affected spouse got something for nothing. Therefore, if a dispute arises as to the character of the property, it is but a small matter to require the beneficially affected spouse to show by a preponderance of the evidence that the transmutation was consensual, which is to say voluntarily consented to with full and fair disclosure.

To conclude, a valid transmutation changes the character of the property as of the date of the transmutation. This can determine management, control and valuation issues. A § 852(a) compliant transmutation is valid unless there is evidence of any unfair advantage, at which point a presumption of undue influence arises in favor of the adversely affected spouse. Rebuttal rests with the beneficially affected spouse to show that the transaction was voluntarily based on full and fair disclosure. The practical effect of the § 721(b) presumption of undue influence is that it only can be used to avoid (or undo) a § 852(a) compliant transmutation; it cannot be used to correct an § 852(a) noncompliant transaction.

Example 14.5: This is an example of how the question of mutual exchange and unfair benefit depends on the circumstances of the exchange. Olive transfers to Franklin separate property securities in ABC Corp. in exchange for cash. The transfer is made by a written document that reads "I, Olive, hereby transfer to Franklin, as Franklin's separate property, 100 shares of ABC Corp. in exchange for their fair market value in cash." Both parties sign the document after full disclosure is made about the exchange. Each is represented by separate and independent counsel. Olive seeks to challenge the § 852(a) compliant transmutation at divorce. Here, reciprocal express declarations were made in writing and acknowledged by both spouses. Each was adversely and beneficially affected by the transmutation. Each was represented by counsel. Neither party appears to have taken advantage of the other's confidence. Olive might argue, in retrospect, that Franklin gained an unfair advantage by giving Olive cash for appreciable securities. But Franklin can counter that the cash represented the fair market value of the securities on the date of the transmutation. Under *Burkle*, when one spouse obtains a benefit from a bargained for exchange with the other spouse, that isn't necessarily the same as obtaining "any unfair advantage" under § 721(b).[26] On these facts, because Olive's transmutation agreement is § 852(a) compliant and because she received fair market value for the shares of stock, the presumption of undue influence in Olive's favor is not raised. The transmutation is valid.

Example 14.6: This example illustrates how gratuitous transmutations give rise to a presumption of undue influence in favor of the donor spouse. Olive gives to Franklin 100 shares of separate property stock in ABC Corp. The gift is made by delivery of a written document in which Olive declares "I hereby give to Franklin, as Franklin's separate property, 100 separate property shares of ABC Corp. stock." Olive signs the document. This gift meets transmutation formalities, but it may not be valid. At divorce, Olive — the adversely affected spouse — can argue that because Olive received no compensation for the shares of stock, Franklin — the benefited spouse — obtained any unfair advantage over her. The presumption of undue influence is raised in Olive's favor. Franklin has the burden to rebut by showing that Olive made the transmutation voluntarily and with an understanding of its consequences (i.e., based on disclosure).

§ 14.03 EXEMPT INTERSPOUSAL GIFTS

Section 852(c) exempts from § 852(a) compliance some personal gifts made between spouses. Exempt gifts remain subject to § 721(b) fiduciary duties.

Section 852(c) provides that a gift of tangible personal property exchanged between spouses is exempt from the § 852(a) written formality requirements if the gift meets two elements. One, the gift must be within the expressly designated category of **"[c]lothing, wearing apparel, jewelry, or other tangible articles of a personal nature that is used solely or principally by the spouse to whom the gift is made."** Two, the gift cannot be **"[s]ubstantial in value taking into account the circumstances of the marriage."**

Section 852(c) uses the phrase **"tangible articles of a personal nature"** rather than "real or personal property," which is the phrase employed by § 852(a). Nevertheless, transmutations of real property are implicitly excluded from the § 852(c) gift exemption on two grounds. One is that transmutations of real property must be in writing and recorded to be effective against third parties, including good faith purchasers and creditors. The second is that gifts of real property are not gifts of personal property as contemplated by § 852(c).

---

[26] *Id.*

Other common gifts of value are not eligible for the § 852(c) exemption. Cash is tangible, but not of a personal nature. Electronically designated funds are neither tangible nor of a personal nature; the same is true for securities.

It is unlikely that any car — even a highly unique collectible — would, could, or should be exempt from the § 852(a) written express declaration requirement. Most cars are not unique; and despite (or perhaps because of) the centrality of the car to California culture, a car is not an article of a personal nature. In *Marriage of Buie & Neighbors*, a court of appeal reversed a trial court decision that a car could be exempt from transmutation formalities. In that case, one spouse, Walter, purchased a $60,000 Porsche with sums on deposit in an account around the time of his birthday. Walter argued that the car was his birthday present. The other spouse, Tatiana, appealed. The court of appeal held that the family court erred when it exempted the Porsche from written transmutation formalities. Important to the court of appeal analysis was the California Law Revision Commission Report comment about Civil Code § 5110.640, the predecessor to § 852(c): "[I]nterspousal 'gifts' are presumed to be separate or community depending on the nature of the property given. . . . [Under § 852(c)] the gift of an automobile, for example, would not create a presumption that the property is separate, *since an automobile is not an article of personal nature within the meaning of the section*."[27] (Italics added by the court of appeal in *Buie & Neighbors*.)

Additionally, car transactions must comply with registration laws, all of which require a written DMV document. In *Estate of Bibb*, the court declined to view a DMV document as a § 852(a) compliant transmutation.[28]

Any change in the character of personal property, including that of an exempt interspousal gift, can be avoided by a creditor if the transmutation was made with the intent to hinder, delay, or defraud that creditor.

Example 14.7: This example illustrates the limits of the § 852(c) exemption for interspousal gifts. Olive leaves a voice mail message giving 100 shares of ABC stock to Franklin for her birthday. This transfer is not § 852(c) exempt property because shares of stock are not tangible, not of a personal nature, and not intended primarily or solely for Franklin's use. Olive's attempt to transmute the shares of stock by making an oral gift to Franklin is void.

Example 14.8: This example illustrates the limits of the § 852(c) exemption for interspousal gifts as to cash. Franklin delivers $10,000 in cash to Olive as a birthday present. This gift is not exempt under § 852(c). Cash is tangible, but it is not of a personal nature. Franklin's attempt to transmute the cash from community property into Olive's separate property is void.

Example 14.9: This example illustrates how gifts exempt from the written express declaration requirement must be personal, tangible, and affordable in light of the marital circumstances. Olive gets a work bonus of $50,000. Olive uses $5,000 of this bonus to buy Franklin a watch. According to § 852(c), this gift is exempt from

---

[27] *Marriage of Buie & Neighbors*, 179 Cal. App. 4th 1170, 1175, 102 Cal. Rptr. 3d 387, 390 (Cal. App. Ct., 4th Dist. 2009), citing 17 Cal. Law Revision Com. Rep. 222 (1984).

[28] *Bibb, supra.*

the transmutation formalities of § 852(a). The gift is a tangible item of a personal nature within the contemplated list of § 852(c) exempt items: **"clothing, wearing apparel, jewelry, or other tangible articles of a personal nature."** Additionally, in light of Olive's $50,000 bonus, the gift is arguably **"not substantial in value taking into account the circumstances of the marriage."** If so, the watch is entirely Franklin's separate property, as of the date of its delivery by Olive to Franklin.

Example 14.10: This example illustrates how an otherwise exempt transmutation can be void if it is too expensive given the circumstances of the marriage. Same as 14.9 except that Olive and Franklin are both unemployed students. Olive obtains a $10,000 student loan disbursement, $5,000 of which she uses buy a watch for Franklin. She delivers the watch to him for his birthday. Dissolution occurs shortly thereafter while Olive is still an unemployed student. Despite Olive's (prior) intention to give Franklin the $5,000 watch, and despite the tangible, personal nature of the gift, Olive can (later) avoid the transmutation. To do so, Olive must show that the watch was (too) substantial in value given the couple's financial circumstances.

§ 14.04 TRANSMUTATION BY OPERATION OF LAW

Generally, community and separate property can be commingled without losing their respective characters. The doctrine of confusion modifies this general rule.

The doctrine of confusion holds that once separate property can no longer be distinguished from community property, the entire separate property contribution is transmuted into community property by operation of law. No reimbursement is allowed to the separate property donor. The rationale is that when a separate property owner so thoroughly mixes his or her property with the community property such that it can no longer be segregated, that property owner is presumed to intend a gift to the community.

The doctrine of confusion is codified in § 852(d). By that provision, no aspect of the statutory transmutation scheme affects the decisional law governing the characterization of commingled property.

§ 14.05 SUMMARY

During marriage spouses can change the character (i.e., the ownership) of property by transmutation. Transmutations can be transfer or by written agreement. Or they can be by exchange of exempt personal gifts between the spouses. The spouses can change the character of separate property to community property, community property to the separate property of one spouse, or the separate property of one spouse to the separate property of the other spouse. A valid transmutation immediately changes the character of the asset or assets in question.

All non-exempt transmutations, to be valid, must comply with § 852(a) formalities. Specifically, § 852(a) requires that the transmutation be made by a written express declaration that is made, joined in, consented to, or accepted by the party who is adversely affected by the transmutation. Transmutations by transfer involve conveyances or deeds that are signed by the adversely affected spouse. Transmutations by agreement involve written agreements that include an express declaration but that otherwise do not convey titled to the transmuted asset or assets. Therefore, a spouse who transmutes his or her property by agreement has an executory duty to transfer record title to the transmuted property.

In addition to being § 852(a) compliant, a transmutation must be consensual and fair. Consent requires voluntariness based on full disclosure, especially about the legal consequences of a transmutation. Where the adversely affected spouse shows that the beneficially affected spouse gained any unfair advantage over the other in the transaction between the spouses, a presumption of undue influence is raised. Rebuttal then shifts to beneficially affected spouse to show that the transaction was voluntarily made with disclosure.

The presence of separate and independent counsel hired specifically for purposes of the transmutation will rebut the presumption of undue influence. Spouses who hire an attorney for estate planning purposes are not represented by independent counsel for divorce planning purposes.

California law recognizes the doctrine of confusion, which is to say transmutation by operation of law. The general rule is that separate and community property retain their character even if commingled. There are exceptions to this rule. The first exception is stated by the doctrine of confusion itself: At the point in time when separate property is no longer distinguishable from community property, then the law presumes that the owner of the separate property intended a gift of that property to the community estate. The second exception is for sums on deposit in an account, discussed in Chapter 5.

Chapter 15

NONMARITAL RELATIONSHIPS

A nonmarital relationship is not a civil marriage; nor is it a registered domestic partnership. A nonmarital relationship doesn't accumulate community property for purposes of dissolution or distribution at death. Parties come to the status of nonmarried cohabitants by different routes.

In some cases, the parties are nonmarried cohabitants because their marriage is void or voidable. A void marriage is the result of any one of three impediments: The parties fail to meet the basic criteria for establishing a valid marriage, the marriage is bigamous, or the marriage is incestuous. A void marriage accumulates no community property. When a marriage is voidable, on the other hand, it is presumptively valid until a judgment of nullity is obtained. A voidable marriage does accumulate community property during its continuance, unless the parties seek to nullify rather than to dissolve the voidable marriage.

The Family Code only applies to void or nullified marriages if one or both of the parties obtain legal recognition as a putative spouse. Then and only then can the parties elect to divide the accumulations of their relationship by reference to the quasi-marital property system. To obtain putative spouse status the petitioner first must prove a genuine and credible belief in the validity of the void or nullified marriage.

The California Domestic Partner Rights and Responsibilities Act of 2003 became fully effective in 2005 [DPRRA]. It permits same-sex partners and different-sex partners where at least one of the partners is over 62 to formalize their domestic partnership by registering it with the State. Once registered, the partners become entitled to the default benefits and protections of California community property law. California residency is not a prerequisite for registering a domestic partnership under California law.

California is now a marriage equality state: The institution of marriage is open to every couple, regardless of the sex or gender identity of the partners.

Increasingly couples have a choice as to how to live together. Each choice brings with it legal issues and consequences. Living together in a committed sexual relationship without marriage or registered domestic partnership is a choice that parties routinely make. These parties are referred to herein as nonmarried cohabitants. Disputes between parties who are nonmarried cohabitants by choice are governed by general law, not by the Family Code.

The term "domestic partners" is defined differently, depending on the context in which it arises. In terms of property rights, the accepted definition of domestic partners is two "single" adults who knowingly live together without the formalization of marriage or registered partnership in a committed, intimate, sexual relationship.

The Legislature has full control of the subject of marriage.

§ 15.01 NULLITY

A valid marriage is a civil contract between two persons based on consent, the issuance of a license, and solemnization.[1]

When the Civil Code of California went into effect on January 1, 1873, marriage was defined as **"[a] personal relation arising out of a civil contract."**[2] That definition still holds today under the current version of Family Code § 300. Parties must be capable of consenting to and consummating marriage. Consent alone is not enough to constitute a valid marriage. **"Consent must be followed by the issuance of a license and solemnization."** For purposes of simplicity, the following materials use the terms marriage and spouse. Notwithstanding that usage, the concepts in this chapter (indeed in this *Understanding* text) apply equally to married persons and to registered domestic partners.

Typically, parties to a valid marriage can produce evidence as to five elements:

(1) Each party had the requisite capacity to consent to the marriage;

(2) The parties obtained a license from the county clerk;

(3) The parties had a ceremony in which they solemnized the civil contract;

(4) Solemnization implies that the marriage is witnessed;

(5) The existence of a marriage certificate means that the parties recorded the marriage license. A marriage license, once recorded, becomes a marriage certificate.

Consent refers to capacity, which in turn refers to mental competence. The level of mental competence required for a valid marriage or a valid registered domestic partnership is low.[3] The level of mental competence required to nullify or dissolve a marriage is equally low.[4] The standard for lack of capacity — looking back at the marriage from the point at which a judgment of nullity is sought — is the same standard used to set aside a contract or a will. This rule was articulated a century ago in *Dunphy v. Dunphy*, discussed below.[5]

The failure to record a marriage license will not invalidate an otherwise valid marriage; nor will recording a marriage license validate an otherwise invalid marriage.[6] However, failure to register a domestic partnership will invalidate a

---

1 Cal. Fam. Code § 300.

2 Cal. Fam. Code § 300.

3 *Dunphy v. Dunphy*, 161 Cal. 380, 383, 119 P. 512 (Cal. 1911).

4 *Higgason, supra*, and its progeny.

5 *Dunphy, supra*, at 383.

6 *Marriage of Cantarella*, 191 Cal. App. 4th 916, 925, 119 Cal. Rptr. 3d 829 (Cal. App. Ct., 4th Dist. 2011).

registered domestic partnership, thus leaving the partners "single" in relation to one another.[7]

[A] Void Marriage

These grounds exist for determining that a marriage is void: The marriage fails to meet the basic requirements for a statutory marriage. The marriage is bigamous, or polygamous.[8] The marriage is incestuous.

A void marriage never comes into existence. Importantly, the parties to a void marriage cannot correct the impediments that make their marriage void, notwithstanding their voluntary cohabitation after the wedding ceremony. By comparison, parties to a voidable marriage can correct the impediment to their marriage by ratifying the marriage after learning about the impediment, with ratification demonstrated by the act of voluntarily living together.[9]

Parties to a void marriage are precluded from using the Family Code to resolve their property disputes, absent a determination of putative spouse status. During the continuance of their void marriage, any transaction between the parties entered into in reliance on the validity of the marriage is also presumptively void.

At the death of a party, a marriage cannot be attacked unless it is proven to have been void from its inception.[10] The ramifications of this rule are discussed in Chapter 17.

[B] Voidable Marriage

During the lifetime of the parties, a voidable marriage is presumed valid unless and until a judgment of nullity is obtained.[11] Once that happens, the parties are precluded from relying on the Family Code to resolve their disputes absent an order confirming one or both parties' status as putative spouse.

At the death of one or both of the parties, a voidable marriage, which is presumptively valid during the parties' lifetimes, is no longer subject to attack. Instead, it becomes valid by operation of law.[12] Thus, at the death of a spouse

---

[7] *Burnham v. California Public Employee's Retirement System*, 208 Cal. App. 4th 1576, 146 Cal. Rptr. 3d 607 (Cal. App. Ct., 3d Dist. 2012).

[8] See, e.g., *Marriage of Seaton*, 200 Cal. App. 4th 800, 133 Cal. Rptr. 3d 50 (Cal. App. Ct., 3d Dist. 2011), where the trial court granted a husband a judgment of nullity on ground of bigamy. The wife appealed. The record showed that that the wife's first marriage had not been dissolved when she entered into a bigamous second marriage. Eventually a final judgment of dissolution was obtained in the wife's first marriage, after which point wife entered into the third marriage. The court of appeal held that the trial court erred in granting the judgment of nullity for the third marriage. The rationale was that since wife's second marriage was bigamous (and without excuse) it had no legal effect; and since wife entered into the third marriage after obtaining a final judgment of dissolution in the first marriage, the third marriage was valid.

[9] Cal. Fam. Code §§ 2200, § 2201.

[10] *In re Gregorson's Estate*, 160 Cal. 21, 116 P. 60 (Cal. 1911).

[11] *McDonald v. McDonald*, 6 Cal. 2d 457, 461, 58 P.2d 163 (Cal. 1936) (in bank).

[12] *Gregorson, supra.*

whose marriage was voidable, only a challenge to the decedent's mental capacity at the time the marriage was contracted can serve as the basis for voiding the marriage. After the death of a party to a voidable marriage, evidence of fraud, financial abuse, duress, and so forth will no longer be grounds for voiding the marriage; these grounds expire after the death of the party who contracted the marriage.

As discussed in Chapter 16, the grounds for establishing a voidable marriage are lack of consent (i.e., lack of capacity), excusable bigamy (as in the case of an absent spouse), unsound mind, fraud, force, and physical incapacity.

Cases on nullity turn on § 300, which states that **"[m]arriage is a personal relation arising out of a civil contract . . ."** between two persons. Questions about the validity of the marriage go to the presence (or absence) of the requisite degree of consent necessary to enter into the marriage. A voidable marriage starts out with a legal impediment that can be corrected by a party's act of voluntarily cohabitating with the other party. Whether ratification occurs depends on the totality of the circumstances. Particularly key is the nonconsenting party's post-marriage conduct relative to the other party. Balancing factors include whether the parties consummated the marriage; whether they lived together as married persons; whether they became parents to biological children, adopted, or co-parented each other's children from prior unions. Also relevant is whether the parties handled earnings, property accumulations, and financial obligations (including taxes) in a joint manner. This last balancing factor is problematic whenever an allegation of lack of capacity due to mental incompetence is raised.

Finally, during the lifetime of the parties, strategy plays a role in deciding whether to nullify or dissolve a voidable marriage. A judgment of nullity supports the strategy of keeping the parties accumulations out of the community property system absent a subsequent determination of putative spouse status. A judgment of dissolution supports the strategy of using the community property system to dissolve the parties' accumulations.

[1] Lack of Capacity

Lack of capacity is an impediment to a valid marriage. Minors lack capacity to marry, but so too can adults.

Dunphy v. Dunphy is a controlling case on the capacity required to consent to marriage.[13] In that case, a judgment of nullity was granted to James, the only son of wealthy San Francisco parents, in relation to his voidable marriage to Lydia. Even by the standards of the day, the trial record showed that James suffered from a severe case of alcoholism. During a "drinking spree . . . preceded and followed by drunken revels" James married Lydia.[14] Six days after the wedding ceremony, James filed a petition of nullity alleging lack of consent due to intoxication. Lydia denied James's claims about the level of his intoxication over the entire six days they cohabited: She argued that even if James had been too intoxicated during the

[13] *Dunphy*, *supra*.

[14] *Id.* at 388.

ceremony to consent to the marriage, James had moments of sobriety during the six days that the parties lived together in which he did give his consent to the marriage. The trial transcript was 650 pages long. It included the testimony of three medical experts, and numerous lay witnesses, all of whom testified about the circumstances surrounding the marriage. They told of how there had been no engagement, no wedding ring, no wedding presents; that James and Lydia agreed one morning to marry; that, on the same day, James and Lydia picked up some friends in James' car; and that they drove to the then-small town of Redwood City, where they obtained a license from the local justice of the peace who immediately married them.

At issue was whether James consented to the marriage. The California Supreme Court explained that the law requires consent, but consent may be given in a lucid (sober) moment either during the ceremony, or in a lucid moment during a period of voluntary cohabitation with the other party. In *Dunphy*, James alleged that he was too intoxicated during the ceremony to consent to marry; and he remained continuously intoxicated over the six days that he and Lydia stayed together, thus negating Lydia's counter allegation that James voluntarily consented to the marriage by voluntarily cohabitation. James's friend Curtis was a key witness. When asked whether James appeared to understand the relation and obligation of marriage, Curtis's answered that James "told [him] he had not wanted to marry the lady, that the marriage had taken place, in effect, at a moment's notice, that he didn't know what he was doing at the time, and that he thought a thousand dollars would 'call it off.' "[15]

The trial court granted a judgment of nullity. Lydia appealed. The California Supreme Court reluctantly affirmed the trial court holding that there was sufficient evidence in the record to support the judgment of nullity. And yet, the court of appeal noted that, under the preponderance of evidence standard, a different fact finder could have interpreted the mountain of evidence in Lydia's favor.

Generalizing from *Dunphy*, intoxication can compromise one's consent to marriage. Continued intoxication can too. But once a lucid moment prevails, the issue becomes whether the party formed the requisite intent to consent to the marriage. Lack of capacity due to intoxication is a transitory impediment to consent, easily lifted by a lucid moment of sobriety.

[2] Excusable Bigamy: Marriage "Suspension"

A marriage is voidable on excusable bigamy grounds when a person who is married, has not heard from a spouse who **"[w]as absent and not known to the party commencing the proceeding to be living for a period of five successive years immediately preceding the subsequent marriage for which the judgment of nullity is sought"** or the absent spouse is **"generally reputed or believed by the party commencing the proceeding to be dead at the time the subsequent marriage was contracted."**[16]

---

[15] *Id.* at 386.

[16] Cal. Fam. Code § 2210(b)(1) and (2).

The mere absence of a spouse is not sufficient to raise a presumption of death. *Estate of Harrington* controls: In that case, Amelia's husband, John, left Michigan a week after their 1874 marriage to find his fortune in San Francisco.[17] At first John wrote to Amelia, but eventually all letters stopped. Twelve years later, believing John to be dead, Amelia subsequently married James, in Michigan, in 1886. After Amelia's second marriage, rumors surfaced that (first spouse) John was alive, at which point Amelia physically separated from (second spouse) James. When John died in California in 1900, Amelia traveled to California to assert her status as John's surviving spouse for purposes of the disposition of his estate. Amelia contended that because she was married to John when she married James, her marriage to James was absolutely void under Michigan law. Amelia was unable to confirm her characterization of Michigan law, which left the California probate court to decide the validity of the second marriage under California law.

The court first invoked a rule still in operation today: A voidable marriage is presumed valid unless a judgment of nullity or dissolution is obtained during the lives of the parties. By that rule, Amelia's second marriage was ruled bigamous, but since the bigamy was excusably contracted in Amelia's good faith belief that John was dead, Amelia's second marriage to James was deemed voidable, not void. A voidable marriage is presumptively valid absent a judgment of nullity, which Amelia never obtained.

As for Amelia's first marriage, the court held that Amelia's marriage to John was "suspended" once she contracted the second (voidable) marriage with James. In the case of excusable bigamy, a suspended first marriage ceases to be binding when the excusably bigamous marriage is contracted. The suspended marriage continues in that status until one of the involved parties to that suspended marriage seeks a judgment of nullity or dissolution; or, unless the excusably bigamous party seeks a judgment of nullity or dissolution for the subsequent marriage. The policy behind recognizing the doctrine of suspension, wrote the court, was to prevent polygamy from being sanctioned by law.[18]

[3] Fraud

Fraud in inducing a person to give consent to the marriage is a ground for nullifying a marriage. However, nullification based on fraud is granted only in extreme cases, especially if the marriage has been consummated.[19] The policy here is twofold. One, marriage is defined as a personal relation arising out of a civil contract; therefore, the petitioner who alleges fraud must prove that he or she relied on the false representation or concealment *specifically in giving his or her consent to marry*. Two, a judgment of nullity granted on the basis of fraud has the unintentional consequence of encouraging additional litigation over title to any

---

[17] *In re Harrington's Estate*, 140 Cal. 294, 73 P. 1131 (Cal. 1903).

[18] *Harrington, supra.*

[19] *Millar v. Millar*, 175 Cal. 797, 167 P. 394 (Cal. 1917) (in bank) (husband petitioned for judgment of nullity on ground of fraud alleging that wife had no intention to consummate the marriage, married husband for obtaining support and property, and did not consummate the marriage; judgment granted).

property that was obtained or transferred by the injured party in reliance on the validity of the voidable marriage.[20]

To date, fraud sufficient to nullify a marriage must involve misrepresentations or concealments of a sexual or procreative matter. *Marriage of Ramirez* is a recent example where one court of appeal restated "the long standing rule" that "neither party may question the validity of the marriage upon the ground of express or implied representations of the other with respect to such matters as character, habits, chastity, business or social standing, financial worth or prospects, or matters of a similar nature."[21] Likewise, "concealment of incontinence, temper, idleness, extravagance, coldness or lack of represented fortune will not justify an annulment."[22]

Some recent cases follow this rule as well. In *Meagher and Maleki*, the petitioner sought a petition of nullity on the ground that during their engagement the respondent misrepresented his wealth in such a way as to induce the petitioner to give him control of her property.[23] The trial judge denied the petition for nullity. It ruled that the husband's misrepresentation went to his financial worth, not to the essence of the marriage relationship itself; therefore, the marriage was not voidable because the respondent's misrepresentations did not induce the petitioner to give her consent to the marriage. By this decision the parties' marriage was adjudged valid. *Marshall v. Marshall* involved a similar petition and outcome, with the added twist of creditors pursuing the husband into the marriage.[24]

In *Marriage of Johnston*, wife petitioned for nullification on the ground that she was unaware of husband's severe drinking problem until after the marriage.[25] Finding the wife credible, the trial court nullified the marriage; it also voided a real property transfer that the wife made to the husband after the wedding occurred. On appeal, the judgment of nullity was reversed; a judgment of dissolution was entered instead. Consequently, the parties' property rights were determined under the ordinary rules of community property. The court of appeal interpreted prior case law in this way:

> "If a shoe salesman's false representation that he owned his own shoe store fell short of 'fraud sufficient to annul a marriage' . . . or a future husband's statement that he was a 'man of means' (when he was really 'impecunious') was not enough . . . how much less so are the grounds here, where the husband turned out to be, in the eyes of his wife, a lazy, unshaven disappointment with a drinking problem. In California, fraud must go to

---

[20] *Marriage of Ramirez*, 165 Cal. App. 4th 751, 757, 759, 81 Cal. Rptr. 3d 180 (Cal. App. Ct., 4th Dist. 2008), citing *Meagher & Maleki, supra*, at 3; *Millar, supra*; *Marshall v. Marshall*, 212 Cal. 736, 300 P. 816 (Cal. 1931) (in bank) (wife petitioned for judgment of nullity on the ground of fraud; wife alleged that husband falsely represented himself as a person of financial status, and wife had relied on that false representation in marrying husband; petition denied).

[21] *Ramirez, supra*, citing *Meagher & Maleki, supra*, at 3.

[22] *Ramirez, supra*, at 757, citing *Marshall, supra*, at 739–40.

[23] *Meagher & Maleki, supra*, at 3.

[24] *Marshall, supra*.

[25] *Marriage of Johnston*, 18 Cal. App. 4th 499, 22 Cal. Rptr. 2d 253 (Cal. App. Ct., 4th Dist. 1993).

the very essence of the marital relation before it is sufficient for an annulment."[26]

Misrepresenting one's willingness to have sex with the other party after the wedding, or concealing one's lack of willingness to have sex with the other person after marriage, and then not (in fact) consummating the marriage is an example of fraud sufficient to nullify a marriage.[27] So too is a promise to bear or co-parent children made with no intention of keeping that promise.[28] More recently, a petition for nullity was granted in a case where the respondent fraudulently concealed his sexual involvement with the petitioner's sister.[29] The evidence showed that the purported groom entered into the marriage to gain permanent resident status in the U.S. However, the immigration issue was not the basis for nullifying the marriage. Instead, the judgment of nullity was granted on the evidence of the groom's concealment of his ongoing infidelity and his misrepresentations about his willingness to be faithful to the woman he was marrying.[30]

In sum, the question asked and answered for determining fraud sufficient to nullify a marriage is this: Had the petitioner known the facts misrepresented or concealed, would he or she nevertheless have consented to enter into the marriage contract?

[4] Force

Obtaining consent by force is grounds for a judgment of nullity, but only if the force causes the party to consent to the marriage against his or her will. Where a marriage is entered into voluntarily, by definition consent cannot be obtained by force. Additionally, if the parties voluntary live together after the wedding ceremony as spouses — engage in an ongoing sexual relationship — they essentially waive the right to seek annulment of the marriage on this ground.

Consent is lacking only when a marriage is entered into without the consent of both parties. As the age of consent is 18, California no longer allows child marriage. Thus marriage by force necessarily involves criminal circumstances, as illustrated by the case of *Marriage of Weintraub*.[31] In *Weintraub* plaintiff sued for reinstatement of spousal support from a former husband. Plaintiff based her claim against her former husband on a judgment of nullity granted in the intervening marriage. The court described how that nullified intervening marriage was contracted:

---

[26] *Id.* at 502, citing *Mayer v. Mayer*, 207 Cal. 685, 694–95, 279 P. 783 (Cal. 1929) (in bank); *Marshall, supra*, at 737–38.

[27] *Millar, supra.*

[28] *Maslow v. Maslow*, 117 Cal. App. 2d 237, 255 P.2d 65 (Cal. App. Ct., 2d Dist. 1953) (ground for nullity by fraud exits where party makes a promise to have children and the person has no intention of keeping that promise), citing *Millar, supra*, at 242.

[29] *Ramirez, supra.*

[30] Reversed by *Ceja, supra*, at 1120, on the putative spouse issue related to husband's first marriage, but not reversed on the issue of the voidability of the *second* marriage due to fraud, which is what the above discussion is about.

[31] *Marriage of Weintraub*, 167 Cal. App. 3d 420, 213 Cal. Rptr. 159 (Cal. App. Ct., 2d Dist. 1985).

"On December 17, 1981, Wife was abducted . . . by force, physical beatings, and threat of physical harm and taken to Arizona, where, on December 20, 1981, against her will and as a result of coercion, physical beatings, intimidation and threats upon the safety of her family, Wife went through a marriage ceremony with [the perpetrator]. Wife returned with [the perpetrator] to her residence in California where for two months she was 'virtually held captive' . . . until February 22, 1982, [when] she managed to leave her residence, contact an attorney and obtain restraining orders removing [the perpetrator] from her home. Through her attorney, she obtained on March 16, 1982, a judgment in Los Angeles Superior Court annulling her marriage [to the perpetrator] on the ground that the marriage was obtained by force.. . . No criminal charges were filed against the [perpetrator] despite police reports made by Wife. [The perpetrator] left the jurisdiction and became the subject of FBI investigation."

In *Weintraub*, the trial court found that the petitioner was induced by force to marry her kidnapper. That finding, which led to a judgment of nullity, was upheld on appeal, as was the reinstatement of the petitioner's spousal support from her former spouse. The court of appeal cited the relation back doctrine as the basis upon for reinstating the spousal support order against the former spouse — the order that was in effect prior to the null intervening marriage. The policy served was to provide equity for the petitioner who was the victim of a heinous and violent crime.

[5] Physical Incapacity

The California judicial putative spouse doctrine was first recognized in *Coats v. Coats*, where a judgment of nullification was granted on the ground of physical incapacity.[32] In *Coats*, the parties were married for eighteen years when the husband successfully petitioned to annul the marriage on the ground of the wife's physical incapacity. Following that action, a subsequent action was brought to divide the parties' accumulations. The husband, Lee, argued that wife, Ida, was not entitled to the accumulations of an annulled (voided) marriage. Ida argued that given her good faith belief in the validity of the marriage, she was entitled to some portion of the accumulations from the long term marriage. The trial court awarded Ida $10,000. Lee appealed. Eventually the California Supreme Court upheld the trial court judgment by affirming Ida's putative spouse status under the common law of California. Eventually, as discussed in Chapter 16, the putative spouse doctrine was codified; today it is part of the Family Code.[33]

In *Coats* the marriage was adjudged null on the basis of physical incapacity. Physical incapacity as a ground for annulment relates to the incapacitated party's inability to engage in so-called "normal copulation;" a condition sometimes referred to as "legal impotence."[34] In *Stepanek v. Stepanek*, for example, the wife was 38 and the husband was 66 when they contracted marriage. The wife petitioned for annulment a couple of weeks after the wedding ceremony on the ground of the

---

[32] *Coats v. Coats*, 160 Cal. 671, 118 P. 441 (Cal. 1911) (in bank).

[33] Cal. Fam. Code § 2251.

[34] *Stepanek v. Stepanek*, 193 Cal. App. 2d 760, 14 Cal. Rptr. 793 (Cal. App. Ct., 1st Dist. 1961).

husband's incurable "impotence." The husband cross-petitioned for an annulment alleging fraud; he contended the wife entered into the marriage with the intent to conceal that she was "unwilling or unable to have matrimonial intercourse." The trial court granted an annulment on grounds of the husband's physical incapacity: Specifically it found that husband was unable to achieve and sustain an erection. The husband appealed. On appeal the trial court judgment was reversed.

Stepanek clarifies the elements of proof required to nullify a marriage on physical incapacity grounds:

(1) The petitioner must prove that the parties have not had sexual relations during the marriage; and

(2) There must be sufficient medical proof that the physical incapacity is incurable.[35]

As to the first element, the court explained that "the law's test is simply the ability or inability for copulation, not fruitfulness . . . the inability need be only for normal copulation, not partial, imperfect, unnatural or painful copulation . . . and the inability must only exist as to the particular spouse."[36] In other words, incurable physical incapacity is person-specific. One could nullify one marriage on physical incapacity grounds, and subsequently go on to have a fulfilling sex life with another.

In conclusion, the underlying rule is that a void marriage is void from the start, whereas a voidable marriage is presumptively valid, unless and until a judgment of nullity is obtained.[37] Based on this rule, in a void marriage the parties do not transition from single status to married status. In a voidable marriage the parties are nonconclusively presumed to have transitioned from single status to married status. In a legal marriage the parties do transition from single status to married status.

§ 15.02 REGISTERED DOMESTIC PARTNERS

On September 19, 2003, then California Governor Gray Davis signed Assembly Bill 205 into law. AB 205 is California Domestic Partner Rights and Responsibilities Act of 2003 [DPRRA]. DPRRA became fully operative in 2005.

Prior to the passage of DPRRA, domestic partnership was a local or county matter. California cities and one county passed domestic partnership laws in the following (chronological) order: West Hollywood (1985), San Francisco (1990), Cathedral City (September 1991), Berkeley (October 1991), Sacramento (1992), Palo Alto (1995), Oakland (1996), Laguna Beach (1997), Arcata (1998), Los Angeles County (March 1999), the City of Los Angeles (May 1999), and Santa Barbara County (July 1999). Registered domestic partnership became available statewide by Family Code § 299, which was passed in 1999, and became effective in 2000. Finally, in 2003, DPRRA was passed; it became fully effective by 2005. Pursuant to DPRRA persons who were registered under a city or county ordinance were required to

---

35 *Id.* at 762.

36 *Id.* at 762–63.

37 *McDonald, supra.*

re-register their partnership with the Secretary of State.

California is a marriage equality state. However, state registration of a domestic partnership is still available. State registration was and still is required for a valid registered domestic partnership.[38] State law preempts local ordinances.[39]

DPRRA is significant because it grants to registered domestic partners all the rights and responsibilities of marriage. Additionally, one of the more significant aspects of the DPRRA is that it has no residency requirement: Couples from all over the U.S. and (perhaps) even the world can elect to register as domestic partners under California law if they meet the basic requirements of § 297.

Once registered with the state, DPRRA offers registered domestic partners the same community property rights as married couples in California.[40] As with a marriage, this means that in any registered domestic partnership there is community property, separate property, commingled property, and the need (or option) to refer to California community property law.[41] Similar to spouses, registered domestic partners may not alter their legal relations except with respect to property; thus the California Premarital Agreement Act [CPAA] applies to preregistration agreements.[42] Management and control rights for community personal and real property are identical to those of spouses; joint obligations for debts incurred from the date the partners first register with the state are also identical.[43] Property transferred between partners is not "a change of ownership" for tax reassessment purposes; this means that the transmutation laws governs transactions between registered partners, who — like spouses — are in a confidential relationship relative to each other.[44] In 2006 California tax law was revised to require registered domestic partners to file either joint or separate California *state* income tax returns.[45] Furthermore, a surviving registered domestic partner has the same status as a surviving spouse for purposes of the intestacy code.

Below are additional ways in which a registered domestic partner has the same rights as a married person.[46]

- parentage issues;[47]
- employee benefits, such as unpaid leave to care for a registered domestic

---

[38] *Velez v. Smith*, 142 Cal. App. 4th 1154, 1169, 48 Cal. Rptr. 3d 642 (Cal. App. Ct., 1st Dist. 2006).

[39] DPRRA 2005 § 299.3 authorized the Secretary of State to notify registered domestic partners of the change in the law.

[40] Cal. Fam. Code §§ 297.5(a)–(b), (k)(1), 721, 1100(e), 1101.

[41] Cal. Fam. Code §§ 297.5, 752, 770.

[42] Cal. Fam. Code §§ 297.5(a)–(b), (k)(1), (2), 1620.

[43] Cal. Fam. Code §§ 297.5, 760, 1110(a), 1100(e), 1101 (personal property), 1102 (real property), 297.5(k), 910–16.

[44] Rev. & TC § 62(p); *Strong v. State Bd. of Equalization*, 155 Cal. App. 4th 1182, 1186, 66 Cal. Rptr. 3d 657 (Cal. App. Ct., 3d Dist. 2007).

[45] Amended version of Cal. Fam. Code § 297.5; Rev. & TC § 17024.5.

[46] This list is derived from CALIFORNIA DOMESTIC PARTNERSHIPS (2008), which has extensive commentary on immigration rights, medical rights, rights upon death, parentage rights, and so forth.

[47] Cal. Fam. Code §§ 297.5, 3010 et seq.

partner, and paid family leave under the Paid Family Leave Insurance Program;

- unemployment benefits if one follows one's registered domestic partner to a new location;[48]
- the right to use necessary force to protect a partner from wrongful injury;[49]
- rights to receive information about one's partner;
- medical decision making and hospital visitation rights;
- confidential communications privilege;
- general benefits: joint club memberships, right to receive absentee ballot for a partner, right to appear on behalf of one's partner in small claims court, right to defend one's partner's rights if both partners are sued, right to be notified if one's partner is being held involuntarily in a medical facility, right to obtain patient-related information subject to federal law;
- access to one's partner's certified birth and death records;
- standing to bring wrongful death or loss of consortium claims;
- public employee benefits such as CalPERS and CERA and county employee death benefits.[50]
- right to claim discrimination under state law based on marital status;[51]
- nearly all the same rights as former spouses, including post-termination support rights like spousal support;[52]
- control of partner's human remains;
- burial rights;
- homestead protection against creditors for the surviving partner;
- simultaneous death provision protection;
- surviving spouse status under the Probate Code.[53]

This list is a non-inclusive list. But it is a useful reminder of the web of default legal protections that extend — across the board — to married persons.[54] If a full

---

[48] Cal. Gov. Code §12945.2; Cal. Unemp. Ins. Code § 1030(a)(4).

[49] Cal. Civ. Code § 50; Cal. Pen. Code § 197.

[50] Cal. Gov. Code § 31780.2.

[51] Cal. Fam. Code § 297.5(f).

[52] Cal. Fam. Code §§ 297.5(a)–(b), (k)(1), 720, 4320. Differences between spouses and former domestic partners include jurisdictional and venue rules, calculations regarding the length of the relationship for purposes of support, enforcement issues with out-of-state ex-domestic partners, and ERISA issues.

[53] Cal. Prob. Code § 6401 and Cal. Fam. Code § 297.5(i) state that DPRRA does not amend or modify **"[a]ny provision of the California Constitution or any provision of any statute that was adopted by initiative."** The Probate Code was not adopted by initiative, therefore every reference to "spouse," "widow," "widower," and "marriage" in the Probate Code or in cases interpreting the Probate Code include domestic partners, a surviving domestic partner, and a domestic partnership.

[54] Such a list presumably could be compiled only by surveying the entirety of the California Codes on a statute-by-statute basis.

list of benefits were assembled, a registered domestic partnership would entitle the partners to every benefit on it and hold them to every obligation, just as if they had opted for marriage. The extensiveness of the partial list also makes clear why it is that a valid registered domestic partnership must be formally recognized under § 299(a), and once recognized, formally terminated.

Registration of a domestic partnership is with the Secretary of State. The prerequisites are set forth at § 297: **"Domestic partners are two adults who have chosen to share one another's lives in an intimate and committed relationship of mutual caring."** A domestic partnership **"shall be established in California when both persons file a Declaration of Domestic Partnership with the Secretary of State . . ."** The parties must share a **"common residence"** even if one or both maintain an additional residence. Neither can be married to another person, related by blood in a way that would give rise to a void marriage, or under 18 years of age. The institution of registered domestic partnership is limited to **"persons of the same sex"** of any age; or persons of opposite sexes where **"one or both are over the age of 62."**

Termination of a valid registered domestic partnership is accomplished by filing a Notice of Termination of Domestic Partnership with the Secretary of State. To file a joint notice, partners must meet the criteria set forth at § 299(a); these criteria parallel the joint petition for summary dissolution process discussed in Chapter 16. Otherwise, as with marriage, under § 299(d), **"the superior courts shall have jurisdiction over all proceedings relating to the dissolution of domestic partnerships, nullity of domestic partnerships, and legal separation of partners in a domestic partnership."** Residency is not required to file a petition: Registered domestic partners, no matter where one or both are domiciled, can file for a petition in a California superior court **". . . even if neither domestic partner is a resident of, or maintains a domicile in, the state at the time the proceedings are filed."**

Finally, under § 299(e): **"Parties to a registered domestic partnership who are also married to one another other may petition the court to dissolve both their domestic partnership and their marriage in a single proceeding, in a form that shall be proscribed by the Judicial Council."**

One significant caveat arises from California's transition to a marriage equality state: The various obligations that can be created by personal transitions coinciding with legal transitions require that the parties carefully assess the status of their prior and current domestic partnership(s) and marriage(s). As with marriage, only a final dissolution judgment can return a registered domestic partner to the status of an individual person. And only a final judgment of nullity can make provide clear evidence that a voidable registered domestic partnership did not change one's personal status from a single person to a registered domestic partner. *Estate of Wilson* is on point.[55]

Once in the superior court, the rights of registered domestic partners **"shall"** be adjudicated by the same doctrines that apply to married persons, and for the same

[55] *Estate of Wilson*, 211 Cal. App. 4th 1284, 150 Cal. Rptr. 3d 699 (Cal. App. Ct., 1st Dist. 2012).

policy reasons.[56]

Example 15.1: This example illustrates how parties in other jurisdictions can take advantage of California community property law. Steiner and Toklas live in a U.S. state that does not recognize same-sex marriage and that does not have a registered domestic partnership law. They decide to register their domestic partnership in California. Under the DRPPA, Steiner and Toklas are registered domestic partners in the state of California, notwithstanding that neither is a resident of California. As such their legal rights and obligations relative to the registered domestic partnership are set forth under California community property law.

Example 15.2: This example illustrates how parties in other jurisdictions can choose California's robust registered domestic partner legislation (DPRRA) over their own jurisdiction's legislation. Steiner and Toklas live in a U.S. state that does not recognize same-sex marriage and that does not have a *robust* registered domestic partnership law. Steiner and Toklas decide to register their domestic partnership in California. Under the DRPPA, Steiner and Toklas are registered domestic partners in the state of California, notwithstanding that neither partner is a resident of California. Under DPRRA, the registered domestic partners' legal rights and obligations are identical to those offered to married persons by the California community property system.

Example 15.3: This example illustrates the human rights aspect of DPRRA. Steiner and Toklas live in a country that is hostile to same sex partners. That country does not recognize same-sex marriage and it does not have a registered domestic partnership law. Steiner and Toklas cannot change their domicile. They decide, however, to register their domestic partnership in California. After several years of living as registered domestic partners, Steiner and Toklas decide to break-up. Steiner and Toklas meet the requirements for filing a joint Notice of Termination of Domestic Partnership with the California Secretary of State. Under the DRPPA, the registered domestic partnership of Steiner and Toklas may be dissolved by the summary process available under DPRRA. Steiner's and Toklas' status as single persons is reinstated upon receipt of a final notice of termination.

Example 15.4: Same as Example 15.3 except that when Steiner and Toklas seek to terminate their registered domestic partnership, they do not meet the requirements for filing a joint Notice of Termination of Domestic Partnership. Nevertheless, and notwithstanding the fact that neither is a resident of California, Steiner and Toklas may file a petition for dissolution of their domestic partnership in a California superior court.[57]

---

[56] Cal. Fam. Code § 299(d).

[57] DPRRA changes prior law on this point. Under prior law, RDPs could file a joint "Termination of Domestic Partnership" in all cases. However, after 2005, termination by filing notice is not available in all cases. *See* § 299.3. Where it is not available, the parties must seek dissolution of the registered domestic partnership in a California superior court.

§ 15.03 NONMARRIED COHABITANTS

The Family Code does not govern the management, control or distribution of property acquired by nonmarried cohabitants. Their property issues are governed by general contract and property law. Express contracts between nonmarried partners are enforceable so long as they do not involve sexual services as consideration. Absent an express contract, the parties' conduct determines whether they had an implied or tacit understanding between them as to property matters.[58]

The term nonmarried cohabitant is defined in different ways, depending upon the context. Under the Domestic Violence Prevention Act (DVPA), the term nonmarried cohabitant is broadly defined as persons who live together, including those who may not have a sexual relationship.[59] Under the Penal Code, a nonmarried cohabitant is more restrictively defined as one of two unrelated adult persons who live together for a substantial period of time in a somewhat permanent relationship.[60] Cal. Penal Code § 13700 lists the following balancing factors as relevant for determining whether parties are cohabitants: sharing sexual relations while living together; sharing income or expenses; joint ownership of property; whether the parties hold themselves out as spouses or domestic partners; the continuity of the relationship; and the length of the relationship.

Case law also defines the term nonmarried cohabitant.[61] For purposes of distributing property at the end of relationship, a nonmarried domestic partner is one of two adults who make a choice to share their lives with each other in an intimate and committed *sexual* relationship. A nonmarried domestic partner may or may not believe that he or she is married to the other partner.[62] A person who has a good faith belief in the validity of a marriage that turns out to be invalid is a nonmarried partner; and he or she is also eligible for putative spouse status. Otherwise, nonmarried cohabitants, as opposed to spouses or registered domestic partners, are generally single persons who know or have reason to know they are not married or formally registered as domestic partners.

That said, nonmarried cohabitants share a residence. They typically share finances, including income and expenses, earnings and accumulations. They may share joint ownership of property, including bank accounts, and so forth. Nonmarried cohabitants may co-parent their own or each other's children. They may recognize the other partner as part of their extended family structure. They may even hold themselves out as married persons. However, since California does not permit informal, or "common law," marriage, the mere fact of holding themselves out as married persons or domestic partners will not make either or both eligible for putative spouse status.

Some nonmarried cohabitants may not want their relationship to be confined by Family Code rights and obligations. For this set of nonmarried cohabitants, the

---

[58] *Marvin v. Marvin*, 18 Cal. 3d 660, 134 Cal. Rptr. 815, 557 P.2d 106 (Cal. 1976) (in bank).

[59] *See* Chapter 11.

[60] *See* Chapter 11.

[61] *Marvin, supra.*

[62] *See Alderson v. Alderson*, 180 Cal. App. 3d 450, 225 Cal. Rptr. 610 (Cal. App. Ct., 1st Dist. 1986).

knowledge that they are single persons living together precludes default application of some but not all of the Family Code to the dissolution of their partnership. The quasi-marital property provisions are not available to the couple, but the DVPA provisions are. The DVPA applies equally to domestic partners, spouses, and registered domestic partners, notwithstanding the fact of marriage, as do most provisions of CAMPAL. The one CAMAPL provision that is not applicable by default to nonmarried cohabitants is the special community property presumption for sums on deposit in an account.

In seeking to enforce a contract between them, there is no requirement that a nonmarried cohabitant allege a long term relationship. However, evidence of such a relationship may corroborate allegations about expectations with respect to property issues that arose from the other partner's conduct. Expectations deriving from conduct may be especially important in cases involving support in exchange for lost opportunity costs (such as when one forgoes a career in order to assist the other or to engage in unpaid domestic tasks such as housekeeping or childcare), the support of children born to the partnership, and post break-up support.

In conclusion, the California Family Code does not regulate the distribution of property between nonmarried cohabitants, even where equity may otherwise seem to demand that it should.[63] A comparative example clarifies this point. In Washington, depending on the totality of the circumstances, the equitable relationship doctrine can be invoked to give nonmarried cohabitants the protections of civil marriage when their relationship terminates by break-up or death. But California does not follow the equitable relationship doctrine.[64] When nonmarried cohabitants break up, each individual's property rights are governed by the Civil Code or by the common law of contract, property, and tort. So, for example, while the Family Code uses presumptions to void a transaction between spouses that was obtained by any undue influence, the Civil Code treats consent not freely given as **"not absolutely void,"** thus requiring the nonmarried claimant to prove his or her right to rescission as to any agreement that he or she made with the other partner.[65]

The California approach makes clear that California preserves a third option for persons who seek to live as intimate partners without marriage. Thus, in California, assuming all other requirements are met, two persons can marry one another[66] or they can register their domestic partnership.[67] Otherwise, they can retain their status as single persons *in relation to each other*, and live as nonmarried cohabitants.

---

[63] *Marriage of Cary*, 34 Cal. App. 3d 345, 109 Cal. Rptr. 862 (Cal. App. Ct., 1st Dist. 1973), where the parties knew they were not married, and yet they petitioned to nullify their "marriage" under the Family Code in a petition stylized for Family Code purposes as "*Marriage of Cary*," rather than as a civil code action, *Cary v. Cary*. The parties, despite knowing that they were not married, used the same family name. *Cary* was reversed by *Marvin*, *supra*, thus precluding nonmarried cohabitants from relying on the Family Code. *See also Taylor v. Polackwich*, 145 Cal. App. 3d 1014, 1021, 194 Cal. Rptr. 8 (Cal. App. Ct., 2d Dist. 1983).

[64] *Marvin*, *supra*.

[65] *See* Cal. Civ. Code § 1566.

[66] Cal. Fam. Code § 300.

[67] Cal. Fam. Code § 297.

[A] The Right to Contract: *Marvin* Cohabitation Agreements

Marvin v. Marvin is the landmark case that held that nonmarried cohabitants may enter into contracts with each other over property notwithstanding the fact of their sexual relationship.[68] In *Marvin*, plaintiff Michelle alleged that she lived with defendant Lee Marvin from October 1964 through May 1970, during which time the parties acquired — in Lee Marvin's name — substantial real and personal property, including motion picture rights worth over $1 million. Michelle also alleged that Lee made an oral promise to Michelle "to provide for all her financial support for the rest of her life" in exchange for unpaid domestic services (housekeeping). Michelle ultimately failed to establish the existence of a contract.[69]

In *Marvin*, the California Supreme Court held that adult nonmarried cohabitants who live together in a sexual relationship are as "competent as any other persons to contract respecting their earnings and property rights."[70] The court went on to say that "[i]n the absence of an express contract, the courts should inquire into the conduct of the parties to determine whether that conduct demonstrates an implied contract, agreement of partnership or joint venture, or some other tacit understanding between the parties."[71] Thus state policy was set: "The courts should enforce express contracts between nonmarital partners except to the extent that the contract is explicitly founded on the consideration of meretricious sexual services."[72]

After *Marvin*, express, oral, implied, and tacit agreements between nonmarital cohabitants are enforceable. The contract need not be in writing absent a Civil Code provision specifically requiring otherwise.[73] Contracts may be oral, implied or by tacit understanding. Contracts based on tacit understanding are contracts of mutual assent, and as such they too require proof of offer, acceptance, and consideration. Uncertainty as to the terms of the contract may be resolved by extrinsic evidence.

Byrne v. Laura extended *Marvin* to oral agreements for support.[74] In *Byrne*, the surviving partner alleged a *Marvin* contract for property and support. On that basis, she argued for (1) summary probate on the basis of an oral joint tenancy agreement; and (2) lifetime support enforceable against the decedent's estate. The motion for summary probate was denied; the oral agreement for lifetime support

---

[68] *Marvin, supra.*

[69] *Marvin v. Marvin*, 122 Cal. App. 3d 871, 176 Cal. Rptr. 555 (Cal. App. Ct., 2d Dist., 1981).

[70] *Id.* at 672.

[71] *Id.* at 672.

[72] *Id.*

[73] Cal. Civ. Code §§ 1619–22.

[74] *Byrne v. Laura*, 52 Cal. App. 4th 1054, 1063, 60 Cal. Rptr. 2d 908 (1st Dist. 1997) (surviving nonmarried partner seeks summary probate on basis that parties had an oral joint tenancy agreement and a *Marvin* contract for lifetime support; summary probate proceeding disallowed but trial court upheld on decision to enforce *Marvin* contracts after the death of a party).

was enforced as against the decedent's estate.[75]

Bergen v. Wood reversed a trial court decision to enforce an alleged oral *Marvin* contract for future support. In *Bergen*, the fact that the parties were lovers, but not cohabitants, took their contract out of the *Marvin* rule.[76] Relying in large part upon *Whorton*, the court in *Bergen* suggested that while the plaintiff's services as defendant's social secretary would have been consideration *if the parties had lived together*, since they didn't live together, the consideration was inseparable from their sexual relationship. This made the *Marvin* contract for future support alleged in *Bergen* unenforceable for lack of consideration.

[B] Consideration

Nonmarried cohabitants are not married or registered as domestic partners. For that reason any agreement they enter into must be supported by consideration that is independent of their sexual relationship. A gratuitous promise, without consideration, is not legally enforceable.[77] Moreover, lack of consideration is an affirmative defense to a *Marvin* contract.[78]

Marvin clarified what sort of exchange can be used as consideration to support a contract between nonmarried cohabitants.[79]

At one end of the consideration spectrum, the parties need not contribute property as consideration for the contract; but at the other end, they must exchange something as consideration for the contract. A promise to contribute sweat equity or a promise to perform "homemaking services" is defined under *Marvin* as "adequate consideration for a contract" between nonmarried cohabitants.[80] One party's promise to divorce a current spouse may be sufficient consideration.[81] To repeat an often quoted phrase from *Marvin*: "so long as the agreement does not rest upon illicit meretricious consideration, [nonmarried cohabitants] may order their affairs as they choose, and no policy precludes the courts from enforcing such agreements."[82]

---

75 *Marvin, supra*, at 674.

76 *Bergen v. Wood*, 14 Cal. App. 4th 854, 18 Cal. Rptr. 2d 75 (Cal. App. Ct., 2d Dist. 1993). *But see Milian v. DeLeon*, 181 Cal. App. 3d 1185, 1193, 226 Cal. Rptr. 831 (Cal. App. Ct., 4th Dist. 1986) (cohabitation was held not to be a prerequisite to *Marvin* contract enforcement where the court found that the parties anticipated marriage and took property in joint title despite unequal contributions to purchase).

77 *Kurokawa v. Blum*, 199 Cal. App. 3d 976, 245 Cal. Rptr. 463 (Cal. App. Ct., 2d Dist. 1988) (*Marvin* contract alleged after 12 year period of separation; the attorney for the contract claimant was Marvin M. Mitchelson, the same attorney who represented the contract claimant in *Marvin*, supra).

78 *Taylor v. Fields*, 178 Cal. App. 3d 653, 665, 224 Cal. Rptr. 186 (Cal. App. Ct., 2d Dist. 1986).

79 *Marvin, supra*, is rejected by *Silver v. Starrett*, 176 Misc. 2d 511, 674 N.Y.S.2d 915 (S.Ct. 1998).

80 *Marvin supra*, at 670.

81 *Feldman v. Nassi*, 111 Cal. App. 3d 881, 886–87, 169 Cal. Rptr. 9 (Cal. App. Ct., 2d Dist. 1980).

82 *Marvin, supra*, at 674.

Whorton v. Dillingham extended the *Marvin* holding on consideration in three ways.[83] One, it clarified additional types of consideration that might support a *Marvin* contract. Two, it applied *Marvin* to a same-sex nonmarried cohabitancy. Three, it confirmed that the same rules apply to all cohabitants, regardless of their gender.

In *Whorton*, Donnis and Benjamin split up after 7 years of living together. Subsequently, Donnis sued Benjamin for breach of an oral pooling agreement. Donnis alleged the terms of the agreement as follows: (1) Donnis was to be Benjamin's "chauffer, bodyguard, social and business secretary, partner and counselor in real estate investments . . . constant companion, confidant, traveling and social companion, and lover . . ." in exchange (2) Benjamin would give Donnis "a one-half equity interest in all real estate acquired in their joint names . . . , financial support for life, bank account access with positive balances maintained, rights of withdrawal for savings accounts, credit card authorization," and (3) Donnis alleged that "the parties specifically agreed that any portion of the agreement found to be legally unenforceable was severable and the balance of the provisions would remain in full force and effect."[84] The trial court dismissed Donnis's contract claim for lack of consideration. Donnis appealed. The court of appeal reversed. It held that although the parties did have a sexual relationship, and that sex was an express term of the contract, the sexual component of the consideration was severable from the remaining portions of the oral agreement which were supported by consideration, namely Donnis's services to Benjamin as chauffeur, bodyguard, secretary, and business partner.

Whorton explicitly extended the *Marvin* doctrine to same-sex partners by distinguishing Donnis's and Benjamin's contract from the contract in *Jones v. Daly*, a case in which a surviving cohabitant sought to enforce an oral *Marvin* agreement against a decedent's estate. In *Jones*, the contract was held unenforceable for lack of consideration where the services provided were limited to "lover, companion, homemaker, traveling companion, housekeeper and cook . . . ."[85] The difference between *Whorton* and *Jones*, said the court, was that in *Jones*, the "sex and other services naturally flowing from sexual cohabitation were an inseparable part of the consideration for the so-called cohabitor's agreement," whereas in *Whorton*, the oral *Marvin* agreement would have been recognized as supported by consideration had Donnis and Benjamin not been sexual partners.[86] Another perhaps more important difference between the two cases is that in *Whorton* the *Marvin* contract claim arose in relation to a break-up, with Benjamin willing and able to testify on his own behalf, whereas in *Jones*, the *Marvin* contract arose as a claim against a decedent's estate. That said, *Marvin* contracts are enforceable against a decedent's estate, but they must be established by clear and convincing proof.

During a breakup, a *Marvin* breach of contract claim is filed as a civil action, not as family court action. The parties litigate their claims without the aid of the

---

[83] *Whorton v. Dillingham*, 202 Cal. App. 3d 447, 248 Cal. Rptr. 405 (Cal. App. Ct., 4th Dist. 1988).

[84] *Whorton, supra*, at 447, 450–51.

[85] *Jones v. Daly*, 122 Cal. App. 3d 500, 176 Cal. Rptr. 130 (Cal. App. Ct., 2d Dist. 1981).

[86] *Whorton, supra*, at 455.

general and specific presumptions that assist spouses and registered domestic partners. However, a *Marvin* claim can be consolidated with an existing family law case, as for example when the nonmarital partners subsequently marry.[87]

Indeed, the principal benefit of a nonmarried cohabitancy is also its principal drawback: The state of California expresses no compelling interest in the equal or fair division of property acquired during an informal domestic partnership. Only cohabitant contracts supported by consideration will be enforceable. Moreover, while the housekeeper's contribution need not be established in the context of the community property system, in the *Marvin* context, the housekeeper's contribution, while sufficient consideration to support a cohabitation contract, must be established by actual proof.

Therefore, as was done by the plaintiff in *Whorton*, it is important for a *Marvin* contract claimant to:

(1) Separately *itemize* the services that are the consideration for the contract.

(2) *Identify* those services as the kind that people outside of a committed intimate relationship ordinarily would provide for monetary compensation.

(3) *Distinguish* those services from sexual services, or from any other form of consideration that is "normally attendant to nonbusiness cohabitation," or services that are "naturally flowing from the sexual cohabitancy."[88]

Additionally, the party seeking equity must have clean hands.[89]

The statute of frauds is not a defense to a *Marvin* contract.[90] The theory is that as between two nonmarried cohabitants, the partner seeking to enforce the contract has provided services over the course of the relationship, and in reliance on a promise made by the other partner. For that reason, the doctrine of estoppel precludes the use of a statute of frauds defense so as to any prevent fraud and unjust enrichment that would result if the contract were not enforced.

[C] Breach

Generally, a *Marvin* contract concerning the distribution of property is breached when one partner terminates the relationship, and the alleged promises are not performed.[91] If the promise is performed, as with a *Marvin* contract for support, breach occurs when the support payments stop.[92] *Marvin* contract obligations survive the subsequent marriage of the original nonmarital partners to each other or to third parties.[93] The Family Code structures support only if the *Marvin* agreement so provides;[94] otherwise, the parties are free to structure

---

87 *Nelson v. Nevel*, 154 Cal. App. 3d 132, 139, 201 Cal. Rptr. 93 (Cal. App. Ct., 2d Dist. 1984).

88 *Whorton*, *supra*, at 455, also distinguishing *Taylor*, *supra*, which involved different-sex partners.

89 *Taylor*, *supra*, at 666 (both parties cannot be *in pari delicto*).

90 *Marvin*, *supra*, at 674; *see also Byrne*, *supra*, at 1067–68.

91 *Whorton*, *supra*.

92 *Cochran v. Cochran*, 56 Cal. App. 4th 1115, 1120, 66 Cal. Rptr. 2d 337 (Cal. App. Ct., 2d Dist. 1997).

93 *See Watkins v. Watkins*, 143 Cal. App. 3d 651, 655, 192 Cal. Rptr. 54 (Cal. App. Ct., 3d Dist. 1983).

94 *Friedman v. Friedman*, 20 Cal. App. 4th 876, 884, 24 Cal. Rptr. 2d 892 (Cal. App. Ct., 1st Dist.

support obligations in any way consistent with public policy. To reiterate, California does not follow the equitable relationship doctrine. Therefore, no matter the equities, a nonmarital relationship in which the parties know or should have known that they were not married will not be dissolved by the terms of the Family Code.[95]

The statute of limitations for *Marvin* contracts differ depending on the claims. The statute of limitations for an oral or implied contract is two years.[96] An action based upon rescission is two years; this includes claims for rescission where the ground is fraud or mistake.[97] A written contract, dissolution of an implied partnership, or contract action based on liability, obligation, recovery of assets, or equity all have a four year statutory period.[98] Other statutes of limitations may apply. An oral contract may be revived.[99]

Even where household services are exchanged for property or support, a *Marvin* contract is not governed by the Labor Code.[100] The rationale is that a *Marvin* contract is a cohabitation agreement, not an employment agreement.

If a *Marvin* contract involves promises about property titled in one of the partner's names, the burden is on the party asserting the *Marvin* agreement to rebut the presumption of record title found in the Evidence Code by clear and convincing proof.[101]

[D] Remedies

Damages for breach of a *Marvin* contract vary.

First, a constructive trust or a resulting trust can be used to demand return of property wrongfully detained.[102] This remedy does not require that the parties be in a fiduciary relationship to each other. A constructive trust protects against unjust enrichment. It can arise in the case of wrongful detainer or wrongful acquisition; the standard of proof is clear and convincing evidence.[103] Likewise, quasi-specific performance is available through the use of a constructive trust.[104]

1993), distinguished by *Kilroy v. Kilroy*, 35 Cal. App. 4th 1141, 41 Cal. Rptr. 2d 812 (Cal. App. Ct., 2d Dist. 1995).

[95] *See* commentary on *Cary*, *supra* note 63.

[96] Cal. Civ. Proc. Code § 339(1).

[97] Cal. Civ. Proc. Code § 339(3).

[98] Cal. Civ. Proc. Code §§ 337(1), 343.

[99] Cal. Civ. Proc. Code § 360, cited in *Kurokawa*, *supra*.

[100] *Whorton*, *supra*.

[101] *Tannehill v. Finch*, 188 Cal. App. 3d 224, 227, 232 Cal. Rptr. 749 (Cal. App. Ct., 4th Dist. 1986), declined to extend by *Murray v. Murray*, 26 Cal. App. 4th 1062, 31 Cal. Rptr. 2d 855 (Cal. App. Ct., 1st Dist. 1994).

[102] Cal. Civ. Code §§ 2223, 2224; *Taylor*, *supra*.

[103] *Toney v. Nolder*, 173 Cal. App. 3d 791, 795–96, 219 Cal. Rptr. 497 (Cal. App. Ct., 1st Dist. 1985).

[104] *Byrne*, *supra*.

A resulting trust, by contrast, arises when one party pays the purchase price for an asset and title is taken in the other partner's name.[105]

Compensatory damages are available.[106]

Specific performance is available.[107]

Quantum meruit is available.[108]

If established, an agreement for ongoing post-breakup financial support — known commonly as "palimony" — will be enforced.[109]

[E] To Marry or Not

Unmarried adults are not married or related by affinity, consanguinity or adoption. They neither owe nor are owed duties, and they are not eligible for family protections under the Family or Probate Codes. Unmarried cohabitants are not eligible for status as each other's surviving spouse, heir, or next of kin for purposes of intestate distribution. Instead, at the death of a cohabitant, a *Marvin* contract claimant asserts his or her claims as a creditor of the decedent's estate.

At the same time, neither do nonmarried cohabitants feel the weight of default marital and familial legal obligations (at least in theory). For example, nonmarried cohabitants are not expected or required to support each other. They are not necessarily obligated to disclose information to each other. They are not required to equally share or divide any property that one might acquire during the cohabitancy. Instead, they contract at arm's length, before, during, and after the cohabitancy, which means that they have the choice to create (or to refrain from creating) a confidential relationship in fact. Additionally, any oral or implied agreements that nonmarried cohabitants might enter into — whether to pool or not to pool resources, to share or not to share earnings, to jointly accumulate or not to jointly accumulate property, to support or not to support each other — are enforceable, notwithstanding the absence of important terms such as how to define a contribution to purchase, or — once defined — how to calculate proportional ownership shares, and so forth.

For all of the above reasons, it is useful if not imperative for nonmarried cohabitants who wish to care for each other to use written agreements to record their property expectations and agreements. Estates must be planned in detail and kept current. Health care directives in relation to each other must be explicitly expressed. All agreements and understandings must be carefully considered and documented.

Agreements between nonmarried cohabitants are *not* governed by the CPAA; however, the CPAA is available *as a model* for achieving a best practice. In other

---

105 *Nelson, supra.*

106 Cal. Civ. Code § 3333.

107 *Byrne, supra.*

108 *Marvin, supra.*

109 *Id.*

words, any contract between nonmarried cohabitants is more predictably enforceable if it is reduced to writing, signed by both cohabitants, supported by adequate consideration, and amended or revoked as necessary. Consideration is not necessary for prospective spouses' premarital contracts because those contracts will become enforceable on the date of the (valid) marriage. By sharp contrast, the contracts of unmarried cohabitants become effective once they are supported by adequate consideration; this is the case for all agreements, amendments, revocations, and transmutations as well.

Furthermore, agreements between spouses must be in writing, whereas agreements between nonmarital cohabitants need not be in writing. The general rule is that *Marvin* recognizes the enforceability of express, oral, implied and tacit agreements between nonmarried cohabitants. The only exception is on an asset-by-asset basis, or when the Civil Code specifically requires that an agreement be in writing.

The following is a *noninclusive* list of example subject matter concerns that can be contracted for in advance of or during a nonmarital cohabitancy:

- Disposition of property in the event of a death or breakup;
- Pooling agreements, including expectations about proportional shares, contributions to purchase, maintenance, and taxes;
- Agreements about what economic contribution each partner will make (or has made) to the relationship;
- Monetary considerations for tasks like caretaking, homemaking, and childcare;
- Agreements about the payment and responsibility of debt during the relationship;
- Agreements about reimbursements;
- Health insurance agreements, if any;
- Guardianship rights in the event of a loss of capacity;
- Health care directives in the event of a loss of capacity;
- Expectations about continuing monetary support between living cohabitants in the event of a break-up;
- Expectations for recording an act of abuse under the DVPA, should such an act occur;
- Expectations about continuing monetary support for a surviving cohabitant from the estate of a deceased cohabitant.

[F] Domestic Violence Issues

Cohabitants are subject to liability to each other for statutory torts that allow remedies for listed acts of abuse, domestic violence, invasions of privacy, and so forth. Nonmarried cohabitants are also subject to liability to each other for common law intentional and negligent torts.

In a 2002 settlement stylized as *Jane Doe v. John Roe*, a Los Angeles Superior Court approved a tort settlement between former unmarried cohabitants in a case alleging assault and battery.[110] Plaintiff alleged that the intentional torts occurred when the defendant: (1) threw a glass table at the plaintiff, thereby cutting her feet; (2) stalked, threatened, and harassed her, thereby causing emotional distress; and (3) filed, without plaintiff's knowledge, a lien in the form of a second deed of trust against their joint tenancy condo, thereby causing plaintiff emotional distress. Plaintiff claimed $2,200 in past medical expenses and $25,000 in lost earnings. She settled for $5,000 on the assault and battery claim, and clear title to the joint tenancy condo, plus attorney's fees. The settlement was (eventually) satisfied with the joint tenancy property when the plaintiff accepted a four part settlement:

(1) $40,000 (from the defendant's equity in the joint tenancy condo);

(2) A deed conveying defendant's interest in the condo to plaintiff;

(3) The avoidance of the deed of trust lien on plaintiff's property; and

(4) A reconveyance from the deed of trust holder that cleared title to the real estate in plaintiff's name only.

§ 15.04 SUMMARY

A void marriage is void from the start. However, parties have the right to petition for a judgment of nullity so as to clear up the record.

A voidable marriage is presumptively valid. This gives the parties the option to seek a judgment of nullity or a judgment of dissolution at the end of the relationship.

California offers registered domestic partnership status to same-sex couples. It also offers registered domestic partnership status to different-sex couples where one or both of the partners are over 62-years of age. There is no residency requirement for registering as California domestic partners. This makes California community property law available to persons in other jurisdictions who meet the California eligibility requirements for registering their domestic partnership. A domestic partnership may be terminated by jointly filing a notice of termination (if eligibility requirements are met) or by seeking an order from a California superior court. Again, California residency is not required to terminate a domestic partnership registered in California.

Parties who live together in a sexual domestic relationship, who are not also married or registered as domestic partners, are referred to as nonmarried cohabitants for purposes of California law. Nonmarried cohabitants have the right to enter into a *Marvin* contract to determine their rights during and after a period of cohabitancy. A *Marvin* contract is enforceable if it is supported by consideration distinguishable from the parties' sexual relationship. Upon breach, a number of remedies are available.

---

[110] *Former Condo Co-Habitants Settle Battery/Partition Claims*, California Jury Verdicts Weekly, Nov. 4, 2002, at 5.

Following is a list of differences between nonmarried cohabitancy and marriage (and registered domestic partnership).

Nonmarried Cohabitants	Married Persons and RDPs
• Eligible for DVPA protections	• Eligible for DVPA protection
• Eligible for CAMPAL	• Eligible for CAMPAL
Otherwise:	**Otherwise:**
• Not held to rights and obligations during partnership	• Rights and obligations determined by the Family Code
• Not deemed to be in a confidential relationship as a matter of law	• In a confidential relationship as a matter of law
• Not eligible for dissolution by the rules or presumptions of the Family Code	• Dissolution determined by the rules and presumptions of the Family Code
• No right or obligation to disclosure upon break-up or death	• Disclosure rights and obligations appear throughout the Family Code
• Not eligible for post break-up support as a matter of right	• Eligible for spousal support as a matter of right and in furtherance of a strong state policy
• Not eligible for putative spouse status or for quasi-marital property system protections	• Putative spouse doctrine and quasi-marital property system provide equitable protections when necessary
• Not eligible for surviving spouse status or designation as an heir or next of kin in an intestacy distribution	• Deemed a surviving spouse for purposes of intestacy
• Not eligible for tax benefits by virtue of relationship status	• Eligible for related tax benefits
• No right to make medical decisions for each other. Power of attorney for health care, medical directives, and financial directives are imperative	• Have the right to make medical decisions for the other spouse or RDP

Part VI

TERMINATION OF MARRIAGE

Chapter 16

JUDGMENTS OF DISSOLUTION, LEGAL SEPARATION, AND NULLITY

Under the civil law, a matrimonial regime came into existence on the date of the marriage. That matrimonial regime served the purpose of holding the community property that the spouses — as partners — acquired during their marriage. The matrimonial regime was independent of the marital relationship; thus, when the marriage ended by dissolution, the parties were returned to their status as individuals and the matrimonial regime terminated. Once the matrimonial regime terminated it could no longer acquire property. Its accumulations and holdings had to be dissolved and distributed to the partners.

California no longer uses the phrase matrimonial regime. Instead, references are made to the community or to the community estate. The community estate holds community property. The community estate is liable for its partners' obligations. And the community estate can be altered or terminated by contract or court order.

The community estate is terminated by one of the following events:

- An enforceable premarital agreement providing that acquisitions during marriage are separate property rather than community property;
- Living separate and apart;
- A judgment of legal separation;
- A final judgment of dissolution;
- A change of domicile to a non-community property state; or
- The death of a spouse.

This chapter covers the termination of the community property estate by dissolution. At dissolution, equal division is the rule. The intended policy is family protection and the efficient settlement of estates.

§ 16.01 VALIDITY OF MARRIAGE

California is a marriage equality state as of June 28, 2013.[1] Any two persons have the right to marry in California regardless of their gender upon the date of marriage.

---

[1] *Hollingsworth v. Perry*, 133 S. Ct. 2652 (2013) (holding that proponents of Proposition 8 did not have standing to appeal District Court's order declaring the proposition unconstitutional). For a detailed timeline of the case, including original documents (full text of all pleadings, documents, and opinions), see https://ecf.cand.uscourts.gov/cand/09cv2292/. *See also In re Marriage Cases*, 43 Cal. 4th 757, 76 Cal. Rptr. 3d 683, 183 P.3d 384 (Cal. 2008); *U.S. v. Windsor*, 133 S. Ct. 2675 (2013) (holding that all legally

A valid marriage is a civil contract between two persons based on consent, the issuance of a license, and solemnization.[2] California does not recognize informal — so-called "common law" — marriage. Nor does it recognize informal — so-called "common law" — divorce.

When a marriage license is filed, it becomes a marriage certificate.

To establish a marriage, § 300 et seq. provides that the parties must be capable of consenting to and consummating marriage. Consent is required because marriage is **"[a] personal relation arising out of a civil contract."**[3] But consent alone is not enough to constitute a valid marriage. **"[T]he issuance of a license and solemnization"** are also required. The failure to record a marriage license will not invalidate an otherwise valid marriage;[4] nor will the filing of a marriage license validate an otherwise invalid marriage.[5] However, failure to register a domestic partnership will invalidate the partnership, thus leaving the prospective partners with the status of nonmarried cohabitants.[6]

Capacity — mental competence — is required to contract a valid marriage. The threshold for capacity is low. Capacity must be sufficient to allow a party to consent to the marriage. A person can consent to a marriage when he or she understands — in a lucid moment — the nature of the marriage contract, its duties and its responsibilities. An alleged lack of capacity can only serve as the basis for a judgment of nullity of it bears directly on the incapacitated party's ability to give consent to the marriage. The standard for nullifying a marriage based on lack of capacity is the same standard used to set aside a contract or a will; this rule was articulated a century ago in *Dunphy v. Dunphy*, discussed in Chapter 15.[7] The "lucid moment" line of cases starts with *Briggs v. Briggs*.[8]

In addition to formal marriage, California continues to offer Domestic Partner Registration for same-sex couples and for couples of opposite sex where at least one of the partners is over 62 years old. Under DPRRA, registered domestic partners have all of the rights and obligations of spouses under the Family Code.[9]

The advantages of the community property system take effect on the date of a valid marriage.[10] During the continuance of the marriage, the parties have a community estate, which exists until one or both spouses continue to live separate

---

married couples must be treated equally by the federal government). On June 26, 2013, the U.S. Supreme Court struck down Section 3 of the Defense of Marriage Act (DOMA), which had required the federal government to treat same-sex couples as unmarried partners. The Supreme Court ruled that DOMA Section 3 violates the United States Constitution's guarantee of equality. State litigation on marriage equality continues at this time.

[2] Cal. Fam. Code § 300.

[3] Cal. Fam. Code § 300.

[4] Cal. Fam. Code § 306.

[5] *Cantarella, supra.*

[6] *Burnham, supra.*

[7] *Dunphy, supra*, at 383.

[8] *Briggs v. Briggs*, 160 Cal. App. 2d 312, 320, 325 P.2d 219 (Cal. App. Ct., 2d Dist. 1958).

[9] Cal. Fam. Code § 297 et. seq.

[10] Cal. Fam. Code §§ 300–310 governs the validity of a marriage.

and apart without intending to resume the marriage. Notwithstanding separation, the parties remain in the community property system until they obtain a final judgment of dissolution or nullity.

§ 16.02 TERMINATION OF MARRIAGE

In accordance with the methods set forth in § 310:

Marriage is dissolved only by one of the following:

(a) The death of one of the parties.

(b) A judgment of dissolution of marriage.

(c) A judgment of nullity of marriage.

A final judgment of dissolution is *always* required to change a party's status from married to single. Under § 2300, **"the effect of a judgment of dissolution of marriage when it becomes final is to restore the parties to the state of unmarried persons."**

Dissolution and legal separation are authorized by statute. Each presumes a valid marriage.

[A] Grounds for Dissolution or Legal Separation

By the Family Law Act of 1969, California adopted no-fault dissolution procedures that went into effect on January 1, 1970. The transition from a fault based petition process to a no-fault one made important changes in the prior law, the most notable of which is that a person seeking to dissolve their marriage is no longer required to prove that his or her spouse had been adulterous, extremely cruel, or neglectful. Neither are intemperance, desertion, or a felony conviction grounds for dissolution. Under the prior law flagrant acts of fault resulted in a greater share of the community estate for the innocent spouse. No-fault dissolution eliminates the economic incentive for reaching a specific determination about why a marriage has ended.

Today, § 2310 allows only two grounds for dissolution or legal separation:

(a) **Irreconcilable differences which have caused the irremediable breakdown of the marriage** and

(b) **Incurable insanity.**

"Evidence of specific acts of misconduct is improper and inadmissible" in a dissolution or legal separation petition or proceeding.[11] This rule extends to depositions and discovery proceedings.

Courts are liberal in finding irreconcilable differences. Pursuant to § 2334, **"[i]f it appears that there is a reasonable possibility of reconciliation, the court shall continue the proceeding for the dissolution of the marriage or for a legal separation of the parties for a period not to exceed 30 days."** Practically

[11] Cal. Fam. Code § 2335.

speaking, a dissolution proceeding would be paused on § 2334 grounds only in an unusual case. Such a pause might happen, for example, if both spouses are present in court, one spouse expresses an intention to reconcile, and the other spouse remains silent. But even in such a case, if the silent spouse begins to express an intention to go forward with the dissolution, the outcome is and should be that the dissolution proceeding moves forward. In any given break-up, there can be a fine line between disappointment, false hope and stalking: Section 2334 delays a dissolution proceeding only if there is or appears to be a genuine hope on both spouses' part to reconcile. The dissolution may be restarted after the continuance period.

Otherwise, "irreconcilable differences" is the ground alleged in a majority of petitions for dissolution.

The second ground for granting a dissolution, **"irreconcilable differences,"** is defined in § 2310(a) as those differences **"which have caused the irremediable breakdown of the marriage."** In *Marriage of Walton*, the court held that the statutory phrase "irreconcilable differences . . . refers to the existence of substantial marital problems which have so impaired the marriage relationship that the legitimate objects of matrimony have been destroyed and as to which there is no reasonable possibility of elimination, correction, or resolution."[12]

The phrase **"incurable insanity"** is defined in § 2312. Incurable insanity is a condition that requires **"[p]roof, including competent medical or psychiatric testimony, that the insane spouse was at the time the petition was filed, and remains, incurably insane."** Importantly, a dissolution of marriage granted on the ground of incurable insanity does not relieve a spouse from **"[a]ny obligation imposed by law as a result of the marriage for the support of the spouse who is incurably insane . . . ."**[13]

Example 16.1: This example illustrates the plasticity of the phrase "irreconcilable differences." Zoe and Ritch get along well when they marry in San Francisco California, but they soon realize that their paths lead in different directions. Still, they continue to like each other. Zoe would like to end the marriage because she wants to marry Truett. In order to be reinstated as a single person, Zoe must obtain a final judgment dissolving her marriage to Ritch. Only then can Zoe lawfully marry Truett. Zoe's basis for petitioning for dissolution of her marriage to Ritch is irreconcilable differences. Zoe may have spousal support obligations to Ritch after the dissolution of their marriage.

Example 16.2: This example applies "irreconcilable differences" to Domestic Registered Partnership terminations. Same as Example 16.1 except that Zoe and Ritch are registered domestic partners in California. In order to terminate their registered domestic partnership, they must petition for dissolution of the partnership by a court proceeding.[14]

---

[12] *Marriage of Walton*, 28 Cal. App. 3d 108, 118, 104 Cal. Rptr. 472 (Cal. App. Ct., 4th Dist. 1972). This definition is echoed in the cases on living separate and apart.

[13] Cal. Fam. Code § 2313.

[14] Cal. Fam. Code § 299(a).

Example 16.3: This example underscores that California does not permit "common law" divorce. Zoe and Ritch validly contract an informal (common law) marriage in Texas, a state that recognizes common law marriage. They move to California, where they decide to split up. California will give full faith and credit to Zoe and Ritch's common law marriage. However, in order to terminate that common law marriage, Zoe and Ritch — now residents of California — must obtain a final judgment of dissolution. Only a final judgment of dissolution can restore Zoe's and Ritch's respective status as unmarried persons. Until they obtain a final judgment, neither can lawfully marry again. No community property state recognizes common law divorce.

Example 16.4: This example illustrates the restrictiveness of the phrase incurable insanity. Zoe and Ritch get along well when they marry in California. They continue to like each other. Zoe develops a mental condition that requires full time professional care. Ritch petitions for dissolution alleging that Zoe's mental condition constitutes incurable insanity. For Ritch's petition to be granted, Ritch must present credible medical evidence concerning the existence and incurability of Zoe's mental condition. After dissolution, Ritch's remains responsible for Zoe's support out of statutory obligation, not judicial discretion.

[B] Residency Requirement for a Judgment of Dissolution

At least one of the parties to the marriage must be a resident of the state in order to file for a petition for dissolution in California. In fact, a judgment of dissolution may not be entered unless at least one of the parties **"has been a resident of the state for six months and of the county in which the proceeding is filed for three months"** immediately before the filing of the petition.[15]

[1] General Rule

The residency requirement is mandatory for obtaining a judgment of dissolution. But it only applies to (at least) one of the spouses. Therefore, spouses may have separate domiciles when the California resident files for dissolution in a California court.

[2] Residency Exemption for Same Sex-Spouses

There is an exception to the residency requirement for same-sex partners who were married in California, but then moved to a state that does not recognize same-sex marriage. This exception is by a 2011 amendment to § 2320.

Under § 2320(b), if a same-sex marriage **"[w]as entered in California"** and at the time the parties seek dissolution **"[n]either party to the marriage resides in a jurisdiction that will dissolve the marriage"** the spouses can nevertheless obtain a judgment of dissolution in California. For purposes of this statute: **"If a jurisdiction does not recognize the marriage, there shall be a rebuttable presumption that the jurisdiction will not dissolve the marriage."** This is a statutory presumption stated at § 2320(b)(1)(a).

---

[15] Cal. Fam. Code § 2320.

[3] Determining Residency

Domicile or residence is a matter of fact, not legal presumption.[16] The factual elements required to establish residency appear at Cal. Gov. Code § 244:

> **In determining the place of residence the following rules shall be observed:**
>
> **(a) It is the place where one remains when not called elsewhere for labor or other special or temporary purpose, and to which he or she returns in seasons of repose.**
>
> **(b) There can only be one a residence.**
>
> **(c) A residence cannot be lost until another is gained.**
>
> **(d) The residence of a parent with whom an unmarried minor child maintains his or her place of abode is the residence of such unmarried minor child.**
>
> **(e) The residence of an unmarried minor who has a parent living cannot be changed by his or her own act.**
>
> **(f) The residence can be changed only by the union of act and intent.**
>
> **(g) A married person shall have the right to retain his or her legal residence in the State of California notwithstanding the legal residence or domicile of his or her spouse."[17]**

[C] The Petition for Dissolution: *In re the Marriage of ____ and ____*

California dissolution cases are entitled as *In re the Marriage of Spouse and Spouse*, not as *Spouse v. Spouse*. Court cases refer to parties by first name, not by last name. Courts do this out of the need for clarity, not out of disrespect to the parties. This text follows the same practice.

A dissolution petition shall include the following information:[18]

- Whether the petition is for dissolution or legal separation;
- Information relevant to the marriage, as listed in § 2330, including "**[t]he date of marriage; the date of separation; the number of years from marriage to separation; the number of children of the marriage, if any, and if none a statement of that fact; and the age and birth date of each minor child of the marriage.**"

There is a minimum six-month waiting period "**from the date of service of a copy of summons and petition or the date of appearance of the respondent,**

---

[16] Cal. Fam. Code § 2322.

[17] In 1976, Cal. Gov. Code § 244(g) was amended to be gender neutral.

[18] Cal. Fam. Code § 2330.

whichever occurs first" and a final judgment of dissolution.[19]

This six-month period can be extended for good cause.

Likewise, the six-month period can be functionally expedited by converting a separation proceeding into a dissolution proceeding. The key to this conversion strategy lies in § 2321, which turns on the fact that there is no statutory residency requirement for filing a petition of legal separation, as there is for filing a petition for dissolution. Therefore, a new arrival to California can file for and be granted a judgment of legal separation immediately upon entering the state: A judgment of legal separation can be granted if both parties consent to it, or if the respondent does not appear.[20]

Once a judgment of legal separation is granted, the petitioner then amends the petition for separation to one for dissolution when the six month residency requirement is met. Pursuant to § 2321(a), the date of the filing of the amended petition **"[s]hall be deemed to be the date of commencement of the proceeding for the dissolution of the marriage for purposes only of the residence requirements of Section 2320."** One caveat: Consent and notice issues do not factor into a judgment of legal separation, whereas as they do factor into a judgment of dissolution, which is a proceeding for which service of petition and summons is required.[21]

Thus, assuming notice and consent procedures are followed when converting a separation proceeding into a dissolution proceeding, § 2321(a) makes it possible for a person arriving in California to accomplish all of the following within six months of moving to the state. He or she can immediately file for legal separation. He or she can immediately seek spousal support while waiting to meet the six month residency requirement for petitioning for a judgment of dissolution. He or she can immediately obtain a restraining order under the DVPA to prevent the other spouse from disposing of property, changing insurance beneficiaries, and so forth. And he or she can convert the petition for legal separation into a petition for dissolution.

[D] The Necessity of the Final Judgment of Dissolution

Divorce is not automatic in California. Instead — and this is an important detail that can be easily overlooked — the parties' marital status is terminated and their status as an individual person is restored only by court action in the form of a final judgment of dissolution.

Therefore every judgment of dissolution **"[s]hall specify the date on which the judgment becomes finally effective for the purpose of terminating the marriage relationship of the parties."**[22] If an appeal is taken **"the dissolution of marriage does not become final until the motion of appeal has been finally**

19 Cal. Fam. Code § 2339.

20 Cal. Fam. Code § 2345.

21 Cal. Fam. Code §§ 2331, 2332 (requiring that if the legal separation or dissolution proceeding is based on incurable insanity, notice must be served on a spouse's guardian or conservator).

22 Cal. Fam. Code § 2340.

disposed of . . ." but even so, the parties' marital status is terminated by the judgment absent special circumstances.[23]

A person can lawfully remarry after his or her status as a single person is restored.[24] A judgment of legal separation does not terminate the parties' marriage, and hence it does not restore the parties' status to that of single persons. The rationale here is that the parties must proceed forward to convert the petition for legal separation into a petition for dissolution.[25] The mere passage of time will not do that. Nor will the mere passage of six-months from the date of the filed petition for dissolution restore the parties' status to that of single persons. Only a final judgment of dissolution can terminate a marriage, restore the former spouses to their status as single individuals, dissolve the community estate, and distribute it.

A court has the authority to postpone the termination of the parties' marital status to a later date.[26] This might be necessary or desirable where for, example, the parties want to file joint tax returns for the year, or preserve employer sponsored health insurance access. When the court retains jurisdiction of the date of termination of marital status, the parties are not divorced, notwithstanding the fact that their community estate has been terminated and dissolved. To the contrary, the parties are still married. And, therefore, neither is free to remarry until their marital status itself is terminated by a final court judgment.

On the flip side, a court has authority to bifurcate the issue of marital status from property issues.[27] In this scenario, the court issues a judgment terminating the parties' marital status, but then retains jurisdiction over the property issues. The result is that each party's marital status is terminated, their single status restored, and their consequent ability to contract for a subsequent marriage re-established. In this scenario, a party is free to remarry as of the date of the final judgment that terminates their marital status, even if they remain obligated to continue on with the dissolution of their former community property estate.

For many employed former spouses, this bifurcation strategy can raise complications in relation to certain types of assets. For example, if one or both parties remarry before the property issues of the previous marriage are resolved, joint tenancies or community property titles may be automatically severed, thus defaulting to tenancies in common. Or, there may be — by the fact of one or both former spouses' divorce and/or remarriage — automatic severance of concurrent interests, automatic revocation of non-probate transfers, the loss of surviving spouse status under the Probate Code, life insurance issues, the loss of survivorship rights for certain retirement assets, and so forth.[28]

---

[23] Cal. Fam. Code § 2341.

[24] Cal. Fam. Code § 2343.

[25] Cal. Fam. Code §§ 2321, 2347.

[26] Cal. Fam. Code § 2343.

[27] Cal. Fam. Code § 2337.

[28] *See McDaniel, supra; Lezine, supra.*

To put it bluntly, timing is an important consideration in a bifurcated dissolution. And the reason for being blunt is that notwithstanding any benefits, traps for the unwary exist. For that reason, experienced attorneys are active in proposing motions that assist courts to customize court orders, on an asset-by-asset basis, as to property with indemnification rights, beneficial designations rights, rights of survivorship, rights of withdrawal, and the like. Specific court orders protect each former spouse's property interests and expectations relative to the other former spouse during the continuance of the dissolution proceeding and beyond.

§ 16.03 SUMMARY DISSOLUTION

California offers some parties who are willing to file a joint petition a summary dissolution process.[29] Parties often don't consult an attorney when they seek this option. And even when one or both spouses does consult an attorney, the consulting attorney may not (and probably will not) become the client's attorney of record.

In a summary dissolution, the final judgment dissolving the marriage may be entered six months after the parties jointly file a petition for dissolution. At that time, a notice of final judgment is sent by the clerk to each party's last known address. Only that final judgment **"[r]estores to the parties the status of single persons, and either party may marry after the entry of the judgment."**[30] Only that final judgment adjudicates **"[t]he rights and obligations of the parties with respect to the status of the marriage and property rights."**[31]

Because the summary judgment process starts with a jointly filed petition for dissolution, it is based on an ongoing agreement between the parties who, because they are still married, owe each other quasi-fiduciary duties.[32] The enforceability of this agreement depends on the presence of each parties' continuous consent to engage in the summary judgment process.

Importantly, the terms of the parties' agreement constitute **"a waiver of their respective rights to spousal support, rights to appeal, and rights to move for a new trial."**[33] For that reason, either party may terminate a summary dissolution proceeding unilaterally, at any time before the entry of the final judgment.[34]

Only parties who meet *all* of the following elements listed under § 2400 can file a joint petition for summary dissolution:[35]

1. Either party meets the jurisdictional residency requirements.
2. The ground for dissolution is irreconcilable differences.
3. No children were born of the marriage, and neither party is pregnant.

---

[29] Cal. Fam. Code § 2342.

[30] Cal. Fam. Code § 2403.

[31] Cal. Fam. Code § 2404(a).

[32] Cal. Fam. Code § 721(b).

[33] Cal. Fam. Code § 2404(b).

[34] Cal. Fam. Code § 2402.

[35] Cal. Fam. Code § 2400 is indexed for inflation.

4. **"The marriage is not more than five years in duration as of the date of separation of the parties."**[36]
5. Neither party has real property, with the exception of the lease of a residence, and if there is a lease:
   a. the lease does not have an option to buy, and
   b. the lease terminates within one year of the date of the filing of the joint petition.
6. There are no unpaid obligations in excess of $4,000 incurred by either or both of the parties **"[a]fter the date of *their* marriage, excluding the amount of any unpaid obligation with respect to an automobile."**[37] (Italics added.)
7. **"The total fair market value of community property assets** [excluding encumbrances and cars including any deferred compensation or retirement plan] **is $25,000 and neither party has separate property, excluding all encumbrances and automobiles, in excess of twenty-five thousand dollars ($25,000)."**[38]
8. The parties have executed a written agreement about the division of the assets and the assumption of community liabilities.
9. The parties waive any rights to spousal support, to appeal, and to move for a new trial.[39]
10. The parties have read instructional literature provided by the § 2406.
11. The parties desire that the court dissolve the marriage.

The summary dissolution proceeding is adjusted for inflation.

§ 16.04 SPOUSAL SUPPORT

The obligation of spousal support is restated yet again at § 4300: **"Subject to this division, a person shall support the person's spouse."** Under § 4303, an obligee spouse can bring an action against the obligor spouse to enforce that duty. Temporary or permanent spousal support is available on a discretionary basis.

California allows permanent (long term) spousal support. In determining a permanent spousal support order, **"the court shall consider all of the following circumstances"** listed at § 4320. There are fourteen (14) circumstances total. Together these circumstances allow the court considerable discretion to determine whether and in what amount spousal support should be ordered, and to whom. The last discretionary circumstance gives the court a broad grant of authority in the form of a catch all phrase. Here is a paraphrased list summarizing the fourteen circumstances:

---

[36] Cal. Fam. Code § 2400(a)(4), amended in 2010 to substitute **"as of the date of separation of the parties"** for "at the time the petition is filed."

[37] Cal. Fam. Code § 2400(a)(6).

[38] Cal. Fam. Code § 2400(a)(7).

[39] Cal. Fam. Code § 2400(a)(9) and (10).

(a) The extent to which the party seeking support has the earning capacity **"[t]o maintain the standard of living established during marriage."**

(b) The extent to which a party seeking support contributed to the other party's **"[e]ducation, training, a career position, or a license . . . ."**

(c) The ability of the supporting party to pay spousal support.

(d) The needs of each party **"[b]ased on the standard of living established during the marriage."**

(e) The obligations and assets of each party, including separate property.

(f) The duration of the marriage.

(g) The ability of the supported party to **"[e]ngage in gainful employment without unduly interfering with the interests of dependent children in the custody of the party."**

(h) The age and health of the parties.

(i) Documented evidence of any history of domestic violence **"between the parties or perpetrated by either party against either party's child."**

(j) Tax consequences to each party.

(k) The **"balance of the hardships"** to each party.

(l) The goal that the supported party shall become self-supporting over time.

(m) The criminal conviction of an abusive spouse.

(n) **"Any other factors the court determines are just and equitable."**

Cohabitation can be the ground upon which to terminate a spousal support award. Under § 4323 if the supported party begins to cohabitate with an intimate partner, a rebuttable presumption arises of a decreased need for spousal support from that person's former spouse.

Attempting to murder or solicit the murder of the other spouse relieves the injured spouse of spousal support duties. Under § 4324 **"[t]he injured spouse shall be entitled to a prohibition of any temporary or permanent award for spousal support or medical, life, or other insurance benefits or payments from the injured spouse to the other spouse."**

California permits temporary orders of spousal support. And whereas domestic violence is one of fourteen requirements that a court shall consider in determining a permanent spousal support award, domestic violence is the only issue that the Legislature mandates the trial court to consider in determining whether to order temporary spousal support.[40] This mandate is found in § 4325, which provides that **"[a]ny award of temporary or permanent spousal support to the abusive spouse otherwise awardable . . . should not be made."**[41]

A spousal support order can be terminated under the § 4325 presumption even if the parties' settlement agreement specifically provides that spousal support is not subject to modification or termination. In *Marriage of Cauley*, a former supported

---

[40] Cal. Fam. Code § 3600.

[41] *See also Cauley, supra.*

spouse was convicted of domestic violence against the former supporting spouse. The trial court terminated a spousal support order, notwithstanding the nonmodifiable spousal support clause in the parties' marriage settlement agreement. The termination of spousal support was based on the former supported spouse's conviction for domestic violence against the former supporting spouse. The trial court relied on the § 4325 presumption, which had not been rebutted in the case. The court of appeal affirmed saying that § 4325 applies, even where the parties have a nonmodifiable settlement agreement. The rationale given was that, in light of the facts of the case, the policy in favor of enforcing spousal support agreements was outweighed by the "significant public policy against domestic violence."[42] To paraphrase the court, one should not have to fund one's own abuse.

§ 16.05 FAMILY CODE PROTECTIONS FOR A PUTATIVE SPOUSE

The putative spouse doctrine is an equitable doctrine first recognized by the courts, and later codified by the Legislature in 1969 as part of the Family Law Act in § 2251. The express language of § 2251 provides:

> **(a) If a determination is made that a marriage is void or voidable and the court finds that either party or both parties believed in good faith that the marriage was valid, the court shall:**
>
> > **(1) Declare the party or parties to have the status of a putative spouse.**
> >
> > **(2) If the division of property is in issue, divide . . . that property acquired during the union which would have been community property or quasi-community property if the union had not been void or voidable. This property is known as "quasi-marital property."**

Putative spouse status is a court granted status requiring proof of two elements. One, evidence that the marriage the party thought was valid turned out not to be. Two, substantial evidence of the petitioning party's genuine and honestly held belief in the validity of that marriage. The California Supreme Court recently held that the § 2251 good faith standard is subjective, not objective; and that it is to be determined after consideration of the totality of the circumstances.[43]

A party who obtains putative spouse status gains important protections parallel to the protections extended to spouses by the Family Code. Putative spouse status allows the petitioner access to the quasi-marital system for purposes of characterizing and dividing accumulations and for assessing rights and liabilities. The rules of the quasi-marital system are the same as those used for community property and quasi-community property. The quasi-marital property system extends to putative registered domestic partnerships.[44]

---

[42] *Id.* at 1106.

[43] *Ceja, supra*, at 1120.

[44] *In re Domestic Partnership of Ellis & Arriaga*, 162 Cal. App. 4th 1000, 1009, 76 Cal. Rptr. 3d 401

Additionally, a putative spouse may be included in the category of surviving lawful spouse for purposes of intestate distribution and wrongful death claims. He or she may obtain a spousal support award, notwithstanding the invalidity of the marriage.[45] He or she may obtain control of the quasi-marital property under the Domestic Violence Prevention Act. And he or she may obtain attorney fees and court costs. Pursuant to § 2255: **"The court may grant attorney's fees and costs . . . in proceedings to have the marriage adjudged void and in those proceedings based upon voidable marriage in which the party applying for attorney's fees and costs is found to be innocent of fraud or wrongdoing in inducing or entering into the marriage, and free from knowledge of the then existence of any prior marriage or other impediment to the contracting of the marriage for which a judgment of nullity is sought."**

For purposes of property division, these protections clearly extend to a good faith putative spouse under the rubric of the quasi-marital property system. But do they extend to a wrongful spouse too?

In a nullity proceeding involving a foreign divorce, at least one court of appeal has held that quasi-marital property protections also extend to the party who knew about the impediment.[46] The rationale is that once the § 2251 elements are met as to at least one person — that is once one person is deemed a putative spouse — the marriage becomes a putative marriage, and division must proceed against the backdrop of California's no-fault policy.[47] By this rationale, the quasi-marital property is divided in accordance with the Family Code, notwithstanding the presence of a wrongful party who knew or should have known about the impediment to the marriage. The California Supreme Court has not yet considered the accuracy of this interpretation.

Whether and when a non-putative spouse may seek the protections of the quasi-marital system are questions still open to interpretation. For that reason a spouse who knows about the impediment of a void or voidable marriage must be prepared to bring any property related claims against the other party under the Civil Code. Moreover, the party who knows about the impediment may not be adjudged a "surviving spouse" for purposes of Cal. Prob. Code § 78, which determines a married person's rights to intestate succession, non-probate transfers, capital gains calculations, wrongful death actions, and other family protections.

§ 16.06 THE JUDGMENT OF NULLITY

A void marriage is unlawful from the start. A void marriage never comes into existence. Therefore, the parties never form a community property estate. Nevertheless, an innocent party can claim protection as a putative spouse.

(Cal. App. Ct., 4th Dist. 2008), disapproved by *Ceja*, which holds that a subjective standard is used to determine putative spouse status and distinguishing, and criticizing *Velez*, *supra*, at 1174.

[45] Cal. Fam. Code § 2254.

[46] *Marriage of Tejeda*, 179 Cal. App. 4th 973, 102 Cal. Rptr. 3d 361 (Cal. App. Ct., 6th Dist. 2009) (involving a bigamous marriage in which husband was aware that he was still married to his first spouse when he married a second spouse), disapproved by *Ceja*, *supra*, on other grounds.

[47] *Tejeda*, *supra*.

By contrast, a voidable marriage is presumed valid until it is adjudged void. A voidable marriage does come into legal existence.

[A] Void Marriage

A marriage can be void on one of these grounds: (1) failure to meet statutory formalities; (2) bigamy or polygamy; and (3) incest.

Bigamy can arise from different factual situations. Generally, a bigamous or polygamous marriage is entered into when one or both parties are still married to a different (third) person. A bigamous marriage is void from the start.[48] So too is a polygamous marriage. More commonly bigamy is accidental. This happens when a marriage that is entered into when one of the purported spouses is still involved in a dissolution proceeding with a third person. A marriage that is contracted before the issuance of a final judgment of dissolution in a prior marriage has been held to be void (not voidable) under § 2201.[49] A bigamous marriage cannot be corrected after the fact by voluntary cohabitation.

Incest occurs when the spouses are too closely related to each other. A marriage between a parent and a child; siblings; an ancestor and a descendant of any degree (grandparent-grandchild, uncle-niece, aunt-nephew); and a half-sibling and a half-sibling are all statutorily defined as incestuous.[50] Depending on the degree of consanguinity, an incestuous marriage may also form the basis of a criminal complaint.[51] An incestuous marriage cannot be corrected or ratified after the fact by voluntary cohabitation.[52]

Notwithstanding the fact that, legally speaking, a void marriage never comes into existence, parties to a void marriage are permitted, if not encouraged, to seek a judgment of nullity. This provides public notice of the non-existence of the marriage.[53]

[B] Voidable Marriage

A voidable marriage is presumed valid. The parties have the option to nullify or affirm the marriage. They do this either by petitioning for a judgment of nullity or (alternatively) for a judgment of dissolution.[54] Upon filing a petition to nullify the marriage, a court has the discretion to deny that petition and to enter a judgment of dissolution instead.

---

[48] Cal. Fam. Code § 2201.

[49] *Marriage of Campbell*, 136 Cal. App. 4th 502, 509, 38 Cal. Rptr. 3d 908 (Cal. App. Ct., 6th Dist. 2006).

[50] Cal. Fam. Code § 2200.

[51] *People v. McCollum*, 116 Cal. App. 55, 2 P.2d 432 (Cal. App. Ct., 4th Dist. 1931) (holding that age is not an element to the crime of incest).

[52] Cal. Fam. Code §§ 2200, 2201.

[53] *See Seaton*, *supra*.

[54] *McDonald*, *supra*, at 461.

To petition for a judgment of nullity a specific ground must be alleged. The petition is entitled *In re the Marriage of* _____.[55] The grounds are set forth in § 2210:

- The petitioning party "[w]**as without the capability of consenting to the marriage . . .**" when it was contracted;
- The petitioning party was unaware that the other spouse was still married to a different person;
- Either party was "[o]**f unsound mind . . . ;**"
- Consent "[w]**as obtained by fraud . . . ;**"
- Consent "[w]**as obtained by force . . . ;**"
- Either party was, "[a]**t the time of the marriage, physically incapable of entering into the marriage state, and that incapacity continues, and appears to be incurable.**"

To obtain a judgment of nullity, the petitioner must prove two elements. First, the petitioner must prove that the marriage was entered into under one of the above listed statutorily enumerated defects. Second, the petitioner must credibly rebut any evidence that he or she "[f]**reely cohabitated with the other as husband or wife**" after learning about the defect to the marriage.

Here are some key differences between a judgment of nullity and a judgment of dissolution:

Judgment of Nullity	**Judgment of Dissolution**
• not private: petition states ground for nullification	• irreconcilable differences is a privacy screen
• declares that marriage was never lawful	• marriage was lawful, but it was legally dissolved
• relates back to the date of the marriage; the parties were never married	• terminates the parties' marital status in the future
• no waiting period from petition to final judgment	• six-month waiting period from petition to final judgment
• no community estate comes into existence, no spousal support available, no court costs or attorney's fees available	• community estate comes into existence at the date of the marriage , discretionary spousal support available, court costs and attorney's fees available for some claims
• quasi-marital property protections available upon one or both parties being deemed a putative spouse	• Family Code protections are available by default, absent an agreement between the parties.

Additionally, a court has the discretion to apply the "relation back" doctrine to restore rights that were lost due to the null marriage. The question of voluntariness determines whether a party to a nullified marriage is able to

---

[55] Cal. Fam. Code § 2250.

reinstate or revive spousal support from a marriage that preceded the voidable marriage. If the nullified marriage was voluntarily entered into by the party who relinquished spousal support from a previous marriage, courts have (so far) held that spousal support cannot be reinstated, notwithstanding an intervening marriage that is adjudged null. *Marriage of Weintraub* is the exception; in that case a court of appeal held that a trial court has the authority to reinstate a prior spousal support order when the ground for the judgment of nullity in an intervening marriage is in force.[56]

If the petitioner was of unsound mind at the time of the marriage, a judgment of nullity may be filed by the petitioner, or by a relative or conservator of the petitioner, at any time *before the death of either spouse*.[57] Once the party who is alleged to be of unsound mind dies, the marriage, which was presumptively valid during the life of the spouse, becomes valid.

Proving a voidable marriage is discussed in Chapter 15.

§ 16.07 DIVISION OF ASSETS AND LIABILITIES

In California, the Family Law court is one of law and equity. Personal fault with respect to how the marriage ends is not a factor in deciding whether the parties are entitled to a divorce. The ground upon which one can petition for dissolution does not undermine the equality of ownership principle.

Nevertheless, the current law on management and control and fiduciary duties does intersect with the law on the division of community property. A breach of a fiduciary duty that results in an impairment of community property may result in a judgment that will have an actual effect on how community assets are divided and liabilities assigned.

Generally, parties attempt to reach a written marital settlement agreement outside of court. Marital settlement agreements are discussed below. Parties also have the option to orally stipulate to property issues in open court.

If for some reason the parties cannot agree on the division of property, the court must divide the property equally using an asset-by-asset approach, subject to applicable law, statutory guidelines, and modifications.

As long as the spouses are married, their respective interest in the community property are **"present, existing, and equal,"** as set forth in § 751. During the dissolution process, however, the court is required by § 2550 to **"divide the community estate of the parties equally."** Accomplishing equal division includes characterizing, valuing, and dividing the community property and quasi-community property assets in such a way that might appear to result in a seemingly unequal division of assets or liabilities. This is especially so once the quasi-community property is included in the community estate, reimbursements are determined, and debts are confirmed. So, for example, under § 2601 and § 2602, a court is empowered to award an asset entirely to one party or to award additional property to one party,

---

[56] *Weintraub, supra.*

[57] Cal. Fam. Code § 2211(c).

or to award an offset to one party. As for debts, a court may assign excessive debts **"taking into account factors such as the parties' relative ability to pay"** (§ 2622), assign personal injury damages (§ 2603), and otherwise assess other parties' rights and remedies provided by statute.

Excessive debts are those that exceed the community estate. As discussed in Chapter 12, when community funds are exhausted, creditors are given statutory authority to marshal available separate property. During marriage, community property liability is not determined by reference to a family purpose — i.e., whether the debt was or wasn't incurred for the benefit of the community — as it is in some community property jurisdictions. Instead, during marriage, if community property funds are exhausted, the spouses' separate property estates become liable. This supports the California policy to protect creditors' rights. Creditors cannot be blocked from reaching one or the other spouse's available separate property assets just because (as the saying goes) the community property well has run dry.

During a dissolution proceeding, however, the question is not whether a creditor can reach community or separate property assets, but rather which spouse will assume the debt upon exiting the marriage.

At the end of the marriage **"the court shall characterize liabilities as separate or community and confirm or assign them"** accordingly. Community debts are typically those incurred by one or both spouses during the marriage. Community debts that remain unpaid at trial are generally divided, but may also be confirmed to one or the other party, depending on their relative economic circumstances. Separate debts are those **"not incurred for the benefit of the community"** under § 2625, which also mandates that separate debts **"shall be confirmed without offset to the spouse who incurred the debt."**

Debts incurred by a party after separation but before the final judgment are covered by § 2623(a). Debts incurred by a party for the **"common necessaries of life"** of either spouse or the children of the marriage, **"shall be confirmed to either spouse according to the parties' respective needs and abilities to pay at the time the debt was incurred."** Whereas under § 2623(b) debts for **"nonnecessaries . . . shall be confirmed without offset to the spouse who incurred the debt."**

A court is statutorily directed, during the dissolution process, to confirm debts typically on the basis of when the debt was incurred: before marriage, during marriage, or after separation. For debts incurred in the period after separation but before the final dissolution judgment, § 2626 gives a court jurisdiction to **"order reimbursement in cases it deems appropriate . . ."**

Between the parties, debts and monetary obligations, like reimbursements due, require different treatment. Separate property is protected by the California Constitution. Therefore, a court cannot award the separate property of one spouse to the other spouse in a dissolution proceeding. This is one very practical reason why characterization is important. What a court can do, however, is to impose an equitable lien against the separate property of a spouse. The equitable lien secures any court ordered reimbursement or support obligation. Equitable liens are widely used in community property systems generally, and by the Internal Revenue Service.

Upon the commencement of a dissolution proceeding, the entire community estate becomes subject to the court's discretion. The community estate is defined under § 125 as both the community and quasi-community assets and liabilities of the parties. In the case of a putative spouse, a court has jurisdiction over all quasi-marital property.

Ideally, community estate would be inventoried, with all assets and liabilities included in the inventory, and all valuations accurately reported. But history is replete with examples of less than ideal behavior during divorce. For that reason, a court is empowered to make any orders the court considers necessary to carry out the purposes of equal division. A court may suspend either spouse's rights to manage and control community property. Or, a court may deviate from the general § 2552(a) mandatory rule of valuing assets and liabilities as of the time of trial, opting instead to value them in accordance with § 2552(b) **"for good cause shown . . . at a date after separation and before trial to accomplish an equal division of the community estate of the parties in an equitable manner."** A court may issue restraining orders in the use and disposition of community property: By this same power, for example, a court can order an abusive party to leave the marital home *and* continue to pay the mortgage. In cases where one spouse transfers property with the intention of impairing or otherwise defrauding the other spouse's interest in the community estate, a court is empowered to void the transfer, or compel an inventory or appraisal, or grant (or deny) an order to defer sale of the family home (§§ 3800–08).

As discussed in Chapter 10 § 1100(e) holds spouses to a fiduciary duty **"until such time as the assets and liabilities have been divided by the parties of by the court."** Thus upon separation, it is imperative that the parties understand that they have continuing fiduciary duties that last until an enforceable marital settlement agreement is reached or a final judgment of dissolution becomes effective.

As for real and personal community property, § 721(b) holds the parties to quasi-fiduciary duties **"[i]n transactions between themselves,"** including those that result from dissolving the community estate. Section 721(b) is particularly clear on the standard of disclosure that spouses owe each other, and § 2556 reflects how important the § 721(b) duty is by its grant to a court of **"[c]ontinuing jurisdiction"** over any community estate asset or liability that was **"[o]mitted or not adjudicated by the judgment."** Omitted assets shall be equally divided unless, upon a showing of good cause, the interests of justice require otherwise. The state has a strong policy in favor of final judgments, but it has an equally strong policy against upholding a judgment tainted by fraud. Therefore, a court has jurisdiction to address the ownership of the asset that one party failed to disclose during the dissolution process. This issue is discussed in more detail below.

Any breach of fiduciary duty, no matter its source, that leads to a past, present, or future impairment of the community estate is actionable under § 1101(a), which provides: **"A spouse has a claim against the other spouse for any breach of the fiduciary duty that results in impairment to the claimant spouse's present undivided one-half interest in the community estate. . . ."** Remedies are provided when the impairment involves **"[a] single transaction or a pattern or series of transactions, which transaction or transactions have caused or will**

cause a detrimental impact to the claimant spouse's undivided one-half interest in the community estate." *See* Chapter 10.

As mentioned previously, parties can agree in writing or by oral stipulation in open court to a voluntary division of the community estate. However, if the parties do not agree, and if in the court's opinion the total value of the community and quasi-community property in controversy does not exceed $50,000, the issue of **"[t]he character, the value and the division of the community estate"** may be submitted to arbitration.[58] An arbitrator's decision is non-appealable.

Finally, under § 2604: **"If the net value of the community estate is less than five thousand dollars ($5,000) and one party cannot be located through the exercise of reasonable diligence, the court may award all the community estate to the other party . . ."** The court may also make the award conditional, as it sees fit.

§ 16.08 JUDGMENTS TAINTED BY FRAUD, DURESS, AND UNDUE INFLUENCE

The Legislature has codified the California public policy on reaching final judgments in the division of the community estate in § 2120, which states:

> **The Legislature finds and declares the following:**
>
> > **(a) The State of California has a strong policy of ensuring the division of community and quasi-community property in the dissolution of a marriage . . . , and of providing for fair and sufficient child and spousal support awards. These policy goals can only be implemented with full disclosure of community, quasi-community, and separate assets, liabilities, income, and expenses . . . , and decisions freely and knowingly made.**

This policy is premised on the understanding that decisions are freely and knowingly made by the parties, with full disclosure. Where there is **"nondisclosure"** or **"other misconduct"** the state's policy in favor of **"assuring finality of judgments must be balanced against the public interest in ensuring property division of marital property, in ensuring sufficient support awards, and in deterring misconduct."**

Grounds for and timing issues related to setting aside a (tainted) final judgment are set forth in § 2122:

- **"Actual fraud"** has a 1 year statute of limitations **"within one year after the date on which the complaining party"** discovered or should have discovered the fraud.
- **"Perjury"** has a 1 year statute of limitations **"within one year after the date on which the complaining party"** discovered or should have discovered the perjury.

---

[58] Cal. Fam. Code § 2554.

- **"Duress"** has a 2 year statute of limitations after the date of entry of judgment.
- **"Mental incapacity"** has a 2 year statute of limitations after the date of entry of judgment.
- **"Mistake"** has a 1 year statute of limitations after the date of entry of judgment, and then only in some circumstances.
- **"Failure to comply with disclosure requirements . . . shall be brought within one year after the date on which the complaining party discovered, or should have discovered, the failure to comply."**

By the express terms of § 2123, a judgment **"may not be set aside simply because the court finds that it was inequitable when made, nor simply because subsequent circumstances caused the division of assets or liabilities to become inequitable, or the support to become inequitable."**

§ 16.09 MARRIAGE SETTLEMENT AGREEMENTS

The statutory authority for marital settlement agreements is found in § 1620 and § 3580. Marital settlement agreements are made in contemplation of dissolution, legal separation, or nullity.

A martial settlement agreement is a transaction between the spouses, therefore it must be compliant with § 721(b), for any property, and § 1100(e), for community personal property. Remedies for breach are set forth in § 1101. Additionally, under §§ 2100–2113, effective to any proceeding commenced on or after January 1, 1993, each party to a marital settlement agreement has a continuing duty to update and augment disclosure declarations to the extent that there have been material changes.

Spouses are in a confidential relationship until the property has been divided, whether by an enforceable marriage settlement agreement or a final judgment.[59] If one spouse takes any unfair advantage of the other in negotiating a marital settlement agreement — just as with transmutations — a presumption of undue influence arises in favor of the adversely affected spouse. Rebuttal requires the advantaged spouse to show that the adversely spouse entered into the agreement voluntarily and with full disclosure.[60] As discussed in Chapter 10, two common practices guard against nondisclosure: formal discovery, which is costly, and the inclusion, in the marital settlement agreement itself, of a warranty that each spouse has complied with his or her statutory duties to disclose the existence and valuation of community property.

The parties may reach a marital settlement agreement by litigation, arbitration, collaborative law, or mediation.

---

[59] *Bonds*, *supra*.

[60] *Bonds*, *supra*; *In re Marriage of Haines*, 33 Cal. App. 4th 277, 293, 39 Cal. Rptr. 2d 673 (Cal. App. Ct., 4th Dist. 1995); *In re Marriage of Lange*, 102 Cal. App. 4th 360, 364, 125 Cal. Rptr. 2d 379 (2d Dist. 2002); *In re Marriage of Mathews*, 133 Cal. App. 4th 624, 630, 35 Cal. Rptr. 3d 1 (Cal. App. Ct., 4th Dist. 2005).

[A] Collaborative Law

The **"[c]ollaborative law process"** is recognized, sanctioned and defined by § 2013 as **"the process in which the parties and any professionals engaged by the parties to assist them agree in writing to use their best efforts and to make a good faith attempt to resolve disputes related to the family law matters** [governed by the Family Code] **on an agreed basis without resorting to adversary judicial intervention."** In a collaborative process clients and their lawyers collaborate as a team to share information in confidential problem solving sessions. The goal is to work problems out cooperatively. However, if either or both parties later decide to pursue litigation, both collaborative attorneys must cease their representation. When this happens, the clients must hire new counsel.

Under § 2013, parties may use a collaborative law process to resolve any matter governed by the Family Code, over which the court is granted jurisdiction by § 2000.

Example 16.5: This example illustrates the collaborative law process. Zoe and Ritch decide to seek dissolution. They hire collaborative lawyers. Together, with their lawyers, Zoe and Ritch cooperate with the professionals in their lawyers' collaborative practice group to reach an agreement. Meetings, documents, work product, and jointly hired experts' reports are all confidential, and thus inadmissible in a later court proceeding.

[B] Family Centered Case Resolution

Family centered case resolution is set forth at §§ 2450–2452. The idea, set out at § 2450, is to expedite litigation, reduce costs, and focus on early resolution by settlement. The Judicial Council has adopted a statewide rule that advances the goals of §§ 2450–2452 by requiring courts to develop and implement family centered case resolution as of January 1, 2013.[61] The stated goal that the Judicial Council hopes to meet on or after January 1, 2014 is to have 90% of cases disposed of within 18 months of the date the petition for dissolution, legal separation, nullity, or parentage is filed.[62]

Under the case management rules of the Family Code, a court reviews dissolution, legal separation, nullity and parentage cases after their initial filing and in certain increments thereafter. The purpose, as set forth under § 2540(b), is to determine, based on a stipulation of the parties, **"[w]hether case management shall be undertaken and a case plan ordered."** Courts either note that milestones are met, as determined by resolution conferences, or they order a case management conference.

Case management conferences are not evidentiary hearings. However, pursuant to § 2451, they may decide important topics related to:

- Early neutral case evaluation;
- Alternative dispute resolution;

---

[61] Cal. R. Ct. 5.83(c)(1).

[62] Cal. R. Ct. 5.83(c)(5).

- Limitations and suspensions of discovery;
- The use of telephone conference calls for communications between lawyers and to hear contested motions;
- Modifications or waivers of procedural requirements;
- A requirement that any expert witness be selected by the parties jointly or appointed by the court; and
- Bifurcation of issues for trial.

Case conference plans can call for arbitration, which is a trial in which the arbitrator acts as the judge, or for mediation.

[C] Mediation

Mediation is a process whereby the parties reach a marriage settlement agreement [MSA] with the assistance of a neutral third party. The parties may or may not be represented by counsel during the mediation process.

Prior to starting mediation, parties typically indicate agreement, in writing, on several important matters. They acknowledge that the mediation, all communications between them and the mediator, and all documents prepared for the mediation are privileged and confidential and, therefore, may not be introduced into evidence in a later civil proceeding between the parties.[63] A later civil proceeding includes a dissolution, tort action, or property claim. They agree that the mediator may not testify unless all parties to the mediation expressly consent to the waiver in writing. They agree to share the expenses of mediation equally. And they agree that the mediation agreement will not become binding or enforceable until each party has sufficient time to obtain the advice of independent counsel.

Kieturakis is a case that complicates the simple view of mediation as a win-win, party-determining process.[64] The case arose when former wife, Anna, filed to set aside the nearly two year old dissolution judgment on the ground that it was based on an MSA agreement that was obtained through fraud, duress, and lack of disclosure. Anna submitted a declaration detailing a history of domestic abuse. As to the mediation, she declared that "she had 'acted under tremendous pressure,' " that included threats, to participate in mediation unrepresented by counsel, and that she had been "intimidated by [her husband] into signing the MSA."[65] Husband, Maciej, responded by making it clear that he had no intention of waiving confidentiality for any communications or documents related to the mediation. However, during the trial to set aside the dissolution judgment the parties vacillated on their willingness (or not) to waive confidentiality by allowing the mediator to testify. Eventually, the mediator was called to testify under seal, notwithstanding her objections.

---

63 Cal. Evid. Code §§ 1115–1128, 1119.

64 *Marriage of Kieturakis*, 138 Cal. App. 4th 56, 41 Cal. Rptr. 3d 119 (Cal. App. Ct., 1st Dist. 2006), discussing Cal. Evid. Code § 1115 and Cal. Fam. Code § 2122.

65 *Kieturakis*, *supra*, at 64.

The trial court found that the MSA favored Maciej insofar as he was awarded, among other assets, the entirety of valuable royalty payments that he had disclosed but not included in his income for purposes of calculating Anna's spousal support. The trial court did not find Anna's declarations of undue influence completely credible, nor did it find that Maciej had failed to comply with mandatory financial disclosure requirements during the mediation. On these findings, the trial court denied Anna's petition to set aside the final dissolution judgment pursuant to § 2122. The trial court did, however, apply the § 721(b) presumption as the basis for granting Anna's request for increased support. Even so, the trial court was unsure about the application of § 721(b) to a mediated MSA agreement. Therefore it reserved jurisdiction to modify its decision pending the court of appeal's review of the intersection of § 721(b) and Cal. Evid. Code 1115 et. seq., which is a series of provisions that treat all communications, negotiations, or settlement discussions among mediation participants as privileged and confidential unless waived in writing by all parties.

The court of appeal reversed and held that, in the mediation context, the § 721(b) presumption yields to the state's policies in favor of mediation and finality of judgments. Several reasons were given. One, the mediation process is voluntary and self-determining. The mediator recognizes it as his or her professional duty to assess whether the parties' participation in the process is voluntarily or not. If one party is being coerced into mediation by the other party, the mediator's professional duty is to observe that dynamic and to bring it to the parties' attention with the goal of establishing or restoring voluntary participation in the mediation process. Failing to do so, the mediator becomes duty bound to end the mediation. Two, applying the presumption of undue influence to mediated agreements undermines the practice of mediating marriage settlement agreements. And three, this in turn interferes with the widespread acceptance of mediation in marital disputes.

In light of these reasons, the court held that "the presumption of undue influence cannot be applied to marital settlement agreements reached through mediation."[66] In reaching its decision, the court considered the history of domestic violence between the parties, the mediator's testimony, Anna's attorney's testimony that the Anna was clearly intimidated by Maciej, and psychological evidence for and against a finding that Anna exhibited battered-spouse syndrome.

The court also explained that what goes on in the mediation is confidential and privileged. Parties may waive the mediator's privilege, but unless they do so, the integrity of the process is presumed. Absent an express waiver, the mediator cannot break confidentiality by testifying to establish the parties' agreement, reveal information about or from the mediation, or otherwise comment on the relationship dynamic between the parties.[67] This privilege, with its assurance of confidentiality, encourages parties to seek out a mediated outcome (rather than a litigated one) as a viable way to strive for an advantageous outcome. *Kieturakis*

---

[66] *Id.* at 85.

[67] *Simmons v. Ghaderi*, 44 Cal. 4th 570, 582, 80 Cal. Rptr. 3d 83, 187 P.3d 934 (Cal. 2008) (in bank) (implied waiver does not apply to mediator confidentiality); *Cassel v. Superior Court*, 51 Cal. 4th 113, 123, 119 Cal. Rptr. 3d 437, 244 P.3d 1080 (Cal. 2011) (in bank).

concludes with the pronouncement that "if there is a price to be paid in fairness to preserve mediation confidentiality, the cases have required that it be paid by parties challenging, not defending, what transpired in the mediation."[68]

And yet, even if one agrees with the court's willingness to presume the integrity of the process, mediation confidentiality must be recognized as a double-edged sword. On one hand it encourages candid discussion between the participants. On the other hand, it can present a problem when the parties hope to refer to the mediation process as evidence of their agreement in any later civil court proceeding between them.

With respect to the parties, one attractive benefit of mediation is cost: It is less expensive to mediate than it is to litigate. Other benefits are that discovery is entirely voluntary in mediation, and the process is private. The parties are theorized as self-determining decision makers. And the process is idealized as one of candid discussion based on voluntary disclosure that gives the parties the opportunity to hammer out a creative, tailored, and interest driven outcome. The win-win nature of a paradigmatic mediation might even suggest that the parties can still be on talking terms when all is said and done. In other words, the promise of a successful mediation is that it gives either and both parties an opportunity to exit a marriage in a way that works for them and with a division of property that they believe to be fair (enough).

Mediation has systemic benefits as well. It relieves the strain on underfunded courts. It encourages finality of judgments. It makes parties aware of just how beneficial cooperation can be to reaching an interest driven outcome, especially where children are involved. If the parties do not reach a mediated agreement, a court will step in to divide property with a mandate to divide assets equally on an asset-by-asset basis, as discussed in Chapter 2. There is a corollary mandate: The court is not required by law to take the parties' preferences or desires into account. A mediated agreement, therefore, has a higher chance than a court order does of being perceived as fair by the parties. Indeed, many a court opinion starts with the adage that because both parties were unhappy, the opinion must have been fair. Mediation seeks to turn that adage on its head: If both parties were happy with the outcome, the mediation process must have been successful.

Notwithstanding the many benefits of mediation, parties must be on guard for potential risks as well. In addition to being cost effective and quick, mediation attracts those who are interested in "conscious uncoupling," especially since mediation is widely praised as a process by which the parties can reach an outcome based on their own sense of fairness.[69] But mediation is a direct conversation between the parties. If that conversation should end, the parties will be required to assume new costs related to pursuing another mode of dissolution, like litigation or arbitration.

Mediation may appeal to a party who hopes to rush an agreement past the other party. The promise (and often the reality) of mediation is that the parties — plural

---

68 *Kieturakis*, *supra*, at 87.

69 Gary Friedman & Steven C. Neustadter, *Mediation*, *in* California Marital Settlement and Other Family Law Agreements §§ 2.1–2.46 (Jon E. Heywood ed., 3d ed. 2014).

— are in control. However, another reality can (too predictably) lurk, namely that one party is willing to use obvious or subtle intimidation tactics over the other to gain control of the process.

Additionally, the parties might request that the mediator opine on the law. But the mediator is not an advocate for either of the parties. What seems fair in a face-to-face mediation conversation may turn out to be incorrect, or unfair to one party over time, or completely contrary to the time tested community property rules. Hence mediator statements and beliefs about how a court might divide a particular asset, while seemingly sensible in the moment, might turn out to have long term financial costs for a party who is too willing to be accommodating of the other side's point of view at the expense of his or her own.

Plus there may be hidden power imbalances. If the parties do not disclose a history of domestic violence, for example, the mediator may not be made fully aware of the existence of subtle issues of coercion, duress, or undue influence. All couples have unproductive patterns of conflict.[70] Some couples' patterns are based on historic undercurrents of abuse, coercion, and deception that may continue to determine the parties' conduct no matter how cooperative the parties appear to act in the mediation room. In *Kieturakis*, the court interpreted undue influence as a term "broad enough to subsume all of the grounds for relief" for purposes of setting aside a final dissolution judgment under § 2122, including fraud, perjury, duress, mental incapacity, mistake (mutual or unilateral), and failure to disclose.[71] Given the state's interest in mediation, *Kieturakis* recognized that unless and until these grounds are proven — which of course requires breaking confidentiality — even a party who becomes aware, after the fact, of how subtle forms of undue influence might have compromised the mediation process cannot invoke the benefit of an evidentiary presumption that would otherwise be available to him or her.

Parties may be aware of their unproductive patterns of communication, or they may not. They may be in denial about the way in which their relationship dynamics pose impediments to a fair and voluntary decisionmaking process. And where there is psychological denial, the dynamic may be too subtle for even a well trained mediator to detect. In *Kieturakis*, for example, Anna testified about the history of domestic abuse in her marriage, and yet she also testified that "she thought mediation was supposed to lead to a fair agreement, and that [the mediator] would be looking out for her interests during the process." Based on Anna's naïve and contradictory hope for mediation, she (perhaps) underplayed her concerns about the parties' history of domestic violence to the mediator. The mediator may have been informed about the parties' history of domestic abuse, but it was the mediator's (empirically questionable) assertion that issues involving domestic violence were (and can be) abated by the structure of the mediation process itself.

More benignly but equally risky are everyday personality issues that may get in the way of voluntariness. One party may appreciate the mediator's style, while the other party may find it too controlling or too emotionally distant (or close) or even intimidating, in which case important information or options may not get

[70] *Id.* at § 2.18.

[71] *Kieturakis, supra.*

expressed, revealed, explored, or vetted. In *Kieturakis*, Anna perceived, for example, that one member of the mediation team spent a greater amount of time listening to Maciej's financial plans relative to hers.

Finally, there are very real risks related to informational inequalities, particularly in today's world of ubiquitous electronic communication. Electronic abuse issues are discussed in Chapter 11.

Kieturakis also involved the effect of an illegal disclosure in the mediation process. Illegal disclosure is (obviously) wrongful conduct. As such, illegally obtained evidence — hacking into someone's e-mail, for example — is inadmissible in a dissolution proceeding, but possibly admissible in a mediation process. In other words, an overreaching spouse cannot use illegally obtained evidence in court; if he or she tries to do so; the parties' advocates will challenge the admissibility of that evidence. But illegally obtained evidence can shape or otherwise form the basis of a mediated or negotiated agreement, especially if the parties do not have advocates present to object to the introduction of that information. A number of legal outcomes are possible when one spouse illegally obtains information against the other spouse for purposes of negotiating a marriage settlement agreement outside of mediation, and such a judgment of dissolution can be set aside under § 2122. But the same might not be possible if that same judgment is based upon a mediated MSA process.

Negotiations based on electronically obtained illegal information, in particular, are subtle and problematic in today's electronically reliant world.

By this point in the text, it should be evident that the property issues related to winding up a marital partnership can be complex, emotionally driven, and vulnerable to the relational history and habits of the parties. The parties may be aware of some of their issues; but probably — if they are like most of us — they are simultaneously unaware of other issues. The issues that don't rise to awareness can be as likely to influence the outcome of a mediation process as those that do. For instance, the parties may feel an incentive to rush the mediation along to buy peace, and the mediator may even encourage them in that aspiration in the name of cooperation. Still, what happens down the line when one or both parties realize that in the rush to reach an agreement, important rights were negotiated away? Rights that could have eased a financial transition from married to single life, or from middle age to older age, or from health to sickness, and so on? In other words, the temporal loss attendant to dividing property without an advocate present could consign a party to a lifetime of financial struggle or even poverty. If and when that happens, what good was a premature peace bought at an exorbitantly high price?

Example 16.6: This example illustrates the mediation process. Zoe and Ritch decide to seek dissolution. They hire a third party neutral to assist them in reaching a mediated agreement. Together, in the presence of the third party neutral, Zoe and Ritch discuss their issues. When asked, the mediator discusses the probable application of general law to any particular question Zoe and Ritch might raise. Eventually Zoe and Ritch reach an agreement that serves as the basis for their final judgment of dissolution.

Example 16.7: This example illustrates the presumption of voluntariness that arises as in a *fairly disclosed* mediation process. Zoe and Ritch seek a divorce. They decide to mediate their property issues with an experienced mediator. Each spouse makes full, fair, and ongoing disclosure. Neither spouse waives the right to disclosure. Neither spouse waives the mediator's privilege. As a result of the mediation, the parties execute an agreement in anticipation of a final dissolution procedure; that agreement does not waive mediator confidentiality. Subsequently, Zoe challenges the mediation agreement on the ground that the mediation process was impeded by Ritch's undue influence. Without more, the mediation agreement cannot be challenged on undue influence grounds. The rationale is that the mediation process is presumptively fair, since disclosure — which is a proxy for voluntary consent — was made. The mediator is not available to testify otherwise. Any marriage settlement agreement or judgment based on the mediation agreement remains enforceable.

Example 16.8: This example illustrates how a search of public websites, which is legal, can influence the mediation outcome. Same Example 16.7, except that after the mediation concludes Zoe goes to Ritch's public LinkIn profile. From that site, Zoe finds out — for the first time — that Ritch boasts a number of clients for a business that Ritch failed to disclose during the mediation process. Ritch concedes his lapse in disclosure as to this client list, but claims that otherwise disclosure was fair because the business was reasonably discoverable by a simple Internet search. Zoe may prevail in challenging the mediation contract or any judgment based on it: Ritch had an ongoing duty to disclose the existence of a business in which the community did or may have had an interest in. Zoe did not waive the right to disclosure. And Zoe could not have reasonably obtained adequate knowledge of the undisclosed business or its financial obligations from a public social media page. Zoe has grounds for setting aside any judgment that is based on the mediation agreement. The mediation contract was the result of undue influence due to Ritch's failure to disclose; and this undue influence compromised Zoe's voluntary consent to any mediated agreement. Under § 721(b), which presumably would apply where disclosure was absent, the burden should be on Ritch to rebut that presumption with proof of the voluntariness of the contested agreement.

Example 16.9: This example illustrates how electronic trespass is illegal and results in inadmissible evidence that can influence the mediation process. Zoe hacks Ritch's computer to access Ritch's e-mail account. Zoe finds e-mails between Ritch and her (Zoe's) therapist on the subject of Zoe's mediation strategy. In California, Zoe's actions are illegal and tortious in relation to Ritch. Any marital mediation agreement that was reached on the basis of the illegally obtained information makes the contracting process involuntary. Not only does Ritch have a cause of action in tort against Zoe, but the illegally obtained information is inadmissible in a court proceeding. And yet, without emphasis on a formal discovery process, the source of Zoe's information might not have been located, and thus might have made its way to the mediation table. Formal discovery can be and is an important part of the dissolution process; and the process of mediation depends on the parties to fully disclose accurate information on a voluntary basis. Thus mediation poses clear risks when one or both parties are not willing to comply with the mandatory disclosure requirements of §§ 1101(e), 721(b), and 2100–13.

Example 16.10: This example illustrates how electronic information gained from a non-password protected source is legal. Zoe searches the hard drive on a family computer that is not password-protected. On that hard drive, Zoe finds files detailing Ritch's undisclosed transfer of $100,000 to a Swiss bank account for lover Laurel's benefit. Ritch's failure to disclose the $100,000 makes the mediation agreement subject to challenge. Under § 2122, Zoe can move to set aside a dissolution judgment based on the mediated MSA. The evidence about the $100,000 transfer is admissible in court, even though — had Zoe not found evidence of Ritch's transfer — it would not likely have surfaced in the mediation, and (yet) had it surfaced in mediation, the sanctions attending Ritch's transfer might not have been fully explored.

Example 16.11: This example illustrates how negotiations based on illegally obtained information can terminate a mediation. Zoe hacks Ritch's password-protected e-mail account on that same family computer. In this example, Zoe's actions are illegal or tortious in relation to Ritch. The evidence about the $100,000 transfer is not admissible in court. Even so, with respect to the mediation process, Zoe's acquisition of this evidence compromises the mediation process in Zoe's favor, notwithstanding the fact that Ritch made a substantial unauthorized gift of community property. In this example, the parties must at least consider terminating the mediation, even if they can successfully "talk out their problems" in mediation.

§ 16.10 SUMMARY

In sum, in an action for dissolution, the court has broad discretion on a wide range of issues. This *Understanding* concerns itself primarily with property issues. However, in a dissolution proceeding, a family court has the power to adjudicate the property rights of the parties as well as a broad grant of discretion to set spousal support, child support, attorney's fees and court costs where appropriate. A trial court also has the authority to restore one or both spouses' former name, one's status as an individual, and other related premarital rights. Additionally, a court has discretion to grant domestic violence restraining orders and monetary awards.

The state of California has expressed a strong interest in the use of alternative dispute resolution approaches, like collaborative law and mediation, in dissolution proceedings. A goal expressed by the Judicial Council is to eventually have 90% of petitions for dissolution, legal separation and nullity disposed of within 18 months of the date that they are filed. Mediation is key to meeting this goal, but it is not without risk in some cases, especially those where domestic violence (as broadly defined by the Family Code) has been, is, or may be present.

Chapter 17

DEATH

When a marriage terminates by the death of a spouse, the state has a strong interest in expediting the administration of the decedent's estate, since the spouses own community property in undivided interests. A clear and firm legal structure for dealing with a deceased person's property is important to making sure that administration moves smoothly.

Testamentary rights are created and recognized by the state; they are not natural rights. The decedent's right to devise is that person's right to dispose of property by devise, at death, after accounting for obligations to support a spouse, children, and (in California) indigent parents. A person's testamentary right contains within it the right to make lifetime transfers (via inter vivos gift), agreements about rights of survivorship in title (in concurrent titles), and to make beneficial designations by contract (via P.O.D. designations).

By contrast, the right to descent belongs to the decedent's intestate heir or heirs, not to the decedent. The right to descent comes into play with respect to any and all of decedent's probate property that does not pass by will or nonprobate transfer. The intestate heir has a right to receive property from a decedent's intestate estate in accordance with the state statutes of descent and distribution.

In the case of a married decedent, all property is subject to characterization as community or separate.

§ 17.01 THE DECEDENT'S PROBATE ESTATE

A person who dies leaving a valid will dies testate.

At a person's death, that person's property must be collected into a probate estate. By law, the probate estate is comprised of all property that the decedent died owning. A property owner has the right to dispose of property prior to or at death, whether by inter vivos gift, beneficial designation or right of survivorship. Property disposed of by these types of nonprobate transfers passes prior to the formation of the decedent's probate estate; therefore it is not collected into the probate estate, and not available to the decedent's estate creditors.

[A] THE DECEDENT'S PROBATE ESTATE

Nonprobate transfers are *excluded* from the decedent's probate estate. 
Joint property with the right of survivorship: • joint tenancy with the right of survivorship • community property with the right of survivorship At decedent's death title passes by operation of law to the joint tenant.
Contractual assets: • life insurance • deferred benefit accounts • bank accounts with the right of survivorship • other beneficial designations At decedent's death title passes by beneficial designation, subject to the surviving spouse's equitable interest (if any).
Trust property and other valid inter vivos transfers • trust designations • inter vivos gifts

All property that the decedent owns after death makes up the probate estate.

Nonprobate transfers are made before or at death. Testamentary transfers pass by will.

Any property not passed by inter vivos gift, will, or nonprobate transfer passes through the intestacy statute.

[B] Options and Characterization of Property

In the context of marriage, the surviving spouse has important options.

First, other than by a final judgment of dissolution, death is the only other way to terminate a marriage. Death is also when the decedent's probate estate comes into existence and a personal representative (executor or administrator) is appointed to settle that probate estate. A decedent can name an executor of his or her choice in a will; the surviving spouse may or may not be named executor. In the event of intestacy, however, the surviving spouse or domestic partner is entitled to priority of appointment as the administrator.[1]

The decedent's personal representative gathers the assets of the decedents, characterizes them, and pays the decedent's taxes, probate expenses, and debts. Only after the bills are paid, does the personal representative distribute any remaining property in accordance with the decedent's valid will, which includes any codicils.

A married decedent's estate is made up of:

- the decedent's one-half community property interest in each community property asset; and
- the decedent's separate property.

Whether property is characterized as community property or separate property determines how it will be disposed of in the event of a probate process.

Property disposed of by will or intestacy is comprised of the decedent's one-half of the community or quasi-community property and his or her separate property.[2] Property disposed of by intestate succession is property that passes under § 6401, as discussed below.

A surviving spouse has the option to forego a probate proceeding, or to administer the decedent's estate. Under Cal. Prob. Code § 13502(1), the surviving spouse **"may"** opt for a probate administration as to **"The one half of the community property that belongs to the decedent . . . , one-half of the quasi-community property that belongs to the decedent . . . , and the separate property of the decedent."** All of the options and concepts discussed here also apply to registered domestic partners under § 297.5(c).

If the surviving spouse elects to administer the decedent spouse's estate, the decedent's creditors can prove and possibly collect on the decedent's unpaid debts, assuming there are sufficient funds.

The decedent's estate is settled in a specific order. Each category of takers can claim only what remains in the probate estate after the previous category's claims are satisfied. Once property is exhausted, any subsequent takers in the queue will be unable to collect against the estate due to the lack of assets.

Here is the order in which the decedent's probate estate is settled (i.e., paid out).

---

[1] Cal. Prob. Code § 37 provides: " **'Domestic partner' means one of two persons who have filed a Declaration of Domestic Partnership with the Secretary of State pursuant to Division 2.5 (commencing with Section 297) of the Family Code, provided that the domestic partnership has not been terminated pursuant to Section 299 of the Family Code."**

[2] Cal. Prob. Code § 6101.

- Taxes;
- Administration expenses, including court costs and attorneys fees;
- Debts;
- Scheduled family protection expenses:
    - o exempt property under Cal. Prob. Code § 6510
    - o homestead property (the family dwelling set-aside) under Cal. Prob. Code § 6520
    - o the family allowance under Cal. Prob. Code § 6540;
- Gifts to the will beneficiaries and substitute beneficiaries;
- Intestate distributions
- Escheat if the decedent has no heirs.

The surviving spouse may elect to contractually assume an obligation for which the decedent was liable. If so, this obligation arises by contract between the surviving spouse and the creditor. If the surviving spouse decides to do this, he or she should quickly notify the decedent's creditor (as with a credit card issuer) to close the account. The surviving spouse also should report the decedent's death to credit reporting agencies.

Otherwise, creditors generally have one year in which to make a claim against the decedent's estate.[3] But if the surviving spouse had **"actual knowledge"** of the debt prior to the expiration of the one year period and the personal representative **"failed to provide the creditor asserting the claim . . . with a timely written notice of the probate administration** [the statute of limitations is extended to four years]."[4]

California has adopted some but not all, of the Uniform Probate Code (1969) provisions. One important adopted provision applies to nonprobate beneficial designations (P.O.D. designations) that name a former spouse or domestic partner.

The general rule is that a nonprobate transfer to a former spouse fails if the former spouse is not the decedent's surviving spouse due to a dissolution or annulment of the marriage. Cal. Prob. Code § 5600(a) provides that in: **"[a] nonprobate transfer to the transferor's former spouse, in an instrument executed by the transferor before or during the marriage, fails if, at the time of the transferor's death, the former spouse is not the transferor's surviving spouse as defined in Section 78, as a result of the dissolution or annulment of the marriage."** Exceptions are listed in § 5600(b): irrevocable designations; revocable designations for which there is **"clear and convincing evidence that the transferor intended to preserve the nonprobate transfer to the former spouse;"** and court ordered designations to the former spouse. Where a nonprobate transfer fails Cal. Prob. Code § 5600(c) states the order of succession: **"the instrument making the nonprobate transfer shall be treated as it would if the former spouse failed to survive the transferor."**

---

[3] Cal. Fam. Code § 914(c).

[4] *Id.*

Another exception applies to joint tenancy property held with a former spouse, a former domestic partner and a former nonmarried partner. A joint tenancy between a decedent and any of the above former partners created before or during the marriage is severed if the former spouse is not the transferor's surviving spouse, at the time of death.[5] Additionally, this rule applies to partnerships between nonmarried partners holding joint tenancy title. Otherwise, joint tenancy interests in real property are terminated by affidavit or by establishing the fact of death when a death certificate cannot be located.[6]

CAMPAL provides that beneficial ownership of sums on deposit in certain accounts — see Chapter 5 for the specific types of accounts — pass automatically on death directly to the named beneficiary unless there is clear and convincing evidence that the decedent had a different intention.[7] These sums are not subject to administration in the decedent's estate. As such they are nonprobate transfers.

Joint access safe-deposit boxes between the spouses remain within the access of the surviving spouse by contract. However, the contents in the box must be characterized separately on an asset-by-asset basis. In the event that the surviving spouse decides to administer the decedent's estate, he or she must transfer the decedent's property from the joint access box that the parties' shared during the decedent's lifetime to an estate safe-deposit box.[8]

Nonprobate transfers are probate avoidance devices. Therefore, they are not available to the decedent's *probate* claimants or creditors.

Instate succession to California property for a decedent is governed by Cal. Prob. Code §§ 6400–6414, 6450–6455, effective from 1984 on. Cal. Prob. Code § 6400 provides: **"Any part of the estate of a decedent not effectively disposed of by will passes to the decedent's heirs as prescribed in this part."** The surviving spouse, as defined by Cal. Prob. Code § 78, is counted among the decedent's heirs.[9] However, the surviving spouse has an exalted status relative to the decedent's actual consanguineous relatives (descendants, ancestors and collateral heirs).

A **"surviving spouse"** is the person who is married to the decedent at the time of death per Cal. Prob. Code § 78. A person whose marriage to the decedent was dissolved or annulled is not a surviving spouse for purposes of intestate distribution. Neither is a person who obtains or consents to a final decree or judgment of dissolution (or annulment) the decedent's surviving spouse. A surviving **"domestic partner"** under Cal. Prob. Code § 37 is a person who was in a registered domestic partnership with the decedent at the time of the decedent's death. An **"heir"** under Cal. Prob. Code § 44 is **"[a]ny person, including the surviving spouse, who is entitled to take property of the decedent by intestate succession under** [the California Probate] **code."**

---

[5] Cal. Prob. Code § 5601.

[6] Cal. Prob. Code §§ 210–212.

[7] Cal. Prob. Code § 5302.

[8] See Cal. Prob. Code § 9630 for bank safe-deposit box access information.

[9] Cal. Prob. Code § 44.

McDaniel directly raised the question of how a dissolution proceeding affects a party's status as surviving spouse under Cal. Prob. Code § 78.[10] *McDaniel* involved a contest for an intestate estate. The estate claimants were the decedent's spouse, who sought status as the decedent's surviving spouse, and the decedent's mother. The court of appeal held that the legal spouse was not a **"surviving spouse"** for purposes of Cal. Prob. Code § 78 since the spouses were in the process of dissolving their marriage when the husband died intestate. The court's rationale was that while the final judgment of dissolution had not yet been granted on the date of the decedent's death, a court order terminating the community estate — i.e., all of the parties' marital property rights — was in effect.

§ 17.02 THE DECEDENT'S COMMUNITY PROPERTY

Cal. Prob. Code § 100 provides that **"one-half of the community property belongs to the surviving spouse and the other half belongs to the decedent."** Quasi-community property is treated identically under Cal. Prob. Code § 101.

The probate code definition of community property is consistent with the Family Code definition. Cal. Prob. Code §28 defines **"[c]ommunity property"** to mean property **"[a]cquired during marriage by a married person while domiciled in this state."** The Probate Code has a similarly broad definition of quasi-community property at Cal. Prob. Code § 66. Registered partners have all the same **"[r]ights, protections, and benefits"** as married persons under §297.5, including those afforded to the surviving spouse under Cal. Prob. Code § 100 and § 101.

Therefore, assuming capacity, a married decedent has the right to dispose of his or her one-half of the community property by will.[11] A community property asset that falls into the decedent's estate but is not effectively disposed of by the decedent's will shall pass to the decedent's intestate heirs by the default order of the rules of intestate succession. Succession rules strongly favor the surviving spouse or registered domestic partner.

The surviving spouse's share of community property passing by intestacy is set forth at Cal. Prob. Code § 6401:

> **(a) As to community property, the intestate share of the surviving spouse is the one-half of the community property that belongs to the decedent under Section 100.**
>
> **(b) As to quasi-community property, the intestate share of the surviving spouse is the one-half of the quasi-community property that belongs to the decedent under Section 101.**

Community property may include easily overlooked items; so too might separate property. For example, the general rule is that all causes of action survive death.[12] Thus it is important for the surviving spouse to determine whether the decedent has any such causes of action, and if so whether they must be prosecuted or defended.

---

[10] *McDaniel, supra.*

[11] Cal. Prob. Code § 6101.

[12] Cal. Civ. Proc. Code § 377.20.

Additionally, insurance claims may be due the decedent.

Gifts, low value transfers, or transfers of certain community property items (like furniture, fixtures, clothing, etc.) made without the consent of one or the other spouse can be ratified (by the decedent's estate plan) or avoided (by the surviving spouse) under § 1100(b) and (c). The operative rule as to the decedent's unauthorized transfers is that during the decedent's lifetime, avoidance would have returned the entirety (100%) of the gift to the community estate.[13] But after the decedent's death, a surviving spouse's avoidance can only return to the surviving spouse his or her one-half (50%) community property interest in the property that was wrongfully transferred. Upon avoidance, the decedent's one-half share of the property is thus distributed in accordance with the decedent's wishes (i.e., by gift, will, intestacy). The rationale is that during the marriage, the nonconsenting spouse is protected by the undivided nature of the community property interest, but once the community estate terminates (in this case by the death of a spouse) balancing factors change. After a donor or transferee spouse's death, the law attempts to strike an equal balance between the decedent spouse's testamentary rights and the nonconsenting surviving spouse's ongoing ownership rights.[14]

All of the above factors are balancing factors that may determine whether the surviving spouse elects to administer the decedent's estate.

If a spouse dies intestate, the decedent's community property interest passes entirely to the surviving spouse, on an asset-by-asset basis.

Cal. Prob. Code § 24 defines beneficiaries as interested parties. Beneficiaries must be given notice of probate proceedings.

Example 17.1: This example illustrates disposition of the decedent's estate by will. Jackson, who is married to Heather, dies with a valid will that devises "his house" to Octavia. The house is entirely community property. Jackson's testamentary right extends to his one-half community property interest in the community property house. Thus by Jackson's will, a one-half interest in the house passes to Octavia. Heather has the option to administer Jackson's estate or not. If she does, Jackson's one-half interest in the house may be reachable by Jackson's estate creditors, unless certain family protections can be invoked.

Example 17.2: This example illustrates the decedent's free right of testation as to community property. Jackson, who is married to Heather, dies with a valid will that devises "his house" to his lover Laurel. The house is entirely community property. Jackson's testamentary right extends only to his one-half community property interest in the house, not to Heather's one-half. While Jackson has the right to devise of his one-half interest in the house to Laurel, Heather has the option to administer Jackson's estate (or not). In this instance, because there is a risk of a contest, Heather will have to carefully consider the balancing factors in deciding what to do.

---

[13] *Britton v. Hammell*, 4 Cal. 2d 690, 692, 52 P.2d 221 (Cal. 1935) (in bank), followed by *Harris v. Harris*, 57 Cal. 2d 367, 19 Cal. Rptr. 793, 369 P.2d 481 (Cal. 1962) (in bank).

[14] *Trimble v. Trimble*, 219 Cal. 340, 347, 26 P.2d 477 (Cal. 1933) (in bank), followed by *Harris*, *supra*.

Example 17.3: This example illustrates how community property passes by intestacy.[15] Jackson and Heather are married. They own a house that is entirely community property. The house is titled as "community property." Jackson dies intestate. At Jackson's death, Jackson's one-half community property interest in the house passes by intestacy to Heather, who already owns a one-half community property interest in the house. After Jackson's death, Heather owns the house in its entirety (100%). As surviving spouse, Heather may elect to forego administration of Jackson's estate, per Cal. Prob. Code § 13500 et seq.

Example 17.4: This example illustrates a nonprobate transfer by right of survivorship. Jackson and Heather are married. They own a house that is entirely community property. Title to the house is held as "community property with the right of survivorship." Jackson dies intestate. At Jackson's death, Heather immediately succeeds to full ownership of the house. The house is disposed of outside of the probate process by the right of survivorship in the deed. Heather can clear the title to the house by affidavit.

Example 17.5: This example illustrates how a contractual asset (e.g., life insurance proceeds) is disposed of by beneficial designation determines ownership at the death of the obligor-spouse. Jackson dies leaving a community property life insurance policy. The policy names surviving spouse Heather as the sole P.O.D. beneficiary. Jackson has the right to dispose of one-half of the insurance proceeds by contract at death; Heather has an equitable property right in the other one-half of the life insurance proceeds. Upon Jackson's death, Heather takes Jackson's one-half community property interest in the proceeds by beneficial designation in the insurance contract; Heather already owns her one-half community property interest in the proceeds by equitable right. Jackson's transfer to Heather is a nonprobate transfer free from the reach of his probate estate creditors.

Example 17.6: This example illustrates how a trust designation determines ownership at the death of the settlor. Jackson and Heather settle a revocable trust funded with their community property house. Each spouse names the other as sole beneficiary. At Jackson's death, Heather takes Jackson's one-half community property interest in the house as Jackson's trust beneficiary. Title passes by nonprobate transfer free from the reach of Jackson's probate estate creditors.

Example 17.7: This example illustrates a transfer by inter vivos gift. Jackson and Heather are married. During his life Jackson gives a $30,000 diamond ring, purchased with community property, to his lover Laurel. At Jackson's death, Heather seeks to avoid that gift. Heather can avoid her one-half community property share of the gift ($15,000). Heather also has the option to seek recovery either against Laurel or Jackson's probate estate.[16] If Heather obtains recovery from Jackson's probate estate, then Laurel retains the ring because it was an inter vivos transfer made during donor Jackson's lifetime.

---

[15] Cal. Prob. Code § 6401.

[16] *Fields v. Michael*, 91 Cal. App. 2d 443, 205 P.2d 402 (Cal. App. Ct., 2d Dist. 1949).

§ 17.03 THE DECEDENT'S SEPARATE PROPERTY

Assuming capacity, a married decedent has the right to dispose of his or her separate property by will or by nonprobate transfer.[17] If a married decedent dies intestate, separate property goes to the surviving spouse, subject to sharing with listed heirs. The decedent's descendants can include children who survived the decedent, the surviving issue of children who predeceased the decedent, and posthumously conceived children.[18] For purposes of intestate distribution, posthumously conceived children are children who were in utero within two years of the issuance of the decedent's death certificate, and whom the decedent expressly authorized for posthumous conception. The availability of genetic material that was frozen by the decedent with the intent of making it available for posthumous conception delays the distribution of property by the limitation period noted above.[19]

Any separate property that the decedent does not dispose of by will or by nonprobate transfer is distributed in accordance with Cal. Prob. Code § 6401(c), which sets forth the mandatory default scheme for the decedent's separate property:

> **(c) As to separate property, the intestate share of the surviving spouse or surviving domestic partner . . . is as follows:**
>
> > **(1) The entire intestate estate if the decedent did not leave any surviving issue, parent, brother, sister, or issue of a deceased brother or sister**
> >
> > **(2) One-half of the intestate estate in the following cases:**
> >
> > > **(A) Where the decedent leaves only one child or the issue of one deceased child.**
> > >
> > > **(B) Where the decedent leaves no issue but leaves a parent or parents or their issue or the issue of either of them.**
> >
> > **(3) One-third of the intestate estate in the following cases:**
> >
> > > **(A) Where the decedent leaves more than one child.**
> > >
> > > **(B) Where the decedent leaves one child and the issue of one or more deceased children.**
> > >
> > > **(C) Where the decedent leaves issue of two or more deceased children.**

The surviving spouse divides his or her statutory share of the separate property that passes pursuant to § 6401(c) with the non-spousal taker or takers, who divide their share among themselves.

---

[17] Cal. Prob. Code § 6101.

[18] Cal. Prob. Code §§ 249.5–249.8; *see also* Cal. Fam. Code § 7611.

[19] Cal. Prob. Code §§ 249.5–.8; Cal. Fam. Code § 7611(f).

An ancestral property provision is found at CPC § 6402.5. This provision applies to real and personal property when a decedent dies intestate within a certain period of time after a former predeceased spouse, and leaves no surviving spouse or issue.[20] Under these circumstances, ancestral property of the former predeceased spouse is returned to that former predeceased spouse's consanguineous heirs. This section is an intestacy rule. Like all intestacy rules, it is easily avoidable by a valid estate plan that disposes of the property in question.

Example 17.8: This example illustrates the operation of the state intestacy provisions as to community and separate property where the decedent has no descendants, ancestors or collateral heirs. Jackson and Heather are married. Jackson owns a community property house with Heather. Jackson leaves no heirs other than Heather. Jackson's also owns a family heirloom that Jackson brought to the marriage. That heirloom is a collection of 100 ancient coins of equal value. Jackson dies intestate. Heather is entitled to the entirety of Jackson's community property share of the house. The heirloom collection is Jackson's separate property. Under § 6401(c)(1), all of Jackson's separate property descends to Heather since Jackson has no other heirs.

Example 17.9: This example illustrates the operation of the state intestacy provisions as to community and separate property where the decedent dies survived by a parent, but no descendant. Jackson and Heather are married. Jackson has no children, but he dies intestate survived by his mother, Iris. Jackson owns a community property house with Heather. Jackson also owns a family heirloom that he brought to the marriage. That heirloom is a collection of 100 ancient coins of equal value. Heather is entitled to the entirety of Jackson's community property share of the house. The heirloom is Jackson's separate property. Under § 6401(c)(2)(B), one-half of Jackson's separate property descends to Heather; the other one-half descends to his surviving parent Iris.

Example 17.10: This example illustrates the operation of the state intestacy provisions as to community and separate property where the decedent has one descendant. Jackson and Heather are married. Jackson owns a community property house with Heather. They have one child, Geary. Jackson also owns a family heirloom that he brought to the marriage. That heirloom is a collection of 100 ancient coins of equal value. Jackson dies intestate. Heather is entitled to the entirety of Jackson's community property share of the house. The heirloom is Jackson's separate property: Under § 6401(c)(2)(A), one-half of Jackson's separate property descends to Heather by intestacy; the other one-half descends to Geary, as Jackson's surviving child.

Example 17.11: This example illustrates the operation of the state intestacy provisions as to community and separate property where the spouses have two descendants. Jackson and Heather are married. Jackson is survived by two children, Geary and Gough. Jackson owns a community property house with Heather. Jackson also owns a family heirloom that he brought to the marriage. That heirloom is a collection of 100 ancient coins of equal value. Jackson dies intestate.

---

20 Cal. Prob. Code § 6402.5(a) and (b). The time period is 15 years for real property and 5 years for personal property.

Heather is entitled to the entirety of Jackson's community property share of the house. The heirloom is Jackson's separate property: Under § 6401(c)(3)(A), one-third of Jackson's separate property descends to Heather by intestacy; the other two-thirds descend to Geary and Gough, as Jackson's surviving children.

Example 17.12: This example illustrates the ancestral property provision of the Probate Code. Same as Example 17.11 except that Jackson and Heather are married. They have no children, but Jackson has two children from a prior marriage, Geary and Gough. Heather survives Jackson. However, she dies within five years of Jackson's death, leaving no heirs. Heather still owns her one-third share of the coin collection that descended to her from Jackson's separate property intestate estate under Example 17.11. At Heather death, both Heather's brother Polk, and Jackson's children Geary and Gough, claim Jackson's coin collection. Under Cal. Prob. Code § 6402.5(b)(1), Geary and Gough have a claim, since Heather died intestate without a surviving spouse or issue (descendants). Geary and Gough must, however, meet their burden to show the existence of the coin collection in Heather's intestate estate.[21] In other words, if Heather circumvented this ancestral provision by transferring the coin collection to her brother by inter vivos gift, will, or trust, then brother Polk will prevail over stepchildren Geary and Gough.

Example 17.13: This example illustrates the importance of joint form title in characterizing property at death. Jackson and Heather own a house titled as "joint tenants with the right of survivorship." At Jackson's death, his interest is separate property, not community property. Jackson's interest in the house passes by right of survivorship to Heather, meaning that Heather takes by nonprobate transfer. But the house will be characterized as concurrently owned separate property for tax purposes.

The above rules are based on presumptions. The law presumes that a reasonable decedent would want all community property to go to a surviving spouse, and all separate property to be shared by a surviving spouse and certain consanguineous heirs (blood relatives). Any of the above outcomes can — and routinely are — altered by a valid will. A person can also employ trusts, the right of survivorship, and beneficial designations to circumvent state intestacy provisions, and thus to determine the disposition of assets as part of a comprehensive estate plan.

§ 17.04 THE PUTATIVE SPOUSE AND THE PUTATIVE REGISTERED DOMESTIC PARTNER

Similar to a lawful spouse, a putative spouse is entitled to a surviving spouse's share of any property that passes by intestacy. A putative spouse is also entitled to priority of appointment as an administrator for the decedent's intestate estate. Putative spouse protections extend to putative registered domestic partners as well.[22]

Where the putative marriage was bigamous, the putative spouse is the decedent's most recent "spouse" and the decedent's lawful spouse is usually deemed the one

---

21 Cal. Prob. Code § 6402.5(b).

22 *Domestic Partnership of Ellis & Arriaga*, *supra*, disapproved of by *Ceja*, *supra*, on other grounds.

from whom the decedent is separated. Thus, for purposes of assessing the putative spouse's intestacy rights, Cal. Prob. Code § 28 defines community property as property which is acquired during the marriage. The putative spouse is entitled to one-half of all such **"quasi-marital property,"** as defined by § 2251(a)(2). The decedent's accumulations relative to the lawful spouse are the decedent's separate property, if they were indeed living separate and apart. When factual situations get too complicated, a trial court has discretion to divide the quasi-marital property in such a way that advances justice, consistent with the Family Code. In these instances, the decedent's putative spouse is typically designated his or her surviving spouse for purposes of Probate Code application and protections.[23]

§ 17.05 ELDER ABUSE AND DEPENDENT CARE ABUSE BY MARRIAGE

Elder law is an emerging field. The scope of professional proficiency required for an elder law practice is exceedingly broad and at the same time exacting. As one commentator put it, "[t]here is a profound emotional dimension to elder law practice, in which issues of autonomy, dependence, and endurance in the face of loss are often brought directly into the attorney's office."[24] Thus begins a wide ranging volume on elder law that covers property law, family law, health care law, public benefits law, conservatorship, estate planning, and other areas of law that routinely intersect in elder law practice.

One topic relevant at this point relates back to the validity of marriage question. On one hand, love knows no age or capacity limits. But on the other hand, elder persons and dependent adults are increasingly targets of financial abuse. Cal. Prob. Code § 2950 expresses the California policy of protecting mentally impaired adults from financial abuse. To this aim, California passed the Elder Abuse and Dependent Adult Civil Protection Act [EADACP §§ 15600–15675] as part of the Welfare and Institutions Code. EADACP § 15610.07 includes as abuse:

> **(a) Physical abuse, neglect, financial abuse, abandonment, isolation, abduction, or other treatment with resulting physical harm or pain or mental suffering.**
>
> **(b) The deprivation by a care custodian of goods and services that are necessary to avoid physical harm or mental suffering.**

In the context of marriage, abuse is made possible due in large part to the low standard of mental capacity required to contract a marriage. The financial abuse of elder adults is increasingly being played out in the interplay between void and voidable marriage rules. This issue is discussed in previous chapters.

The low standard of capacity to marry permits a perpetrator to marry an elderly person (i.e., a person 65 or over) or a dependent adult so as to wrongfully ensure for

---

[23] *See, e.g.*, *Estate of Leslie*, 37 Cal. 3d 186, 207 Cal. Rptr. 561, 689 P.2d 133 (Cal. 1984) (in bank); *Estate of Vargas*, 36 Cal. App. 3d 714, 111 Cal. Rptr. 779 (Cal. App. Ct., 2d Dist. 1974).

[24] Susanne B. Cohen & Priscilla Camp, *Elder Law Practice*, *in* CALIFORNIA ELDER LAW, RESOURCES, BENEFITS, AND PLANNING: AN ADVOCATE'S GUIDE, Vol. 1, § 1.11 (Mary Gerber, ed. 2013).

him or herself of the status of that elderly or dependent person's surviving spouse. The perpetrator relies on the Probate Code's exaltation of the surviving spouse for purposes of the disposing of a decedent's estate.

To reiterate the rules discussed previously, a void marriage never comes into existence. A void marriage is limited in circumstance to those for which there was a lack of capacity, incest, or bigamy. There is no married person in a void marriage, and so there can be no surviving spouse at the death of one of the purported spouses. Instead, the decedent's property passes to his or her will beneficiaries or consanguineous heirs. Additionally, due to the invalidity of the marriage, any will provisions that name a "spouse" as caregiver are void, any intestacy claims that are based on "surviving spouse status" are negated, and any default protections that the claimant makes on the basis of the marriage are denied.

By sharp contrast, in the case of a voidable marriage the death of one of the parties does leave a surviving spouse. Upon the decedent's death, the voidable marriage, because it was presumptively valid during the decedent's lifetime, can no longer be attacked by the decedent's heirs unless there is clear and convincing evidence that the decedent lacked the capacity to contract marriage. In other words, a voidable marriage becomes functionally valid at the decedent's death, especially for purposes of disposing of the decedent's property. At that time, gifts made in a will to a spouse take effect, intestacy designations benefiting the surviving spouse over other heirs become operative, and claims for default protections based on marriage must be granted: So, for example, a perpetrator of financial abuse can marry the decedent prior to death and, as long as the marriage was voidable rather than void, be included in the decedent's estate plan as an omitted spouse, be named as administrator, obtain status as an intestate heir, obtain family protections, and so forth.[25] Added to this risk is that California allows confidential marriage certificates.[26] All of these factors heighten the risk of elder financial abuse through the mechanism of marriage.

§ 17.06 THE NEED FOR ESTATE PLANNING

Traditional planning for married persons encompasses a bypass trust and a marital trust. Depending on the married couple's overall net worth, this type of basic estate planning can be important in California, where housing costs are among the highest in the U.S. Additionally, a trust can be used to guard against incapacity.

In a simple traditional plan, two or more revocable trusts are used. The first trust is called a "marital trust" and the second is called a "by-pass trust."

The marital trust names the surviving spouse as beneficiary. Its purpose is to avoid estate tax upon the death of *the surviving spouse*. The marital trust is designed to be funded with an equal amount of the decedent spouse's remaining

---

[25] Cal. Prob. Code § 21610: **"[t]he omitted spouse shall receive a share in the decedent's estate, consisting of the following property in said estate"** including one-half of the community and quasi-community property and the surviving spouse's share of the decedent's separate property as set forth in Cal. Prob. Code § 6104(c).

[26] Cal. Fam. Code §§ 501, 502, 503.

applicable credit amount in the form of community property. The by-pass trust names the surviving spouse and descendants as trust beneficiaries. Marital trust assets receive an adjusted basis — to current fair market value — upon the surviving spouse's death; by-pass trust assets may and typically do not.[27]

Obviously many factors and details influence estate planning. Nevertheless, the basic structure of the traditional plan involves the relatively straightforward but integrated use of mechanisms that pass property by trust designation, probate, right of survivorship, contract beneficial designation, and (perhaps) other inter vivos gifts made outside of trust.

§ 17.07 SUMMARY

A marriage ends when one of the spouses dies before the other. At the death of the first spouse, the other has the option to administer the decedent's estate or not. In an estate administration, property is characterized in accordance with the community property rules.

A decedent who dies testate has freedom of testation as to his or her one-half of the community property. There is no requirement that a spouse devise his or her community property to the other spouse.

The distribution of an intestate decedent's estate passes in accordance with the state's intestacy statutes, which provide that the decedent's one-half of the community property descend to the surviving spouse. The decedent's separate property, if any, is shared between the surviving spouse and other heirs. Registered domestic partners and putative spouses are deemed surviving spouses for purposes of the Probate Code. Spouses who are in the process of dissolution when one party dies may not be eligible for surviving spouse status depending on whether the community property estate is still in existence or not.

A voidable marriage is presumptively valid. For that reason, at the death of one of the spouses the marriage is deemed valid subject to clear and convincing evidence that the decedent lacked the capacity to contract the marriage.

Estate planning can determine the disposition of assets, tax issues related to the disposition of assets, and important family protections.

---

[27] *See* Chapter 2.

TABLE OF CASES

[References are to pages.]

[References are to pages.]

[References are to pages.]

J

K

L

M

[References are to pages.]

N

O

P

R

S

[References are to pages.]

T

U

V

W

[References are to pages.]

Y

Z

INDEX

[References are to sections.]

[References are to sections.]

[References are to sections.]

[References are to sections.]

F

H

L

M

N

P

[References are to sections.]

[References are to sections.]